A FURIOUS DEVOTION: THE LIFE OF
SHANE MACGOWAN

PRAISE FOR *A FURIOUS DEVOTION*

'A brilliant read.'
Tim Burgess

'A deep dive into the legacy of an Irish icon. Richard Balls serves up the most thorough account of the man — and myth — to date.'
Rolling Stone

'Definitive portrait of the former Pogue. Intimate, cooperative... the book's strength is that he lets MacGowan speak, and speak on, perfectly capturing the lyrical, romantic rhythms beneath the rasped whisper.'
Mojo, 4★

'This is the most in-depth and well-written book about the singer to date.'
Sunday Independent (**Ireland**)

'Meticulously researched... balanced and rather excellent biography.'
Hot Press

'The real strength of *A Furious Devotion* is the author doesn't try to sugar-coat any of the stories. He lets MacGowan and the interviewees speak, it's warts and all. *A Furious Devotion* does a brilliant job capturing the "colourful life" the singer has led.'
Louder Than War

'Offers some new glimpses into a complex personality, along with some illuminating snapshots of the ever-more ravaged figure he has cut in recent years.'
Classic Rock 8/10

'The myths have, if anything, been growing of late and a balanced view has been long overdue. Richard Balls' new tome, A Furious Devotion: The Authorised Story of Shane MacGowan is that, and more.'
Irish Examiner

'He has found a sensitive biographer who tells the band's long and delightful story from MacGowan's own mouth.'
Irish Voice

'A fascinating portrait of ex-Pogue and folk-punk pioneer Shane MacGowan.'
Choice Magazine

A FURIOUS DEVOTION: THE LIFE OF

SHANE MACGOWAN

Richard Balls

OMNIBUS PRESS
London / New York / Paris / Sydney / Copenhagen / Berlin / Madrid / Tokyo

CONTENTS

In memory of Dave Lally – a Saint among men

Acknowledgements

One person more than any other made this book happen: Shane's old friend Paul Ronan. When I wanted to interview Shane for my Stiff Records book back in 2012, he set up a meeting in London. We became friends and it was Paul who sounded Shane out about my interest in writing his biography. He gave me invaluable advice, made introductions and accompanied me on trips to Ireland, helping me steadily build Shane's trust. Without him, there would have been no book.

As well as a fount of knowledge, Shane's sister Siobhan MacGowan has been a rock of support. From my first visit to Tipperary, she was full of encouragement and no request was ever too much trouble. Thanks to Shiv and her husband, Anthony Hayes, I spent a wonderful afternoon gathered around the kitchen table at The Commons, listening to stories from her mother's family. That fireside chat in Shane's spiritual home was the perfect place to begin what would be a long and immensely enjoyable journey.

Maurice MacGowan, Shane's father, has also been a great advocate of this book and I am grateful for his backing. He is still sharp and great company, and it was a privilege to share a few pints with him in Nenagh.

Shane and his wife Victoria always made me feel welcome, allowing me to spend time and stay with them in Dublin. Being able to sit and chat with Shane in his home made it possible to talk to him when the time was right. The result was hours of recordings. Victoria kindly gave me a lengthy interview on my final trip to Dublin, during which she provided some telling insights into the man with whom she has spent much of the past four decades.

Dave Lally was a constant voice of encouragement, as well as a great friend prior to his death. A lifelong fan, as well as a friend of Shane's, he put me in contact with people and provided a wealth of information. This book is all the richer, thanks to him, and is dedicated to his memory.

I am also indebted to the following for giving interviews or contributing via other means:

Mark Addis, Justin Bairamian, Shanne Bradley, Mary Buxton, Vicky Cahill, Seán Cannon, Ted Carroll, Joey Cashman, Nick Cave, Johnny Cronin, Michael Cronin, Joy Crookes, Thomas Dolby, Debra Donnelly, Bob Dowling, John Dunford, James Fearnley, Jem Finer, Brendan Fitzpatrick, Bernie France, Finbar Furey, Aidan Gillen, Paul Harriman, Michele Harriman-Smith, Shelley Harris, Merrill Heatley, Darryl Hunt, Tom Kenneally, Noel Kenny, Scruffy Kenny, Ingrid Knetsch, Catherine Leech, Steve Lillywhite, Kathy MacMillan, Glen Matlock, Tomi May, Paul McGuinness, Christy Moore, Lauren Mulvihill, Lisa Mulvihill, Mundy, Cillian Murphy, Maeve Murphy, Fionna Murray, Gerry O'Boyle, Sinéad O'Connor, Trish O'Flynn, Dermot O'Leary, Deirdre O'Mahony, Terry O'Neill, Jane Perry-Woodgate, Philly Ryan, Ann Scanlon, Nick Skouras, Sharon Shannon, Tom Simpson, Jamie Spencer, Mary Taylor, Liam Teeling, Julien Temple, Richard Thomas, Terry Woods.

My sincere thanks also to the editorial team at Omnibus Press. David Barraclough showed great enthusiasm for this book from the moment I pitched the idea, and he and Imogen Gordon Clark were an absolute pleasure to work with.

I would also like to thank Steve Gedge, Sally Minogue, Ken Sweeney, Rob Webb and Jon Welch, who provided information and offered other support.

Finally, I would like to thank my partner Emma Outten for all her wonderful support and for proofreading and editing the final chapter.

Prologue

June 2012, London

Across the road from a private clinic in Belgravia, I wait, watching for the door to open. Shane MacGowan has an appointment and I have arranged to meet him afterwards and interview him for a book about Stiff Records. The rendezvous has been set up by Shane's old friend Paul Ronan, with whom he stays in London. I haven't met Shane before, so don't know what to expect. My instinct tells me to go with the flow.

The heavy door of the exclusive doctor's surgery opens and the two of them emerge. Shane is tall, with a loping gait, his eyes obscured behind thick black shades. I introduce myself and we shake hands, but he's a man on a mission. He sets off gainfully alongside the black railings and it's clear this is no time for conversation. At the end of the pavement, Shane turns into a cobbled side-street. Suddenly, he stops and sways, a gigantic trail of snot dangling from his nose. He snorts it onto the street, takes a slug of water from the plastic cup he's holding before throwing that down and carrying on.

Around the corner, we settle at a small table outside a bistro. Shane is anxious. His appointment has interrupted his drinking and he seems twitchy as he waits for his order to arrive. However, once the waiter returns with his bottle of rosé champagne he relaxes and, when it seems safe to do so, I switch on my recorder and begin asking some questions. Paul helps to steer things along and encourages him to chat. Shane's rambling recollections about the record label that took a chance on The Pogues are punctuated with his notorious snigger – '*tsscchh*' – which sounds like someone gargling with gravel. At one point he falls asleep on the recorder and I have to gently prise it from under him.

He disappears off to the toilet and when after some time he doesn't return, I ask Paul if he's OK. He assures me Shane is fine. But I'm not convinced, and I head to the gents to investigate. Inside, I discover Shane has locked himself in a cubicle and is hammering on the door for help. I encourage him to simply turn the handle, but it's no good, and a key is fetched by the staff to get him out.

His motor skills seem shot. Several times, he clumsily knocks his cutlery through the slats in the wooden table, and I end up helping him light his cigarettes as he struggles to do it himself. Food is spilled down his shirt. He is not drunk, but the years of abuse have taken their toll, as indicated by the carrier bag of medication with which he emerged from the clinic.

It is clear that I am in the company of a highly intelligent, extremely well-read man, with an encyclopaedic knowledge of pretty much everything. There are moments of irascibility, but overall, Shane is good company. He enjoys recounting stories and chuckles away to himself as he remembers funny things that have happened. I ask him to sign a couple of items and he is happy to oblige. 'To Richard. You boring asshole! Shane x', he scrawls in the front of Victoria's book. Paul takes a photograph of the two of us raising a glass. There is no ego at play here. Shane is generous and there is a kindness in his eyes. Definitely.

I want to know so much more about him than his association with Stiff Records and, a couple of years later, I ask Paul, with whom I have stayed in touch, if Shane would be open to me writing his biography. To my surprise, he replies that Shane is not against the idea. And that's how it starts.

June 2018, Dublin

My eyes open and I gaze around blearily. I am on a mattress on the floor of an office and it takes a few moments for the morning fug to lift. Then I remember. I am in Shane MacGowan's flat and although last night was a late one for me, I had left the others to carry on, knowing they would still be at it by daylight. I pull on some clothes and pad along the corridor to the sitting room.

Shane's tousled hair is poking up over the top of his armchair. He hasn't gone to bed and is still watching TV. Sleep is something he does without any routine. It simply comes over him wherever he happens to be. Day blurs into night and night into day. When I leave the flat to go for a walk or to get food or a pint, I leave Shane's World and re-join the one outside. Or that's how it seems.

I wonder if it is possible to find out who this man really is and if I am on a fool's errand. Shane detests being 'interviewed' and asked about his work. He will only talk when he is in the mood. Even then, it is hard to make out what he is saying, especially over the TV, which is never turned off. One documentary maker compared working with him to wildlife photography and it's a good analogy. So, I sit with him and Paul and whoever else is around and wait for an opening. We watch the World Cup, which Shane loves, but mostly violent films. 'We've missed a lovely garrotting,' he complains when I distract him with my questions during *The Godfather*.

One night, I am about to go to bed when Shane asks me to make him a cup of tea. Black with one sugar. I sense he might want to talk, so I fetch my recorder and sit with him, grabbing an unexpected opportunity. I've learned that he can be ill-tempered, his invective erupting from nowhere. One night he tells me he is 'exhausted from trying to explain the bloody obvious things,' and that it is more fun being interviewed by the police. I politely apologise, desperate not to lose a window of opportunity, and hesitantly ask if I can turn the TV down as I can't hear what he is saying. This is a high-risk strategy, given that he could easily react by turning it up even louder.

'Yes, turn it down, but don't fucking go on all night about it,' he growls. 'I've got some great stories about the filth'.

'Well, let's hear them,' I reply. And off we go again, as if nothing has happened.

Over two years I spend a great deal of time with Shane. Sometimes I am just sitting with him, chatting and watching TV. At other times I try to get answers to questions that have arisen through the extensive interviews I have conducted with his family, friends and former bandmates. Some of these never get resolved and probably never will be, but I am determined not to give up in my quest to sort the myths from the truths and better understand this shy and complex man.

CHAPTER 1

The Little Man

'I sat for a while at the cross at Finnoe
Where young lovers would meet when the flowers were in bloom
Heard the men coming home from the fair at Shinrone
Their hearts in Tipperary wherever they go'

'The Broad Majestic Shannon', **The Pogues**

Shane gazed out glassily on the audience which had filled Dublin's National Concert Hall in January 2018, on a night of competing emotions. Gripped in his hand was the Lifetime Achievement Award bestowed on him by the distinguished venue and presented by its patron and the President of Ireland, Michael D. Higgins. Not far from Shane's mind was the memory of his mother Therese who had died just a year earlier. A tear had been shed for her when he had listened to Finbar Furey's sublime rendition of 'Kitty', the song Shane had learned from her as a child. Away from the unbridled excitement in the hall, Shane had quietly watched the performance on a monitor, pride intermingled with grief.

There was no acceptance speech. He sat in his wheelchair listening to the whoops and cheers and looking across a sea of mobile phones. As the President left the stage and the evening ended, Shane simply raised his glass. 'Good night and good luck, tsscchh,' he slurred. A reminder that an artist who has penned so many memorable words is, in fact, a man of very few.

The occasion, as well as recognising his quite unique talents as a writer, underlined the extraordinary nature of the journey Shane MacGowan has made in Ireland. The Pogues were seen as a violation of traditional music by purists, and some in the media, when they gate-crashed the pop scene, with Shane accused of playing to the pissed-up-paddy image that 1980s' Ireland was so desperate to cast off. That the band came from across the water and their singer had more of an English accent than an Irish one only made them more unpalatable. So, as Shane received a standing ovation, both from the sell-out crowd and a line-up of guests that read like a *Who's Who* of Irish music, his unlikely transformation from the rank outsider looking in through the window to national hero was complete. No wonder there were tears in the house.

To those who were there that night and to fans the world over, Shane MacGowan is as Irish as St Patrick himself. Over his career, he has aligned himself ever more closely with his native country and in media interviews has lasered in on the remote cottage where he first encountered people playing traditional instruments and dancing on the stone-flagged kitchen floor. However, The Pogues could never have emerged from Ireland's shores and it was when memories of idyllic childhood holidays in Tipperary were hotwired with those from his markedly different adolescence in London that Shane blessed us with 'The Old Main Drag', 'A Pair Of Brown Eyes' and 'A Rainy Night In Soho'.

'He is as paddy as they come,' says producer Steve Lillywhite. 'But he grew up in England and in London, so he had much more of an English punk-rock way of thinking – from The Nipple Erectors early on – than Irish. So, the fact that he grew up in England, but he was an Irishman – there is a schizophrenia that comes from that as well.'

Many people believe Shane was born in Tipperary and not Pembury, near the quintessentially English town of Tunbridge Wells, Kent. This common misconception was only encouraged by the BBC's 1997 documentary *The Great Hunger: The Life and Songs of Shane MacGowan*, which stated that he was 'born on the banks of the River Shannon in rural Ireland'. This and other subsequent films have concentrated heavily on his mother's family and his time spent at their remote cottage. Much less has been said about his father's relatives, some of whom still live in England, and around whom Shane spent a great deal of his early life.

Their recollections are shared here for the first time, along with those of his closest friends, musicians, ex-lovers and even his former English teacher. Most have never been approached before, despite some of them having had a significant impact on his life and career. While the story of The Pogues has been well-documented, the complete and frequently surprising journey of their notorious frontman, from outcast to national treasure, has never been told.

Until now.

I step into The Commons, a cottage in a remote part of Tipperary, dipping my head under the lintel as I do so, and I am transported back two hundred years. The Sacred Heart statues draped in cobwebs; the abandoned accordion on top of a cupboard; the blackened stone fireplace. No one has lived here for years, but a fire has been lit to warm it through. It is not hard to see why this place came to be so romanticised by Shane; somewhere untouched by time and a world away from the built-up English suburbs where he grew up.

His sister Siobhan, an author in her own right, has kindly arranged for family members to gather here and share their memories of the boy they called 'the little man'. A generous pot of tea – or '*tae*' in Irish – is poured, and I am introduced to them all. His aunts, his cousins. As the stories start to flow, you can almost hear, ghost-like, the music and dancing that once tested the stability of its thick stone walls. This is the place Shane still calls home and where, in the snug bosom of his family, he first sang and played Irish music.

'Shane loved it here and he'd come for months and months at a time,' says his aunt, Vicky Cahill. 'I think he liked the way they lived. He liked their easy-going way of life; he loved the countryside. When he was that little, he didn't realise how much he loved the countryside, but he did. He loved the music and the dancing and the way everybody wandered in and out, and he knew them all.'

The Commons is in Carney, a townland in the parish of Finnoe, about eight miles from Nenagh and three from Borrisokane. It is a traditional 'teachín', a thatched farm worker's cottage that could stand as a heritage centre today. There is a parlour, two small rooms with single beds, and a kitchen on the ground floor. Brave the steep stairs and you find a cramped attic space where Shane's LPs are strewn across the floor. The original structure was apparently extended about ninety years ago, and it is remarkable to think that it was home to Shane's great-grandparents, John and Mary Lynch, and their eleven children: Margaret, Pat, Julia, Ellen, Norah, John, Jim, Mikey, Bridget, William and Tom.

Shane is well-versed in his family's genealogy and always happy to talk about his beloved Commons. 'They moved in with this old woman who was a cousin,' he says of his great-grandparents. 'She was a D'Arcy and the D'Arcys had been run out of Ireland. We were rebels, they were rebels. There was a whole clan of us around the area, and in other areas there would be other clans and we would all get together for bigger things. They moved in to look after this woman and she promised them the house.'

John Lynch became a well-known figure in the area. He was associated with the Irish National Land League which sought to abolish landlordism in Ireland and enable tenant farmers to own the land they worked. He also wrote himself into the history books of the Gaelic Athletic Association (GAA) by becoming the first chairman of the hurling and Gaelic football club Shannon Rovers. A framed photograph of him still hangs on the wall in the parlour and the resemblance to his great-grandson, Shane, is inescapable.

Of the Lynch clan, it was the eldest, John, who worked full-time on the family farm and ended up taking it over. These were hard times in rural Ireland. Everyone had to help, including Tom, who was killed in a tragic accident with the threshing machine. Some of the other Lynch sons worked for North Tipperary county council, while several of the girls were excellent seamstresses, among them Nora and Julia, and Shane's grandmother Margaret, or 'Maggie'. Nowadays, the thought of so many people living cheek-by-jowl in a stone cottage with no inside toilet or bathroom is unimaginable. However, as the light dimmed on nineteenth-century Ireland, such a basic existence was normal in rural communities.

What was less typical, at a time when the Catholic Church still had a barnacle-like hold on the population, was Maggie's decision to leave her husband and move back to The Commons with her two young children. She had met and married John Cahill, a guard at the local station, and moved with him to Dublin where they started a family. Their first child and Shane's mother, Therese Mary, was born on 20 September 1929, and exactly one year later she was joined by her brother Sean. But John was an alcoholic and when the marriage foundered, Maggie and the children returned to The Commons.

'Mum used to say the Lynches were terribly soft and innocent, but Mum and Uncle Sean's mother was a shrewd woman,' comments Siobhan MacGowan. 'She could see through a lot of the old *plámás* [nonsense] that might be going on. She left her husband, which in those days you just didn't do. She was a strong character and she let our dad have it a few times.

'The Lynches very much supported her decision, though, because at one point her husband, John Cahill, wrote to her begging her to come back. She was wavering, and they absolutely forbid it. They did everything in their power to stop her going back to him.'

Shane says: 'He was a drunken guard. The only people who complained about him were a few landlords who objected to him turning up and banging on the door with his nightstick. He would arrive with a bunch of other drunks and demand to be let in. And you always let the cops in, especially if you were open that late already. He was very dominating, but he was also a man with a great heart. Everybody loved him but they feared him if they fucked up. He got kicked out of the guards. He had come down from Westmeath and was a first cousin of Dermot O'Brien, who was a second cousin of mine and a first cousin of Patricia Cahill, a famous singer.'

Therese was a bright pupil at both Kilbarron national primary school and St Mary's convent school, near Nenagh, where she did her secondary education. Her essays were lauded by teachers, just as Shane's would be thirty years later, says Siobhan. She was a fluent Irish speaker who enjoyed studying and an ardent reader. Had university been an option for a young woman in 1940s' Ireland, she would almost certainly have gone on to do a degree. But these were different times.

Not surprisingly, given her upbringing at The Commons, Therese possessed a fine singing voice and she won contests in the Feis Ceoil, an annual celebration of Irish music that continues today. 'The whole family at The Commons were all great singers – my mother was an amazing singer,' Shane says proudly. 'She won the adult singing prize at the main Feis when she was three. She had a mature voice at three, not as mature as it became a bit later, but she never had a little girl voice.'

Catherine Leech, a relative by marriage on Maurice's side, referred to by Shane as Aunty Catherine, adds: 'Therese had a lovely singing voice. She'd sing all sorts of songs; she'd sing Irish songs. All I remember is that I could sit and listen to Therese.'

After leaving school, Therese worked as a secretary, first in Limerick and then in Dublin. In Limerick she attracted the attention of local man Tony Portley, who was studying at University College Dublin, and was a close friend of Maurice MacGowan. Tony was keen on Therese and even gave up smoking so he could afford to take her out. 'She was knocking around with Tony Portley and getting free meals; that's what she did,' says Shane. 'If nobody else was offering one, and it didn't happen that often, she could always get a meal off Tony.'

It was Tony who introduced Therese to Maurice, and it quickly became clear that in doing so, he had made a fatal error. Like Therese, Maurice had a deep passion for literature. He read poetry to her in her small, rented bedsit in Dublin, and they began spending more and more time together. 'Tony realised that he didn't have a chance fairly early,' explains Shane. 'They [Maurice and Therese] were walking out for ages before they actually started courting. My dad forked out a whole week's wages for a copy of *Ulysses*, but she burnt it when she got to the first bit of obscenity! They had this stove and if it went out, they would freeze to death, so they had to keep it going. She could have put one of her Edna O'Brien books in, but instead she put in that brand new *Ulysses* that had just come out and he had spent all his money to get because it was disapproved of strongly by the Church. So, it was very expensive for a book. Mind you, he didn't just rely on a week's wages – he was a very good gambler on the horses. He had a great economic brain.'

Therese was extremely busy in Dublin and earned money from modelling as well as from her secretarial job. On 18 March 1957 she was named Irish Colleen by the *Evening Press* and given front-page billing. 'She did loads of modelling and became Ireland's top model for a while,' Shane says proudly. 'She was on the front of all the papers, pictured with three wolfhounds. That was taken in the same place as Van Morrison laid down with wolfhounds on the cover of *Veedon Fleece*.'

Her striking looks drew plenty of male attention, including that of the poet and novelist Patrick Kavanagh. Siobhan says, 'He saw Mum and Dad walking over Leeson Street Bridge one day and was said to have asked Mum afterwards if she was involved with "that fella". Mum said she was, and Patrick Kavanagh said to her he had thought she was because he saw them shouting at one another and knew they were trying to communicate!' Adds Shane, 'She met Patrick Kavanagh loads of times. He used to pick up girls from the country; he just liked talking to them and writing poetry about them. He was pretty attractive to women, especially girls from the country. He was the prince of Irish writers and poets.'

Therese also did some acting and was offered a tour with a theatre company, an invitation she declined as, by that time, she was set on marrying Maurice. They tied the knot on 1 August 1956 at Kilbarron church, just a couple of miles from The Commons. For their honeymoon, the newlyweds borrowed Maurice's dad's car and drove around Ireland. Maurice remembers staying at the Old Ground Hotel in Ennis, County Clare, and stopping off at the Galway Races during their two-week trip.

Although they had much in common, Maurice's upbringing in suburban Dublin had been very different from Therese's life in a remote village and it is one that offers another perspective on his son's Irish heritage. Shane's great-great-grandfather, John MacGowan, was a leading house builder who developed parts of Ranelagh in south Dublin, where there was once a MacGowan Terrace named after him.

He married Belinda Lysaght, a daughter of landed gentry whose surname would later be given to Maurice, Shane and Siobhan as a middle name. One of John and Belinda's children – referred to in the family as the 'Ranelagh five' – was Shane's great-grandfather William and it was his conversion to Catholicism to marry Jane White that ended the Protestant MacGowan line. The marriage is said to have been a disastrous one and he more or less deserted his wife and two sons William and Noel. Such was William's ill-feeling towards his father that he later changed his name to Maurice.

Shane's grandfather took law exams as a youngster but eventually joined the civil service and worked his way up to be deputy registrar of the Land Registry. After taking early retirement, he returned to his interest in legal matters and became a barrister. He married Eileen Green, known as Lena, who came from a steel-making family in Sheffield and who had had a difficult start in life. Her mother had died young and her father was an alcoholic, leaving Lena to be raised by her stern maternal grandfather.

The couple had four children: Sybil, Madeleine, William (Billy) and Maurice. Sybil married Belfast man Rene Harriman and, when he got a job in a London bank, they moved to Tunbridge Wells in Kent, where she started The Childrens Salon. The clothing company is run today by her daughter Michele Harriman-Smith and is a global online empire named Childrensalon. Billy trained as a surgeon and became a professor and registrar at the Royal College of Surgeons in Dublin. Madeleine tragically succumbed to tuberculosis, which claimed the lives of many thousands of people in Ireland in the first half of the twentieth century. She died aged just 18.

Maurice Matthew Lysaght MacGowan was born in Dublin on 7 October 1929 and his sharp intellect was clear from a young age. Billy found that while he read comics in bed, his younger brother was devouring huge encyclopaedias from the family's generously stocked bookshelves. So advanced was his reading age that he gained early entry to Belvedere College, a Jesuit school for boys in the heart of the city, where he excelled. At University College Dublin he was awarded first-class honours in his BA and MA, both of which were in political economy and national economics. His BA was put on show at an exhibition.

Maurice had a particular flair for Latin and Greek, writing his own translations of the Greek plays, and he would later take Shane and Siobhan to professional performances of them in London – to their dread! Later in life he penned a series of satirical plays and poetry under the pseudonym of George Geneva, which he now says will serve as his epitaph: 'Have a laugh on George Geneva, whose pseudonym he never needed, as all his works went quite unheeded.'

After completing his studies, Maurice worked in stocks and shares for a firm in Dublin owned by the Brenninkmeijers, the Dutch family who had founded the C&A clothing chain. The company clearly considered him an asset because, when the Dublin operation was closed, he was offered a position at its headquarters in London's Marble Arch. Maurice was to be head of personnel administration, designing pension schemes, salary structures and taking on other economics-related work. So, following his job offer, he and Therese took the big decision to emigrate to England.

'There was very little employment really,' said Therese in the documentary *If I Should Fall From Grace With God*, broadcast on the Irish channel TG4. 'Many, many people had to go abroad to either England or America or somewhere else to actually earn a living and Maurice was one of those really. So, we had to go to London.'

A farewell party was held on 29 August 1957 and Maurice and Therese, who was now pregnant with Shane, followed in the footsteps of so many in Ireland by emigrating to England.

Initially, the young couple found it hard to adjust to life in a small, rented flat. 'We started off in Ealing, which I hated with a great hatred,' said Maurice in the same documentary. 'Coming from Dublin it was a real dreary London suburb.' However, as was common for the Irish diaspora, Therese and Maurice had relatives who had already settled in the UK and could help with their transition. Sybil and Rene were about an hour and a half away in affluent Tunbridge Wells and Maurice and Therese would regularly visit their large, detached home in Madeira Park, bought in 1953 and referred to in the family as 'Mad Park'.

Britain was experiencing a cold winter in 1957 as the Queen was preparing to make her very first televised Christmas speech. Through the snow, Maurice and a heavily pregnant Therese drove to Kent to wait for the arrival of their first baby. His parents and his brother Billy and his family had come over from Dublin so they could be there for the birth, and as Maurice and Therese would be staying at Madeira Park, it was decided the baby should be delivered at the nearest maternity hospital. Shane says: 'It was my dad's idea to visit them for Christmas to cut out the cost, tsscchh', "because you've got to think of the baby now".'

Shane Patrick Lysaght MacGowan was born on Christmas Day 1957 at Pembury hospital. As a 'Christmas Day baby', his arrival was duly reported in the local press and he was the subject of plenty of attention. Therese recalled: 'Because he was the Christmas baby, the matron, the doctors, the nurses, the mayor actually, came to give him gifts. And he was photographed and hung up on the wall in the hospital – a sign of things to come.' [1]

But the festive mood on the maternity ward meant Therese was overlooked by the staff, according to Maurice. 'He was the Christmas baby, and all the buggers were celebrating,' he remembers. 'Therese was roaring in pain and she got very little attention; she never forgot that. They were very poor with her.'

When Therese left hospital, they returned to Sybil and Rene's at Madeira Park, but there was no cot for Shane, leading to a family legend that was passed on down the years. Paul Harriman, Sybil's son and Shane's cousin, says, 'The story is that when she came out on Boxing Day, they came back here, and Billy and Joan were already here with their son Nick – Shane's first cousin – who had the cot. So, Shane was put in a drawer of the chest of drawers, which was very sensible.' His sister Michele, who still lives in the house, adds, 'My mother was quite into it, putting babies in drawers who came to stay the night!'

Shane's birth certificate shows that his proud parents registered him on 2 January 1958, with Rene and Sybil's home at 23 Madeira Park given as their address. Maurice's profession was recorded as company executive.

In fact, the first two years or so of Shane's life, aside from holidays, were spent at the ground-floor flat in Woodfield Avenue, Ealing. It was here that baby Shane made a great impression on Miss Lamb, an older woman who lived upstairs, and a photograph from this time shows the two of them together, Shane brandishing a toy knife. 'Miss Lamb was an old servant of the Brenninkmeijers, and she was a great character,' says Maurice. 'She knew them all from when they were little and she'd talk about "little Willie", William Brenninkmeijer. She adored Shane. "Mother Two", she called herself.'

Shane was about three when his family moved to Tunbridge Wells. They rented part of 50 Claremont Road, a large, terraced house close to Madeira Park, with Shane going to a local playschool. The following year they relocated to Saltdean in Brighton, where he started at St Martha's convent school in Rottingdean.

Shane's sister Siobhan was born on 22 February 1963. Perhaps typically for a small child who suddenly has a rival for their parents' attention, Shane's initial reaction wasn't positive. 'I think when you are the younger sibling you come into a readymade family,' says Siobhan. 'For me, it was Shane, Mum and Dad straight away. But when Shane met me, I'm told he wasn't impressed with this interloper!'

The MacGowans' stay in the coastal village was short-lived and the following year they returned to Tunbridge Wells, this time buying their own house. Maurice's grandfather in Dublin had always rented and didn't believe in owning his own house, a philosophy Maurice had himself adopted. However, Therese wanted them to have their own place, and they bought their first home. Number 6 Newlands is a large, detached house in Langton Green, a quintessentially English, middle-class suburb with neat lawns and driveways – a galaxy away from The Commons. Shane has said his only happy times as a child were spent on his holidays in Tipperary, but Siobhan remembers this chapter of their life in England with great affection.

'The house at Newlands had four bedrooms,' she says. 'I think the houses were built in the sixties, so for then it was a modern housing estate. I loved it because we were very happy there. We had a typical English model house with an A-roof. It had latticed windows and out the back was this big wood, which I can't believe they've now cut down. In our back garden we actually had a wood. It was unreal; beautiful. Shane had a white cat called Mulligan – that was our first cat. Mulligan disappeared for a few weeks and then he was found at the back of a drawer and still in good form.'

Shane paints a less than favourable view of the place to which they moved: 'Tunbridge Wells is a grotty, London overspill town. There is a top end of the town where they've got The Pantiles, which they built because the king started coming there – one of the Hanover kings – because there was a spa there. So, they built pantiles there and shops and stuff. So, there was good housing going pretty cheap around there. Newlands was the first estate we lived in; they were still building it then.'

For the family as a whole it was a happy time. Maurice had a stable, well-paid job, Therese liked the area, and Sybil, Rene and their children lived nearby. The family dynamic was a good one and Shane was close to both his parents. 'He was very attached to both me and Therese and we had good fun – we were like pals,' says Maurice. 'He was my sidekick; we'd laugh and joke together.'

Maurice and Therese were both outgoing and sociable and, when they weren't entertaining, they were round at the Harrimans. Siobhan and Shane got on famously with their cousins and family parties were a regular occurrence, Rene playing the piano and Maurice always full of talk and with a drink in his hand. By this time, Frank Leech (a distant relation on the MacGowan side), his wife Catherine and their young son John had also moved to Tunbridge Wells to be near Sybil and Rene. They too were close to Shane when he was growing up, particularly Catherine. Maurice and Therese also attended St Augustine's church in Tunbridge Wells and Father Bill Howell was a frequent visitor to Newlands, playing football with Shane and Siobhan on the lawn. Siobhan recalls Fr Howell and her mother engaging in good-natured debate about social and moral issues and Therese challenging some of his ideas.

Overall, Shane's childhood mirrored that of so many youngsters growing up in 1960s' England. Saturday teatime, he and Siobhan would settle down to watch *Doctor Who* and both had toy Daleks. Shane had a Scalextric, of which Siobhan was very envious, and they careered around the house in Batman and Robin outfits. Board games on the dining room table often brought the whole family together and brought out Shane's fiercely competitive spirit.

'We used to play Monopoly a lot on the table in the dining room and Shane did not like losing at all,' says Siobhan. 'He also used to cheat at cards when I played with him because he didn't like losing. Dad had this card game called The Racing Game. My dad was mad into racing horses, liked betting on them, and we enjoyed that.'

Shane had a wicked sense of humour and would say and do things for sheer devilment, something he would continue into later life. 'On Christmas Day, when I was about 6, Santa Claus apparently bought me Witchy Poo pens, which were pens with witches' hats on them, and put them at the end of my bed,' remembers Siobhan. 'I went rushing into Shane, who was in his room, and went, "Shane, Shane, look what Santa Claus bought me." And he turned around and said, "There is no Santa Claus." [she laughs] He told me that on Christmas morning. So, I rushed in to see Mum and Dad and said, "Shane says there's no Santa Claus," and then I heard all this shouting in the background. I didn't believe him at that stage.'

Siobhan recalls another dastardly trick he played on her. 'There was this dark-haired, very fat boy, that I was in love with for some reason,' she says. 'I had seen him in a school play which I think Shane was in as well. I was saying, "Shane, Shane, will you tell him I said. "Hello"? And Shane was going, "Fuck off." Anyway, a Valentine's letter came for me which said, "Not to be opened until February the fourteenth". So, I was all excited and when I opened it, it said, "Fuck off, you annoying little cow. Love from…" whatever his name was. And Shane was like, "Hee-hee!" So, he had planned this. He was such a bastard!'

Shane was and remains family-oriented, however, and he could be protective towards his younger sister. Siobhan says, 'We had next-door neighbours, and they had a little girl who had a tea set and I was mad on this tea set. I was doing what I shouldn't have been doing, which was sneaking through their gate to play with the tea set. Then one day her brother put an elastic band on the gate so that when I opened it, it sprang in my eye. I went wailing home and Mum had me on her knee, and Shane said, "Where's the fucking bastard? I'm going to kill the bastard."'

Overall, with an older brother she looked up to, Siobhan has fond memories of her early childhood. 'He could be a bit grumpy with me,' she remembers, 'but I wouldn't have been grumpy with him in those days because I think I was probably just a bit of an adoring little sister. He was older than me. I would have said we got on well in those days. My impression of it is that I just loved him.'

On moving to Langton Green, Shane was enrolled at a local school. But it wasn't through the gates of a state primary school that he walked on his first day, but the fee-paying Holmewood House. Set in thirty acres of rolling countryside on the Kent border, it had been opened as a boys' school just after the Second World War. Some pupils boarded there but, as the MacGowans lived nearby, Shane was a 'day boy'.

The decision to send him to a private prep school was Therese's and one that Maurice went along with reluctantly. 'She wanted our first boy to go to public school,' he says. 'I wasn't a bit happy about it. I went along with her on the boy, but I didn't go along with her on the girl. But she wasn't so worried about private education for a girl. That was the way it was in those days.'

Shane also emphasises it was at his mother's insistence that he went to public school. 'Holmewood was producing young gentlemen and cricket was more important than most things,' he explains. 'I was dragged along there to meet [the headmaster] Bairamian and see if I wanted to go there, although it wasn't up to me. My mother dragged me in. She wanted me to mix with the fucking English middle-class who were trying to be upper-class, like the nouveau riche, trying to get there. But most of them were too thick. They didn't do much writing or thinking or creating. Their parents were not rich, they were not poor. They thought it was important their children got the Holmewood House name, which was supposed to be a really good name.'

The headmaster at Holmewood, the flamboyant Robert 'Bob' Bairamian, shared Maurice's love of Greek and Latin and was, according to Shane, 'heavily into Irish books'. The ambitious Armenian was just 24 when he took charge, but he already had a reputation for getting the best out of his pupils. He was quick to identify and encourage Shane's extraordinary talents when he joined the school and he never forgot him. 'He was very unusual indeed, one of the most unusual personalities I've ever, ever met,' he told the BBC in 2018. 'I thought he would end up in the drama scene.'

Shane sniggers as he reminisces about his seven years at Holmewood and is at pains to stress this was no Eton or Harrow. 'It was a tip when I went there!' he says. 'The toilets were fucking filthy; they were like a slum. There were really old classrooms and stuff, and it was *Goodbye Mr Chips*. Well, they were trying to do that, but it wasn't *Goodbye Mr Chips*. We liked some of the teachers and we disliked most of them. But we thought they were funny because we reckoned they were all wife-swappers and alcoholics and chain-smokers who didn't know the answers to most of their own questions.'

Holmewood admittedly didn't fit the stereotype of an English public school when Shane was enrolled in 1964. From the outset, Robert Bairamian had welcomed pupils from different countries, including Nigeria and Ghana. He had spent the first ten years of his life in Cyprus and his Armenian father served as chief justice of Sierra Leone and a judge of appeal in Nigeria. At his funeral in 2018, a message was read out from the President of Ghana, Nana Akufo-Addo, who had been taught by him in the 1950s. Shane recalls mixing with black, Pakistani and working-class English pupils, and says Bairamian was interested in anything and anyone who might raise Holmewood's profile.

'Schools were like that all over the place, everywhere where they wanted the name to get money out of people, and if they could be bullied into playing cricket maybe they would like it and be really good cricketers. Anything that would put the place on the map. Also, he was offering places to blacks, Irish, Asians. It wasn't a school like that. It was a tip disguised as a school like that. There was a small handful of brilliant teachers and the kids weren't generally interested. Nobody likes school. I would have preferred it if I'd got hit with a cricket bat a few times. I used to get my kicks really fucking him [Bairamian] up.

'When Bairamian arrived, it was big news. There was a black guy there who was really into reggae and could really dance to it. But Bairamian didn't think that was Holmewood. It wasn't really a place where you could skank the way through the night, smoking ganja. But we used to take our dicks out, tsscchh, and see who could get the biggest erection and the black guy had a huge one. The chemistry class had this thing for measuring things rising and he hit the end of the dial. It was fucking twelve inches long and he was fucking 11 years old. His voice had broken, and he had a moustache, and he looked really good as well. He looked like a fucking reggae star. Holmewood was good like that. There was no attempt to make it a fucking elitist thing. It was the sixties and Bairamian was a modernist.'

Shane's upbringing may have seemed conventional for the time, but he was not, especially when it came to reading. He devoured books and exhibited an appetite for literature way beyond his age. Maurice, hugely literate himself, often read with him and nurtured his interest in heavyweight classic novels that few children of his age would have attempted. Therese was also a great reader and she encouraged his love of books, which he was always happy to discuss with others.

Maurice remembers: 'We read and discussed books a lot together. We would laugh a lot at Joyce. We read out the funnier passages from *Ulysses* and with *Finnegan's Wake* – I managed one page and he alleged he'd read two! We both liked the passage in *Finnegan's Wake* where God was called "Guv"; we laughed a lot at that and KMRIA [Kiss My Royal Irish Arse] in *Ulysses*. Back then, we probably considered *Dubliners* his better work. Both Therese and I would be reading writers like Evelyn Waugh and Graham Greene and he would read them also. We also enjoyed the mobsters in Damon Runyon. We read Sean O'Casey, D. H. Lawrence, and Dostoyevsky (*The Brothers Karamazov*), and Voltaire and Sartre. This was all up to age 12; he had a very advanced reading age. We had a great meeting of minds up until age 12, and then Shane progressed on to more modern things and writers that I'd find challenging, like Günter Grass.'

Siobhan recalls: 'I was drawing one time while we were watching *Doctor Who* and I drew a tree with pink leaves and a blue stem. And Shane went, "No, no, that's brown and that's green." And I went, "Huh?" And he said, "It's all right, you're a surrealist." I suppose he was about 10. He was reading widely, and Dad was giving him the books to read, and he didn't give him children's books; he gave him books by Irish writers and other classic writers. So, he was reading grown-up books. Dad would have had a big influence on that and that started young, Dad's handing him books. They shared a very close relationship at that stage. Shane read a lot of what Dad would be giving him and they talked a lot about all that kind of stuff.'

Catherine Leech also had regular conversations with young Shane about books and recalls him being 'very intellectual'. 'He was great fun and he used to read an awful lot,' she says. 'Shane actually introduced me to Samuel Beckett. Shane read everything and his daddy never stopped him reading and never said to him, "You're not to read that." He was just naturally clever, but then so was his daddy.'

His cousin Michele has fond memories of babysitting him and she was astounded at the level of books he read. 'He was a softie. He had beautiful curly hair and we just used to laugh. He was just a really nice kid to look after. We used to play with games and Shane used to read bits to me of what he was reading. That's when I used to think, I'm not quite sure what the hell that was all about... I was trying to get through *Ulysses* because I was thinking, I've got to be able to read this. So, I tried to be as clever as he was, this little squirt!'

Aged 11 and a half, Shane was reading *The Devils* by Dostoyevsky, *The Grapes of Wrath* by John Steinbeck and *A Portrait of the Artist as a Young Man* by James Joyce. His writing was also precocious, and so highbrow were his reading lists that some of his teachers were suspicious. How many children of his age would possess such an imagination, let alone be able to bring such extraordinary ideas so powerfully to the page? And was it really likely that during the school holidays he was reading works by Dostoevsky and Nietzsche?

Holmewood English teacher, the late Tom Simpson, was initially sceptical of Shane's claims, but when he came to mark the stories Shane had written, he knew the school had a literary genius on its hands. Even at age eight and a half, he says, Shane was simply 'brilliant'.

'It is extraordinary that quite a lot of staff and boys didn't appreciate him at all,' said Tom, in an interview for this book. 'Holmewood didn't shut him down, but they did not realise what an amazing talent they had. Some of them I think didn't believe it. "Did he really write that? I don't believe it." But I did believe it because I had seen a lot of it in his own handwriting... I said to Bob, "We have an amazing young man here and we have got to do something about it." I think Shane did enjoy his last few years at Holmewood because eventually the rest of the staff began to realise how brilliant he was. I pushed it a bit.'

Shane remarks: 'He [Tom Simpson] was a tortured artistic genius. He realised I could probably write better stuff than him with a bit of help...I wasn't interested in what I was writing about in the essays, but I was good at writing about history and stuff about what was going on in America: the Vietnam War, the Black Panthers, the riots and killings, and the Ku Klux Klan. I was interested in that sort of thing. I wasn't interested in fucking G. I. Joe and cricket.'

It is testament to the indelible impression Shane's words made on his English master that Simpson kept many of his handwritten stories and one of his exercise books, convinced his star pupil would one day be famous. I collected them when I went to meet him and returned them to Shane and his family, something Tom had always wanted. The stories, penned in a large and distinctive hand during his time at Holmewood, offer a fascinating insight into the development of a unique songwriter. They show that the subjects which animate him today – the Catholic Church, rural Irish society, war – inspired him just as deeply as a child. The essays written during his time at Holmewood also illustrate how Shane learned young the value of listening in on conversations .

In 'Dusk', which appeared in the school journal *The Holmewoodian*, he named-checked 'Paddy McGrath, madman of the Puckane district' and described the exchanges between locals coming and going on asses and carts. '"Even' to you, Mick." "Even', Pat. How's the missus? Thought she had a cold." All off to some place.'

Overheard gossip supplied fodder for a piece entitled 'From the Top of the Hill'. On seeing a local pub was closed, he concluded the landlord 'must have got pissed last night as he always does. One night he came home and threw chairs at his wife and child. They had to leave the house.' Even at 12, Shane was soaking up stories about people and committing them to paper.

Coarse language and the vernacular peppered his stories. 'Get moving, you bitch of an ass' and 'Gerroff, you bloody cur!' form part of the colourful dialogue in 'Dusk'. In 'Man Drowning', he wrote: 'Look at the beach. A woman and a kid. She's asleep. Stupid cow.' He used the vocabulary of the man and woman in the street and his storytelling was more authentic for it, just as his songs would be. 'You scumbag, you maggot,' slurs one of his drunken characters famously in 'Fairytale Of New York'.

Like his English teacher, Maurice and Therese had also thought Shane might end up writing books. 'We knew he was brilliant at writing and English and all that kind of thing, and Maurice said, "I suppose you'll probably earn your living as a writer,"' recalled Therese. 'He said, "I will, Dad, but not in the way you're talking about. I'll earn my living," he said, "through music, writing through music because that's the way you communicate with people nowadays. It's a much wider form of communication." I remember him saying that.' [2]

Maurice added, 'Well, I suppose, you see, I thought it might be more in the book form, rather than in the song form. But that's before 12. I knew around 12 it wasn't going to be that because there was Bob Dylan blowing one ear out and the Grateful Dead blowing the other. I knew there was something going on there.' [3]

Catherine Leech always took a great interest in Shane's progress and wondered if he might write books. But she was not surprised when he went on to forge a career in music. 'That's what I would have expected because he didn't just suddenly become like that,' she said. 'It would have been part of him. It was bound to come out some way because he came from such a musical family.'

As well as Shane's natural gift for writing and his unusually candid style of prose, Tom Simpson also remembered his pupil's wry sense of humour. 'I can remember him taking the mickey out of the headmaster,' he said. 'A lot of the other boys there were listening, and the headmaster asked him a question and Shane wasn't quite sure what the answer was. So, he took a coin out of his pocket and threw it in the air and said, "Do you want heads or tails?" Bob did not know what to do and he looked at me and I was hysterical with laughter. Shane wasn't being rude because he could take the mickey out of anybody.'

Shane has also not forgotten the incident, 'Well, I thought it was the best idea. I didn't want to be wrong, and we loved taking the piss out of him.'

Justin Bairamian, Bob's son and director of BBC Creative, found bound copies of *The Holmewoodian* in his late father's possessions. They included stories Shane had written between the ages of 9 and 13 that were striking in their maturity. 'They are bizarre pieces, as you would expect,' says Justin. 'Tom always said that he wrote like an 18- or 19-year-old at the age of 9 or 10 and he was one of the brightest English students he ever taught. He has always remembered him fondly... The reason he kept all the work is because he admired it so much. He certainly wouldn't have done that with a lot of boys.'

Many children of Irish families brought up in England felt a lack of identity. They weren't Irish because they hadn't been born in Ireland and didn't live there, but they weren't English because they had Irish parents and relatives. The tradition of going back to the family homestead during school holidays, where they would spend weeks playing on the farm or in the fields, reinforced their sense of Irishness. However, as the holidays ended, they had to board the ferry and return to their English schools, friends and culture. Several people who would bond with Shane later in his life came from Irish families and felt similarly conflicted.

For Shane, the contrast between the aspirational suburb of Tunbridge Wells – where people tended their neat lawns and washed their cars in the drive – and the carefree, pastoral world of The Commons, could not have been starker. But it was in this rustic cottage, wrapped in the warm embrace of his adoring aunts and assimilated into farm life by his uncles, that young Shane found his identity. 'He loved Ireland – he still loves Ireland,' says Catherine Leech. 'All Therese's family were around, uncles and everything, so it was ideal for Shane as a little boy because you have great freedom in Tipperary.'

Shane first remembers going to The Commons when he was 'two or three, probably younger' and was just three months old when his parents took him to Tipperary to show him off. He loved it immediately and his parents, who like so many had left their native country behind with great reluctance, gave him every opportunity to spend time there. 'At The Commons, we were surrounded by relatives, Irish relatives and friends, and they used to come over and visit wherever we happened to be living in England,' says Shane. 'Then I might go back with one of them or I might go back with my parents.' Therese said: 'We tried to leave Shane in Ireland as much as possible when he was young. During his holidays he always returned to Ireland... his heart and soul always lay in Ireland and Tipperary. That's where his spiritual home was – his heart was there.' [4]

The journey from Kent was arduous. Shane and Siobhan would cover themselves with a blanket on the back seat of the car and write and draw to pass time on the long drive to Holyhead in Wales, where they would catch the ferry to Dún Laoghaire in County Dublin. They would spend some time with Maurice's parents in Dublin before driving to Tipperary, always arriving in the dark. Uncle John would be waiting for them at the gate and tears would run down the faces of their aunts as they hugged and kissed them and excitedly swept them inside. Their visits would be more eagerly anticipated than Christmas and were a highlight for all the family members still living there. When they came to leave, the tears would flow all over again and holy water would be sprinkled over them to keep them safe.

The Commons was a microcosm of bucolic life in Ireland and Shane drank in every drop. His aunts and uncles involved him and Siobhan in everything they did on the farm and, as a result, they felt part of it. They lent a hand with the threshing, played happily in the bales of hay, herded geese, rode horses bareback and looked after calves – experiences that few children back in Tunbridge Wells would have had. Two collies lived on the farm and the children were 'given' one each: Shane had Peter and Siobhan's was Paul. 'Shane got the really smooth, sleek collie and I got the one with all the matted fur who couldn't get off the floor!' laughs Siobhan.

They loved the freedom and Shane – who never missed an opportunity to prank his sister – took full advantage of what was an exciting environment. 'When we were doing the hay over at Tom's, the way they did it meant there used to be a big hole in the middle and I came down with tea and pancakes for the men,' remembers Siobhan. 'Shane didn't want me there, so he picked me up and threw me in the hole. I couldn't get out and there was a search party going around. In the end, they heard me shouting from inside the hole and that's what he did. He also used to put my face in cowpats!'

Shane didn't just direct his mischief at his younger sister; his cousin Debra Donnelly also remembers the playfully wicked side of his nature. 'When we were small, probably about 7 or 8, I remember he was very like the Lynches in that he would tease,' she says. 'We were up in the attic and I heard a noise and I said, "What's that?" and he said, "It's the banshee and it's coming to get you." That was the relationship we had. If the turkeys were going to chase anybody, he would make sure they chased me.'

Shane and Siobhan were spoiled rotten by their uncles and aunts, who missed Therese desperately after she and Maurice emigrated to England, as they did her brother Sean and his family. Vicky Cahill, Sean's widow, comments: 'The thing is that Sean and Therese were their pride and delight. Once somebody else got them they didn't have quite so much hold on them, but it was their offspring [Shane and Siobhan] and they couldn't do a thing wrong.'

Siobhan remembers the Lynches as 'very soft, very sensitive, lovely people' who showered the children with attention. Aunty Ellen did most of the cooking and she would spend a lot of time with Shane, whom they referred to as 'the Little Man'. 'As a child he was a very bad eater and at The Commons they used to make him a little dish that he would eat called "savoury",' says Siobhan. 'Aunty Ellen made it and it was hard-boiled egg, cabbage, mashed potato and butter.' Mary Taylor, another of Shane's aunts, confirms: 'Auntie Ellen always made Shane his lunch or dinner and he wouldn't have anybody else's.'

Asked who most influenced Shane at this formative time in his life, Siobhan replies: 'I think all of them, but if I was going to pick one it would be Aunty Nora. They used to walk to Mass together and he used to hold her hand. He loved all of them really.'

Nora was the one who would make Shane have a wash when he was little and changed his clothes. Debra also has fond memories of her aunt: 'I remember there was an old couch out in the garden and one afternoon, when everyone was out working in the farm, she made me afternoon tea. We had tea and Swiss roll and she let me pour the tea. Everyone was really busy, but she just made time.'

Religion was still at the heart of Irish life in the 1960s and the Lynches were staunch Catholics. Nora was constantly saying prayers, tuned in at six o'clock every evening for the broadcast of the Angelus on RTE (Raidió Telifís Éireann, the Irish national broadcaster), and walked to Mass every morning at Kilbarron church, praying the rosary on the way.

Shane was happy to escort her: 'I would go to Mass with Aunty Nora or I might go with the family. Mass is a social event, people met each other there and the pubs opened half an hour before the chapel bell sounded for Mass, so you could have a few drinks and hang around smoking until the last minute. Everybody would be looking shifty, wondering what they should leave out of confession and wondering if they'd notice if they didn't go to confession. I enjoyed going to confession because I simply said, "I was rude to my mother, but I apologised," or, "I lied to my mother, but I apologised," and various bullshit like that.'

Shane's exposure to such devout Catholicism at a young age left a lasting impression. 'I might have become a priest if I hadn't been a singer,' he said [5]. Alongside 'free-thinking Catholicism', he has explored Taoism, Buddhism and Zen over the years. The Sacred Heart of Jesus and a statue of Mary holding Jesus have pride of place on the mantelpiece of his flat in Dublin to this day and he wears a crucifix around his neck.

'I love the way Shane talks about Irish Catholicism because I think that is something that is absolutely essential to Shane and who he is – that rural Irish Catholic,' says Ann Scanlon, journalist and author of *The Pogues – The*

Lost Decade. 'He is very spiritual and that is something we both have quietly in common. He did describe himself many times to me as a religious maniac and it's that thing of when you're a kid, and you feel close to God and all the angels and saints, and some of us never lose that.'

The Commons was a paradise for Shane and he hated going home. While Siobhan would spend maybe three weeks of her summer holiday there, Shane would spin it out for as long as he could, often staying for the duration. Siobhan says: 'He would stay there for six weeks and we'd pick him up off the bus and he'd smell of the fire and he'd have the cap on and all that kind of stuff. So, he did stretch it out, he did love it there and was very influenced by it all.'

Shane says: 'It's a magical place because it's probably a hundred years out of date, the whole kind of thing, and it's great. It's a real home and it had been the family home for a couple of centuries. The house was about four hundred years old and it started off as one big flagged-floor room with a big hearth fire with pots and pans on hooks and all the cooking was done there. I played hurling out in the fields with friends and my older relatives. The girls play a version of the game called camogie, but we played girls because we didn't mind. It's really sexual watching a girl running around with knobbly knees and big tits smacking the shit out of the opposition! It's really violent, really fast, really skilful – the Irish warrior spirit.'

The Commons was an 'open house' and was legendary in the area as a place for singing and dancing at night. Maurice was aghast when Therese first took him there to introduce him to her family and couldn't believe the amount of talking that went on. Shane's aunt Mary Taylor says her husband was equally taken aback by the scenes. 'The first time he came here the place was full,' says Mary. 'He said to me, "What's the occasion, is it a birthday?" and I said, "No, it's an everyday occurrence." All the neighbours were always here. And they used to have the crossroads dancing and when that finished when it got dark, everybody came back here for the rest of the night.'

Everyone in the room had to play, sing or recite something. A wide-eyed Shane found himself in the middle of these impromptu sessions and was a willing participant. 'Shane would stand up on the table and sing,' says Siobhan. 'But that wouldn't have been an unusual thing because everybody would be taking a turn. So, Aunty Ellen played the accordion, somebody would sing a song and they'd make him sing. You were just called to do it.'

Shane's aunt, Monica Cahalan, said: 'He was singing from a very early age and acting as he was singing songs. Do you remember the "Hole in the Bucket"? Do you remember that song? Oh, lord, when he was only two-and-a-half he was at that, and it was a scream to look at him. He was amazing.' [6]

Therese said her young son soaked up the music and the atmosphere of The Commons and it was those childhood experiences that inspired him to perform Irish music. 'Every weekend and sometimes in the middle of the week you had music, you had dancing, set dancing on the old kitchen floor, and you had songs,' she said. 'So, he absorbed all that wonderful traditional Irish music and singing and dancing through his pores when he was at a very formative age. And it had a tremendous influence on him, on his love of Irish music and on his desire really to do something for Irish music as well.' [7]

Shane recalled: 'Everybody would sing here in this room and play music and dance and, on Friday, Saturday and Sunday, the door was open all night and it would be a place to go for a session. It was a constant session for the whole weekend. I would be put upon the table from the earliest days I can remember and told to sing what songs I knew. My repertoire gradually increased, so I did my first gig when I was three.' [8]

Although it would be many years before he would fuse his extraordinary words with music, Shane was still at primary school when he first picked up a guitar and began to learn his first chords. And it was during visits to Tipperary that he got his first taste of playing with other people. 'I played music with ballad groups in Ireland,' he explains. 'I started playing when I was about 9. I got chord books and struggled with a crappy guitar and then I went to one lesson. The guy showed me how to play "Careless Love" and another good song. I had the basics and there were people I played with and I thought the best way to get better is to keep playing it with other guys at school. We played Fairport Convention songs and we tried to play Led Zeppelin. We did play Black Sabbath because they're a lot easier.'

The Commons has been a place of reassurance for Shane throughout his life, a remote but resolute rock in a frequently torrid sea. He has shown it off with deep pride, as some people do their children, and visits are more like pilgrimages. Girlfriends have been taken there, one after another, The Popes rehearsed there ahead of their first major show, and Shane and his friend Joey Cashman lived there during the 1990s. Journalists have rarely, if ever, been told about his upbringing in England, but have been frequently regaled with stories about Tipperary. In the 1997 BBC documentary *The Great Hunger: The Life and Songs of Shane MacGowan*, Shane was filmed in the kitchen at the cottage where he said he only ever had 'happy times'.

Places in Shane's beloved Tipperary have been namechecked in song after song: Cloughprior in 'The Sick Bed Of Cuchulainn'; Finnoe, Shinrone and the River Shannon in 'The Broad Majestic Shannon', and Nenagh in 'Medley', 'Paddy Rolling Stone' and 'Back In The County Hell', not to mention the cast of local characters who populate 'B&I Ferry'.

The rich musical education he received on his trips to Ireland was augmented at home through his dad's record collection. The family used to have regular 'music nights' and Maurice would play records by traditional groups The Dubliners, The Clancy Brothers and The Fureys, as well as Dixieland jazz and rock'n'roll. Maurice remembers Shane liking The Rolling Stones when they saw them on TV when he was still quite young and says he was 11 or 12 when he 'got seriously into music'. Shane's cousin Michele was six years older than him and immersed in music and the hippie culture. Siobhan says her brother 'idolised her' and she was a big influence on him.

His mother's family at The Commons remember Shane's growing obsession, not just with Irish music, but rock'n'roll. 'He was a devil,' says Vicky Cahill. 'He used to come over here for his holidays and he would want to play the records. He collected all the Rolling Stones records out of my collection and took them back with him. He probably sold them.'

In the spring of 1971, Shane went to his first live concert – Mott The Hoople at Tunbridge Wells Assembly Hall. Maurice drove him there but wasn't allowed to accompany his son into the venue. 'I had to drop him there just outside and fuck off or I would have ruined his cred,' he says. 'He really enjoyed it and I collected him, and he was all stiff when he came out of the place.'

Shane remembers, 'It was madness and it was brilliant. It was deafeningly loud because it was the first live rock gig I'd been to, but they weren't a heavy metal band, they were a fucking punk band. They were loud, fast and also melodic. I saw them when the second album *Mad Shadows* came out – really early days. I'd read about them in the pages of the music papers, there were interviews with them and they were really getting to the younger crowd who were getting bored with progressive music. There was a split in the crowd really because there was another lot who were really into Bowie and him dressing as somebody else and being Ziggy Stardust and anti-sexual and all that shit.'

Just how much music and popular culture was coming to mean to Shane was illustrated when he heard on 18 September 1970 that Jimi Hendrix had died. The event also underlined how hard bad news hit him. His reaction was to completely shut himself off, a mechanism that would trigger whenever members of his own family passed away. 'When Jimi Hendrix died, I remember he went into his room and he was lying on his side with his face to the wall and he laid there for twenty-four hours,' says Siobhan. 'He was absolutely devastated. When the Lynches started to die, that's exactly what he did, but he lay on the sofa with his face into it and he just lay there. He went into shutdown.'

Shane's prodigious talent for English and his noticeably mature writing style hadn't just made Tom Simpson and Bob Bairamian at Holmewood sit up and take notice. When Shane was 13, one of his stories entitled 'To Mac, a Bus', won a prize after being entered for a competition in the *Daily Mirror*. As well as receiving £10, Shane had his composition published in a book called *Children As Writers*, featuring the best of the entries.

His literary success, along with a photograph, made the front page of the *Kent & Sussex Courier*. Readers were told how Shane had been writing since he was 5 years old and harboured ambitions of a career in writing. His favourite author was James Joyce and he also enjoyed studying European translations of works by authors such as Jean-Paul Sartre and Thomas Mann. 'I started with stories about space and science fiction when I was five or six,' Shane told the paper [9]. 'When I was ten, I started getting some meaning into my work in the way of self-expression and social commentary.' Holmewood's literary star had even produced a short novel, although he had discarded it, and he hoped eventually to go university to study philosophy.

Characteristically, Shane wasn't especially proud of 'To Mac, a Bus' and didn't understand what the fuss was about. However, his headmaster knew he had a prodigy on his hands and now Shane had received national recognition for his writing.

'Bob Bairamian knew people came along every now and then, and he wasn't that surprised,' remarks Shane. 'I was Irish and the Irish have got a legendary talent for storytelling and the use of words, whether it's Irish words or English words. I won a newspaper prize for a short story, which wasn't very good, I don't think. It was about a bunch of Irish dossers sitting on a bench and it was called "To Mac, a Bus". My dad told me that in the birth announcements in the older Irish press, when you were announcing a baby born to a well-known person about town, a man or a woman, it would say "To Shelagh, a son". Mac gets run over by a bus at the end of the story, so it was called "To Mac, a Bus".

'I was about 13 by then and about to leave. I think Holmewood hassled them to come down and do a story about a local boy and they went for it.'

Maurice well remembers Shane's prize-winning essay and his part in it: 'I wrote the title to the one that won the *Daily Mirror* award – "To Mac, a Bus". I wasn't too impressed because it was the *Daily Mirror*, but I was a bit snobby about literature in those days.'

Shane's education was now moving to secondary level. Therese's driving ambition for her son had influenced the decision to have him schooled at Holmewood and she still wanted the best education available. Bob Bairamian, meanwhile, was aware that if Shane could get a place at a prestigious school, it would be a feather in Holmewood's cap. It is said that he suggested Westminster School for Shane's high school. He was accepted and awarded a partial scholarship.

'Holmewood helped me get into Westminster because I would have been one of the few who had ever gone there,' comments Shane. 'It's a prestigious school, but it's not for clowns. There's no straw boaters and boat races and all that shit. It's nothing like Eton or Harrow. It was for anybody who had done some real learning and doesn't fuck up all the time.'

Catherine Leech was extremely proud of her young nephew's achievement, but not surprised. 'It was natural that he would get in really,' she says. 'Maurice and Therese were both very clever and Maurice let Shane read, which was a very good idea.'

By the time he knew he would be going to Westminster, Shane's attention had drifted well beyond the quiet countryside and the classrooms at Holmewood. His magpie eyes were fixed firmly on the north part of the town that 'always had more violence and aggro', a record shop and a Wimpey bar, which was 'very cool in those days'.

Shane recalls: 'The Beatles drank whiskey and coke, and everybody drank whiskey and coke when they found out that's what The Beatles drank. It was showing off, drinking whiskey and coke and expensive drinks like that. You're thinking as an adolescent. You want to be independent; you want to pick up women, you want to go to good-time gigs and dances, you don't want to work until you have to. And when you do have to, you want to get paid, and school is slavery. But luckily, they were satisfied with grabbing my essays off me and sending them up to Westminster and trying to blag me in there, yeah? Westminster depended on its academic fucking reputation, in other words you had to have a brain cell or two.'

Tom Simpson knew Shane was more than academically equipped to meet the rigorous demands of Westminster. However, in contrast with Bob Bairamian, he considered it an unsuitable choice for his prize-winning pupil and didn't think he would blossom there as he had at Holmewood. 'It's not one of the schools I would have said, "Shane must go there,"' said Tom. 'Once I knew he was going there, I thought, This is not your scene. I knew a lot of Westminster people because I played cricket and it was never for Shane. I thought it was sad he did not go to a decent school which appreciated him.'

Maurice was extremely proud of his son's academic achievements, but he felt that with the intellect he possessed, he didn't need to attend such a school to thrive. There was also the not-insignificant matter of the fees he would end up paying. 'Westminster was Holmewood's idea, in conjunction with Therese, at the cost of my pocket – which was horrific,' he says.

By the time Shane was admitted to Westminster, the MacGowans had already decided to move to London. Maurice was tired of his commute and wanted to be closer to the office. He preferred the urban cut-and-thrust of London to the suburban mundanity of Tunbridge Wells and was fascinated by the capital's ancient history. So, in 1971, the MacGowans sold their spacious home at Newlands and moved into a rented flat in a house in Boyne Park, Tunbridge Wells, while they waited for their new home in London to become available.

For the family, the move would prove disastrous and for Shane it would be the prelude to one of the most traumatic periods of his life.

CHAPTER 2

Shane O'Hooligan

'Every time that I look on the first day of summer
Takes me back to the place where they gave ECT
And the drugged-up psychos
With death in their eyes'

'Dark Streets Of London', **The Pogues**

Shane was a teenager already obsessed with pop music when the MacGowans moved into their London home in the Barbican. As Britain spent its last pounds, shillings and pence before decimalisation at the beginning of 1971 and The Troubles in Northern Ireland spiralled out of control, it was the records of Cream, Black Sabbath, Creedence Clearwater Revival, The Rolling Stones, Pink Floyd and other bands that thundered from his eerily lit bedroom, competing with the daily soundtrack of the construction work outside.

'He got into music big-time at the Barbican and he would have records going all day long up in his room,' recalls Maurice. 'The big one was Bob Dylan and that was the time I got to like Bob Dylan too. I was a real square, sort of pretending to be literary, and I got to love Bob Dylan and still do. I got to love all that rock music, especially when combined with country. My mind was opening. Siobhan was just next door and she'd watch the people entering the den. The music coming out of there was shattering.'

'We had a Black Sabbath poster up in the toilet,' says Siobhan. 'Mum and Dad were like that, so we introduced the culture around the house. Shane used to play his records all day, all night, used to study *Sounds*, *NME*, *Melody Maker*, and a lot of his hippie friends were around the flat all the time.'

A far cry from Tunbridge Wells and a whole world away from The Commons, Willoughby House was a terraced block in the Barbican, a complex seen as being at the frontier of modern housing. The flats were built in the brutalist style and on land which once housed a Roman watchtower, something that appealed to Maurice's love of urban environments and his preoccupation with history. It also meant a much shorter commute to his office in Marble Arch and more opportunities for a post-work pint. For Shane, it was edgy and cool. 'It was right next to the East End,' he says. 'You didn't have to have a lot of money for some of the flats there. The caretaker had a free flat and he got tips from people at the top of the tree. Although they didn't make a big deal out of it, there were people like Roger Moore and Kenny Everett, and a few really famous criminals in there.'

Much of the Barbican had been built in the 1960s, but the three, now iconic, tower blocks were still being built when Shane and his family arrived. The last of these wasn't completed until 1976, so as the four of them were trying to acclimatise to their new surroundings, the constant clamour of building work was going on all around them. 'You would be inside your flat and you could shut it out if you wanted,' says Shane. 'But me and my old man liked leaving the side window open so we could hear all the racket, the mixers and the scaffolding, walls being knocked down.

'They were a real ostentatious design, like stairs and another set of stairs leading to the main bedroom. Me and Siobhan had a room each and there was a kitchen and a garbage disposal unit, which would stink the place out. You put everything in, and it chewed it all away, cabbage and rotting food. There was no natural light: it had strip-lighting. I had a green light. I was very psychedelic. I was well over the edge of psychedelia. I was next door to Jim Morrison when he was already dead. He'd visit sometimes in my fevered imagination. It was a great place to play The Doors, I must admit, really loud.'

Shane not only had to adjust to what he saw as a 'space-age' environment; he also started at Westminster School. His love of literature and natural gift for writing had helped win him a part-scholarship to one of the most historic and prestigious establishments in the country. *The Record of Old Westminsters* records that he began as a dayboy at the school in January 1972, joining Ashburnham House.

Situated in the grounds of Westminster Abbey, the school's history stretches back to the early fourteenth century. Six British prime ministers were taught there, along with poets, philosophers, novelists, high court judges, scientists and other notables. Alumni include former deputy prime minister Nick Clegg, actresses Helena Bonham Carter and Imogen Stubbs, actor and director John Gielgud, broadcaster Louis Theroux, and playwright Stephen Poliakoff. Joining Shane in the roll call of singers and musicians who went there are Thomas Dolby, Dido and Mika.

However, for a teenager already dabbling with drugs and who was drawn to the seamier side of life, the staunchly traditional Westminster was wholly unsuitable. 'Westminster was awful – they were such wankers,' remarks Shane. 'I didn't want to go, but Holmewood wanted to get me in. It was good for me and he [Bairamian] liked the idea of a "foreigner" getting into an English gentleman's school.'

Recalling his initial days there, Shane says his instincts were 'to stay out of the classes for as long as I can, tsscchh, and I'm definitely not doing any sports because they didn't do football. They just did boating, which they called water. We went to Grove Park near Bromley on the train. I was not really into it at first, but then when I tried on one of the uniforms, the uniforms were brilliant. With my hair as long as it was, I looked like the guy out of The Yardbirds.'

The move was doomed to fail from the outset. Shane was fully immersed in his hippie phase when he walked through the doors of Westminster that winter. Then 14, he had shoulder-length hair and he was thin, existing on a diet of bananas and beans. His only real focus was the music he was listening to and the records he was buying, but he used his comprehensive knowledge of music to try to fit in.

One of his classmates Thomas Dolby (real name Robertson) says, 'I think he tried to listen to what the other Westminster kids were listening to at the time – Yes, Genesis, Pink Floyd, ELP, The Allman Brothers – because there was a lot of analysis of them. But you could tell it was not what he was passionate about.'

His yearning to be accepted wasn't helped by the fact that the way he looked and sounded made him stand out like a sore thumb. In The Pogues, he would make a virtue of his oddness, his taxi-door ears and rotting teeth. But as a rake-thin teenager in the most English of schools, he was self-conscious. 'He was awkward, a bit embarrassed about his accent and his teeth, and didn't really seem to fit in,' says Thomas. 'But he was clearly very intelligent.'

Shane's love of pranks also ensured he drew even more attention. When a group were taken to the Mendip Hills for orienteering, he told Thomas that if they turned up in drag, the staff would make them stay on the bus and they would get out of it. In the event, Thomas chickened out and Shane ended up leading some of the others to a pub where they weren't discovered until late in the evening.

In class, Shane never missed an opportunity to play a joke. Thomas recalls: 'He and I sat at the back row of Mr [Alan] Howarth's English class, whispering. Shane had read the books, but he did not participate in discussions. One day Mr Howarth, who later became a cabinet minister under Margaret Thatcher, was talking about Emily Brontë or something, and wanted to humiliate us. So, he asked me what figure of speech a certain word was. I wasn't paying attention. Shane leaned over and whispered, "It's an onanism." So that's what I said out loud! "Robertson, come to the front of the class and look up 'onanism' in my dictionary, and read it out loud, please." Well, it turned out to mean masturbation, or ejaculating outside of the vagina, so I was a laughing stock. It took me a few years to realise the irony of that prank, given Shane's background, and the fact Howarth was a bit of a wanker.'

Outside the classroom, Shane made sure others would never forget him. He was in a gang that conducted 'inquisitions' on fellow pupils, and he was in charge of making them talk. 'If they wanted to get information out of somebody, they sat next to them and I did the interrogation and I might put a fag or two out in his face, tsscchh,' he claims. 'There were lots of different things you could do, like squeeze his nipples and you could dump nettles in his pants and rub them in until he's screaming. And there's no dock leaves nearby, which instantly relieve it, but they wouldn't have relieved this! You've got two guys guarding him from getting away in any direction except backwards, which is a really stupid idea. You just jump on his face a few times and kick him in the balls continuously. We just liked to give it sexy names like Minister for Torture. If they wanted me to perform at my best, I had to be Minister for Torture, tsscchh.'

Despite Shane's notoriety, Westminster was tolerant of pupils who were different, providing they were clever, says Thomas Dolby: 'Shane was thought to be a troublemaker. He had terribly yellowed fingers and teeth, and the teachers loved to point that out. But as public schools went, Westminster was pretty liberal. They tended to allow for different strokes, and Shane was a scholar, and scholars were respected for being very smart and sometimes being from less affluent backgrounds.'

Shane was without question a remarkable writer, continuing to pen pieces that went way beyond his age in terms of style and subject. It wasn't just his ability, but his appreciation of eccentric characters and gruesome stories that made his essays, and later his songs, so vivid. He revelled in life's depravity and soaked up detail to use in his fiction. Ted Craven, his house master at Westminster, who taught English and history, seemed boring to many of his students, droning on endlessly about his days in the Royal Navy. To Shane, however, it was a rich vein of material that he could mine. In his teacher's ramblings, he heard something they didn't.

'He would go into graphic descriptions of degrees of seasickness: before the bile starts coming up and different colours of bile, and you just had to encourage him to keep talking and the lesson was over before you knew it,' Shane recalls of his teacher's anecdotes. 'And you got some great detail. I mean, he helped me a lot with my songwriting. It was like Coleridge – "The Rime of the Ancient Mariner", except that it was on a Second World War ship that he served on. First, you have green bile, which is not pleasant, then you have blue bile and then black bile. It would be great to pour that stuff into glasses and serve it up as absinthe in a West End club.'

At home, Shane spent most of his time listening to music and reading about his favourite bands and artists. A green light bulb hung from the ceiling, giving his room a strange glow, and he would sit at his desk assiduously cutting out articles from the music press. His extensive collection of records was kept on a large bookcase and, sometimes when he was out, Siobhan would sneak in and play them. He watched *Top of the Pops* every week and knew all about the mainstream music scene in Britain, but by devouring the music press he was exposed to the alternative scene in the US and its punk prototypes. At Westminster, his evangelising about these obscure American bands shocked his prog-loving peers.

'A group of us used to sneak out to a coffee bar in Victoria and spend most afternoons nursing a single cup of tea and discussing music,' recalls Thomas. 'Shane was always there, smoking Woodbines. We respected his knowledge of music, and he always knew all the trivia from the backs of album covers and the lyrics. One day Shane walked in, in the middle of an intense discussion about Soft Machine *III* [*Third*] or some such. "It's all crap!" he slurred. "All

33

that progressive rock bullshit." We all gasped. "Even the Beatles and the Stones – they're just a bunch of old tossers." We were dumbstruck – this was sacrilege. "Well, what should we be listening to, Shane?" He listed a bunch of bands we'd never heard of. "Iggy and the Stooges. The MC5. Johnny Thunders." Our collective outrage was very similar to that of the mainstream music press when, a year or so later, the Sex Pistols came on the scene.'

Not surprisingly, London's West End exerted a vortex-like pull on Shane, and Thomas remembers going with him on a few occasions to Virgin Records on Oxford Street. They would request a record and then sit on one of the old aircraft seats, listening to it on headphones and admiring the cover. The pair also used to head to Kensington Market, where they would indulge Shane's heightened interest in drugs. Thomas remembers them buying hash and speed from the dealers who hung out there, and smoking joints in alleyways. Shane was also beginning to use acid, although Thomas never took it with him.

Shane had started dabbling with drugs in Tunbridge Wells and at the Barbican his parents adopted a liberal stance to him taking them with his mates, even dealing with some of the chaotic scenes that came with it. One of his closest friends, Jez, had a girlfriend called Sarah, who Shane also liked. During a bad acid trip, she tried to throw herself off the balcony and had to be dragged to safety. Jez, meanwhile, was always being picked up for drug offences and other misdemeanours and Maurice would go down to the police station and bail him out.

Maurice and Therese's thinking was that, if their son was going to experiment with drugs, it was better that he did it at home. 'It was a big hippie culture anyway and an awful lot of people were doing it, so I don't think they thought they were fighting this big demon at that time,' says Siobhan. 'We weren't talking about the kind of stuff you see now. It was mainly dope and they were also taking LSD because Sarah had a bad trip. Mum and Dad weren't keen as such, but they wanted to contain it as much as possible. Shane and Sarah did start going out at that time, putting on Mum's pink jacket and putting make-up on and going down to Piccadilly Circus and all around there, and they weren't keen on that.'

Shane's parents may have taken a lenient view of his experimentation with drugs at the Barbican, but the police did not. He and his school-friend Charlie were arrested after someone saw them smoking weed outside the Barbican and reported them. Charlie had nothing on him, but Shane had been carrying his supply. 'I was caught with speed, grass, acid and a gram of tobacco, all in a tin box, which I didn't have hidden down my trousers,' he explains. 'I knew I should, but it was in the courtyard of the flats where I lived.'

The upshot was at just 15, Shane found himself on a charge sheet for the first time and up before the juvenile court in Tower Hamlets. Maurice accompanied his errant son to the hearing. 'It was hysterically funny,' says Shane. 'My dad was with me and I remember us laughing our heads off quietly and jabbing each other. Councils like to try and be ahead of the time, modern and aware of social issues that make people do irresponsible things. There was a black main beak who was probably afraid he'd get lynched if he really started laying down the law with white guys who had been caught with loads of drugs.

'The black guy was the main one, trying to pretend he was devoid of prejudice. Then there was an old woman, who was horrible to me. She had glasses and was knitting like Madame Defarge, tsscchh. The magistrates run the Earth when you're in the fucking juvenile court – they can put you away for two years' probation. They fined me five pounds, which was very severe for a juvenile delinquent. My dad had to pay it. I thought it might be much worse. Then came a year's probation and that meant I couldn't go to Ireland. But I sorted that out with the probation officer I got sent to. They are usually really good guys and if you explain to them, "While I'm in London, I'm always going to be surrounded by criminal influences and things are going to be hard going. I just need to get away to Ireland and get the city and the hate out of me..."'

As for how his parents reacted to his first criminal conviction, Shane says: 'My old man said, "I hope you remember this when I'm trying to live without a pension," tsscchh. My mother was just glad I didn't go to prison. I could have been sent to prison if they were real assholes, especially when they knew I was Irish. But the black guy made the point that he was more powerful than a paddy and the old bag felt she was saving society from an untamed savage who needed saving.'

Shane wasn't just expanding his own hallucinogenic horizons at Westminster. He was involved in a small drug distribution network which took orders from other pupils and their friends and sourced them from shady characters in the West End, some of whom were, according to Shane, associates of Charlie Kray. One of their regular suppliers was a doorman at a rock venue where Shane frequently hung out.

'I was hanging out with the other guys in the drug-dealing organisation. It was a small organisation with a lot of customers, and we kept it within the school or friends of people in the school. But they might come and buy a large amount and we knew they were selling to people we hadn't met, and the school had sussed that out. They had already got rid of the previous head of the racket, the term before I came. So, I was approached immediately to replace him, as one of the point men.'

First-formers were among their customers, but Shane says the 'more exotic' shopping lists came from students further up the school who wanted 'heroin, cocaine, acid, mescaline, Nepalese temple balls, things like that. They became special customers and I used to make friends with them.'

His teenage crew were also thieving to order, charging 'commission' for booze, records and other shoplifted items. Then they would hotfoot it down to Petticoat Lane Market in the East End with their illicit earnings and sort themselves out with the coveted clothes and shoes they couldn't afford to buy in the trendy shops up town. 'It was all fucking hot, so you could get it for practically nothing,' says Shane. 'I got an amazing, beautiful pair of real winkle-pickers for five quid.'

Westminster was already aware of his drug-peddling in school and his court appearance brought things to a head. So, just fourteen months after he had joined the school, Shane and his dad were summoned to see the headmaster, Dr John Rae. Maurice recalls the occasion vividly: 'I always remember the meeting was on a Good Friday; we often laughed at that. The headmaster was called Dr Rae, a character like Jacob Rees-Mogg, or Smog, as we call him. He intoned about Shane's misdemeanours: he'd been up to tricks in school, as well as a court appearance for smoking weed in the Barbican. Rae said he couldn't possibly keep Shane in the school, which I was quite pleased about, as I knew Shane had no need of whatever they had to teach, it was all within him.

'It was quite clear to us that he wasn't going to go down the conventional route, so he would need no qualifications; he had no academic aspirations at all. His knowledge of English was fantastic at that point, he couldn't be taught on that, he'd be teaching other people. I can't remember my exact words, but I perhaps thought the headmaster a little too august for me to start flinging the F-word about. I probably thought he might collapse. But I know I was forceful about not wanting him in that bloody, perhaps "fucking", school. Anyway, I told him to shove it, and the meeting came to a somewhat abrupt end.'

Recalling the dramatic end to his time at Westminster, Shane says, 'My mother wasn't surprised I got kicked out. We'd seen it coming. My dad was really relieved and so was I. Me and him were at a meeting with Rae and he had a go at Rae about being a racist fucker. Rae had been on my back from the start because I was Irish. He was trying to take it back to what it had been a few years before and the school motto was that it produced English gentlemen. I used to say, "I'm Irish and I want to be an Irish gentleman," and they might have laughed, and they might not. But the other kids would laugh.'

Shane's expulsion might not have concerned Maurice and Shane, but it did nothing to dispel the storm gathering at home. Therese had never adjusted to life in their fifth-floor flat and the Barbican's brooding, oppressive atmosphere was taking its toll on her health. Therese had always felt uneasy about the move, but she hadn't opposed it because she didn't know exactly what she thought about it, according to Siobhan. Almost as soon as they arrived, however, she began to suffer with anxiety and depression.

'She wanted to get out of London as soon as we got there,' Maurice recalls. 'Therese had been brought up in rural Ireland and a flat with no garden and little fresh air or natural light made her feel claustrophobic and depressed. She did seek help from a doctor and was prescribed Valium, which helped the symptoms but did nothing to lift her malaise. After much toing and froing, she began seeing a psychiatrist who gave her Marplan, an antidepressant.'

Her nephew Paul Harriman worked in legal practice at Gray's Inn at that time and often called round to see Therese. 'I used to see them a lot in the Barbican and he [Maurice] was really very difficult,' says Paul. 'I think she hated it and Maurice loved it because he was in the city and there was the culture of the city that he loved. Maurice just carried on, so there was a lot of tension. She literally couldn't stand it and it was a fortress to get in there. In those days it was the latest thing, but to Therese it was all concrete and you had various strange people living there.'

Catherine Leech adds, 'It was a lovely flat, but the place was a prison. You had to open locks to get in and there were long corridors.'

Despite her failing mental health, Therese responded to Shane being drummed out of Westminster by helping him get a job at the local supermarket. So, while she was at home in bed taking medication for depression, he was stacking shelves and unloading delivery lorries. 'It was a family supermarket and they employed young people, boys mainly, well underage and money-in-the-hand,' he recalls. 'The black economy – good for everyone. Sometimes it was quite heavy labour, but mostly monotonous shelf-stacking. But every time a lorry came in, there would be massive boxes containing big family tins of beans and all the other stuff, and at Christmas they put out jars of gherkins and they went like the clappers. At that age, ten quid a week was a really good wage.'

His supermarket gig was to be the first of a string of temporary jobs he took. But Shane wasn't yet done with education, despite his unceremonious departure from Westminster. He attempted to get a place at Kingsway College in Camden, which was attended by Simon John Ritchie before he emerged in the Sex Pistols as Sid Vicious. But they refused him – he believes on 'racial grounds' – and instead he ended up at Hammersmith College of further education, which he says was 'bottom of the heap'.

'I was doing English language and literature, history and French,' says Shane. 'They used essays I wrote, on the rare occasions I turned up to class, to read out to classes in Westminster.'

Shane was 16 when he started there in September 1974. The college was in an old Victorian building next door to Cadby Hall, the famous Lyons factory, and the smell of cakes and biscuits permeated the air. It predominantly served the surrounding area, which made it a melting pot of youngsters from different ethnic backgrounds, especially West Indian and London Irish. Shane's interest in studying was practically non-existent and enrolling for A-levels was more about appeasing his mother than satisfying any academic desire on his part. His world continued to revolve around taking weed and LSD in his bedroom, while extending his record collection and his encyclopaedic knowledge of the music scene. And it was this obsession that made him hit it off with classmate Bernie France, who would become a lifelong friend.

Bernie was a year or so older than Shane and had been expelled from not just one but two schools before winding up at Hammersmith. They were in an art class when they first met, and it was Shane's startling appearance that singled him out. 'We were doing a still-life of some stuff on a table and this guy walks in, really thin, very tall, dead white face and long hair, dressed in a style which I wouldn't call hippie but a freak. Freaks were into these bands that weren't hippie but revolutionary, so The Deviants, the Pink Fairies and, to an extent, Hawkwind... He had this style which was a sort of school blazer, a choker thing round his neck, really thin trousers and pointy boots. I thought, OK. So, we're drawing away and at the end of the class he comes over and he's drawn me. I was dressed in this Dr Feelgood kind of way, a bit of an untidy mullet and leather jacket with a suit lapel, a bit *Life On Mars* I suppose.

'We got talking and my first question was, "What music do you like?" I knew he was going to say: The Stooges, the Pink Fairies – so, bang, we hit it off! Then we met another friend of mine called Anthony Goodrich, whose nickname was Moysy Boysy, a guy from Maida Vale I had known years ago. Me and Shane were hanging out in the first couple of weeks and we saw a guy with *NME* and the headline was MOTT THE HOOPLE SPLIT, and so we were like, "Oh, come here, I want to read that." I was looking at him and he was quite a distinctive-looking guy and I said, "Did you live in Maida Vale and is your name Anthony?" and it was him.'

Bernie remembers Shane's attendance as being sporadic and he was around less and less as the year went on. When he was in college, the conversation was invariably about music and together they read the music press from cover to cover to find out more about the bands they were drawn to. In that year, 1974, David Bowie released *Diamond Dogs* and glam acts like Roxy Music, The Sweet and Slade were leaving the imprint of their platform boots all over the UK Top 40.

But it was bands redrawing the boundaries of rock on the other side of the Atlantic that were of more interest to Shane and Bernie. They both loved MC5 and The Stooges, groups that had burst violently out of Michigan and whose insurgency and white-hot energy would fan the flames of punk. Flamin' Groovies and Velvet Underground had also appeared on their radar and the music press provided the only available insight into these trailblazing acts.

Shane and Bernie were forever drawing. They were influenced by underground comics featuring works by American artists like S. Clay Wilson and Robert Crumb, which were 'quite violent and hallucinogenic'. In the absence of photos of bands like MC5, they drew their own posters and record sleeves. They also, fleetingly, created their own group, the name of which would later provide the title of a song performed by The Nips and The Pogues.

'We formed Hot Dogs With Everything, but we never ruined it by actually putting it into action!' says Bernie. 'It was an idea and we did song names and drew album covers. It was me and Shane and Charlie and whoever else was with us at the time. It was always "about to happen". We didn't need instruments; we were banging on the tables, singing to each other. I suppose I would have played guitar.'

Shane continued to go over to Tipperary whenever he could, and his cousin Lisa Mulvihill remembers being intimidated by him. 'I was always a little bit scared of Shane because he was ten years older than me,' she recalls. 'So, when he came back at 16 and he was a punk rocker, I was 6 or 7. I was petrified. All I can remember is him sitting on the floor and he used to have really long nails and really artistic hands and he'd be strumming the guitar.' Debra Donnelly also remembers Shane from this period: 'When he first came during teenage years, he had his hair very long and he would wear Uncle John's vests and combat jackets.'

Sundays saw Shane and his cronies at the Implosion nights at the Roundhouse in Camden. Freaks of all ages got off their heads to light shows and witnessed an exotic roster of acts like Hawkwind and the Pink Fairies. These underground shows started at three o'clock in the afternoon and drew long queues which would snake around the venue on Chalk Farm Road. Not only did DJ Jeff Dexter's legendary, LSD-fuelled shows feature some of the biggest names in rock, they became a crucible for those who would spearhead the revolution that was to come. Mick Jones of The Clash, John Lydon of the Sex Pistols and Poly Styrene of X-Ray Spex were among those who, along with Shane, were drawn to these marathon music sessions.

Even on these trippy Sunday evenings, where ice creams were served and people would lie down amid the strobe lights, Shane would still find himself targeted because of his looks and behaviour, says Bernie. 'There were factions and it was violent and if you didn't look right… Shane particularly used to get loads of kickings because of the way he looked and also because of the way he would react to people. I got done in a couple of times. I know some black guys gave him a kicking because he was wearing a rockabilly southern [US] flag in Camden.'

Shane spent less and less time at college, preferring to take drugs with his mates in his bedroom and attracting attention from the police. Therese was still struggling with life at the Barbican, her depression frequently confining her to her room, and she and Maurice had little influence over their unusual and wayward son. History was about to repeat itself, to no one's surprise.

'The last time I saw Shane at college was the day he got kicked out,' says Bernie. 'He was sitting on the stairs drawing a be-bop musician on the wall with a felt pen – beret, striped T-shirt and playing a saxophone. The principal of the college, who was this classic *Guardian*-reading, "We're going to help the kids" type, just fucking flipped. "Shane. You come in here off your head. Get out now and never come back!" He pushed her to the edge, which is great. And he just kind of laughed and then left... He was much bolder than me; I would never do anything like that. So, I think I was beginning to become quite in awe of his boldness.'

Shane's preoccupation with drugs wasn't just responsible for his second expulsion in two years. It was having a serious impact on his own mental health. He was drinking as well as taking acid and a variety of pills, a cocktail that made him anxious. He suffered hallucinations and strange shapes appeared on his bedroom wall, freaking him out so much he was scared to go to bed. The family GP prescribed Valium and, while this did reduce his anxiety and helped him sleep, the other illicit substances he used continued to affect his mood and behaviour. Worried that their son was heading for a breakdown, Maurice and Therese asked Shane if he thought he needed professional help. He agreed that he did.

Maurice says: 'We went to a guy in Harley Street and he recommended Bethlem [Royal Hospital, Beckenham]. So, we went down there, and Shane ended up in a sort of home at Beckenham. You'd go down to see him and there were a whole lot of 'out of it' people there, playing table tennis to keep themselves occupied. We were worried about Shane at that stage, really worried. But he was his own man then; it was difficult to get through to him. I think he blamed me for a lot.'

Recalling this traumatic stage in his life, Shane said: 'The doctor had put me on Valium – a hundred milligrams a day – because I had a nervous breakdown after my mum had one. That's a heavy dosage, but it's not as heavy as what he had her on. She was on real zombie stuff, yeah? I used to go up every morning and kick her to see if she was alive. I had to go into the drug ward of a mental hospital... called Bethlem, one of the big ones in London.' [1]

Shane was 17 in 1975 when he was admitted as a patient to Bethlem, the oldest hospital of its kind in the world. The evening before he went in,

Shane and his friend Pete had been to The Hope & Anchor, Islington, to see Ace, who had tasted chart success the year before with 'How Long'. It was the last night out Shane would have for a long time as his in-patient treatment at the hospital would last six whole months.

Siobhan was 12 when her brother was admitted and says it had a 'devastating effect' on her. When they went to see him on his 18th birthday, Shane was 'pretty anxious and upset', but when Maurice and Therese asked him if he wanted to come out, 'he decided to stay or, at least, not make the decision to leave'. It wasn't until two months later that he left Bethlem and the memory of that visit is still painful for her.

'That was just dreadful,' she says. 'I went in and I just couldn't talk. I remember just staring out the window and there were no words to describe how I felt. I remember coming out and listening to "Bohemian Rhapsody" on the radio and that's how I felt. That song described exactly all the tumult of emotions going through me. That really messed me up actually.'

For Shane, it must have been a daunting experience. He was placed on a mixed ward with people with severe drug and alcohol dependencies and had to give a urine sample each day to show he was clean. Occupational therapy involved painting and there were group sessions where patients were encouraged to talk about their addictions and problems. Doctors allowed Shane to have his guitar and he taught a young girl who was being treated for schizophrenia to play. He was also allowed on outings in the company of a nurse and says he fell in love with a young Irish woman who took him to see Man at the Fairfield Halls in Croydon and the film *Jaws* [2].

Shane would later write about 'the place where they gave ECT / And the drugged-up psychos with death in their eyes' in 'Dark Streets Of London'. A song recorded much later called 'Pinned Down / I'm Alone In The Wilderness' also appeared to refer to his time on the wards of Bethlem. The lyrics made a lasting impression on Pogues accordionist James Fearnley when they recorded it during the sessions for *Hell's Ditch*. 'Shane does this rant about these being kids pinned down in an institution,' he says. 'Whether that had been his experience himself, I wouldn't know. But there was something that touched a nerve with him to do with young people and children having life go horribly wrong and seeing the worst that life can throw you, and I guess he'd seen it.'

Years later, Shane would talk candidly to his partner Victoria Mary Clarke about his lengthy spell in hospital and his experiences there. She told me that he speaks 'quite fondly of hospital' and thinks he 'enjoyed quite a lot of it'. 'Shane didn't have it [ECT, or electroconvulsive therapy]. They kept threatening him with it, but they didn't do it. They were all having it, all of them. Except the doctor he had was actually quite cool and he was lucky... Shane was on Valium, but he came off it in hospital, so he was actually on nothing when he came out. It was useful for him. He doesn't look back on it with regret or anger.'

Others he has talked to about his life at Bethlem say the episode left its scars. 'He was always fearful of being sectioned,' says Pogues bassist Darryl Hunt. 'I remember when I first met him in the early days, he talked about that. His biggest horror was being sectioned because it's your own family putting you into a serious space – quite frightening.'

Maurice says the doctor looking after Shane had taken a dim view of what he had seen as his lenient parenting and admits he had little influence over his son. However, Shane responded well to the treatment he received and was in a much better place when he finally left.

'Actually, he seemed to get on quite well there, he made quite a few friends, got pally with people, even played table tennis!' comments Maurice. 'And the nurses took a shine to him. A doctor interviewed me and suggested that I should have been or be stricter with him. But I had a liberal view and at that age I didn't feel I should tell him what to do. But I did talk to him, tell him to forget about the drugs, just have a few drinks like me. I tried to reason with him. He was quite well when he came out; had cleaned himself up.'

By the spring of 1976, the whole family was at a crossroads. Therese could no longer cope in the Barbican's concrete maze and was desperate to get some peace away from the constant barrage of building work. She took the bold decision to move back to Tunbridge Wells on her own.

Her niece, Michele Harriman-Smith, paid Therese regular visits at this time and says the move was good for her state of mind. 'She said she had to be in touch with the Earth,' she says. 'It was only a one-room place she rented, with a little bit of garden outside, but it was enough. She loved it. I used to tell her all my problems and she talked to me about how difficult it is if your soul isn't in touch with the Earth.'

With Maurice now paying rent in Tunbridge Wells and London, he moved out of the Barbican with Shane and Siobhan into a cheaper flat, owned by a family with a connection to Paul Harriman. St Andrew's Chambers in Wells Street was off Oxford Street and relocating to the West End meant Shane was better placed than ever to pursue his obsession with music and earn a few quid from temporary jobs. 'At the top of Tottenham Court Road there was an Alfred Marks temp bureau,' Shane recalls, 'and you got in there early in the morning and sat and waited and got called up and sent off to a job. It could last for ten months or three months or just a few days. I had some pretty dirty jobs, but amazingly interesting jobs. I worked at the Hudson Bay warehouse where all the fur skins come in.'

Soho had a plethora of record shops and, when Shane wasn't at the manpower agency waiting for his next assignment, he was painstakingly digging through crates of albums and singles. One of his favoured haunts was Rock On in the open-air market in Chinatown, and he quickly got to know Roger Armstrong, Phil Gaston and Stan Brennan, who helped run the stall for owner Ted Carroll.

Ted recalls: 'They used to say he would come in and dribble on the records. Even then he couldn't speak clearly... He looked like he did on the front of The Nips' singles: short hair, ears sticking out, bad teeth, dribbling, mumbling, grumbling. He used to wear suits a lot because he had some kind of job in the city, office boy or junior, I don't know.'

Phil Gaston said: 'One day Shane walked into the stall and he was slightly shook-looking, is what I'd say. He had matted long hair down to his shoulders, heavily caked with one thing or other, I don't know what, and he looked a bit dazed. He said that he had been in hospital. I knew he was on pills or something like that, but he was lucid whenever he started talking and he just started hanging around the shop.' [3]

Shane's family life had fractured, he was not in education and there was no telling what direction his life was going to take. This was also the year that saw Britain go bust and opportunities for young people were few and far between, whether or not you'd been turfed out of college. But in a pub back room, everything was about to fall into place for Shane.

The Nashville was in West Kensington and had been a country music venue before becoming part of the pub rock network. It was there, on 3 April 1976, that Shane says he headed to see his first gig since leaving hospital.

Headlining were The 101ers, the four-piece band fronted by Joe Strummer and already in the sights of Chiswick Records, the label formed the previous year by Ted Carroll and Roger Armstrong. But it was the first group on that night which completely blew Shane's mind and changed the course of his life. '...I went to see the 101ers at The Nashville and the Pistols were the support band,' said Shane [4]. 'I just couldn't believe it. There it was. The band that I'd always been waiting for, playing Stooges numbers and Dolls numbers. I just thought, This is what I'm all about, and I started following them.'

Shane wasn't the only one to have an epiphany that night. Pennies were dropping all over The Nashville, even on stage. Joe Strummer said later, 'The 101ers had been playing for two years or so when the Pistols burst onto the scene, and when I saw them, I realised you couldn't compare the Pistols to any other group on the island, they were so far ahead... And I knew we were finished. Five seconds into their first song I knew we were like yesterday's papers, I mean, we were over.' [5]

In England, Shane had always felt like a square peg. He never got anywhere with girls at discos because of how he looked, and he was regularly beaten up, apparently because of his outspoken support for the IRA. Despite his best efforts, he felt he never fitted in. His time at The Commons – where he always felt so at home – remained precious to him. He was and still is fundamentally shy and that had always made him feel awkward around other people. In his teens, however, he embraced a new emotion that would shape his behaviour and his outlook on life. Hate.

Being Irish in Britain in the early 1970s was to live under a cloud of suspicion. The IRA's bombing campaign, particularly the horrifying attacks on pubs in Guildford, Woolwich and Birmingham in 1974, put anyone with an Irish accent at risk of verbal or physical assault. Shane's sense of injustice at such discrimination would have been amplified by the republican songs he learned on his trips to The Commons and the stories about his predecessors helping 'the cause'. Constant news reports about The Troubles on television would have intensified his resentment.

When I ask him if the 'hate' he had earlier reported to his probation officer had been real, his reply is forceful. 'Oh, yeah. It was The Troubles, for fuck's sake. They [the British] were murdering young people,' says Shane. 'If two or three youths were holding a meeting, they were getting put in the Maze [a high-security prison near Belfast which housed Republican and Loyalist prisoners] and ended up doing dirty protests.'

Catherine Leech says Shane's deep sense of pride in his Irish roots and his willingness to challenge any discrimination had set in at an early age. 'Shane would come back from Ireland and he'd have a real Irish accent,' she says. 'We lived at that time on the Edgware Road and Shane used to come and see us. We had an off-licence and somebody came in and said something about Ireland and Shane was very annoyed. He was only a little chap, but he jumped up and said, "Don't say that". Of course, the man had no idea why Shane was so defensive, but I don't think he was long back [from Tipperary].'

The anger he felt as a result of The Troubles was mixed with anxiety over his mother's illness, the splintering of the family and the deterioration of his own mental health. So, when he was unexpectedly confronted with the fury and nihilism of a band fronted by a London Irish lad, it was a life-changing moment. 'And that's when I saw God,' said Shane. 'I saw this little red-haired paddy up there pouring beer over his head and sneering at the audience shouting insults at him. And then he'd launch into this loud, raucous rock'n'rollin' number with foul lyrics; I thought this was the pop band I'd been waiting for all my life.' [6]

His new home just off Oxford Street put Shane at the eye of punk's storm. The 100 Club, The Roxy, The Marquee and The Vortex were all a stone's throw from the flat, while others were a bus or tube ride away. The stagnant waters of British pop were being violently stirred up, and a delirious Shane flung himself in. Punk gave him a channel for his anger and a feeling of acceptance and belonging he had never experienced outside of The Commons. He still attracted attention with his unconventional looks, but punk was inclusive and a welcoming home for life's outsiders. Whether you were performing on stage or pogoing in the sweat-sodden mass below, being different was a virtue, not a crime.

Some of the gigs Shane went to would become legendary, although they were sparsely attended. Jordan, Siouxsie Sioux, Sid Vicious, Steve Severin, Soo Catwoman and Helen of Troy were already part of its colourful cognoscenti and on 23 October 1976 Shane MacGowan took his place in punk's hall of fame. Fliers for the gig at the Institute of Contemporary Arts on The Mall promised 'A Night of Pure Energy', and it more than lived up to its billing. Snatch Sounds and Subway Sect warmed up the crowd for headliners The Clash and by the time they took to the stage Shane was in the crowd canoodling with Jane Crockford (now Perry-Woodgate), known as 'Mad Jane', at the feet of guitarist Mick Jones. The next anyone knew, blood was gushing from one of his earlobes and *NME* photographer Red Saunders, who was standing nearby, began snapping.

CANNIBALISM AT CLASH GIG read the headline above the *NME* review, with a picture of blonde-haired Jane raising a gloved hand to Shane's ear. Beneath it was another showing Shane smeared with blood and grinning as Jane lurched at someone else in the crowd. Describing the incident, writer Miles wrote: 'A young couple, somewhat out of it, had been nibbling and fondling each other amid the broken glass when she suddenly lunged forward and bit his ear lobe off. As the blood spurted, she reached out to paw it with a hand tastefully clad in a rubber glove, and after smashing a Guinness bottle on the front of the stage, she was about to add to the gore by slashing her wrists when the security men finally reached her, pushing through the trance-like crowd who watched with cold, calculated hiptitude.'

Jane, who would later play bass with all-girl group the Mo-Dettes, recalls the episode: 'Rat Scabies – who I'd always teased because I always called him a loud-mouth bighead – had bought me a pint. But I had these latex gloves on, and I'd had the pint and it just slipped right through. So, I don't know if I still had the broken glass or then I had a bottle and, it wasn't my fault, but I managed to break that as well, again with these latex gloves it dropped. So, I'm like, "Oh look." We were at the front of the stage and maybe we got nudged. I didn't do it on purpose. I was very drunk and shoom… and the blood! I was sort of holding it and I was trying to drink the blood and so everybody said that I bit it, but no, I hadn't. The next thing I saw, it was in the *NME*. But it gave him a kickstart, didn't it?'

Ted Carroll was also at the ICA that night and witnessed the gory aftermath. 'There was claret all over the place,' he recalls. 'It was just at the end of the gig, during the last number, I think. The lights came on and there was Shane bleeding profusely, but it didn't look like he was bleeding to death. I didn't give any thought to getting him to hospital; they were all drunk anyway and I thought it would probably take care of itself, which it did. But it was good publicity and it definitely helped because there were photographs of him and he was very distinctive with those flapping elephant ears.'

He adds: 'Everybody knew Shane. I mean Shane is a sociable sort of person. He's not aggressive or egotistical, so he got on with everyone and he was everyone's mate. He was one of those people who was a face.'

Jane says that while the episode ended up being blown out of all proportion in the music press, Shane never made out it was anything other than 'just fun'. She admits she found Shane charismatic and attractive and that others were drawn to him. In contrast to Sid Vicious, to whom she was close, he didn't have a violent side, and his kind-heartedness came out through the songs he would go on to write. 'I would say, if you looked at Shane MacGowan and you looked at Sid Vicious, Shane was like the Joe Strummer to John Lydon: the angel and the devil,' says Jane. 'You've got these two lanky, tall characters. Sid was seriously flawed, seriously fucked-up, with a junkie mother and his upbringing. He had a good heart, but you couldn't see it. Whereas Shane, once he started writing, had that belief in himself and was able to get out there. You just saw this big heart and this beauty in him, which is very attractive.

'People would love that and to be around him. He had a sparkle. I mean, we were having a sparkle moment that night before I drank too much and probably fell over. I don't remember what happened afterwards. I haven't got a clue. But we were having a sparkling moment and it was fun – he was so much fun.

'I had some really good moments with Sid as well, but not so much. They were more violent against other people. I showed him how to be violent as well. Shane didn't have violence in him. I did. I grew up going to the football matches and chasing people. I'd run with the boys. I think Shane went a totally different route because of the music, but Sid never got to that point. He couldn't release anything through words and music.'

Shane's notoriety soared after the article appeared and, within a few weeks, the self-styled 'Shane O'Hooligan' had produced his own punk fanzine, *Bondage*. All six pages were handwritten on foolscap paper and he used safety pins to attach pictures he had torn out of the music press. Jon Savage, who later wrote *England's Dreaming*, was hawking his own zine, *London's Outrage*, around punk gigs at the time and had run into Shane at a Damned gig at The Hope & Anchor. He had free access to a photocopier, so he copied it for Shane, who then went round places he knew, getting it printed up in return for some free copies. A picture taken by a press photographer in the kitchen at Wells Street shows Shane proudly holding up his handiwork.

A photo taken from a Sex Pistols flyer adorned the cover and there were reviews of teen band Eater at the Hope & Anchor and The Jam, who Shane had seen at Upstairs at Ronnie Scott's and then three nights later at The Marquee. Shane was lavish in his praise of the soul-influenced trio and rubbished claims by some that their matching suits were derivative. Of the Ronnie Scott's gig, Shane wrote: 'Pogo-dancing broke out and from then on things got better and better, with "In The City" for a second time, "Route 66" and "Faking Your Love" [sic], climaxing in Paul Weller going mad and throwing his amp to the people in the front who tore it to bits. I was really inspired by the violence of their act – it was fucking great.'

Shane also took the opportunity to vent about the infamous episode on Thames TV's *Today* show, when host Bill Grundy goaded the Sex Pistols into swearing. 'Since when did EMI or any of those old cunts put "public duty" before their precious money or the security it gives them?' he ranted. 'What it really is, is they feel that security is threatened just by what the Pistols represent.' On the final page, Shane said it was handwritten because he didn't have a typewriter, but 'anybody who uses a typewriter is a GIRL'. 'I don't like fanzines anyway, there [sic] boring and unconstructive, but it's better than reading *THE SUN*,' he said.

Siobhan recalls how she and Shane had been watching the *Today* show with their mum when the Sex Pistols turned the air blue. 'When Johnny Rotten went, "Shit," she [Therese] just roared with laughter,' she says. 'She thought he was hilarious.'

After being blown away by the Sex Pistols at The Nashville, Shane had become a fixture at their shows and original bassist Glen Matlock remembers him well. 'To be honest, Shane wasn't the most handsome bloke in the world back then,' he says. 'He reminded me of a character from The Bash Street Kids… All the little gigs he was around at; you'd see him at lots of things. He was one of the few people on the scene. He wasn't in the Bromley contingent, but he might as well have been. He had a bit of Sid [Vicious] about him in the way that he jumped around a little bit too much, just to get a bit more attention. I never saw him create trouble or anything.'

In the months after he had left hospital and discovered punk, Shane had been working, drifting from one temporary job to another. For a while, he worked at The Griffin Tavern, a large Irish pub next to Charing Cross station, although he was much more suited to being on the other side of the bar. Between paid employment and nicking stuff from the back of restaurants in the West End with his mates, he generally had cash in his pocket for records and gigs. There were, inevitably, run-ins with the law. One night he and his pal Peter Gates were chased and caught by police after bricking the window of Bourne & Hollingsworth, the large department store on the corner of Oxford Street and Berners Street. At Marlborough Street Court, the pair said they had been drunk and didn't know what they were doing. The magistrate was unmoved and ordered each of them to pay fines and compensation totalling £340. The drunken escapade was reported in the *Marylebone Mercury* on 9 July, under the headline EXPENSIVE NIGHT OUT.

But given how concerned his parents had been about his preoccupation with drugs and its effect on his mental health, to see him embracing punk was a blessed relief. 'Punk was very anti-drug and anti-hippie, so actually we were pleased about that,' says Siobhan. 'He wasn't really interested too much [in drugs] at that stage. It was music, music, music, the dancing all night, the anarchy of it.'

Shane wasn't just living and breathing the punk scene, he was influencing it. Its sudden explosion had left the major labels playing catch-up and A&R departments were scouring the clubs and hole-in-the-wall venues in London hoping to nab the next big act before their competitors. Chris Parry from Polydor was smarting after missing the Sex Pistols, who went to EMI, and The Clash, who were picked up by CBS, and was desperate to make it third time lucky. The tip-off he so urgently needed came from Shane, who had his finger firmly on the punk pulse. Thanks to him, Polydor made one of the signings of the late 1970s.

Chris Parry recalled, 'He came up to me one day, he said, "Chris, don't worry about missing out on The Clash and the Sex Pistols, there's a really good band playing, they're opening up Saturday night at The Marquee."' [7] Top of the bill at the Wardour Street club on 22 January 1977 were rock also-rans Bearded Lady, but the support was the band Shane was forever eulogising about – The Jam. 'Everyone knows Saturday night opening up is just a dead spot, but I went, and I saw this band and I just really was impressed with Paul Weller.' A month later Polydor signed them for £6,000.

(Right) Maurice and Therese MacGowan were married on 1 August 1956 at Kilbarron church, just a couple of miles from The Commons. For their honeymoon, the newlyweds borrowed Maurice's dad's car and drove around Ireland (MacGowan family).

(Far right) Therese MacGowan with baby Shane in his pram (MacGowan family).

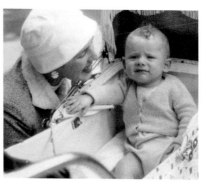

(Far left) Shane on one of his treasured childhood visits to The Commons. Back L–R: John Lynch, Jim Ralph (family friend), Shane, Jim Lynch, Willie Lynch. Front L–R: Puppe Harriman (cousin), Maggie Lynch (Shane's grandmother), Nora Lynch, Monica Lynch (MacGowan family).

(Left) Maurice and Therese with young Shane (MacGowan family).

(Right) Back: John Lynch and Siobhan MacGowan. Front: Shane with family friends.

(Right) Siobhan, Therese and Shane at Monica Cahalan's farm in Tipperary, with Willie Lynch leading a calf in the background (MacGowan family).

(Above) Shane and Siobhan at Newlands (MacGowan family).

(Above left) 'Holmewood was producing young gentlemen and cricket was more important than most things.' Shane at Holmewood House school, Tunbridge Wells (MacGowan family).

(Above) 'He got into music big-time at the Barbican and he would have records going all day long up in his room.' Back L–R: A family friend, Joy Harriman, David (family friend), Shane, Therese, Maurice. Front: Puppe Harriman (sitting) and Siobhan (MacGowan family).

(Left) Nineteen-year-old Shane with his punk fanzine *Bondage* at St Andrew's Chambers, Wells Street. All six pages were handwritten on foolscap paper, and he used safety pins to attach pictures torn out of the music press (Sydney O'Meara/Getty).

(Right) Shane and Shanne Bradley with a sheep in tow outside Buckingham Palace in a still from *The Punk Kebab Documentary*, filmed in 1977.

(Above) Shane with Therese and Maurice at their home in Tunbridge Wells (MacGowan family).

(Right) Shane on the floor of the Harlesden Coliseum, London, during a punk gig on 11 March 1977. The following month the picture graced the cover of *Sounds*, with Shane hailed as one of the 'images of the new wave' (Ian Dickson/Redferns).

(Above) The Nips pictured at The Moonlight Club, West Hampstead, 21 April 1979. L–R: Shanne Bradley (bass guitar), John Grinton (drums), Shane (vocals), Larry Hinrichs (guitar) (Justin Thomas).

(Above) Shane in a classic pose at the microphone during the Pogue Mahone days (Ray Vaughan).

(Right) 'He had the energy, that's what it was about, and we got on really well.' Shanne Bradley and Shane on stage during a Nips gig at Billy's, Meard Street, Soho, 22 January 1980 (Justin Thomas).

(Right) A teenage Shane at Soho Market, 1979 (Kathy MacMillan).

(Above) Pogue Mahone performing at the London Irish Centre in Camden in 1983. L–R: James Fearnley, Jem Finer, Andrew Ranken, Shane, Spider Stacy (Kathy MacMillan).

(Left) Shane and Spider Stacy on stage at The Hope & Anchor, London (Kathy MacMillan).

(Left) Siobhan, family friend Sarah Capp, and Shane after a gig (Ray Vaughan).

(Right) L–R: Jem Finer, Spider Stacy and Shane (Ray Vaughan).

(Right) Shane on cloakroom duties at the 100 Club, Oxford Street, with then girlfriend Merrill Heatley (Ray Vaughan).

(Below) L–R: Unknown, Maria Ryan and Trish O'Flynn from The Shillelagh Sisters, Slim Cyder (Clive Pain) from The Boothill Foot-Tappers, and Shane (Ray Vaughan).

(Above top) The Pogues. L–R: Andrew Ranken, James Fearnley, Cait O'Riordan, Jem Finer, Spider Stacy, and Shane (Joe Bangay/Arena/PAL).

(Above) Scruffy Kenny, Shane and Noel Kenny behind the bar in a pub in Nenagh, Co Tipperary (Scruffy Kenny).

(Left) Shane and Cait O'Riordan (Lisa Haun/Michael Ochs Archives/Getty).

The band knew Shane as the guy who pogoed about in a sweaty Union Jack shirt and Paul Weller was desperate to buy it off him. Shane played hardball and eventually sold it to him for £500. Not bad, given he had got it from a tramp. 'Mine was a real Carnaby Street '67 job,' said Shane. 'I wore it to all The Jam gigs, 'cos I knew Paul Weller would crack sooner or later and give me a ridiculous amount of money for it. He offered me a Rickenbacker [guitar]. I said, "No, I couldn't part with it." I'd got it from this old tramp. I was trying to get the most I could, and eventually he offered me £500. I said, "You're done!" Half a grand for a fucking mod shirt!' [8]

While Shane was roving the West End, invigorated by the bands that vented the hate that had been building up inside him, his mum was recovering after her mental breakdown. Living away from her own family might once have seemed unthinkable, but the relative peace of Tunbridge Wells was just what the doctor ordered. She was so relieved to have escaped the constant noise of building work at the Barbican and to be able to sit in a garden, taking in the fresh air. Maurice and Siobhan stayed with her at weekends and, every Sunday, she would accompany them back to London and stay over in Wells Street, where she would see Shane.

Therese was delighted he had thrown his lot in with punk, after the effect his drug-taking had had on his mental state, although she got a shock when she arrived one weekend and saw his new look. As Siobhan recalls, 'Me and Dad went down to Tunbridge Wells one weekend and came back up with Mum, and Shane's hair was all cut off and white-bleached, and Shanne [Bradley] had done it for him. And we screamed, I think – I screamed, anyway. But Mum did say as we were walking out, "Shane, you'll have to get famous now to justify that haircut," because she had to walk alongside him looking like that.

'Punk was a good thing for Shane; it had a lot of positive energy and he could do something, he belonged to something. It was very non-sexist because all the girls cut off their hair, all the boys cut off their hair. So, it was really wonderful, and Mum and Dad had no problem with that at all.'

Over Christmas 1976, Maurice and Siobhan moved down to Tunbridge Wells to live permanently again with Therese. Shane, meanwhile, stayed behind and prepared to fully unleash himself on London's virulent punk scene.

CHAPTER 3

King Of The Bop

'And though you never once gave it away
I can still remember those crazy days
We'd dance all night and sleep all day
In the old West End everybody was dancing'

'Gabrielle', **The Nips**

Fireworks were exploding and screeching across the night sky, but it was to the sound of The Clash that Shane and Shanne Bradley's stars collided. They were both faces on punk's speed-fuelled and now rapidly expanding scene, Shane enjoying new-found notoriety following the 'ear-biting' episode, and Shanne having been an eyewitness at its violent birth. But it was when The Clash headlined 'A Night of Treason' at London's Royal College of Art on Bonfire Night 1976 that fate brought them together.

'I just saw him across the bar with big ears and I thought, What the hell?' recalls Shanne, who was there with friends from her fashion course at St Martin's College of Art. 'He used to get called Plug sometimes, like the Bash Street Kids character – and it's not very nice to say that. He was around. You noticed people because there were so few of us. But by that time, it was building up.'

Shane has been referred to as one of the first punks, but Shanne says he was a comparative latecomer to the party. She had seen one of the Pistols' very first shows towards the end of 1975 at St Albans College of Art and had booked them to play other shows there. After she had seen The Damned's incendiary debut at the 100 Club on Oxford Street, she had hastily arranged for them to perform at the college after the Pistols pulled out. The teenager from Hertfordshire with the closely cropped, dyed hair had also adopted the punk DIY ethos, learning the rudiments of the bass guitar from Fred Berk of Johnny Moped and The Damned's peroxide prankster Captain Sensible.

In fact, Shanne insists it was courtesy of her that Shane first saw the Sex Pistols. 'He was never into the Sex Pistols then. He was a Dr Feelgood fan. He didn't even see the Pistols with Glen Matlock. I took him to see them for the first time at the Notre Dame Hall, off Leicester Square. Not the first time they played but the second. Sid was on bass and that's the first time Shane ever saw them. He said, "Don't tell anyone."'

Certainly, the gigs by The Jam and Eater that Shane reviewed in *Bondage* came after his first encounter with the woman who would play a big part in his life. However, the blood-letting incident through which Shane had writ his name large in the pages of the music press had taken place two weeks earlier. What is beyond dispute is that as punk provided a suitably chaotic finale to 1976 in a Britain gripped by unemployment and strife, Shane and Shanne were at its epicentre and desperate to graduate from the sticky, glass-strewn dancefloors to the stages graced by their heroes.

Shanne (as Shanne Skratch) had tried to form a band with friends Ray Pist and Claudio Chaotic Bass, christened The Launderettes because their basic recordings sounded like a washing machine. But by the spring of 1977, she was scouting for new conscripts and asked Shane the question he had been waiting for. She recalls: 'He used to go mad at gigs, so I said, "Do you want to audition for my band?" and he said, "Oh, that's my dream. I've always wanted to be in a band." I said, "Well it's my dream too."'

Arriving for his audition at Shanne's cold bedsit in Stavordale Road, Highbury, Shane needed no encouragement, unleashing a torrent of energy and attitude. Shanne says: 'He knocked on my door and I opened it and he charged in and started rolling around on the carpet doing a really good Iggy impersonation. He proper screamed and everything and I just went, "Yeah, you're it, you're the frontman. Perfect." He had the energy, that's what it was about, and we got on really well.'

It's easy to see why Shane's family were delighted at the positive impact of punk on his life. A year earlier he had spent six months on a hospital ward and had emerged with little purpose and plenty of anger. What he saw and heard around London's intimate venues gave him an outlet for those feelings and an inclusive environment where – probably for the first time in his life – he was accepted for who he was.

'I suppose I was always made to feel a bit of a wanker at school and I always found it hard to pick up girls at discos cos I was so ugly,' he said [1].

'I mean, the punk thing fuckin' changed my life. It didn't matter that I was ugly... nothing mattered. It was good.'

The band Shane would spearhead with such ferocity already had a name – The Nipple Erectors. After seeing a performance by Jobriath, regarded by some as the American Bowie, Shanne had dreamed about a band wearing rubber suits with nipples and decided it would be a 'ridiculous name' for a group. They rehearsed for about a year at her flat. Drummers and guitarists came and went, while Shane and Shanne provided the nucleus of the group and embarked on what would be a tempestuous relationship.

In April 1977, Shane graced the cover of *Sounds* as one of the 'images of the new wave'. In the photograph, he is wearing a jumper and a pinstriped jacket and lying flat on his back on the floor of The Coliseum in Harlesden, with an arm outstretched. That summer, he and Shanne were invited by a friend studying at the International Film School to appear in a short, low-budget film entitled *The Punk Kebab Documentary*. So, as punk gate-crashed The Queen's Silver Jubilee celebrations, Shane and Shanne were seen in its opening scene outside Buckingham Palace with a sheep on a rope and the Sex Pistols' 'God Save The Queen' blaring forth.

Shane, then 19, has dyed-red hair and is wearing an overcoat and dark shades, while Shanne has tightly cropped hair, panda bear make-up and an old jacket. They are filmed leading the sheep away, Shane smacking its rear as they go. Joe Kerr, a friend of Shanne's, then joins them as they board a train with the sheep and head to the country, where pitta bread falls from heaven with the recipe for the perfect kebab. This seals the sheep's fate and the trio gorge themselves on their kebabs, only to have the recipe stolen by a café owner while they sleep. The fifteen-minute cinematic oddity was consigned to obscurity, but it captured Shane in his punk prime; a study in surliness and hiding behind thick shades which would later become part of his trademark look.

Before the end of what was a tumultuous year for music, and Britain as a country, Shane finally made the transition from audience to stage. The Nipple Erectors made their thunderous debut at The Roxy in Covent Garden on 17 September 1977, with guitarist Roger Towndrow and drummer Arcane Vendetta completing a line-up that would constantly ebb and sway.

'I would say it was one of the best punk gigs I have seen,' wrote teenager Mark Jay in the fanzine *Skum*. 'There was no barrier between the audience and the band... Shane, rocking the mic backwards and forwards, fag end hanging out of his mouth... Shanne on bass stumbling about half-drunk... storming through "Downtown", "19 Wasted Years", "Stupid Cow" (about Shanne), "Urban Success", "Abuse", and then... "Poxy Poser"... Shane sings 'You're a poxy poser – you, you, you", pointing his finger at the seething mass of sweaty pogo-ers at the front of the stage. Halfway through the set, Captain Sensible came in with loads of red and white roses, and we all started pelting the band with them.'

One of Shane's regular hangouts around Soho was The Cambridge in Cambridge Circus. A London landmark on the corner of Charing Cross Road and Shaftesbury Avenue, the pub was a meeting point in the late 1970s for art students, punks and scene influencers like Malcolm McLaren. It was also within stumbling distance of Wells Street.

Shane and Shanne were interviewed there for a piece in *Skum*, in October 1977. Shane appeared on the cover standing at a urinal with a cigarette dangling from his mouth. In one of his first interviews, he gave mostly facile responses. 'Rolf Harris and Cliff Richard,' he replied when asked about The Nipple Erectors' influences, while Shanne cited The Jam, the Sex Pistols, the Ramones and Wayne County (later Jayne County).

There was no particular image he was trying to create on stage and it was 'bad enough trying to hold a mic', he said. The band had no political opinions and just wanted to 'earn as much money as possible for doing fuck-all!'

On stage, the pair had a natural chemistry and off it their relationship was deepening. So much so that they almost marked 1977 by getting married. 'We went together to Finsbury Town Hall and booked it and met the registrar,' says Shanne. 'It was serious and we were going to do it. But his parents phoned up my mum and said, "Maybe they should think, wait a bit."'

Asked how she felt when their plans were abandoned, Shanne says: 'I didn't really think about it. I just thought it will happen later on. We were so busy enjoying ourselves, going round town or just being in, doing music. We just get on really well.'

Siobhan recalls: 'Shanne used to come around to our house and they were going to get married. They were older than 17, but they were still very young and for some reason they asked if they could marry. Their idea was to get married in gorilla suits. But Mum and Dad said, "No, you're way too young," and it probably had an influence at that time.'

Punk's DIY philosophy had spawned myriad bands who were all jockeying for position, but Shane's infamy as 'that guy who got his ear bitten off' meant there was an immediate buzz of interest around The Nipple Erectors. And one thing was abundantly clear – Shane was ambitious. He may have come across as flippant, but he saw the group as a serious endeavour and, to borrow a Paul Weller title, he yearned 'To Be Someone'. He told *Sounds*, 'If I don't make any money, I'm gonna wanna know why,' and he meant it.

'As shy and sensitive as he was, there was also great confidence,' says Siobhan. 'He had a lot of confidence and was very driven, and when you are driven you don't care what's in front of you. You're going to go there.'

Phil Gaston and Stan Brennan had taken on the management of the band and made sure there was no shortage of gigs. The Nipple Erectors became a fixture on the live scene in London, playing venues like The Music Machine in Camden, The Hope & Anchor in Islington and The Moonlight Club in West Hampstead. They also performed much further afield and in October 1978, they made a bit of punk history when they crossed the Irish Sea to play in Belfast. 'The Nipple Erectors played The Harp Bar in Belfast in 1978 which, during The Troubles, was the first venue to allow both Protestants and Catholics to mix,' says Shanne. 'We went on a tour and were shown the Shankill Road and the Falls Road. The venue had bomb catchers on the windows so nobody could lop a bomb in during the gig. Terri Hooley put the gig on, and we stayed with him and signed copies of our record in his shop, Good Vibrations.'

Phil and Stan's aptly named Piss Artistes management company conducted most of its business from a public telephone box at the end of Gerrard Street in Chinatown, and they used their network of contacts to promote the group and get them work. By 1978, up-and-coming bands could get a single pressed up and delivered to shops without the involvement of the major labels. Phil and Stan formed their own label, Soho Records, and booked the group into Chalk Farm Studios to record 'King Of The Bop' and 'Nervous Wreck'. The band were worse for wear during the session and Shanne was so drunk she passed out in the toilet. 'Then I remember being incapable of getting up,' she said. 'I could hear this horrible noise, and it was Shane doing his vocals.' [2]

A photograph of Shane wearing a teddy boy drape jacket and exuding rock'n'roll swagger adorned the sleeve, but the record went largely unnoticed. A reviewer who saw them at The Moonlight Club, West Hampstead, not long after its release, said they were 'the sort of band who should care but don't'. The decision that summer to change their name to The Nips, however, suggested otherwise. 'It was supposed to be sexist, which I could never understand since everybody's got them, but we had to shorten it from The Nipple Erectors to The Nips,' commented Phil Gaston [3]. 'All The Time In The World' became the follow-up single three months later under their less provocative new moniker. But it fared no better and Shane's open question on the reverse of the sleeve, 'Why hasn't John Peel given us a session yet?', failed to elicit a reply.

Shane may have been focused on achieving success and immersed in life in London. However, his thoughts never wandered far from Tipperary. He sent regular updates to his family, keen for them all to know what the band was doing, and clearly proud of the songs they were playing. 'What I do remember is how important it was for him as he was developing because he sent Dad a tape of The Nips,' says Debra Donnelly. 'He was very anxious that everybody should hear it and it was important they were involved with his music. Dad used to love it; he was so pleased. Shane would always want them to know what he was doing; he wanted their approval, I think.'

He was also keen for Shanne to meet his family in Ireland and, in summer 1978, she became the first of his long-term girlfriends to be taken on a pilgrimage to The Commons. She vividly remembers the long journey from London to Tipperary and the Spartan conditions at the cottage. 'It was an experience, going on the train and the boat, and with Shane at the bar,' she says. 'The bus took several hours to Nenagh and I don't even know how we got to The Commons. Then we were all stuck there, apart from his aunty Monica. There was no toilet, no heating. Luckily it was the summer, but it was raining most of the time. Welcome to Ireland! You had to go out in the fields and find a dock leaf; that's what Shane told me to do.'

By now, the two of them were living together. When Shane had left Wells Street, he had lived at a flat in Hammersmith, but he had eventually moved his stuff into Shanne's bedsit, immortalised in the Nipple Erectors song 'Stavordale Road, N5'.

'I think I just got fed up,' says Shanne. 'I've got a diary from '77 and it's like two or three pages of, "Where the fuck is Shane?" We didn't have telephones or anything, so I think he just moved in because it was easier.'

The band continued to gig regularly and look for opportunities to move to the next level. While the untamed energy of punk had inspired them, their sound was more in keeping with the new wave, due in part to the playing of guitarist Gavin Douglas, who joined in the spring of 1979. He had spent six months attending auditions, but none of the bands appealed to him until he replied to an advertisement placed by The Nips. 'The audition was in Covent Garden, in a dingy basement rehearsal studio,' recalled Gavin [4]. 'Something gelled. A young woman with blonde hair was playing some brilliant melodic bass lines; it was the one and only Shanne Bradley. A guy with big ears was screaming down the mic. This man was Shane MacGowan, famous for having his ear bitten off at an early Clash gig!' After the audition, he was left waiting nervously while the band went out with their manager. When they returned, he was told he had the job, and their next gig was supporting The Jam at the Rainbow Theatre in Finsbury Park.

Gavin also played on what would become one of The Nips' best-remembered songs, 'Gabrielle', which was released on Soho Records in October 1979. An unashamedly pop song, its breezy three-chord progression was reminiscent of 'Best Friend's Girl' by American band The Cars, and there was no shortage of opportunities to promote their radio-friendly song. In January they supported Dexys Midnight Runners at Camden's Music Machine and Athletico Spizz 80 at The Nashville, Kensington. The following month they opened for mod band The Purple Hearts at The Moonlight Club and Stiff Records' Wreckless Eric at The Marquee. When Dexys announced the second part of their 'Dance Stance' tour, starting that February, The Nips were confirmed as the support on several dates around the country.

Phil and Stan were ambitious for the band and arranged with Ted Carroll and Roger Armstrong to license them to Chiswick Records. The label was home to Johnny Moped, Radio Stars, Drug Addix (featuring a teenage Kirsty MacColl as 'Mandy Doubt'), and The Radiators From Space, among others. But when 'Gabrielle' was given a reissue by the label, it flopped, leaving the band deflated.

Shane was bitter and he made no bones about it when the press caught up with him. 'It's a good tune, but Chiswick fucked it up and I am fucking ashamed to have been associated with a silly pop record,' he raged to *Zigzag*, three months later. There would be no more of 'that R&B shit' from The Nips, he announced. In future, his songs would laser in on those inhabiting the capital's seedy underbelly. 'In the future I want to play disturbing dance music – really strange stuff, but not fucking arty... Trash is what we're really all about... the Soho part of London, the side that's full of pimps, whores and junkies.'

That month, after a gig at The Rock Garden in Covent Garden, The Nips announced they were splitting up. Shanne told *NME* it wasn't just the lack of progress that had caused it to implode. They were 'sick of each other' and Shanne hated the music they were making. 'Shane and I just weren't communicating,' she confessed to journalist Adrian Thrills. 'We were beating each other up all the time.'

Frustration in and around the group was deepening and as the recriminations began, manager Howard Cohen was sacked. Shane was as disheartened as anyone at the group's failure to make a greater impression on the UK's buoyant punk scene. However, he had always avoided confrontation and his natural inclination was to rally to defend someone who was under attack. So, he was dismayed when that frustration spilled over in the direction of their jettisoned manager. When The Nips played their supposed swansong at The Music Machine in Camden, Shane's friend Deirdre O'Mahony says, 'We shocked Shane because Howard had been sacked as the manager and everybody was very angry that they were splitting up and that Howard had apparently made a mess of it. I remember getting really carried away with that anger and being really quite aggressive towards Howard, and Shane was really upset that Howard was being attacked. He was so shocked that everyone else was so angry.'

As Shane was left licking his wounds, Britain's music scene was undergoing a sea-change. A mod revival was in full swing, spearheaded by groups like The Jam, The Lambrettas and Secret Affair, and teenagers were discovering Motown, Stax and other soul records from the 1960s they had missed first time round. Shane's taste in music had always been very

catholic and he was as fanatical about soul and reggae as he was punk. He
was still spending any money he had at the record stalls and shops around
Soho and beyond, and he was working in one as he contemplated his next
move.

Rocks Off (not to be confused with Rock On) had opened a small shop
in Hanway Street, between Oxford Street and Tottenham Court Road.
And when Shane was sober enough to turn up, he could be found behind
the counter. 'He could talk intelligently about any kind of music with our
punters,' said Stan Brennan. 'But his drinking – and at that stage, it was
still mostly drinking – was getting in the way of him working. Sometimes
he would turn up at three in the afternoon stinking of booze, pretty rough
looking, when he was meant to have been in at ten. I went a lot of extra
yards to keep him working. It was like a charity, really.' [5]

Just as things had unravelled for The Nips, so had Shane's relationship
with the woman he had once vowed to marry. And although there was
animosity between her and The Nips' former managers, she remained
close to Shane and a few months later suggested they rekindle the group.
This time they would be managed by Howard Cohen and Shanne's new
boyfriend, John Hasler, once a member of Madness. Gavin Douglas was
not involved and auditions for a new guitarist were held on 30 June 1980.

One of those who responded to the ad in *Melody Maker* to join a 'name
band' was James Fearnley. Hauling his Telecaster into Halligan's rehearsal
rooms on Holloway Road, he remembers being 'a little bit disappointed'
the moment he first laid eyes on Shane. 'I had come up from Teddington
and, when I walked in and realised who this was – Shane O'Hooligan at
this time – I thought, Oh, shit,' says James. 'But then he was so arresting
as a person to look at and Shanne and Shane were almost homonymous –
the two of them were a presentation. Shane was the one that you looked
at, but not far behind was the shadow of Shanne Bradley, who was fairly
intimidating in her own right. But to me, he was just totally fascinating to
look at. I was relieved to have Terry Smith, who was playing drums at the
time, in the room with me as a kind of conduit for this weather system at
the end of the room that could ground itself through him to me, so I could
actually figure out what was going on.'

Afterwards, Shane and Howard Cohen joined him in a nearby pub and
invited him to join the band. James said he would, on the proviso that they

would find him somewhere to live. Shane said it shouldn't be a problem. Jem Finer, then Shane's flatmate, says: 'I can remember them doing these auditions and Shane coming back and saying, "There was this northern bloke, but he was actually a really good guitar player, a bit like Wilko [Johnson].'

James had officially joined The Nips. However, his real initiation was to come – a night out drinking with its legendarily thirsty singer. The pub crawl began on Holloway Road and then swiftly moved to King's Cross. There didn't seem to be a landlord in the area who didn't know Shane – and not all of them wanted his custom. That didn't bother Shane, who seemed unable to stay still for very long. No sooner had they got to one pub and ordered their pints, than Shane was off to the next one.

James says: 'I wonder if the restlessness that first time I met him for a drink was because it was so difficult for him to settle in one place because nobody wanted him where he turned up. The first pub we went into, the guy says, "You're not coming in here." So, he was this sort of peripatetic figure going around London and walking really fast everywhere. It was so difficult to keep up with him, not just that night, but whenever I went out drinking with him, you had to virtually skip to keep up with him. He was always on the move some place, and fast.'

Maybe he was keen to impress James, but Shane was garrulous on this first night out with his new band member and he talked freely about his family in Ireland and his time spent at The Commons. James was also struck by the fact that it wasn't just Shane's body that couldn't keep still. It was his mind too. 'Something I've always been aware of is that it's as if someone's continually ringing a triangle in his ear and he has to cope with that while he talks to everybody else,' says James. 'Which isn't to say that he's distracted all the time, but I think it's just some bell being rung and that's with him the entire time.'

The first show with The Nips' new guitarist was at The Rock Garden in Covent Garden. As a group they were still an unknown quantity for him, and James didn't know what to expect as he strapped on his Telecaster. When he stepped forward to join Shane on the vocals for 'Hot Dogs With Everything', he was surprised to hear the crowd shouting it back at them. But it was Shane's wild, Iggy Pop-like performance that left the deepest impression.

'The entire audience seemed to be on the edge of the room,' he recalls. 'Shane was wearing this smoking jacket and he just got off the stage and decided he was going to go into some sort of paroxysm in the middle of the floor. It was fucking amazing. It was like, "If no one else is using the floor, then fuck you, I'm going to use it and I'm going to writhe around in it." It was fantastic. It was shocking, but really funny to see somebody do that.'

James ended up sharing a house with Shane in Burton Street, a dead-end street in King's Cross. Shanne had shared a flat there with Shane, but by the time The Nips had reformed, she had moved out and had married John Hasler. James says: 'It took me a while to piece together what the actual relationships were. I discovered later, when I came across the instrumental The Pogues did called 'Shanne Bradley', how devoted Shane was to her.

'Shanne presented to me as so impassive and I want to put words like cruel on to it, but these are my projections on to her and they're probably not what she was. I found her a bit weird and it made me want to impress her because I could get nothing out of her. The two of them together were scary and a unit and I was on the outside of it.'

Jem Finer saw The Nips perform and he had been particularly impressed with this incarnation of what he says was Shanne's band. He believes a deal was almost secured with Stiff Records, to which label The Pogues would eventually sign. But the maverick label, run by Dave Robinson, plumped for Tenpole Tudor instead.

Paul Weller had designs on the band signing to Polydor and paid for them to record a demo at the label's studio in Bond Street. He produced the four tracks, 'Happy Song', 'Nobody To Love', 'Ghost Town' and 'Love To Make You Cry'. Polydor passed, but Paul knew the band, and Shane in particular had something, and he invited them to open for The Jam at a couple of their shows. The first was on 3 November at Queens Hall, Leeds and the second on 12 December at The Music Machine in Camden, where Shane joined Paul on stage for a cover of Martha Reeves and The Vandellas' 'Heatwave'.

'I always looked at Paul to be a kind of mentor for Shane. I don't know how true that is, but Shane had a lot of time for Paul and Paul seemed to have some time for Shane,' says James Fearnley.

By the time these shows came around, Shanne was heavily pregnant. At The Music Machine, she wore a yashmak, and the rest of the band were made to wear her mum's nighties. Behind the drumkit that night was Jon Moss, who was deeply unimpressed. Less than two years later he was at the top of the charts with Culture Club and in a relationship with Boy George.

Siobhan MacGowan was among those who saw what would be The Nips' last public gig. 'The audience were gobbing at Shane,' she says. 'He was getting covered in gob, but he just kept on and on singing.'

Shane and James Fearnley did get up and perform with The Jam at their annual private Christmas party at The Fulham Greyhound, but their show at The Music Machine proved to be their last hurrah.

The Nips had hoped Paul Weller would be able to do for them what Bruce Foxton, The Jam's bassist, had done for The Vapors after spotting them playing in a London pub. He had taken over their management with Paul's dad, John, and their single 'Turning Japanese' had become a huge hit, reaching number three in March 1980. Paul did offer The Nips the chance to record for Respond, the label he set up in 1981 as a kind of English Motown. But the sessions never took place. It was over.

Richard Thomas, a promoter and a friend of Shane's from King's Cross, rated the group and Shane's songs. But he says the UK's live scene was small and overcrowded and The Nips found themselves cut adrift on the post-punk swell. 'They were very good, but you never thought that Shane would come from them and The Pogues would come from them,' he says. '"Gabrielle" was a great single, but there were so many of those bands around then. They got lost in everything.

'Compared to what it is today, it was a very small scene. It was like that really until the late eighties. I mean, The Smiths never played to more than five thousand people in this country and Joy Division played to even fewer. With huge bands now, everyone thinks you must have done endless nights at the O2 or something, but it was nothing like that at all. U2 were always on a major label, REM were on an American indie label and they might have been the first band to play Wembley, although The Pogues might have done it just before them – and that's Wembley indoors... So the biggest place The Nips headlined was probably The Hope & Anchor.'

Shanne gave birth to a daughter, Sigrid, in March 1981, but she wanted to keep The Nips going and she had some fresh ideas about the direction they should take. 'I had been to Crete and I just loved it,' she says. 'I fell in love with Greece and the music, the Cretan style and the rhythm of it, and I wanted to incorporate it into the music I was doing. So, I told Shane about all this and he said, "Well, I would like to incorporate more Irish music." We had played "Poor Paddy" in The Nips and my landlord had lent me an album of Irish rebel songs. I had been learning tenor banjo as well and had been going to traditional Irish sessions. So, we had this little outfit with the Scottish fiddler player David Rattray and John Hasler on stand-up drums, but I had a lot of personal issues going on, including being homeless, and I just said, "I can't do this right now."'

Time had finally been called on The Nips, but the seeds of what was to come had started to take root.

Burton Street in Camden looms large in the story of Shane MacGowan and The Pogues. The short-life housing project behind the British Medical Association and near Euston brought him together with the soon-to-be Pogues' banjo player and his co-songwriter, Jem Finer. It was also while he was living there that Shane met the next woman in his life, Mary Buxton, who he went out with for two years and who accompanied him on a drunken ride from squats and punk dives to mainstream success.

Like lots of women who came into Shane's orbit, Mary found him physically attractive and his company addictive. In no time at all, she found herself hopelessly in love with him. Speaking about her life with him for the first time, she says: 'He was good looking and he is incredibly strong. He was already quite well-known, and I've got a little problem with "trophies". And he is so incredibly interesting. I really fell for him.'

By her own admission, Mary was an alcoholic and had been going through a tough time when she became involved with Shane. 'My mum died in late 1977 and she was a rampant alcoholic and it was all very unpleasant. I think I was in a breakdown because I had a very nice relationship in Kilburn, but I couldn't deal with it – not the first mistake of my life in that regard. I left there to move to Burton Street, and I knocked that relationship on the head once I started going out with Shane.'

Life with Shane was a relentless social whirl, his restlessness and inexhaustible thirst meaning the couple were always in a pub. The Boot on Cromer Street, The Skinners Arms on Judd Street, The Norfolk Arms on Leigh Street. His lanky frame was part of the furniture in these and other watering holes, all of which were within staggering distance of his bottle-strewn flat, which also had its own bar set up in one corner.

Mary sat and listened in awe as Shane and Spider laced drinking sessions with lengthy discussions about the Second World War. They shared a passion and an encyclopaedic knowledge of the subject, and there was an electricity when they were in the same room. Mary and Shane would also sit up late into the night talking about history, politics and even *Doctor Who* – another subject he knew everything about. 'He had watched all those programmes as a child and he remembered them word-for-word,' says Mary.

Shane and Mary went to gigs regularly, and Camden Palace was a favourite haunt. Formerly known as The Music Machine, where The Nips had performed, it had been relaunched in 1982 and adopted by the new romantics. Shane knew a lot of people in clubs and venues across London and he saw his socialising as business, as well as pleasure, says Mary. This and her collision course with alcohol meant they would often become separated on nights out and drunkenly make their way home on their own.

'For our first date we went to Dingwalls, and I remember this because I was so happy,' says Mary. 'But I was an alcoholic and obviously there's quite a lot of beer in Dingwalls. So, we lost each other and only met up in the flat at about eight o'clock the next morning. This was the constant story of our relationship because he was completely in his own world and actually had a lot to do because he was a professional. Shane was mixing with people he needed to mix with and then had little old me, who was basically having a nervous breakdown and drinking to black out. Unfortunately for him, he must have had to listen to a lot of shit about my childhood. He was kind and he would listen for hours. He had very caring parents, so I think he was quite sympathetic to someone who hadn't been looked after. I was quite feral.'

Shane's pride in his Irish roots was evident and he talked openly about his own childhood experiences. Mary got the firm impression that while he had fond memories of his visits to Tipperary, he had 'blocked out shitty old Tunbridge Wells'. However, he did take her to his parents' house in Kent for Sunday lunch and to meet his family in Ireland.

Says Mary, 'In the first flush we went and stayed at The Commons and that was when his uncle Sean was around. He was in a mobile home, as far as I remember, somewhere nearby. They were proper old-style farmers with their sheep outside, and we had ducks' eggs for breakfast, which Shane loved. They were quite straight, and you had to behave properly in that house. I loved it there because I just wanted a family and anyone who was going to give me breakfast, I just lapped it up. There were some great pubs in people's living rooms, and we did have a laugh. We would walk for miles down these lanes and you would get all the stories about what had gone on for the last hundred years... He was just so happy there.'

For a time, Shane had a job in the staff bar at the National Hospital for Neurology and Neurosurgery in Queen Square, Bloomsbury, where Mary also pulled pints. The two of them had keys and were sometimes left in charge of the place, with chaotic consequences. 'The bar was open most of the day and right up to about midnight because obviously hospitals are twenty-four-hour places and the staff need a drink, as do the bar tenders! So, we were running this bar and it was just completely insane. I was working the day John Lennon was shot, and it was just absolute mayhem. We were the only two staff members. We were absolutely, totally smashed, and we were best mates with everybody in there.'

Shane remembers it well: 'I'd come in and get the keys and open up and I was meant to shut at three o'clock in the afternoon at the latest, two if possible. There were a few doctors who came in who were regulars and then there were all the hospital porters, black and West Indian and Asian guys. Mary had been running it and then she jacked it in, and I got the job. These guys would come in and they left when I felt like it. I wasn't that worried about them staying and it was ages before we got caught by this woman. We were still going at six o'clock when we were meant to be out of there at two or three. They were all hard drinkers, and they'd line up against the bar and they'd all be drinking rum and pep or rum and coke. By the time I'd served the first round, the second guy would be shouting for the second round.

'I got a stripping down from this bitch who was the entertainment director of the hospital social club. But they needed someone, so they couldn't just sack me. Mary was better at getting them out of the place because it's like mum telling you to get out. But how the fuck could I tell them to get out? I didn't want them to get out to start with. I was getting a drink every time they had one and that was once every five minutes or less!

67

'There was a Scottish doctor who liked his whiskey and he used to keep buying me drinks, and one time I got really pissed. *A Sense of Freedom*, the film about Jimmy Boyle, had been on a couple of nights before, and for some reason I got worked up. Another doctor who was with him mentioned it and they were talking about it. I don't know what I thought they were saying, but I fucking attacked this big Scottish guy. I got the wrong end of the stick about what he was saying. He just pushed me back and told me to calm down.

'The next morning, I met a mate of mine because I was drawing the dole at the same time. I knew I had done something awful, but I couldn't remember what. So, he told me and took great pleasure out of that. "You started a fight with that Scottish doctor, and it was something about the Jimmy Boyle film, and he was agreeing with you!" This was years ago when I used to get out of my mind. I haven't been that drunk in years.'

When he had moved to number 32 Burton Street in the summer of 1978 from a squat in Kentish Town, Shane joined an established close-knit community, and the room he initially moved into was next to that of Jem Finer. The quietly spoken graduate found Shane 'funny and clever' during their drinking sessions at The Norfolk Arms. They formed a close bond, discussing their shared interests in literature, music and films.

Jem reflects fondly on the early days of an enduring friendship: 'We hung out and would go to gigs and the pub, and then have these late-night drinking sessions after the clubs. When you live next door to someone, you are witness to a lot of behaviours and likes and dislikes, and a lot of the music that he played was Irish folk music. So, we would come back late at night and put on The Dubliners or The Clancy Brothers. He always had a very strong relationship to traditional music and Irish traditions from being a kid and being asked to sing at parties and weddings.

'While he was in The Nips, he was still playing that. We all had very broad tastes and we listened to the music of the pubs and clubs and late-night restaurants. It was Turkish music, Greek, Irish, country and western, as well as whatever was going on, so post-punk and the beginning of the northern Factory Records scene, like Joy Division and then New Order after that. So, there was this big melting pot.'

Shane recalls: 'It was the house that Jem built. People used to come round after the pubs and gigs and we'd be up late with his missus and other heads. They'd be smoking bongs and it would be Nepalese temple balls and really good fucking dope and grass and everybody used to get completely stoned and we'd drink some wine and listen to music... Jem was obsessed by country and bluegrass and we were both obsessed with jazz, from Dixieland through Chicago, and swing. My old man was a jazz freak. Jem was also a ballad freak and he was mad on The Dubliners, The Clancys, The Fureys, and he also listened to Woody Guthrie and Pete Seeger. He liked melody and he liked rhythm and that's like me.'

Jem wasn't a musician and he'd always been led to believe there was no point him picking up an instrument, his childhood piano teacher declaring him tone deaf. He had been brought up in Stoke-on-Trent and had studied at Keele University in Staffordshire before being drawn to London. His epiphany came when he met Matt Jacobson, who was playing bass in a band called The Millwall Chainsaws. He told Jem anyone could play a musical instrument and, with the DIY ethos of punk still thick in the air, Jem was inspired to try. Burton Street was awash with embryonic bands and cellars used as rudimentary rehearsal studios. By the time Shane moved in, Jem was playing bass in The Petals, which was fronted by Shane's old friend Pete Petal.

Jem was full of admiration for Shane's drive and the effort he put into his songwriting, even if some of his behavior got on his nerves. 'I hesitate to use the phrase "pop star", but he wanted to be successful,' he says. 'I wouldn't like to try and say what his motives were, but he is an incredibly talented guy. There is something that used to really annoy me. He would just take my guitar without asking. So, I would go home and my guitar wasn't there and I would find it in his room with a broken string. I'd say, "You fucking twat." Sometimes he was there playing it and I would have to negotiate to get it back. I don't know why he didn't actually have his own guitar, but anyway, fair enough, it was always interesting to listen to the process of how he would write songs. This was when it didn't even occur to me to write songs. He had been doing it for a long time and for me it was an education to look and listen and learn this craft. He was very meticulous and hard-working.'

A little later, Cathy Cinnamon – a schoolteacher who lived in their house – wanted to record some of the songs she was writing. A band was formed from the Burton Street crowd; the duo who would go on to write so many memorable songs found themselves playing music together for the first time. Jem says: 'I think I played guitar in it and Shane played bass, and this guy called Ollie Watts, who was the drummer from The Millwall Chainsaws, played drums. I think there were a couple of other people. We actually did a recording session and it went a bit skew-whiff and we did Cathy's songs. But we also did songs of our own, which were more like industrial, funk jam sessions. It was the time of Joy Division and A Certain Ratio and all this weird, industrial, northern funk. My only memory of it really is that I was trying to play weird, abrasive funk licks and these dubby bass lines. We went to Rough Trade to try and get a deal with them because Shane knew the guy who ran Rough Trade, and he had the cache to walk in there with the tapes. But I think he came out quickly and that was the end of that...

'There was an idea in the air – and I'm sure it was Shane's – that after that last version of The Nips stopped, rather than start a new version again, he was thinking about starting a band playing Greek music. And eventually there was this idea to play traditional songs, but with a ferocity and punk energy. So, the band that we had played with Cathy Cinnamon recording was the nucleus of the band that first played these songs, which was called The New Republicans.'

James recalls Shane's preoccupation with Greek music being driven by Shanne: 'When I went round to visit him, he was talking about a Roman emperor, Gladiator, new romantic type band, and I said, "So what type of music are we going to play?" He said, "We're going to play fucking Cretan music." Shanne Bradley had been playing stuff or she had given him a tape before The Men They Couldn't Hang started and she was interested in Cretan music. So, it came out of his relationship with her. But I think it started to fly with him because he played me this Cretan music and it was just like this loop thing, a line of music. He said, "It's like fucking Irish music." So, the jump from Cretan music to Irish music wasn't far, but there was also the way that it linked a repetitive loop of something. He was so obsessed with the band Loop and loved any music that just went round and round.'

Ironically, it was at a new romantics hangout in the West End that the group managed to land a booking. Shane and Ollie Watts were drinking at Cabaret Futura, the avant-garde mixed media club in Soho established by scene influencer Richard 'Kid' Strange, where some of the new wave of electronic bands made early appearances. 'We called ourselves The New Republicans as a piss-take of the new romantics,' says Shane. 'Me and Ollie, who was the first drummer, were at Cabaret Futura and Soft Cell were on. A couple of days later they had a Top 10 hit and then a number one. Ollie went up to Richard Strange and said, "'Ere listen, mush. We're The New Republicans and we play Irish ballads and rebel songs and we're playing here next fortnight." And Richard Strange said, "Oh, all right. What are you called?" "We're called The New Republicans." "As in Irish republicans?" "Yes!"'

So, in the spring of 1981, the group that would eventually become The Pogues made its first public appearance. Jem was away in Italy at the time, so joining Shane on stage at the trendy West End hangout was Matt Jacobson on bass, Ollie Watts on drums and Pete 'Spider' Stacy. Spider had sung during the rehearsals, but on the night, he lost his voice and Shane took over the vocals, while thrashing away furiously on an acoustic guitar. Their repertoire didn't contain any of the songs by Cathy Cinnamon, for which rehearsal sessions had been booked, but traditional Irish songs that would feature in The Pogues' early sets, such as 'The Auld Triangle', 'Down In The Ground Where The Dead Men Go' and 'Poor Paddy'.

Recalling the group's shambolic debut, Shane says: 'A load of squaddies were there and objected to the republican song we were singing and pelted us with chips, which was getting off lightly, I thought. The manager, who was Irish, came rushing up and said, "I don't want to get in trouble with the fucking army and the police; I like this club. We're turning down the lights." So, we had the plugs pulled on us, but we went down well... People were looking confused or delighted. The Raincoats [post-punk band] were looking confused.'

Shane's friend Deirdre O'Mahony was in the audience that night with her boyfriend Phil Gaston and couldn't see it going much further. 'There was only myself and Phil and maybe about four other people in the audience that actually knew the band, and there was a whole bunch of squaddies there, and it was just mad. I remember looking at the band and thinking, Jesus, what are they at? Nobody's ever going to go to this, nobody's ever going to get this. It was so wrong, it was so stripped-back and, of course, that was the essence of The Pogues. That was the heart of what they did, and it got you – it really did. Everybody was so wasted, and Shane didn't care… It was Shane and Spider that I remember. Spider was really out of tune on the whistle, he could hardly play it. You did know you were watching something extraordinary, but I never thought it would ever become popular.'

The Troubles in Northern Ireland were reaching a critical point in 1981. Republican prisoners in Long Kesh – or the Maze as it was known – had begun a second series of hunger strikes and the election of one of them, Bobby Sands, as an MP had made it a cause célèbre. Prime Minister Margaret Thatcher remained steadfast in refusing to give special category status for paramilitary prisoners and, when Sands died on 5 May, it received worldwide media attention. Damian O'Neill, lead guitarist with The Undertones, wore a black armband when they recorded a *Top of the Pops* performance of 'It's Going To Happen!' on the same day.

London was on edge. The IRA had carried out a series of bombings through the 1970s and in January 1981 had blown up the barracks at RAF Uxbridge, although no one was killed. Just months after The New Republicans performed Irish rebel songs in the middle of Soho, devices were set off at Chelsea barracks and the Wimpy bar on Oxford Street.

This was no time to be Irish in Britain, especially in the capital. Discrimination was rife. Anyone with an Irish accent could attract suspicion and some deliberately kept a low profile. But not Shane. He had always been immensely proud of his Irish heritage and never hid it from anyone. His accent was unequivocally English – London, even – but as he held sway in The Cambridge he would talk openly about The Troubles and flaunted his Irishness.

'What struck me about Shane and the others, like Trish O'Flynn [of The Shillelagh Sisters], who had grown up here, but were from very strong Irish backgrounds, was that they really embraced their identity,' says Deirdre. 'They were very aware of their Irishness and they didn't see it as a source of embarrassment. And actually, I don't think I was alone. That sense of, "Let's escape all that embarrassing stuff around being Irish" and being considered "less than" and from "the country", because I was from Limerick – the height of sophistication! I suppose the reason I'm making a point about this is because it began my own education about my own identity. The conversations that used to take place in the pub between the

Northern Irish mob, myself, Shane and Spider, were just really taking apart who we were, what it was to be Irish…'

Something else about Shane that won Deirdre's admiration was his willingness to spend time talking not just to the in-crowd, but to people who were important to those he knew. Her mum paid a surprise visit to London for Deirdre's 21st birthday and when she took her to The Cambridge to introduce her to her friends, Shane sat talking to her for ages.

'Shane turned up and he blew me away because, unlike the rest of my friends, he didn't ignore her,' Deirdre remembers. 'He sat down and made a point of talking to her for a very long time and she was totally blown away by this. But family and the relationship with family and how you behave around your family… he didn't care about what was cool or what wasn't cool. It was just important. I think he makes a point of including anybody he sees as excluded.

'I always remember if anybody was keeping anybody else out, or not being as inclusive as they should be, Shane was on to it like a laser. He could have been wasted, but if he perceived anybody being left out, he was on it. And he could be really scathing. Family was hugely significant to him and that way, which is a kind of country way, that you take the whole person and their extended family as part of who you know.'

By 1981, Shane, Jem and James all moved out of Burton Street, after Camden council declared the houses unsafe and everyone had to leave. James relocated to Mornington Crescent and Jem got a flat in the Hillview estate in King's Cross. Shane moved into a flat above a corner shop north of King's Cross station – a place that would pass into legend among those who knew him.

'The builders were knocking away and kept coming and eventually they were knocking away in the houses next door either side and it started acting like the Leaning Tower of Pisa,' says Shane. 'It was like being on a ship in a storm and we were rolling around the flat, you know what I mean? They had demolished everything and now they wanted to demolish us. But we stuck it out because we wanted to be re-housed and I got a really good flat on the fourth floor, on the corner of a block of flats in Cromer Street.'

Shane's peripatetic life in London was in stark contrast to that of the rest of his family, but he still went to Tunbridge Wells when his chaotic timetable allowed. Therese was much happier since resettling there and

Siobhan was studying and working at local pubs. Local teenager Shelley Harris got to know Siobhan during this period and spent a lot of time at the MacGowans. She fondly remembers the friendly atmosphere and the parties that went on there.

'After the pub closed, we would end up at "Magoogan Hall", our nickname for Therese and Maurice's,' recalls Shelley. 'We were always welcomed, and Therese and Maurice were often part of the party. Maurice would enjoy a drink or two and was known for being the last man standing. Therese would have a cup of tea. As parents, they weren't typical, and they enjoyed our company and engaged with us. Therese was a kind, warm lady, and many of us would sit and talk to her about the woes of youth… she was always compassionate about whatever was troubling us. When he was visiting Tunbridge Wells, Shane would come to the pub where Siobhan worked and would sit and talk to us all.

'A happy memory for me was being with them one Christmas evening. Therese insisted we all did a turn. She sang a beautiful Irish song, then Shane and I were encouraged to do "The Sailor's Hornpipe". He played on his penny whistle and I danced, much to everyone's amusement… simple pleasures surrounded by family and friends with warmth from the open fire.'

When he was in a state to make it there, Shane could still be found behind the counter at Rocks Off, buying, selling and playing records, and immersed in music. Siobhan MacGowan often spent the day there with him instead of going to college. 'I used to hang around with him and then I'd go and get him his favourite sandwich – a brown bread, fried egg sandwich with lots of black pepper,' she says. 'He was very animated in the record shop and he was living in Cromer Street. He lived there for quite a while. You used to ring on the doorbell, and he'd open the window and drop down the key from the top window so you could let yourself in. He just had it like a pit. It was really awful. His bed was on the floor and the kitchen was full of bottles, with no food going on, and the bathroom was full of bottles.'

Whatever was buried beneath the mountains of empties, it wasn't his sense of purpose. The New Republicans might have gone down in flames, but Shane now had a clear vision for his next band. Cretan music had given way to traditional Irish songs and Jem was now back from his travels and keen to be involved. In the evenings he went to Cromer Street and amid the detritus, Shane taught him the songs he wanted to play.

'There was a lot of talking about what was going to happen next and I was going to be playing guitar,' explains Jem. 'But whatever happened next seemed to take an incredibly long time and I kept saying to Shane, "Well just teach me some of the songs and then when something happens at least I'm ready." I started learning some of the traditional songs like "Poor Paddy", "Peggy Gordon", "Carrickfergus", but he had also started writing and "Streams Of Whiskey" was one. I have an amazing old cassette, which is Shane and I just playing songs together in his room.'

Shane sang and played chords on his acoustic guitar, thrashing the strings with violent intensity. Jem found himself trying to pick out the underlying tune as it if were being played on a banjo. He had never attempted to play one, but his cousin Carol (a former girlfriend of Ian Dury) had one in her flat and it had always intrigued him. He figured that, as he was trying to make his guitar emulate a banjo, he might as well have a go at playing a real one. Although The Pogues were still a way off, a defining part of its sound was now in place.

'Her instrument was the banjo,' says Jem, 'so I used to come down to London and stay with her in her flat and I'd always liked this banjo and the sound of it. So, I thought, Fuck, this is mad, I'll try and play the banjo. By then it was Shane playing guitar and I was playing the banjo, and suddenly we had to start finding the rest of the people for the band.'

There was a real sense that things were coming together, although putting the final pieces in place was going to take time, and Shane and Jem decided to fill the hiatus by busking. Initially, they set up at Finsbury Park or Tottenham Court Road underground stations, but then decided to 'go upmarket' and get a licence to perform in Covent Garden. For this, they had to audition.

'We generally pulled crowds,' says Shane. 'It was raining, and it was early in the morning and it was a Thursday or something. We started playing and we immediately had a fan, right? – an old navvy from Carrickfergus – and he asked us to play "Carrickfergus". Jem and I were both a bit unsure of it, but basically we had it. So, we did "Carrickfergus", and we did it well. Jem was playing banjo and I was playing Irish rhythm guitar, really fast up- and down-strokes, changing chords a lot. It's chromatic and it's on the same scale as Indian and north African music.'

Jem continues: 'Afterwards, we had to go into this guy's office to get our licence and he basically said, "I don't think I've ever had to do this before, but I'm sorry to say I've talked to all the shopkeepers and the feeling is that you really don't have the Covent Garden seal of quality." So, we failed the audition and maybe that galvanised us to find a band!'

The musicians who had taken to the stage with Shane at Cabaret Futura were no longer around. New faces were needed and Jem remembers the search being a slow one. Shane had a notion that he knew a woman who played accordion, but he couldn't remember her name or who she was. Eventually, he gave up on that idea and remembered how James Fearnley sometimes played piano backstage at Nips shows. They borrowed an accordion from a friend and Jem called round to James's flat in Mornington Crescent and invited him to learn how to play it.

At James's first rehearsal at Cromer Street, Shane handed him a cassette tape of the songs they had been rehearsing and writing. These included 'The Clobberer', which would never see the light of day.

Practice sessions took place at the homes of accommodating friends, among them Rick Trevan and Kathy MacMillan. Jem and James were still getting to grips with their instruments and there was a vacancy for a singer, as Shane didn't want to be in the spotlight. A drummer was also yet to be recruited. However, Shane had a clear vision of the music he wanted to play and knew they were on to something with their energetic treatment of the songs he had heard as a child.

Irish traditional music could not have been further removed from the pop music that was dominating the UK charts at the time. However, one group had pushed the door ajar when it came to an acceptance of more traditional instruments in mainstream pop. Dexys Midnight Runners had forsaken their driving, brass-fuelled northern soul for a Celtic sound incorporating fiddles, banjo, accordion and tin whistle. Kevin Rowland and his new-look entourage – in dungarees, berets and neckerchiefs – were first unveiled to the British public with the single 'The Celtic Soul Brothers' in March 1982.

The record received some airplay and peaked at number forty-five. But it was the follow-up 'Come On Eileen', and the accompanying album, *Too-Rye-Ay*, which proved there was a real appetite for their exhilarating take on Irish music. 'Come On Eileen' spent a month at number one, while the album reached number two and enjoyed an incredible forty-six weeks on the chart. *Too-Rye-Ay* remains one of the most iconic records of the 1980s.

Rowland's parents were from County Mayo in the west of Ireland and he was heavily influenced by Irish literature and music. For his group to score such a huge commercial success with a record so connected with his Irish roots was a spur for Shane. 'Dexys were hugely important for Shane,' confirms Deirdre O'Mahony. 'I remember seeing Dexys at The Music Machine in Camden with Shane when "Come On Eileen" was out and Shane played that constantly. He thought that was amazing and I think in no small measure because it was tapping into the same thing. When Shane was working in Hanway Street, I can remember "Come On Eileen" being played a lot.'

Shane says: 'Dexys had done it. They had done the soul thing and they had done the Irish thing. Spider used to play "Come On Eileen" on the whistle, so we started doing it for an encore. I love that whole album.'

More than a year had passed since The New Republicans' one and only show and Shane was desperate to start gigging. But he didn't want to be the frontman any more than he had before. So, a few days before their first show in the back room of a nearby pub, he drafted in Spider to share the vocals with him. The drum stool was, meanwhile, to be occupied by another familiar face – John Hasler – a surprising choice given Shane's previous involvement with Shanne.

As for a name, various suggestions were batted around. The Noisy Boysies was one. The Men They Couldn't Hang was another, although this ended up being taken up by Shanne Bradley's next band. Eventually, the solution came from a phrase Spider had heard Shane use: 'Pogue Mahone'.

CHAPTER 4

Pogue Mahone

'Been drunk as a skunk since I've been home
From bar to bar like a ghost I roamed
I can't forget those things I saw
Been down with the devil in the Dalling Road'

'Down In The Ground Where The Dead Men Go', **The Pogues**

'Last night as I slept, I dreamed I met with Behan,' slurred Shane as Pogue Mahone opened their first show with a song that had the gambolling tempo of a MacGowan pub crawl. The Pindar of Wakefield, on Gray's Inn Road, King's Cross, was just a short walk from Shane's flat in Cromer Street where, heavily intoxicated, he would crash out on a mattress beneath a portrait of his muse, Brendan Behan. As the group didn't need a van, they walked there with their instruments like a gang of outlaws. It was an image that chimed with Shane's love of Sam Peckinpah movies. The game was on.

Shane's concept for the group hadn't stopped at the music and attitude. He also wanted them to look the part. They dressed in 'paddy suits', the black jackets and trousers and white shirts worn by so many Irishmen in London and back home. It was a look that couldn't have been more out of step with the times in the autumn of 1982, when *Top of the Pops* was all glitz and glamour and party clothes.

On the night Pogue Mahone took to the modest stage at The Pindar [now The Water Rats], Culture Club were closing in on the number one spot with 'Do You Really Want To Hurt Me' Other musicians from punk bands had also reinvented themselves for the 'aspirational' 1980s.

Members of X-Ray Spex had formed new romantic act Classix Nouveaux and Adam Ant was part of the frilly-shirted mainstream, six years after his band Bazooka Joe had topped the bill at the Sex Pistols' first-ever show. But here, in a pub back room, Shane's gang was playing music from a different era.

Jem was amazed at how many people turned up at The Pindar on 4 October and how well it went, given the band's full line-up had barely rehearsed together. He had hardly seen Spider since coming back from Italy and developing the band with Shane. But Spider had appeared out of the blue about a week before the gig, when the name of the group was being discussed. Consequently, he looked out of synch with the rest of them.

'We were all wearing suits,' says Jem. 'It wasn't like, "Let's stop wearing jeans and leather jackets and wear suits." We were wearing them anyway. You could get nice suits in second-hand shops. There was a great stall down the end of Portobello Market, just to the north of the Westway, where I got some amazing suits. The pockets would still be sewn up and they were like a fiver. So, the clothing was suits, white shirts, a nice pair of shoes and a normal haircut – no asymmetrical haircuts.

'Spider turned up in a leather jacket, with red hair dye in a bit of his hair. He hadn't been to any rehearsals or learned any songs. He just sort of shouted and snarled and did his best Johnny Rotten microphone manoeuvres. I found that kind of annoying. So, those are my lasting impressions really. I was amazed that so many people had come and there was a real buzz. Although it was kind of ramshackle, it felt like, "There is something really unique in this – this is a new thing," and it flew totally in the face of fashion.'

The consensus was that the recipe was right, it just needed honing. At a meeting, rules were laid down about what people could and couldn't wear. Spider was told to learn the whistle and get his hair cut properly. His then girlfriend, Anya, was not to cut anyone's hair. Jem wrote it all down. A bass player was also needed, and almost immediately Shane stumbled on a solution. He was wandering along Oxford Street when he bumped into Cait O'Riordan and he suggested they go for a drink. They chatted in The Hog in the Pound on South Molton Street, sinking whiskies courtesy of her freshly cashed giro cheque – her unemployment benefit. She was agog as he filled her in about the group's debut at The Pindar and when she slipped into the conversation that she had a bass guitar gathering dust under her bed, Shane wasted no time in signing her up.

Cait knew all about Shane. She had heard 'Gabrielle' on John Peel's Radio 1 show and had gone to Rocks Off to buy it, only to find Shane behind the counter. He knew little about her and she could barely play the bass. But there was something about this skinny, spiky-haired 17-year-old – and possibly the large amount of whiskey consumed – that made him recruit her on the spot.

Jem recalls there was surprise and some scepticism from the other band members when Shane introduced her to them in a pub and she started coming to rehearsals. 'I don't quite know what their relationship was,' he says. 'I think it might have started out as a slightly romantic one, I'm not sure. He might have had ulterior motives for even offering her the job of bass player when she couldn't play a note. We had to teach her and luckily the bass lines were pretty straightforward.'

Her debut at Clapham's 101 Club on 23 October was a baptism of fire in more ways than one. With Cait on bass, the group also had to perform amid rabbit and chicken entrails and other detritus left by wild psychobilly band King Kurt after they lost the toss and had to go on second. But Pogue Mahone rose to the occasion and Spider added to their own visual spectacle by smashing a metal beer tray on his head and knees throughout.

Cait compensated for her inexperience by forcefully swinging her guitar's neck and glowering at the audience. She cut an intimidating figure, with spiky, backcombed hair and a threatening demeanour. When the show finished and most of the audience had left, she spontaneously stepped up to the microphone and sang a couple of Irish rebel songs. In the silence of the almost empty venue came a beautiful voice and possibly a cry for attention.

As 1982 drew to a close, Shane had still been going out with Mary Buxton. She shared his passion for music, as well as the drink, and had her own extensive record collection. They both loved northern soul and on Saturdays they went to the legendary 6Ts Rhythm and Soul Society all-nighters run by Ady Croasdell and Randy Cozens at the 100 Club. Not all nights out were so happy though and, often, Mary's drinking was the culprit. She had stormed out of The Pindar during Pogue Mahone's debut and been mugged at knifepoint on her way home. Reflecting on her alcoholism and her mental state, she admits it was a 'horrible time' in her life. 'I could see why no one would want to take me on and might want to move on to someone a bit less problematic who didn't need digging out of casualty,' she says.

By 1983, Mary had moved to Nottingham to study law. Shane went up to see her and they sought out nightclubs together. But back in London he had other distractions and Mary sensed a shift in their relationship. 'Maybe I thought I was his girlfriend, but maybe I wasn't,' she says. 'I'm not sure when Cait came along, but the writing was on the wall for me then.'

A tightly wound ball of attitude and aggression, Cait had taken more than just musical inspiration from The Pretenders' Chrissie Hynde. She was volatile on and off stage and her involvement with Shane only added to the tension. Spider commented: 'Cait and Shane were an item for a while. The fights in public sort of added fuel to the fire. Their relationship didn't last very long. Apart from the odd fight, it never really got in the way of the band. Cait could be a real loose cannon. She was quite unpredictable. But she was a very, very powerful force in the band.' [1]

Fionna Murray, who was involved in putting on live music nights at The Pindar, recalls: 'Cait was homeless when I first met her. She was quite scary. She was very tall and wore a big overcoat and she was living in one of the hotels around the corner from Hillview. She looked fantastic in the band as the girl bass player.'

Cait took no prisoners and her temper could erupt volcanically. In stark contrast to Shane, who would do anything to avoid confrontation, she met issues head on. John Hasler was a case in point. There had been an undercurrent of dissatisfaction within the band about his drumming, although no one had raised it directly with him. One day, as everyone turned up for a rehearsal at Rick Trevan's flat, Cait exploded at him. James Fearnley described the moment in his memoir *Here Comes Everybody: The Story of the Pogues*. '"I don't understand what the fuck you are doing in this fucking band," she said. "You can't play for shit. Why don't you just fuck off?" John looked at us, from one to the other. "Go on, fuck off!" Cait said. John looked at her with a panicked smile of disbelief, then, cowed and beaten, he left.'

James was aware of Cait's feelings for Shane and wondered whether, by firing the man who had ensnared Shanne, she was showing her love for him. Whatever her motivation, she had driven him out and, given they had gigs booked, the need for a replacement was urgent. Several were tried before Shane and Jem managed to persuade Andrew Ranken, who lived nearby, to join Pogue Mahone.

Shane explains: 'There was a bit of reshuffling and basically we went back to Andrew, who was the first guy we tried out, and thank God for that. And Cait had joined on bass, of course. It was my idea to do it like a rockabilly sound: it gave it a thunderous sound.'

Jem and his long-term girlfriend Marcia were married in March 1983 and the group were booked to play at their wedding reception in a wine bar off Gray's Inn Road. But Cait's frustration at Shane's apparent non-reciprocation of her feelings was to have repercussions. James came across Cait after a gig at The Pindar one night. She was clearly upset and said she had seen Shane going into the toilet with Spider's girlfriend, Anya. Cait failed to turn up to rehearse the night before the reception and it emerged that after Shane, Spider and Cait had gone drinking there had been a row, and she had stormed off. Shane, typically, didn't want to be the one to go over to her guesthouse to talk her around. Instead, Spider was dispatched, but his attempt at brokering a peace proved disastrous. Cait had wanted to know if Shane had finished with her and Spider said he thought this was likely. Unsurprisingly, this didn't appease her, so it was decided that Jem would play bass at his reception as it was too late to draft in someone else.

Cait had to join Jem and Marcia's celebrations and a roster was drawn up for visits to her guesthouse. No one could get a response. When it came to Shane's turn, he was in for a nasty shock. Cait had overdosed on pills. The others were setting up their equipment when he rushed in with the news. Shane was adamant he was not going to go back, as she was 'vicious'. So, as would so often be the case, responsibility for the situation fell to the others. Jem and James sat with Cait and kept her awake while they waited for the ambulance to arrive. After she was taken to hospital, James looked around the room for a note. He found one in the suitcase above the wardrobe. It read: 'Shane, 98 Cromer Street WC1. You can do what you want with stuff'. Shane had stayed at the reception with Spider and Andrew and seemed nonplussed by events. When the band finally took to the stage, Shane strummed his guitar and nonchalantly informed the guests, 'We haven't got a bass player. She's dead.'

Kathy MacMillan, who was very close to Shane at the time, was struck by his inability to deal with difficult situations. 'He hates confrontation,' she says. 'He would run to the other side of the world rather than face confrontation. He might try to mediate or negotiate or whatever, but if it was really awkward, he wouldn't deal with it. He would be off, believe me.'

Trish O'Flynn, saxophonist with The Shillelagh Sisters, also experienced Shane's aversion to conflict. 'There was a time when Cait and I had an argument one night, and Shane spotted what was going on and he disappeared so fast,' she says. 'I just saw him out of the corner of my eye and thought, Yeah, thanks, mate. I think this is maybe part of that softer side of his personality, that he doesn't like confrontation.'

It wasn't that Shane didn't care. These and other women who know him say he is sensitive and such situations upset him. 'He has a vulnerable side, absolutely,' remarks Merrill Heatley, who also went out with Shane and at that time sang with London folk revival band The Boothill Foot-Tappers. 'Something must have triggered that... I don't think he had a great time at school. It was a difficult time and I think punk rock probably saved him.' Trish adds: 'He is a very complex person who had very difficult younger years which have fed into something.'

Their observations are echoed by Terry Woods from The Pogues: "Consider this. He's 61 now and Shane, since I've known him – and I suspect it went on before – has never accepted responsibility for anything. Somebody else does whatever he needs doing – whatever it is. I think it's part of whatever happened to him. Confronting situations is responsibility."

A by-product of Shane's vulnerability and his propensity to opt for the path of least resistance was a growing dependency on others. Those around him would end up doing things for him, from cleaning up his bombsite of a flat to scraping him up off the floor after someone had laid into him. People felt he needed looking after and Kathy MacMillan believes this is one of the reasons why women are drawn to him. Reflecting on his close social circle in the early days, she says, 'It definitely was fifty-fifty men and women in that whole group of people. There was Trish, Merrill, Julie and me, and quite a few of the guys were married or had girlfriends. So, there were a lot of women. One thing that attracted me to Shane was the fact that he needed mothering. I always had maternal instincts towards him.

'The first time I ever saw Shane was at a party in a squat around King's Cross. He was sitting on the floor, back against the wall, fast asleep, mouth open. He was whiter than I've ever seen a living person and it was like, "Oh my God, is that guy OK?" Then a few other people said, "You don't look very well," and then others came by and said, "Oh, it's only Shane. He's like that all the time." I thought, I'll get on with the party and come back and see if he is still OK. And that for me was the start of a long question – "Is Shane OK?"'

Pogue Mahone didn't set out to be part of any scene. Beyond Dexys, no one else was playing Irish music and the patent on hotwiring traditional songs with punk's raw power rested firmly with Shane. Musical trends being what they are, however, they were seen as part of a movement that had grown organically in pubs and small venues, with The Pindar at its centre.

The Heywire Club was a live music night held there on Wednesday nights, run by Fionna Murray, her sister Gerry and friend Sharon James. It launched in 1983 and the concept was to provide a club-style venue where aspiring bands could play. Pogue Mahone got wind of the venture and asked if they could play one night. Fionna said they wouldn't give them a slot without seeing them, so she and Gerry went to check them out at The Hope & Anchor. The band were just about to start as the two of them picked their way down the dimly lit stairs into the cavernous venue. 'As soon as Shane started, Spider bashed the tin tray off his head,' recalls Fionna. 'Gerry and I just looked at each other. It was like the Irish rebel songs of our childhood meeting punk – two things we'd both experienced. We just thought, Oh my God. This is amazing!'

Off stage, Fionna found Shane 'quite gruff', but in retrospect believes this was a cover for his shyness. He also had a persuasive charm that allowed him to take advantage of their innocence as promoters. 'It was quite funny because Shane would have a guest list,' says Fionna. 'We would be charging one pound on the door for three acts and Shane would arrive with a guest list the length of his arm. We were so naive in a way, but we let them in because we wanted to have a social scene and we had to pay the pub to use the room. The pub was getting all this money behind the bar and we were paying for the privilege. We had to get the money back to cover our costs. We were too soft, and Shane was so charming.'

When Pogue Mahone was booked to perform at Heywire, Shane was apprehensive about the presence of Fionna's father. 'Shane was really nervous because my dad was coming down and he was first-generation Irish,' says Fionna. 'They had a bit of a chat at the end and he was quite taken with the fact that my dad had come to see the gig... Some people didn't get what he was trying to do, but Dad really liked it. He liked the fact that Andrew had one drum. It was just so irreverent, the whole thing, and of course it really set off a certain pride in being Irish in London.

'People forget how repressive it was, being London-Irish. There is a funny thing about being second-generation Irish and not being seen as Irish. You know that you're not English when you're brought up in England with Irish parents. But you're not quite Irish either – you're a hybrid.'

Much of the club's clientele emanated from the short-life housing around King's Cross and got to know each other through the gigs. Darryl Hunt lived near The Pindar and played bass in Baby Lotion with guitarist friend Dave Scott, later of Spizzenergi and Athletico Spizz 80. When Cait asked if she could sing with them, they formed Pride Of The Cross and performed songs like Peggy Lee's 'Is That All There Is?' and 'The Day Before You Came' by Abba, sometimes with Deirdre O'Mahony's art as a backdrop. Later, they recorded 'Tommy's Blue Valentine' as a single, a song Phil Gaston had written for Cait because of her adoration for Tom Waits, and Ace Records released it on its Big Beat label.

Among those lured to The Pindar to see the embryonic Pogue Mahone was Shane's old college friend Bernie France. They had been out of touch for a long time and it was through an article in *NME* that Bernie caught up with what he was doing. 'They were playing at The Pindar, so I went there and saw Shane sitting there with a girl on either side. He'd got a flat, Tom Waits kind of hat on, and we sat down and spoke. They went on stage and I thought, Woah, this is really special. Even though it was barely amplified, you could feel a physical energy from it and then, when they stopped and did stuff like "Kitty", it was actually really emotional, and I was thinking it didn't surprise me that he could do that. I was just enormously impressed.'

Pogue Mahone played Heywire several times and a competitiveness developed as they jostled for position with other bands on the scene: The Shillelagh Sisters, The Boothill Foot-Tappers, and The Men They Couldn't Hang, in which Shanne played bass. 'There was a rivalry between The Men They Couldn't Hang and The Pogues,' recalls Fionna. 'You often get that in a scene where there are two bands that are on an equal footing, but one of them is going to go on and make it. I think it was just the strength of Shane's idea and the songwriting that really took them beyond just being a local band. There was a lot of tension between Shane and [Men... vocalist Stefan] Cush. He [Cush] was with Merrill and there was nearly fisticuffs at times.'

Trish O'Flynn laughs: 'I remember when we got our record deal. It was the end of 1983 and we got a Christmas card from Shane that said, "Happy Christmas, you rich cunts!"'

The emergence of bands playing banjos, tea-chest basses, washboards and other instruments associated with skiffle was picked up on by *South of Watford*, a London Weekend Television pop culture show presented by comedian Ben Elton. The Boothill Foot-Tappers, The Shillelaghs, The Skiff Cats and Pogue Mahone were all featured. A camera crew filmed Pogue Mahone at The Fridge in Brixton and did an interview with Shane at The Pindar. Shane lounged on a bar stool, full of rock'n'roll bravado, drinking a pint and drawing heavily on a cigarette. James Fearnley had told his parents to tune in and watch it and his father phoned him the following day. He described Shane as 'a moron' and warned that if the band hitched their fortunes to him, they'd had it.

Trish O'Flynn and her family were equally appalled by Shane's performance. 'At the end, Ben Elton said, "I don't think The Pogues will get anywhere,"' she says. 'The worst thing was they interviewed Shane in The Pindar. I wasn't there, but obviously we all saw the film. We had all sat down with our parents. I was giving up my health-inspecting career and my parents were thoroughly disgusted. I had said, "Watch this programme. It will tell you about all the music and how successful we're going to be." Then Shane comes on and he's effing and blinding all the way through the interview. It was "fuck" every other word and the older Irish were so disgusted. I know Shane was embarrassed about it at the time. He said they kept feeding him beer and he'd swear a bit more. But it was his own fault for drinking and being interviewed. He really had to live it down. Maria, who was the drummer in The Shillelaghs, said her granddad had watched it, who was from Tipperary, and she had a right go at Shane.'

A session for John Peel's celebrated show on Radio 1 had not been without controversy either. A liberal sprinkling of the F-word in 'Boys From The County Hell' prompted the BBC to prevent its inclusion in songs broadcast in April 1984. Cait, meanwhile, overindulged in the BBC bar across the road from the Maida Vale studios and got so wrecked she couldn't play. James ended up playing most of her bass parts and the band slapped a drinks ban on her.

Despite Shane's 'Bill Grundy' moment and Cait's erratic behaviour, a momentum was slowly building. Stan Brennan got the band into Elephant Studios in Wapping to record a single and started a label called Pogue Mahone. 'Dark Streets Of London' was chosen as the A-side, with 'And The Band Played Waltzing Matilda' on the reverse. White label copies were pressed up and sold at a gig at The Irish Centre, Camden, on the eve of St Patrick's Day, 1984.

The previous week, the band had supported The Clash at The Brixton Academy, after Shane had badgered his old mate Joe Strummer into giving them a slot. On Easter Monday, they took part in the Alternative Country Festival at the Electric Ballroom, Camden, with the Boothills and other acts. It was another profile-raising show. However, the occasion was marred by a violent attack on Shane in the venue's toilets and the sight of him emerging from the gents covered in blood was a shock for his new girlfriend, Merrill Heatley. 'He came out and he'd been beaten up really badly,' she says. 'I was like, "Bloody hell, what's happened?" and he said, "Ah, whatever." He wasn't a scrapper, but he was quite often targeted, and I think he probably just used to cave in. I don't think he would fight back. It's sad.'

Explaining the motivation for the attack, Shane said: 'There was a bit of shouting about the IRA, and there was a lot of them. I was lying in a pool of blood in the Electric Ballroom. I've been there before…' [2]

Shane was so badly beaten he was still suffering from concussion the following night when they played the 100 Club, and Spider had to step in to finish the show. Shane would be assaulted many times over, often severely. But for a man so often described as non-confrontational, the question is, why was he targeted? Those who know him say his odd appearance simply drew unwanted attention 'He got beaten up sometimes because he just stands out,' says Mary Buxton. 'He is more bullied, although I don't mean that in a pathetic way. People picked on him because he was different, and you are vulnerable if you're a bit pissed.'

Deirdre O'Mahony also cites his vulnerability as an explanation for the beatings he suffered: 'I remember the night they were supposed to play the 100 Club. I have an awful photograph of him taken at the bottom of the stairs with his face all swollen. He had no defences. He'd be just out there, dependent on the kindness and madness of strangers... He was never afraid to be vulnerable. So, while on the one hand there was the assurance and conviction about his talent, on the other there was a willingness to be really open and vulnerable and not wear the shields that most people would use.'

When Victoria embarked on her relationship with him in 1986, Shane being set upon was simply part of a night out. She says his staunch Irish republican views were one of the reasons he was targeted. 'Whenever we went out, we would get attacked,' she says. 'When it happened when I was there, it was usually because people took exception to his republicanism and they were not necessarily just English people. A lot of Irish people also took exception to it, so he used to get attacked.

'He was very out there in his views at a time when people were being bombed in England. They would jump on him; it happened all the time. I got so used to it that I used to factor it in to a night out and think, Oh yeah, at some point we're going to get jumped. But I wasn't scared of it because he was very good at fighting back. I saw him fight loads of people many times and brush it off, and it was, "On we go to the pub." It was never a problem.'

Shanne Bradley remembers Shane being attacked often during the time they were together, but denies he was targeted for being Irish. 'He is [violent] towards himself because he is self-destructive. He turns it inwards or he uses his mouth and he's been beaten up many times because of it. Not because he is Irish, as it says in the [Julien Temple] film, but because he's got a big mouth. And we used to outrage people with the way we looked, and people wanted to beat the crap out of you anyway. He can be really cutting – he can just cut you to pieces quite easily.

'I remember I went up to see my mum and he called me from a call-box and said, "There's these guys outside circling the phone box and I think they're going to beat me up," and I said, "Oh, no." I didn't hear anything and then I get a phone call and he says, "I'm in the hospital. They've kicked the shit out of me." So, I went back home to where we lived and then I went to see him, and he looked like the Elephant Man. His head was swollen, and his face was unrecognisable. I looked after him until it all went down. It was really frightening actually; really shocking.

'It was Teds who had attacked him in the phone box. We used to go to rock'n'roll gigs together at the Electric Ballroom in Camden that were full of Teds. Back then, it was Teds versus punks. Johnny Rotten was seriously attacked at this time and lots of people were, just for looking unconventional.'

Violent attacks on Shane were not just confined to his younger days. Twenty years after he was given a kicking in the lavatory of the Electric Ballroom, in 2004, it happened in a pub in west London. This time the case went to court. The man admitted assaulting Shane in the toilet, although Victoria says of that later episode: 'That wasn't actually political. The guy thought Shane was hitting on his friend or his friend was hitting on him.'

Shane has always loved women and he could be persistent in his pursuit of them, as Merrill Heatley discovered. He took a shine to her when The Pogues and the Boothills played The Hope & Anchor and she was taken aback at his boldness. 'I think he just said something like, "I'm crazy about you,"' recalls Merrill, who was quite a bit younger than Shane and still lived at home with her mum. 'I thought, It's a bit much. You haven't really said "Hello" yet! But that was what he was like – he was really full-on.'

When their bands did another joint show at the London Irish Centre in Camden, it presented Shane with another opportunity. A disco followed the gig and when the unmistakable opening bars of Nina Simone's 'My Baby Just Cares For Me' were played, he asked Merrill to dance. As they danced together and Shane showed off his moves, she saw him 'in a different kind of way'. They spent the rest of the evening drinking and chatting and at the end of the night they swapped phone numbers. Shane called her and they started going out to gigs and clubs.

The man she got to know over the next year was sensitive and kind. She was particularly struck by how important family was to him and, only a few months after they started seeing each other, he took her to Ireland to meet his mother's relatives. Spider was at Euston station to see them off as they headed for Holyhead. The drinking began as soon as they got on the ferry and Shane embarrassed her by constantly singing Stevie Wonder's 'I Just Called To Say I Love You', the number one hit of the summer of 1984. They arrived in Dublin at six o'clock in the morning and to Merrill's surprise, Shane took them straight to an 'early house' where they could get a drink.

When they finally got to Tipperary, Shane told her she couldn't sleep with him at The Commons because of the local scandal it would cause. Instead, she would have to stay next door with his uncle Sean and aunty Vicky. 'That didn't stop us,' says Merrill. 'I would regularly creep in through the back door the next morning and his uncle Sean, who was a peat farmer, would be putting his boots on,' she remembers. 'He would be getting ready for work and he'd be like, "Oh, hi, Merrill," and I'd usually be a bit hungover and go and crash out for a couple of hours.'

Along with Merrill's collie dog, Molly, they rambled the country lanes of Tipperary, stopping in at pubs run from people's houses. She remembers: 'He was very sweet. We used to go out and walk a lot and he took me to the River Shannon and showed me all around the countryside. One time we were walking and chatting, and I turned around and he wasn't there. I thought, Where's he gone? And he had thrown himself into this ditch which had spring water coming out of it.

'I said, "What are you doing down there?"

'He said, "Oh, I've got a bad ankle, and this is like magical water and it will get my ankle better. It's spring water."

'I was like, "OK... A warning would have been nice." He was there with his trousers rolled up, sorting his bad ankle out and it was the first I'd heard of it...

'We went to a dance one evening. It was really old-fashioned – this was in the eighties – and it was in the backroom of a pub and it had one light coming down. Irish music was playing, and women were dancing with women if they didn't have male partners. It all seemed very backwards to me. Being over there and spending that time with him is something that is a strong memory. It was a lovely time.'

They spent about a month in Ireland and Merrill was struck by the primitive conditions at The Commons. There was no toilet or bathroom and neither of them knew how to light a fire properly. Shane's family wouldn't go into the cottage while they were there, and his aunty Vicky left bags of potatoes and cabbage outside the door. 'He said, "I know how we'll do the fire,"' remembers Merrill, 'and we were scrunching up newspaper and soaking it with paddy whiskey and setting fire to it. We were completely useless!'

It was a welcome break from the intensity of the scene they were involved in back in London. Neither The Pogues nor the Boothills had any live commitments over the summer and Shane was in his element at his beloved homestead, where he was greeted as the prodigal son.

After about four weeks in Tipperary, Shane told Merrill he was heading up to Dublin to see other relatives and friends and it was clear that it was time for her to return to London. By then, she was ready to go home. It had been a wonderful trip and Merrill still treasures her memories of the time she spent with him.

Back in London, Merrill faced increasing competition for Shane's affections – not least from Cait. 'It was always a much better night for me if she didn't turn up,' says Merrill. 'She was obsessed with Shane and he kind of tolerated her. She was a handful, but at that stage she was an important part of the band because she really looked the part, and she was a real ladette. She used to hang around a lot. She moved to be close by and I think they probably slept together.'

Fionna Murray confirms Shane and Cait were romantically involved and says they had a strong bond, despite their ongoing conflict. 'I would say Shane and Cait were pretty on and off a lot of the time, but I sensed a great love between them as well,' she says.

For her part, Merrill remembers Shane being very attentive. He was also a romantic. One evening, the couple were walking through the Hillview estate when Shane, who was wearing a trilby hat, stopped to perform a song and dance routine to a Frank Sinatra song. But the man she had got to know was on the verge of fame and was about to change – some would say for ever.

'I think a lot of his girlfriends after me were there for Shane and who he was becoming,' says Merrill. 'Siobhan said to me a while ago, "I think you had him at his best." We finished because he was getting a bit greedy with women and I wasn't sharing or doing any of that. So it was, "OK, I think now it's time for us to say goodbye." I think that was really hard for him and made him quite obsessive. We lived in a house at the back of Acton and Chiswick and my bedroom was right at the top. The phone would be ringing at three in the morning and I would have to run down all these stairs and, sure enough it would be Shane, pissed and crying down the phone. "Merrill, I'm sorry. Come and meet me."

'"No, sorry. Bye, Shane," and I'd put the phone down.'

A buzz of excitement had been developing around Pogue Mahone. 'Dark Streets Of London' had been picked up by John Peel and other Radio 1 presenters, including David 'Kid' Jensen, also gave it some airplay. A *Music Week* poll of DJs, journalists and record company employees had named Pogue Mahone as a band to look out for in 1984 and Stan Brennan's phone was kept busy with people wanting to interview them.

But although record labels were always looking for original songwriters, a dubious-looking rabble singing Irish rebel songs was a marketing challenge that few wanted. 'I didn't think there was going to be any problem, but I couldn't get a deal anywhere,' conceded Stan. 'Irish music – the labels didn't want to know. Nobody would touch them with a barge pole.' [3]

All except Dave Robinson. When he and Jake Riviera had launched Stiff in 1976, their mission was to release records by the acts they liked, rather than those with commercial appeal. Ian Dury, Elvis Costello and other outsiders had been brought in from the cold by the maverick label, which turned their eccentricities into a virtue. So, when Dave Robinson checked out Pogue Mahone at The Pindar of Wakefield, he knew instantly they would be perfect for Stiff.

Shane commented: 'Stiff were the only people who could understand why people liked going to see us; the only people who were worth a job in the record business. There were all these A&R men going, "The Pogues

93

are going to be huge, but we don't understand why people are going to see them." But Stiff got it. That's why they signed Wreckless Eric, Nick Lowe and The Damned. People thought they were mad when they signed The Damned and Richard Hell because they thought it was just a fleeting fad. But anybody involved in it knew that punk was never going to go away again.' [4]

Stan Brennan went to see Dave Robinson and he then met with The Pogues. A deal was struck, initially for a re-release of 'Dark Streets Of London'. Stiff then agreed to stump up the money for an album on one condition – that they change their name. Pogue Mahone was the Anglicised version of '*póg mo thóin*', Gaelic for 'Kiss my arse'. After some discussion, the group took a pragmatic view and agreed to become The Pogues. After all, The Nipple Erectors had become The Nips and Pogue Mahone's controversial name had already limited the amount of airplay given to 'Dark Streets Of London'. A producer for BBC Radio Scotland had alerted the corporation's bosses to the fact that presenters were saying 'Kiss my arse' in Gaelic every time they read out the band's name. Although Kid Jensen had continued playing the record on his evening show and referred to them as The Pogues, Mike Read refused to play it.

Shane said: 'It took a week or two to reach the old farts at the top and they went "This is unacceptable"' because they'd had that with the Pistols and "God Save The Queen" and Frankie Goes To Hollywood with "Relax".' The Pistols had released their single to coincide with the Queen's silver jubilee celebrations while Frankie's song explicitly extolled the joys of sex. 'They were terrified of getting their fingers burnt again. So, they said they weren't going to ban it, they weren't going to do anything like that. But they were not going to play the record and just pretend we didn't exist unless we changed our name. And people were already calling us The Pogues because "Pogue Mahone" is a bit of a mouthful, so we just changed to The Pogues and got on with it.' [5]

Jamie Spencer worked in Stiff's press department. He had seen the group several times and knew they would be a great fit. At the time, Dave Robinson had been exploring the idea of setting up an offshoot label and saw the newly christened band being its inaugural act. 'The general idea was Stiff would have an incubator label and Robbo was going to sign

The Pogues as the first band on this label,' says Jamie. 'It was to be an independent through Stiff and then, if it took off, they would go on to Stiff. But suddenly there was a lot of interest and they signed to Stiff Records. Robbo was obviously looking for a replacement for Madness and I'm not sure he thought King Kurt would do that. Stiff really upped the ante and The Pogues were the perfect fit in terms of the way they marketed and promoted those typically Stiff bands.'

According to Jem Finer, another label boss had been interested in signing the band. 'The other way it could have gone was Creation, which would have been interesting because Alan McGee was interested in us making a record before we made the record with Stan,' he says. 'I often wonder what would have happened if we had done that. I think it didn't happen because Shane felt a kind of loyalty to Stan.'

Jem was delighted that the band had found a home with a label renowned for its bold and maverick approach. He says: 'I had always been a big fan of Stiff, so it was a real thrill for me to come from being someone who, a few years before, had never thought I could even play a note on an instrument, to putting out records on this legendary label. It was very exciting, I thought, and definitely a good match.'

Shane's prolific writing and the traditional Irish songs in the group's repertoire meant The Pogues had a rich seam of material when they arrived at Elephant Studios to record the album. The finished record would have thirteen tracks – including seven MacGowan originals – and there were yet more that didn't make it.

Stan Brennan was given the nod to produce it, which was a challenge, given the band were best enjoyed in a sweaty pub, washed down with several pints. Pogue Mahone had been as much a feast for the eyes as the ears; Spider thrashing himself with a tin tray, Cait snarling at the crowd and Shane like a lighthouse in a storm – lashed but a shining beacon. Stan would later say he was immensely proud of the recording, although he bemoaned the mastering, which resulted from Stiff's decision to rush-release it.

Spider commented: 'The essence of the band, the way we sound live – I don't know if it's ever been satisfactorily captured. I'm certainly not going to say that's any fault of Stan Brennan as a producer when people like, say, Steve Lillywhite, may equally not be able to capture the essence of the band. I don't think anybody ever could, but I think *Red Roses For Me* comes closest.' [6]

The walls of Shane's flat in Cromer Street were covered with scraps of paper containing lyrics written in his spidery hand. He had a gift for human storytelling and many of his songs name-checked places from his own life, echoing some of the writers he most admired. Van Morrison's sprawling songbook takes in places in Belfast and other locations in his native Northern Ireland: 'Hyndford Street', 'Cyprus Avenue', 'Orangefield', 'Connswater', 'Coney Island'. Tom Waits' lyrics are shot through with place names: 'Kentucky Avenue', '9th & Hennepin', 'Fannin Street', 'Tenkiller Lake'.

Shane's early songs took in as many stops as a London Routemaster. 'Transmetropolitan' is a white-knuckle ride through his city haunts, while 'Dark Streets Of London' and 'Down In The Ground Where The Dead Men Go' cited places with which he has personal and emotionally painful associations.

Jem Finer remarks: 'The thing about Shane's writing is that the songs could only have been written by someone who was looking back at Ireland, and they were very much about London as well. You could take all the places, names, the bars and cafes and streets and make a fascinating Shane MacGowan's London out of them. And that, too, is something I don't think people understand. It's London-Irish; London songs but through this "outsider of Ireland" prism. Most of us in the band were in some way outsiders. People who had grown up feeling a bit alienated. My father is a Jewish guy, and I grew up being ribbed for being a "Yid". So, I had a kind of feeling of being a bit "other" and I think it was quite a powerful thing in the chemistry of that group.'

Kathy MacMillan adds: 'I think I realised Shane was a very gifted songwriter when I heard his first single, "Dark Streets Of London". I can remember where I was: Euston Road, Marylebone Road around midnight, crossing it and thinking of the lyrics. That song blew me away.'

A photoshoot for the album was arranged at the London Irish Centre in Camden and Spider came up with the idea of them wearing long duster coats like those worn by the James-Younger gang in Walter Hill's 1980 western *The Long Riders*. Stiff went with the theme and had them tailored for a princely £100 each. On the front cover the band posed in front of a portrait of John F. Kennedy wearing the gear audiences would have seen them in at gigs. Andrew 'The Clobberer' Ranken was on holiday when the session took place and Stiff's designers rather crassly added a doily bearing his face. A photo of all six of them in their matching pale-grey coats from nineteenth-century America appeared on the back. Shane was holding a walking stick and nursing a heavily bandaged foot, having fallen down a flight of stairs the night before. The coats reappeared on the front cover of 'Boys From The County Hell', the single Stiff chose to release from the record.

The Pogues continued to play gigs around London and one was to prove a date with destiny. On 22 June they played Diorama Arts Centre near Regent's Park. Philip Chevron, a drinking mate of Shane and Spider's, was in the audience and with him was Elvis Costello, to whom he had been singing the group's praises. By the end of the gig, the singer was indeed smitten – but with Cait.

Philip said: 'I dragged Elvis to see them at the Diorama and he spent half the gig saying, "The bass player… isn't she wonderful?" Me being innocent, I didn't realise he fancied the pants off her and was looking for an introduction. Anyway, he took it upon himself then to make his own connections with The Pogues.' [7]

Costello was about to go on tour with The Attractions to promote his new album, *Goodbye Cruel World*, and he invited The Pogues to support them. The opening show was on 27 September at Belfast's Ulster Hall, with dates at Leisureland in Galway and the National Stadium in Dublin to follow. Arrangements were made. The band's gear went ahead of them to Belfast in one of Costello's trucks, ferry tickets were booked, and Darryl Hunt hired a van to drive them to Holyhead. Everything ran to schedule, until they arrived at Cromer Street to collect Shane.

The doorbell was rung by pressing two live wires together and, when there was no reply, people shouted up at his flat. Half an hour passed with no sign of Shane. James threw a handful of gravel at the window and eventually Shane opened it and belligerently yelled down that he was coming. But another thirty minutes went by before he came out, carrying a filthy bag full of bottles, and got in the van. Darryl put his foot to the floor to try and make up for lost time, but they missed their ferry and had to catch a later one.

It was a scenario that would be played out repeatedly through the band's career. On this occasion, James believes the anticipation and added pressure of a major tour was at the root of Shane's tardiness. 'Every situation for Shane is stressful, even the one he is in,' he says. 'But the next one is going to be worse. So, for Shane it was like, "I'm going to stay here and not show up. I don't really want to come downstairs and get in the van and go to Holyhead and join the Elvis Costello opening tour through Ireland, even if it makes my friends wait for hours until we miss the ferry." I totally get that. I don't want to put myself in a situation that has the least bit of stress in it because the least bit of stress for me is nightmarish.'

Outside of London, The Pogues were still relatively unknown. Their only television appearance had been on LWT and, although the album was released ahead of the tour, radio play had been limited. So, opening for such a high-profile act was a major coup. This was a full UK tour taking in twenty-seven shows at halls and universities that dwarfed the kind of places The Pogues were used to playing. The final show was at the Dominion Theatre on Tottenham Court Road.

Shane had little time for Elvis and relations were strained, especially between The Pogues and Elvis's security crew. Shane recalled: 'We nearly got thrown off the tour three times. I did IRA graffiti all over the PA bus and Spider did UDA on the other side. When Costello and that lot were on stage, we used to drink their fucking booze. The guy was in love with Cait, so that's the reason we didn't get sacked off the tour. And we gave him street cred.' [8]

It was a happy period for Shane. He and Spider were an inseparable double-act and a source of constant entertainment. When they weren't dissecting world wars, they were machine-gunning jokes back and forth and showing off their razor-sharp wit. The scheduling of the tour also suited Shane. 'That tour came back to London every week, so that was quite nice,' explains Jem. 'Shane seemed quite all right. He could do all the things he liked doing, which was drinking and staying up late and playing music. I mean, we all had to live in very close proximity in a little van and not the most salubrious lodgings, but it was all new and a novelty. There were ups and downs and the odd row, but it was a formative experience. It started us on the road to being a professional band.'

Siobhan saw the band in London during the tour and knew it was a seminal moment for her brother. 'The very first time I knew that he was going to make it was at Hammersmith Palais where they were supporting Elvis Costello,' she says. 'They weren't famous yet, but they were getting a name and I walked up steps to go into the gig and I heard the audience calling, "Shane, Shane!" Stan Brennan was at the top and I said, "Oh my God, Stan. Did you ever think that was going to happen?" And he said, "Yes, I did."'

CHAPTER 5

Farewell To New York City Boys

'Fare thee well gone away
There's nothing left to say
Farewell to New York City boys
To Boston and PA'

'The Body Of An American', **The Pogues**

Shane has an extraordinary propensity for getting his own way. Sometimes his silence or a hard stare is enough. At other times, it is the sheer strength of the case he makes or the desire he engenders in some to do his bidding. As he is charismatic on stage, so he holds a power over people off it. So, when the redoubtable figure of Frank Murray became the band's manager, a battle of wills commenced.

'People just can't say "No" to Shane,' says Kathy MacMillan. 'He puts up a very good argument and looks at you with those big blue eyes and you just think, Oh, what the hell. And that, I think, was the crux of the problem with him and Frank. He was also an incredibly charming man, very charismatic and used to getting his own way. It was a clash of two alpha males.'

Frank was a hard-nosed Dubliner who had managed the Irish bands Skid Row and Thin Lizzy and believed in his charges working and playing hard. It was during the Elvis Costello tour that he crossed paths with Jem Finer in a pub, and the timing of their conversation was fortuitous. The Pogues had no manager and the burden had fallen largely on their banjo player. After all, Shane could barely be relied on to get himself to rehearsals and gigs. And while the tour had done wonders for their profile, there was no money coming in. If they were going to go professional, they needed to be managed in the same manner and Jem suggested they give Frank a chance. A meeting was arranged at a pub in Camden and it was agreed he would take over.

Shane was sceptical from the outset. 'In the first place, I was the only person who didn't vote for Frank to be the manager,' he said. 'We were on varying terms of friendship with him, but I knew him better than anyone else and at the meeting where we decided to offer him to look after us, he did warn us we'd probably all hate him within a few months. But I never hated him.' [1]

The Pogues had a few weeks off before embarking on a series of dates in early December 1984, branded the Lock Up Your Drinks Cabinet Tour. But from the get-go it became clear that under Frank's stewardship there would be no respite. Jem says: 'After the Costello tour, I felt I couldn't cope with looking after the organisational side of things. Also, I had a young family and it was too much. So, we got a manager, which I found difficult because I didn't agree with a lot of the things he wanted to do. I very quickly thought, Fuck, we've just given away something really precious to the wrong person. He had this very old-school modus operandi, which was you put a band on the road and they do nothing else. So, we started doing tours of this country and then France got very interested in us. We started going to France, and then Germany got interested in us, so we started going to Germany. Any manager would have done it; you get the whole thing working on a higher level and start picking up the phone and saying you won't do certain gigs. That's fair enough. So, immediately after the Costello tour, we started to do our own headline tours, starting with small places and then gradually becoming bigger as the audiences became bigger.'

The Costello tour paid instant dividends. John Peel broadcast a second session on 12 December, with 'Sally MacLennane', written by Shane, 'Navigator', by Phil Gaston, and arrangements of 'Whiskey You're The Devil' and 'Danny Boy'. The following month they appeared again on the influential Channel 4 show *The Tube* and this was followed by five weeks of gigs. Frank had immediately signed them with gig booker Derek Kemp at The Agency – central to his strategy for selling huge amounts of records was to keep the band on the road as much as possible.

Shane says: 'We started to get loads of gigs all over London and the home counties and eventually we did the north and the Midlands, we did Scotland regularly and we did Ireland... The point was to play Irish trad/rock'n'roll to as many people as possible and the fees went up really fast... Young, London-Irish musicians weren't playing sets in bars, but I got thanked by a lot of these people after The Pogues started off because they all suddenly had loads of jobs because we made Irish hip.'

Frank had also successfully brokered a deal for the band to return to Elephant Studios, this time with Elvis Costello behind the production desk. Elvis had been responsible for The Specials' highly successful debut and was involved in Squeeze's *East Side Story*. He was particular about who he worked with and his manager Jake Riviera was cynical about rumours that he wanted to produce The Pogues. Jake checked it out after a call from Frank and rang back to confirm it was true. There was no doubt that Costello's deepening romance with Cait was a key factor, but it was still a coup for the band. Consequently, 'Sally MacLennane' and an achingly beautiful Shane composition called 'A Pair Of Brown Eyes' were recorded and the results were stunning. So much so that Elvis offered to produce the next album and, despite Shane's previous loyalty to Stan Brennan, he agreed.

Shane met Stan and told him he was no longer going to be involved with the group. If Shane felt guilty or sad at his departure, he didn't say. 'He didn't say an awful lot,' said Stan. 'He was very low-key about it. There was a part of me that wanted him to say, "I want you to stay..." I don't know what kind of relationship you really make with Shane. For me, having had the first experience of Howard Cohen and The Nips, I didn't want to get hurt again.' [2]

Kathy MacMillan believes that, as Shane became more successful, the loyalty he had once shown to others began to melt away. She says ruefully: 'I tell you, there is a trail of friends who were a great support to Shane in his developing years and he just dropped them; he moved on and never spoke to them again. And he's very hurtful and very disrespectful to what people have done for him... Stan and Phil, who produced the first album, they got cast aside.'

Elvis Costello was spending as much time as he could with The Pogues and, as a result, was boosting their profile. During a break from recording, they accompanied him on a tour of Ireland, and he even supported them when they played their first big St Patrick's Day gig at The Clarendon ballroom, Hammersmith. Shane was nauseated by the sight of Elvis and Cait making out, notably in the studio when he was 'dry-humping her on the settee in the control room'. But although Elvis wasn't the most experienced producer in town, Shane was positive about his involvement at the time.

'I'm really looking forward to it, you know?' he said. 'I'm not sure just how big an effect he is going to have on how it turns out, because we already know it is going to be quite different from the first one... I don't think that means it will necessarily be any cleaner or more professional, because one of the numbers on it will be the fastest thing we have ever done, and a couple of the others are fairly rough as well. You still know it's The Pogues.' [3]

Elvis later remarked: 'I saw my task was to capture them in their dilapidated glory before some more professional producer fucked them up.' [4]

Lyrically and musically, the compositions that continued to emerge from among the piles of empty bottles, cigarette packets and other rubbish in Shane's working space were as potent as the Irish whiskey that was steeping his insides. They were vivid and poignant and inhabited by real, flawed characters. They also had a timeless quality, and many continue to resonate with fans decades later.

Shane had discovered his precocious talent for writing in English lessons at Holmewood House school and it was clear, even from those early stories that he had a unique style. He had written then of war and conflict and of life's underdogs. No tale was sugar-coated and he didn't spare the reader from life's harsh realities. In 'Euthanasia', he described matter-of-factly a boy who kills his overbearing father with an overdose of morphine. 'He rose, smiling, then caught sight of the deathly pallor of his father's skin, rushed over to the sink and vomited into it,' he wrote. 'Then he cleaned himself up and went out again.' 'Lost In The Crowd' was narrated by a boy trampled to the ground during the Dublin Lockout of 1913. 'He made to get up, but then he felt a sharp pain in his genitals as a cop's boot hit him in the loin. He saw the blue uniform and the baton coming towards him, then seas of darkness engulfed him.'

In his affecting ballad, 'A Pair Of Brown Eyes', a man sitting drunk in a pub meets a war veteran who tells him of the horrors he has seen. But through the hell of war, he kept in mind his lover's brown eyes, prompting the drunk to recall his own lost love as he staggers home.

The stirring stories from Irish mythology that Shane had soaked up on his trips to The Commons were now infiltrating his songs, just as they had his school essays. 'Cuchulain's [sic] Defeat', written at Holmewood, sees the fearless mythical fighter who slayed Cuchulainn's guard dog reinvented at a modern dentist, 'looking no worse for his six thousand years of life', but with rheumatism and in need of dentures. In 'The Sick Bed Of Cuchulainn', the explosive opening track of The Pogues' second album, he finally dies – only to spring back to life demanding a drink.

Shane had always known he could write. But when he discovered the power that music gave his words it was an epiphany. 'Westminster couldn't understand why I was able to write a short story,' he says. 'What's so difficult about making up a story? It's just writing it down and I was good at writing. I can write, I can spell, I can make it flow and when I mixed it with music, it was perfect.'

Inspiration for two other memorable songs on the record was drawn from his life in London. 'Sally MacLennane' was populated with colourful characters from a pub run in Dagenham by his uncle. 'The Old Main Drag' meanwhile was a disturbingly bleak tale told by a teenage boy who finds himself sleeping rough and turning tricks for men in Soho's backstreets. 'In the dark of an alley, you'll work for a fiver/For a swift one off the wrist down on the old main drag', sang Shane. The heartrending story, in which the narrator tells of being 'pissed on and shat on and raped and abused', made for a discomfiting but nonetheless compelling listen.

So vivid were the lyrics they prompted speculation that they had been born out of personal experience. After all, as a teenager Shane had hung about on the 'Dilly' [Piccadilly] with people who were living rough. 'Shane's situation was pretty much hand to mouth back then,' says Kathy MacMillan. 'Life was difficult and not particularly pleasant for him to just get by.'

James Fearnley, who played accordion on the song, said he wondered whether Shane had written about something that had happened to him, but also knew that he could 'understand the experience of someone who could find himself in that kind of life'. 'I do remember at the time there was stuff in the newspaper about a kid who had come down from the north and ended up in that underbelly of London, and they found his body under a bridge,' says James. 'He was only 16, I think, and the reason I say the north is because Shane always explained to me about the dancing bag in "The Old Main Drag" – that it was a thing that they used to take to the Wigan Casino so they could get changed out of their work clothes into their dance clothes.

Shane was adamant 'The Old Main Drag' was based on the experiences of others: 'It isn't necessarily about me... it's what I saw. All the rest of it is just stuff that, if you spend a lot of time living the – I don't know the word for it – "real life" in central London, you see it or it happens to you... I don't like writing about my personal hang-ups like a lot of populists do, I just like giving an impression of real life.' [5]

Years later, a very different light was cast on things. Victoria's book *A Drink with Shane MacGowan* was published in 2001 and the accompanying press release said Shane 'became a rent boy'. Oddly, the book itself contained no reference to this and, when Shane was asked about it in an interview with *The Scotsman* in August 2004, he was quick to refute it. 'That's a load of rubbish,' he said. 'That never happened. It all came from a song I wrote about rent boys called "The Old Main Drag". I knew some people who did it, but I certainly never did it myself.'

Guardian writer Lynn Barber interviewed him around the time of the book's publication and when she questioned him about the explosive revelation that he had been a male prostitute, he was ambiguous.

'I can't believe you were a rent boy. Who would pay to rent you?' joked Barber.

'You'd be surprised,' replied Shane. 'There are women who would climb over their grandmothers to get to a celebrity – Victoria, for instance!' [6] It was a flippant reply and one designed to move the conversation on. But it was not a denial.

A strong clue as to Shane's personal involvement in prostitution had been left in a poem he had written a few years earlier entitled 'No Half-Arsed Buggery'. He had never intended for anyone else to read it, but he left a recital of it on a cassette tape, which he then used to record songs he was working on as Pogue Mahone took shape. It makes for a difficult listen, the elegiac tone in his voice painfully confessional.

> *In the rosy parks of England / maybe we'd go walking*
> *holding hands and making promises / the squeaking and the squawking*
> *Oh, but I swear on that last blowjob / I'll never have another*
> *And I'll have no more half-arsed buggery in the house of love*
>
> ...

Oh, this love, it is a fine thing/but it's only for your parents
And they could have told you years ago/it's only for the morons
And this crazy fucking city is dragging me to damage
For me, no more half-arsed buggery in the house of love.

Shane's admission that that he had turned tricks for men on the streets of London finally came during a conversation with Johnny Depp and Victoria in the film documentary, *Crock of Gold: A Few Rounds with Shane MacGowan*. [7] 'Shane used to do it,' Victoria says when the subject of rent boys is mentioned by the Hollywood actor. There is then a pause before Shane replies, 'Just hand jobs. It was a job in hand [tsscchh].'

Rum Sodomy & The Lash was the unforgettable title given to the group's second album, recalling Sir Winston Churchill's reported opinion of the British Navy. Frank Murray and Stiff enthusiastically took up the nautical theme and ran with it, with the band decked out in Napoleonic uniforms for a photoshoot at Tower Bridge. For the sleeve, Théodore Géricault's painting *Le Radeau de la Medusé (The Raft of the Medusa)* was adapted to incorporate the faces of the band members.

Ever imaginative, Stiff's marketing team went into overdrive. *HMS Belfast* was hired for a launch party on the Thames, the band wore their Napoleonic uniforms and journalists from the music papers were plied with generous amounts of rum. One sub-editor from *Melody Maker* literally went overboard. Shane recalled: 'A journalist fell in the river and had to be picked up by the river police. He couldn't fucking take his drink.' [8]

The record hit shops on 5 August 1985. In less than three weeks it climbed to number thirteen in the UK chart and spent nine weeks in the Top 40. By contrast, their debut album *Red Roses For Me* had reached number eighty-nine and managed just one week in the Top 100. The Pogues were now contenders and the 'Little Man' who had sung on the table at The Commons was now reaching his broadest audience yet.

Bernie France had seen first-hand The Pogues' transition from a band on the radar of those 'in the know' to one enjoying mainstream chart success. 'They started to take off and the last I saw Shane at that time, they had just released *Rum Sodomy & The Lash* and they were about to go out on tour in America,' he remembers. 'I saw them at The Mean Fiddler, and there was such a crush of people, I thought, He's moving on to another place. I remember leaving and walking home and thinking, I might never see him again. I didn't see him then for the rest of his time in The Pogues.'

For many British record-buyers, a group without a whiff of pretence that played rootsy, good-time music was a breath of fresh air, an antidote to the fey, foppishness of the new romantics. The atmosphere at their gigs was one of sheer abandonment, an insight into the energy and intensity of punk for those not old enough to have been there. And there was something rebellious – and typically Stiff – about taking traditional Irish music and making it cool.

'The Pogues made a place where first- and second-generation Irish could get together and just have a bloody good time in London,' comments Shane's long-time friend Paul Ronan.

'People were jumping up and down. It was like a football terrace. People were just dancing a bit at the back or just going wild. It wasn't boring. The other thing I liked about it was that when you went to each gig, you would know a load of fans and it was like a family. They had a very loyal following and they created that quickly because when people enjoyed it, they couldn't get enough of it.'

Paul's curiosity had been piqued after seeing The Pogues on *South of Watford* and he decided to check them out at The Cricketers in Kennington, where promoter Jim Driver was championing their cause. He was 'absolutely blown apart' by what he saw and heard and the following night he went to see them again at The Sir George Robey in Finsbury Park. This time he got chatting to Shane and the pair hit it off instantly.

Paul remembers: 'We were both second-generation Irish, we both used to spend a lot of our time over there and holidays were taken in Ireland. We had a love of the same music, we were influenced by the same things – The Dubliners, The Clancy Brothers and the show bands – and we were a year apart in age. So, we had a lot in common. I started hanging around The Devonshire Arms in Camden Town and we became quite close. I was living in Chichester for a while, but I used to come up for the weekends, and when I had time off, I used to go to quite a few of the universities to see them. I can remember the UEA in Norwich and Reading. When I saw the fans outside of the band's normal London market, they were so into it and I thought, Something incredible is happening tonight, and the hairs on the back of my neck just stood up. It was just an amazing sight to behold.'

The timing of the group's arrival on the UK music scene made them doubly relevant to its Irish communities, especially those in London. Suspicion and mistrust of anyone with an Irish accent remained, leaving many feeling cowed. Yet just as he had been back in The Cambridge years Shane was as 'out there' with his Irishness as was humanly possible. He was unapologetically proud of his heritage; from the traditional instruments and songs he had heard in The Commons as a child to his family connections with the republican movement. So, for those who felt ghettoised and self-conscious in Thatcher's Britain, Shane was a voice for them. In an unsettling time, he was a lodestar.

The Pogues had been on tour with Elvis Costello on 12 October 1984 when the IRA attempted to kill Margaret Thatcher and her cabinet. A hundred-pound bomb exploded in the Grand Hotel, Brighton, where the Conservative Party conference was taking place. Five people died, including a sitting MP, and thirty-one were injured. The blast missed the Thatchers' sitting-room, where she was still working, by inches, but hit the bathroom and bedroom where her husband Denis was asleep. The IRA had come within a whisker of assassinating the British prime minister and issued a chilling statement as people were pulled from the rubble: 'Today we were unlucky but, remember, we only have to be lucky once; you will have to be lucky always.'

Nine days earlier The Pogues had performed at the Brighton Top Rank and that, and their reputation for playing republican songs, drew attention from the police. Shane recalled: 'After the Brighton bombing and all that – we were on the road, luckily – they came round to Stiff to arrest us because we played in Brighton a week before the bomb went off! There was a whole load of bands that they blacklisted, and we were one of them.' [9]

Among the second-generation Irish who felt emboldened by The Pogues was freelance writer Ann Scanlon. Her parents had emigrated to England from the west of Ireland and ran a pub in Lincolnshire. And like Shane, she had grown up listening to Irish music. 'My parents were the only Irish publicans in the area and the pub was a magnet for seasonal workers and those who worked on the Humber Bridge. No one called it the Nelthorpe Arms, they called it Scanlon's pub in Brigg. It had a proper Johnny McCauley, Irish and country jukebox. When I first heard The Pogues, it was like the Sex Pistols hijacking our jukebox, getting drunk with The Dubliners, taking speed with The Tulla Céilí Band and coming down with Johnny McEvoy, who I loved, and Shane loved too.

'Shane said "A Pair Of Brown Eyes" was influenced by Johnny McEvoy's "Those Brown Eyes". My dad had a lot of cousins who were all Irish publicans. His cousin Tommy had the Camden Stores and that is the pub where Shane wrote about the jukebox with Johnny and Philomena singing. So, it was a massive connection… It spoke to me because of my background and also because we had put up with a lot of racism. We had – it's a fact. I remember being at school and there was an innocent lunchtime debate about what butter you had, and I proudly said, "My mum only ever buys Kerrygold." And this girl said, "My mother says that Jacksons supermarket shouldn't stock it because all the money goes to the IRA." Now it's funny: my IRA butter – but, at the time, I had to shut up. After the Birmingham pub bombings, an anonymous caller rang the police station and said they'd planted a bomb in our pub, and I remember being carried out of bed by a police officer. That did happen.'

Ann was was keen to write about The Pogues after seeing them on *The Tube* and being given vinyl copies of their albums by David Gedge from The Wedding Present, who she had interviewed. She touted the idea of a feature to *ZigZag* only to be told that the writer Kris Needs had already been commissioned to do a phone interview. But when he graciously stood down, she called Stiff's press officer Phil Hall. She offered to pay for train tickets for her and a photographer, and he said the label would pay for their hotel and, even more usefully, the bar bill. She met the band at the Rote Fabrik, Zurich, on 31 October and conducted her interview in the early hours, while Shane emptied her minibar.

'My first impressions of Shane were that he was funny and he was clever,' recalls Ann. 'He was Irish Catholic from the countryside and my parents are from Mayo, so that was a big thing we had in common. Obviously, he was highly and tastefully literate and, apart from writing amazing music, he knew so much about music that it was an education. But he was also quite shy, which I find a very attractive quality in people. He really was a scholar and a gentleman in the old-fashioned sense…

'Frank Murray wasn't at the gig, because his wife Ferga had just had a baby, but he arrived later. So, the interview ended up being Shane, Spider, Jem and Terry Woods, and it was about 3 a.m. I think I met Shane at a really good time because he didn't have anything to prove. The Pogues were on a roll and they were a gang and a family. They were like the last gang in town.'

As well as interviewing Shane with other Pogues for *Zigzag*, Ann also got the chance to talk to him on his own for a piece she was writing about the tenth anniversary of punk. She recalls him speaking candidly about his past. 'He was really happy in his childhood, the way he talked about Ireland, and then punk was the greatest thing for him,' she says. 'I remember him saying to me, "Straight out of the loony bin and the first thing you see is a band who look like they've come out of there too."'

Today, Shane is feted in Ireland. But it was not always so. In fact, initial reactions in his beloved Ireland were hostile. *Irish Times* journalist Joe Breen dismissed The Pogues and drew a parallel between his own response to the band and that of contemporary African Americans who preferred modern black music to the blues tradition, which was obsessed with slavery. The Pogues' take on traditional music drew even sterner criticism from musical purists.

On 5 September 1985, The Pogues were guests on the *B. P. Fallon Orchestra*, a show on RTE Radio 2. The programme was recorded in front of an audience of about forty people, including concertina player Noel Hill, writer and performer Joe Ambrose, and promoter and manager of Foster & Allen, Donnie Cassidy. Frank Murray was also in the studio for the session. Fallon was a keen sponsor of the group, but he was also intent on a lively debate. 'This evening we have here as our special guests probably the most controversial group in the groovy world of pop and roll,' he told listeners.

Teeing up a verbal sparring match with The Pogues and their manager in one corner and the purists in the opposing one, the presenter wondered if they felt 'a bit more vulnerable' coming to Ireland and whether it was a case of bringing 'coals to Newcastle'. 'Well, nobody expects the Spanish Inquisition, do they?' Shane fired back when the question was directed at him. Fallon then asked if it was the same as people stupidly saying The Rolling Stones shouldn't go to America and play Chuck Berry songs. The room then collapsed with laughter when Shane came back as quick as lightning, 'Yeah, well, they were right about that!'

The heated exchanges that followed centred on the group's Irishness and what constituted Irish music. It brought to the fore Shane's quick-wittedness and his extensive knowledge and passion for Irish music. When

Fallon asked if they listened to Irish music at all, citing Moving Hearts and Clannad as examples, Shane replied, 'Well, I'm not sure if Moving Hearts are Irish music, generally speaking, apart from the last album, anyway.'

'Well, what would you regard them as?' enquired Fallon.

'It depends if you mean Irish music, music played by people who have lived all their lives in Ireland, or Irish music as some kind of idea of what the Irish tradition of music is or whatever,' explained Shane. 'If it's the second then I wouldn't count Moving Hearts, do you know what I mean? If it's the first thing, then they're an Irish band. In Finland or Germany, it doesn't matter whether you're Irish or not. I just don't understand what's so surprising about a group playing what we are playing, I don't understand what people are so confused by.'

Former Planxty member Noel Hill was exercised by the arrival of The Pogues, a band whose music he thought bore no resemblance to traditional Irish music and who were besmirching its reputation. Meanwhile, labelling as Irish music the rowdy ballad bands that had emerged from drunken sessions in Dublin pubs twenty years earlier was 'a terrible abortion', he contended.

Fellow Irish musician Jack Costello, however, leapt to the band's defence. Ireland had raised its traditional music to a state of sanctity to the point where it was 'inviolable and we can't touch it'. Irish music was strong enough to be played on any instrument and 'used, abused, attacked'. By dint of its history, Ireland had a 'gross inferiority complex where, if anybody touches our music, our religions, our games, they can never do it like we do it.' He praised innovative groups like The Chieftains who had taken it out of small, rural pubs and broadened it, putting it on the international stage.

The ill-tempered session came to a feisty finale with Joe Ambrose describing the behaviour of Cait O'Riordan as that of 'a pig' and accusing her of refusing to reply to genuine questions. 'Rocky' responded by honking noisily into the microphone. 'Is that behaving like a pig enough for you?' she fired back.

Christy Moore was one of the founding members of Planxty in the early 1970s, along with Andy Irvine, Dónal Lunny and Liam Flynn, and he found the wariness and suspicion with which The Pogues were received in Ireland all too familiar. 'When I heard negative reactions to The Pogues, I recalled similar reactions to Planxty when we first arrived,' says Christy.

'There were two particularly vicious Pogues critics at the time, both high-profile, trad players, and I suggested to Shane that he invite them to join the band on tour. That would soon shut them up, they'd soon take the soup!'

Commenting on the furore many years later, Shane said: 'The musicians [traditional Irish musicians] all liked us, B. P. Fallon liked us, but that idiot Joe Duffy hated us. Noel Hill accused us of bastardising Irish music and filling it with obscenity. Whereas I pointed out a few songs which are full of obscenities, which are humorous. Noel Hill was a great concertina player technically, but there wasn't an ounce of soul in there.' [10]

There was no less scepticism when they appeared on RTE1's flagship programme *The Late Late Show*, aired on the same day as the radio show had been recorded. The notoriously conservative host and national treasure Gay Byrne also wanted to know what The Pogues were. After the group had treated the smartly dressed audience to 'The Sick Bed Of Cuchulainn', Gaybo wasted no time in starting his own inquisition. 'Are you the ceili band, Shane MacGowan, or are you the ballad group or are you the punk-rock outfit or what are ye?'

'We're all of them, really,' replied a nonplussed Shane.

Gaybo wasn't to be deterred and, with Bob Geldof looking on, he put Shane firmly on the spot. What did he have to say to criticisms that The Pogues were 'bringing Irish music into disrepute' and were 'playing up the drunken paddy image'? he wanted to know.

'Well, we started out playing in bars and Irish pubs quite a lot, actually, in London, and we did usually get quite drunk,' replied Shane.

'Did you?' asked the seemingly shocked presenter.

'Well, sometimes, yeah. I mean we weren't playing to many people or anything. So, then he [a journalist] just put together these two things, drunkenness and Irishness or London Irishness, and so he called us drunken paddies. It's just a kind of image, a label to hang on people.'

Shane looked genuinely perplexed. However, he didn't react defensively or storm off, as some musicians might. He simply stood disarmingly with his hands in his jacket pockets, denying Gaybo his Bill Grundy moment. For a man so proud of his Irish lineage and making his first appearance on Irish television, with his family watching, this was an uncomfortable ride.

Jem Finer says of Gay Byrne's comments: 'It's a very conservative point of view. The people in Ireland who influenced us, like The Dubliners, thought it was great what we were doing. It was never a problem for me. I have to say, Shane was maybe a lot more sensitive to it and tuned into what people were saying, for and against. So maybe for him, certain people saying we'd brought Irish music into disrepute, he was sensitive to that. My feeling is that on the surface he seemed thrilled that The Dubliners were great supporters and respected the band and his writing and fuck the rest of them. That has to be the position you take, whether you feel it or not. If you project yourself as a rebellious and "fuck you" character – and Shane was always someone who had a mind of his own – you can't really start whinging. And it didn't matter because we were on *The Late Late Show* and the joke was on Gay Byrne, like the joke was on the guy at Covent Garden. He could have been the guy who gave the embryonic Pogues their big break. But instead, he was the guy with the cloth ears who couldn't see it.'

Deirdre O'Mahony says it was because The Pogues were challenging that conservative image of Ireland that they were greeted with such suspicion when they pulled into town with paddy suits and a reputation for heavy drinking.

'That was part of the difficulty The Pogues had in Ireland initially when they first went back because people thought they were taking the piss and that it was disrespectful, which it never was,' observes Deirdre. 'This goes back to attitudes in Ireland to being made to feel "other" and nothing epitomised that more than Irish music. Not the nice Planxty, Bothy Band, Celtic music, but that raw Ronnie Drew, Dubliners, uncool folk music that was somehow seen as a bastard; not respectable enough to be part of a tradition. There wasn't the distance to do it in Ireland. You can't step back from your own culture when you're in the middle of it.'

By the mid-1980s, Ireland was 'trying to remake itself as a sophisticated modern nation' and the arrival of a group rooted in the Ireland of Brendan Behan and The Dubliners was ill-timed, says Deirdre. But rather than hindering Ireland's attempts to modernise and move on, others believed The Pogues would ultimately progress it.

'I think it was really necessary for Ireland, hugely important that it happened,' says Deirdre. 'Phil Chevron used to have big arguments with me on this, but I always remember Bill Graham from *Hot Press* coming over and, as I recall, we went to see The Pogues at The Hope & Anchor and he was absolutely shell-shocked. He didn't know what to make of it. Phil used to say he got it straight away, but I don't think he did. You walked in and it was everything modern Ireland didn't want to be, and that hipster Dublin didn't want to be.'

Elsewhere, there was no such navel-gazing about how Irish The Pogues were or whether or not they were playing traditional Irish music. They blazed a trail across Europe, playing riotous shows in the Netherlands, France, Germany, Switzerland and Scandinavia as Frank Murray's punishing tour schedule continued unabated. Those in and around the band would remember these as halcyon days. But even at this early stage, touring didn't agree with Shane and he couldn't wait to get back to London. By the time they reached Malmö, Sweden, in early November, he was gravely ill and, shortly before they were due on stage at a venue called Kulturbogalet, he was diagnosed with pneumonia. He was admitted to hospital – as he would be on so many occasions – and vocal duties were taken up by Elvis Costello and other band members. 'It was touch and go,' said Shane: 'When the hospital started treating me, they shoved paracetamol up my bum. That felt a bit strange, but some of the nurses were nice.' [11]

The band enjoyed a rare break while Shane recovered before they were off again, playing a Christmas tour of dates around the UK and Ireland. Their larger-than-life manager was holding to his belief that constant performing was the key to commercial success. But his influence on The Pogues extended beyond keeping the tour bus rolling. Earlier in the year he had brought Dubliner Philip Chevron into the fold. The guitarist had played in The Radiators From Space, also managed by Frank, and he was brought in as a stand-in for Jem on the group's first European dates, as Jem's wife Marcia was expecting their first child. Philip didn't know his way around a banjo, but he made his debut in Stuttgart and then joined the band on a subsequent Scandinavian tour. Memorably, he was hospitalised when a mammoth drinking session with James Fearnley on a ferry to Finland caused a near fatal reaction with his stomach ulcer.

Philip proved a perfect fit and when Jem returned from his paternity leave, he joined the group full-time and Shane was relieved of his duties on rhythm guitar. Shane had always been proud of his playing style, which amounted to thrashing violently across the steel strings and had contributed to the energy of many of the early songs. However, while he was put out by the group's suggestion that Philip take over, he admits it had become a

115

distraction on stage. 'They took me off guitar, so then it was just Phil and that was awful because I was bloody good at Irish rhythm guitar. But Phil couldn't play Irish rhythm guitar. He used to use light strings and break them every night, even though he wasn't hitting them. For ages, it had been good for me to have the guitar, but then it started putting me off my singing as we got faster and faster and madder and madder. I couldn't listen to the drums properly and the timing started going out, and it wasn't Andrew. Christy Moore goes out of time all the time, but he doesn't use a drummer.

'But then I switched to the banjo and then I switched to the bouzouki, which is fucking easy to play. It's only got four strings and it's in open tuning. I can't pick at it and pick out tunes like Andy Irvine, like it's meant to be or like the Greeks do. But I can make a bloody good racket which sounds really like it's meant to. I missed playing the guitar, but I didn't miss playing the bouzouki because I took that up after the guitar and flashed it in their faces and said, "Fuck you, assholes. Now Terry, can you tell me how to tune this fucker!"'

Terry Woods was the second of Frank Murray's friends to join the group and the addition of his cittern was to be significant in the development of The Pogues' sound. A Dubliner who liked American country music as well as folk and other styles, he was an acclaimed musician in Ireland who had been at the vanguard of electric folk. He was a member of Sweeney's Men, a popular traditional Irish trio that recorded a version of Pogues' favourite 'Waxie's Dargle'. Along with his girlfriend Gay, he had been a founder member of Steeleye Span and had briefly played with the experimental Dr Strangely Strange. The pair later formed The Woods Band and then performed as a duo until they separated. A five-year hiatus from the music business was brought to a close when his old friend Frank mooted the idea of him joining The Pogues.

Terry's induction was a baptism of fire. The band were circumspect about him becoming one of their number and an initial rehearsal in London didn't go well. The next day he found himself in the ill-tempered debate on RTE radio, with B. P. Fallon demanding to know if he was joining the band or not. They hadn't asked, he replied. But they soon did, and it was precisely because The Pogues strayed so joyously beyond the traditional tramlines of Irish music that he found them so appealing.

'Funnily enough, the music I started off playing was American mountain music,' explains Terry. 'I was put completely off Irish music by my upbringing with the Christian Brothers. I fucking hated them. That's why I never got involved with Comhaltas [set up to promote and preserve Irish music] and the total trad thing. I hear the music, but I hear offshoots as well, and I'm not really interested in "Playing note for note what me granny played, and if she didn't play it that way it isn't good enough". I'd play it, but I want freedom.'

Shane remarks: 'Terry was a really famous Irish musician. He has quite a high voice and when he gets freaked out about something it goes very high. We used to call him The Virginian. He looks like the guy in *The Virginian*: tall, with a hat, a black dustcoat and cowboy winklepickers with spurs, which he wore on the bus!'

No matter how The Pogues perceived themselves, their fans saw them as an Irish group and this fed into their popularity, especially in countries with large Irish communities. Frank might have been criticised for working the band into the ground and later, even contributing to its demise. However, his recruitment of Philip and Terry encouraged the expansion of its musical horizons, says Ann Scanlon. 'Without him, The Pogues would not be the group as we know it,' she comments. 'I totally believe that. He just saw that this was the most exciting thing on the London scene since the Sex Pistols and he brought in Philip Chevron and Terry Woods. He re-emphasised the Irish side, even though a lot of them were saying, "We're not an Irish band." Also, Frank was very connected; he knew the stars, and he was a really great, charismatic man.'

By the end of 1985, The Pogues were the darlings of the music press. *Rum Sodomy & The Lash* was voted number two in *Melody Maker*'s albums of the year and Shane named Chap of the Year. *NME* chose 'A Pair Of Brown Eyes' as the ninth best single and the album came eighteenth in its end-of-year list, and The Pogues also had no fewer than four songs in John Peel's famous Festive 50. Stiff also got in on the act, with Phil Hall chosen by *Music Week* as Press Officer of the Year for his ingenious marketing of the LP.

Christmas brought some well-earned respite from the relentless gigging. But not for long. The group set off on Boxing Day to Ireland for a tour starting at The Bridge hotel, Waterford. Cait got her dates mixed up and missed the flight, so Darryl Hunt had to step in at the last minute.

He played with his back to the audience, reading the bass charts that had been scribbled down and stuck to an amp. She did arrive in time for the next show in Tralee and was all smiles as she showed off her new diamond and emerald engagement ring.

Shane's triumphant return to Ireland with the band of the moment was a matter of immense pride for his relatives. He always made sure they were kept up to date with what he was doing and sent them tickets so they could see his shows. A very special gig was also arranged in a village in Tipperary, close to his beloved Carney, as his aunty Vicky recalls: 'Shane and The Pogues came to Kennedy's pub in Puckane and did a concert there and everybody was absolutely amazed!'

For all the American films he had scrutinised and consigned to memory, Shane had never been to the country itself. In fact, he had never flown. So, it was with wide, staring eyes and a childlike excitement that he arrived in New York in late February 1986 for The Pogues' first US tour.

'It's always been a dream world to me,' he said ahead of his trip: 'Kennedy was a huge hero in my family, because he was Irish American and the first Catholic president of the United States. The late fifties, early sixties, was a great period of hope for everybody in the western world and America represented that. And then, bang! The Vietnam War and John Kennedy, Robert Kennedy, Martin Luther King and Malcolm X, all assassinated. In one decade it went from a dream period of affluence and everybody looking to America to the shit-heap that everything is now. But I want to go there. I'm fascinated by all the different cultures: the Irish, the Italians, the Puerto Ricans, the Japs, they're all American but they still have their own cultures. I'm obsessed with it for loads of reasons.' [12]

The Pogues landed at JFK and were chauffeur-driven to the Iroquois hotel on West 44th Street. They had absolutely no idea how Americans would receive them or even if they had heard any of their records. Their opening show was on 28 February at The World, a fêted venue in Manhattan's East Village with a sophisticated clientele that could be difficult to please. But they needn't have worried. The city in which Shane's idol Brendan Behan danced in the street had been eagerly anticipating their first show. The rich and famous were clamouring for tickets and the *New York Times* and other media outlets were on the phone, begging for review passes. Peter Dougherty, the man credited with bringing rap to MTV, was among those in the audience and he took some video footage. He ventured backstage that night to meet the band and the following year he would direct the video to 'Fairytale Of New York'.

For one band member, the occasion proved all too much. As they waited around for Cait to join them in the hotel the following morning, she was heading to JFK to catch a flight home.

Shane recalled: 'Cait was getting freaked out. Well, she was young, we were all young. She was 18 by the time we first got to America and she knocked Matt Dillon [who would later appear as an NYPD cop in the video to "Fairytale"] down a fire escape! She was a very strong Irish woman and she could be very aggressive. She was really into her rights as a woman and she wasn't into manipulation. And Matt Dillon wasn't doing that, he was just being polite and saying, "I think you're a really groovy chick", you know what I mean? That was enough! She kicked him down the fire escape, tsscchh, and he got up and dusted himself off and came limping back up and said, "I'm sorry if I offended you", and all this, and she said, "Oh, fuck off." But they got on better later on. There was some mate of Costello's there who helped her get a flight back to England, so he was obviously planning to get her out of the group.' [13]

When Cait flew back to London, Darryl took over bass duties for shows at the 9:30 Club in Washington, DC, the 8x10 club in Maryland, and a press show at the legendary Limelight club on the Avenue of the Americas in New York, where *Breakfast Club* actress Molly Ringwald and New York Dolls frontman David Johansen were among the luminaries in attendance.

There were frenzied scenes at Spit in Boston where fans dived on and off the stage and stormed the dressing room after the show. Joseph Kennedy, then running for Congress, and his son John F. Kennedy Jr., had reportedly been discussing a fundraising event in The Metro next door. After finding out The Pogues were playing, they dropped in to see the show. In the Rhode Island capital of Providence, the group headed a four-band line-up at Lupo's Heartbreak Hotel, before returning to New York for a curtain-closer at the Danceteria in Chelsea.

The band had been surprised to find college and other radio stations in the US playing their new EP *Poguetry In Motion* and, by the time they got home to do yet more gigs, it had given them their first UK Top 40 hit, the track climbing to number twenty-nine. The record contained four tracks, all recorded as part of the sessions produced by Elvis Costello: 'London Girl', 'The Body Of An American', 'A Rainy Night In Soho' and 'Planxty Noel Hill', the last an instrumental by Jem Finer, but the others written by Shane. 'The Body Of An American' was one of the songs the group chose to play when they appeared on *Saturday Night Live* in 1990 and later it would be played during police wakes in the HBO series *The Wire*. 'London Girl' received plenty of airplay but 'A Rainy Night In Soho' was the tour de force, a moving, sweeping ballad that would melt even the hardest of hearts.

All the stars were aligning. The Pogues' maiden voyage to America had been a triumph, the press couldn't get enough of them, and they were enjoying their first hit single. Added to that, respected filmmaker Alex Cox was planning a movie featuring the band. He had directed the official video for 'A Pair Of Brown Eyes' the previous year and was now plotting a rock'n'roll documentary which was to be shot in Nicaragua that summer.

A heavy schedule of dates in France and Germany were lined up as the Pogues juggernaut motored on, exhausting audiences and band members alike. But these had to be cancelled suddenly after Shane was involved in another near-death encounter. He and Spider had spent an enjoyable evening with Cox discussing his latest film project at an Indian restaurant when a taxi sent Shane flying as he crossed the road. 'Shane was slightly behind me, and suddenly I heard this bang,' recalled Spider: 'I looked around and Shane wasn't there. There was a taxi very near to where he should have been and then there he was, further on down the road, on his back. The very first thought was, He's dead, but then I saw that he wasn't, almost immediately.' [14]

Shane suffered extensive injuries and underwent surgery in hospital. One arm and one leg had to be kept in casts for a month. The band had needed a rest, but not in such awful circumstances. Recalling the episode, Shane says: 'I got knocked full in the side by a fucking black cab which was doing about fifty on a double-parked road. I could have sued him for thousands. "London Girl" was in the charts at the time and it was playing on the hospital radio and the nurses all started getting more interested, although they were pretty interested anyway.'

Cats are said to have nine lives, but over his forty-year career, Shane has surely used up more, and he and seems to accept such near-misses as a kind of occupational hazard.

'On another occasion it happened when I was working at the Hudson Bay warehouse,' said Shane. 'I wasn't even drunk, just hungover from the night before. I was doing overtime on a Sunday. At lunch-hour, most people used to go across the road to the pub. I was just wandering across and this Renault hit me much faster than the taxi. Again, he glanced me, but it knocked me across the road. I was really lucky. I didn't even realise I had a lacerated arm.' [15]

Shane's friends were nothing if not resourceful. Once he emerged from hospital, a plan was hatched to keep him occupied while the band were off the road. Another group was formed, called Shit, with Shane's best mate Paul Ronan singing and Shane playing guitar as best he could, along with friend Kieran 'Mo' O'Hagan. Paul Scully was on bass and his fellow sound engineer Dave Jordan was behind the drum kit until Frank Murray tried to sabotage the side-project by forbidding him from being involved. He was promptly replaced by Rob McKahey, the drummer from Stump.

Trish O'Flynn from The Shillelagh Sisters was tasked with trying to manage this motley crew and has fond memories of Shit. 'I was the manager because I had a van, so I would drive up to Shane's flat, ring the doorbell and shout, "Get down here, you've got a rehearsal," she says. 'I mean, it was great fun. We did a gig at Wendy May's Locomotion at The Forum in Kentish Town. She was singing in the Boothills, but she had this big northern soul night at The Forum. Shane was a mad northern soul person as well, so we did this gig there. There weren't that many extra people to the usual crowd who turned up. We got paid a few hundred quid, but it certainly wasn't a massive sell-out like Frank was worried about.'

Shane recalls: 'Paul Ronan was doing lead vocals and generally winding up the audience. We had a guest singer and with twenty-five minutes to go he got all the numbers wrong. We had a drummer who couldn't play drums properly on "Twenty-Flight Rock" ... They started pelting us really early on with plastic glasses, which freaked Mo out completely.'

Shit would play a few more times, although Shane's only appearance was at The Forum on 3 May. It was simply a welcome distraction while he waited for his latest injuries to heal and, as time would show, the last opportunity for The Pogues to have any respite from their punishing schedule. By the middle of May they were back on the road, starting with Self-Aid, a huge event held at the RDS in Dublin to highlight chronic unemployment in

Ireland. Elvis Costello, Chris Rea and The Boomtown Rats were among the acts who entertained the thirty thousand fans crammed into the venue. Inspired by Live Aid the previous year, the concert raised millions of pounds for a job creation trust fund.

Shows in France, Finland and the UK, and an appearance on *The Old Grey Whistle Test* followed before they flew to Washington, DC on 24 June. On their previous trip they had dipped their toes in the water, unsure of how those on the other side of the Atlantic would respond. But it had worked wonders for their reputation and now, just a few months later, tickets to see them were like gold dust. The returning heroes played at Nightclub in the capital and then Philadelphia, before travelling to New York to perform at The Ritz. That evening, with the euphoria backstage so strong you could have bottled it, someone walked in who would not only play a key role in the band, but in the life of Shane.

Joey Cashman, who had met the band the previous year, was on his way to see a friend on Rhode Island when he landed in New York and saw The Pogues were playing that night. 'It was only a few blocks away and I thought, I might as well walk up and say "Hello" and then I'll get the bus up to Newport. When I arrived, Darryl was on his knees begging, "Will you help?" The show was wild. I'd never seen anything like it backstage. There were probably as many people backstage as there were at the show, you know? You couldn't move.'

Frank Murray, seeing the urgent need for back-up for what was now an eight-piece band, ended up asking Joey to do the whole tour. The formidable Dubliner with an athletic build and a whip-sharp sense of humour had become part of the crew. He recalls first entering the band's orbit the previous year, on a long weekend away in Paris. 'It was winter and we went over to see Tom Waits, among other reasons. I drive motorbikes, so I had all the leather gear and it was freezing. So, I went into the room with them, and I had all the leather gear on, trousers, gloves, the whole shebang. These guys banged on the door and said I had to go, and I'm going, "What the fuck? I'm the only straight one in here." They thought I was whipping them or something!'

Joey had spoken at that time to Philip Chevron over a meal and offered to roadie for free, providing his costs were covered. That led to him being invited to help Darryl for two consecutive shows at Hammersmith Palais, including St Patrick's night. He was then asked to accompany the band on tours of France and Germany and had his bags packed and ready when the news came through about Shane's altercation with a taxi. Now, in America, Joey had joined the band's inner circle.

'I started off just as the one-man roadie,' says Joey. 'The rest of the crew were like, "I'm a lighting man", "I'm the sound engineer. I do sound" – but I'm like, "That needs doing, I'm going to do it." So, I became tour manager really quickly.'

Joey had been with the group when they had seen Tom Waits at the Casino de Paris in November 1985, and *Rain Dogs*, his bellwether album released earlier that year, was the constant soundtrack in the tour bus on its release. When they returned to the US the following summer, their show at The Vic theatre, Chicago, coincided with a performance of *Frank's Wild Years*, the stage production written by Waits and his wife Kathleen Brennan. The troubadour, who under his partner's influence was busily shedding his drunken hobo persona, was doing back-to-back shows at the Briar Street theatre. Shane and the group went to the first of these before taking to the stage themselves and later that night they were left pinching themselves in disbelief when they ended up drinking with their idol.

'The Pogues were in town and came to see the show,' said Waits. 'Then Kathleen went to see their show. She flipped. You have to give them awards for standing up first of all and anything that follows… afterwards, we all went out to a bar and got up and sang and played all night. Yeah, The Pogues are something else.' [16]

Shane says: 'On the tour after *Rain Dogs* had just come out, we kept sticking it on. I was on a speed comedown and you know how jerky "Singapore" is, if you're coming down off speed feeling a bit paranoid and "Singapore" comes on really loud. That was the first album [Tom] made when he gave up the drink. He had just married Kathleen Brennan and he co-wrote all the songs with her for *Swordfishtrombones* and then *Rain Dogs*. My favourite is "Downtown Train". All the songs on that are great. She wanted to get him off booze and that piano and the lounge thing went with booze. In the end, he became that persona. I've never been a persona; I was just straightforward. We all went and saw him in Chicago in the *Frank's Wild Years* musical, and we kept bumping into him after that. We got on great, us and him. He's a real barrel of laughs, he's like he's always on stage. Mind you, I think I might be on stage all the time, I don't know. Not now, but for a while... We were all fans of his and it turned out he was a fan of us.'

James Fearnley says the actor Aidan Quinn was with the band for the unforgettable night out with Waits, but he doesn't remember Shane being there. 'We went in through the front door of one bar and out through the back door where the van was waiting so we could lose people that we didn't want,' says James. 'I don't recall Shane being around for that at all, which isn't to say that he wasn't. But I just do not remember him being there and I think I would have remembered had he been.'

If Shane did miss out on an evening in the company of one of his heroes, it would not have been out of character. Anyone who knows Shane well will tell you he has no interest in being around the rich and famous, and he can feel uncomfortable on such occasions. He is far happier sitting with locals in the bars of Nenagh or Tipperary than with A-list celebrities, and would sooner talk about a film he has just watched than his own work. While Shane pursued success, he never craved fame for its own sake.

Darryl Hunt observes: 'Shane doesn't have that star-like attitude towards being a personality. He's got his feet on the ground. You often feel that some other people's careers come from their efforts to make themselves well-known, whereas Shane doesn't really do that. He doesn't bother too much about making himself well-known. You get what you get, and he is the same onstage as offstage.'

One night during a lively discussion round at Shane's flat, Joey turned to Shane and said: 'When anyone interesting was interested in you, you'd tell them to fuck off. You said "Fuck off" to Kylie Minogue, you said "Fuck off" to Dave Stewart from Eurythmics. The band [The Pogues] said "Fuck off" to Lollapalooza twice and that's when I left them "in my head".'

Famous people from other fields have had the Shane treatment. In 2009, The Pogues were in Manchester for one of their traditional Christmas shows and staying at the Lowry hotel. Shane was having a drink with his regular driver Brendan Fitzpatrick when they spotted Manchester United stars Paul Scholes, Ryan Giggs and Wayne Rooney, and former players Mark Hughes and Francis Lee. That weekend Giggs had been named BBC Sports Personality of the Year and he was holding a party to celebrate.

Brendan describes what happened next: 'He [Giggs] made his way over to our table and he says to Shane, "You're Shane MacGowan."

'Shane says, "Yeah, who the fuck are you?"

'"I'm Ryan Giggs," he goes.

'"Oh, you're the guy who shags his brother's wife, yeah?"

'He took it fairly well, so that was grand. Shane and myself were on double black Russians, double Bloody Marys – we were having a right go on the drink. I asked Ryan Giggs for a photograph and he politely did that, and he offered Shane and myself tickets for Man United against Wolves on the Tuesday night. He said, "Lads, I'm having a party tonight in Mojo's nightclub and I'd like to invite you as my guests." So, Shane just goes to him, "I'll think about it, all right?" It was classic Shane.'

At two o'clock in the morning, when the hotel stopped serving, Shane decided he wanted to go, and they climbed in a taxi and went to meet up with the footballing legend. 'It was a great night and we ended up in a casino,' says Brendan. 'Giggs didn't play in the game and there was a write-up in one of the tabloids with a picture of Shane and a headline, DON'T BLAME SHANE MACGOWAN!

The atmosphere at many of the US shows verged on hysterical, especially in the cities with a sizeable Irish community. This time they travelled much further, the itinerary including Columbus, Detroit and Chicago and their first foray into Canada for shows in Toronto, Ottawa, Montreal and Quebec. The tour closed on 14 July with a sell-out show at the Hollywood Palace in Los Angeles.

Less than four years after making their debut in the back room of The Pindar of Wakefield, The Pogues were the toast of America.

CHAPTER 6

Straight To Hell

'I am Francesco Vasquez Garcia
I am welcome to Almeria
We have sin gas and con leche
We have fiesta and feria'

'Fiesta', **The Pogues**

Films are Shane's constant companion. Especially westerns. *For a Few Dollars More, The Wild Bunch, Hang 'Em High* and other iconic movies have been devoured endlessly. In hotel rooms and in his flat. Sometimes the end credits will start rolling and he will start watching it all over again. Call round to see him and you can guarantee he will be in front of the television. He might appear to be dozing or out of it, but he is taking everything in.

Some movies he knows by heart and he awaits each violent scene with glee, wanting you to enjoy them with him. Such moments are savoured like a fine wine. 'People wonder why he obsessively watches war movies and it's actually because he feels it,' explains Victoria. 'It's like he's in it. He's putting himself in it all the time.'

Not surprisingly, Shane becomes animated when he reminisces about appearing in *Straight to Hell*, the spaghetti western directed by Alex Cox, shot in Almeria, Spain, which also featured Clash frontman Joe Strummer. 'Me and Spider were the two idiotic fucking hitmen. His death scene was brilliant. He roared and screamed and rolled down the hill and writhed. He was very good at it and he should have kept with it. I would have liked to have kept with the acting.'

Cox's 'deranged punk-western', as one reviewer put it, was to have been called *The Legend of Paddy Garcia*, from Jem Finer's instrumental 'A Pistol For Paddy Garcia'. But probably at Joe Strummer's suggestion it eventually took its name from a single from The Clash's 1982 album *Combat Rock*. *Straight to Hell* was shot during August and September 1986 in the melting, 110-degree heat of the Tabernas Desert, among the sets from some of Sergio Leone's spaghetti westerns. The main set was originally built for the 1973 film *Chino*, starring Charles Bronson, and had also been used in *For a Few Dollars More*.

But while Leone was an undeniable influence, Cox said it was a film by Italian director Giulio Questi that inspired his own spaghetti western. 'Django was this spaghetti-western hero who'd get his hands cut off, his neck broken, or his tongue cut out; really terrible sadistic things would happen to him and yet he'd always triumph in the end,' said the director. 'And *Straight to Hell* is actually ripped off from *Django Kill*, which is the story of this horrible town where the townspeople are worse than the outlaws. It's full of lynchings, gratuitous sadism, cannibalism, homosexuality; and all kinds of good stuff.' [1]

A homage to the spaghetti western had not been Cox's original intention, but rather he had wanted to stage a tour. The politically active filmmaker had organised a concert to raise money for the Sandinistas, the Nicaraguan government then embroiled in a civil war with the US-backed Contras. Most of the musicians who appeared in *Straight to Hell*, including The Pogues, Joe Strummer and Elvis Costello, lent their voices to the event at The Fridge in Brixton on 7 August 1985. So popular was the concert that Cox mooted a package tour of Nicaragua the following summer. But when record labels and video companies passed on the idea, there was no money. As the artists had earmarked the month of August for the proposed trip, Cox decided to take advantage of their availability and make a punk-styled tribute to the spaghetti western.

Alongside Kathy Burke, Elvis Costello and Biff Yeager, The Pogues played members of the McMahon Gang, a coffee-addicted gang of bandits who run the desert town of El Blanco. Other cast members included Dennis Hopper, Grace Jones, Courtney Love, Sy Richardson and Jim Jarmusch. Love had also been in *Sid & Nancy*, Cox's biopic of the doomed Sex Pistols bassist Sid Vicious and his girlfriend Nancy Spungeon, for which

The Pogues had recorded the song 'Haunted'. Posters for *Straight to Hell* promised 'Blood, money, guns, coffee and sexual tension' – all were in plentiful supply in the anarchic desert romp.

Shane probably hadn't seen so much daylight for years and looked incongruous in a large sombrero. But he was in his element acting in just the kind of film he loved watching, playing a crazed bandit alongside his natural sidekick Spider, and drinking vast quantities of Spanish wine. Jem also remembers him spending a lot of time reading and says he was inspired to pen some new songs while in Almeria: 'Shane wrote "If I Should Fall From Grace With God" and "Lullaby Of London" while we were there. He seemed to be reading a lot of Lorca [Spanish poet and playwright Federico García Lorca], which I'm sure he'd read before, but we were in Lorca territory. After that we wrote "Fiesta", which was a direct consequence of staying in this hotel right next to the fairground and being kept awake all night – if you weren't awake all night anyway – by this crazy cacophony. That happened when we got home and I put together some of the tunes from the fairground, misremembered, with a new tune. I basically wrote a song without words called "Fiesta" and then Shane wrote the words for it, which contained some Lorca. So, from a musical point of view it was quite productive.'

For the soundtrack album, The Pogues contributed their take on the theme from *The Good, The Bad and The Ugly*, an a capella version of 'Danny Boy', beautifully sung by Cait and accompanied by the cast, and 'Rabinga', an instrumental written on set by Philip Chevron on a cheap Spanish guitar he bought in Almeria. Two new songs by Shane, 'If I Should Fall From Grace With God' and 'Rake At The Gates Of Hell', were also included on the record.

'They're both cowboy death songs which I wrote for the film,' said Shane. 'The whole idea of "Rake At The Gates Of Hell" is very violent and romantic. It's the sort of thing that your classic maniac gunslinger would be thinking, about anybody who'd ever done anything to them, as they were waiting to go. It's inspired by Marty Robbins, you know, doom and death in the hot sun. And "If I Should Fall From Grace With God" is inspired, I suppose, by gospel/country songs where they have one verse about God and the rest of it is about killing all the others.' [2]

Alex Cox said later that Spider, James, Jem and Philip delivered the best of The Pogues' performances, while Elvis Costello was 'a natural actor of great subtlety'. Shane enjoyed acting but, said Cox, 'wasn't such a natural actor. He's a poet, rather than a thespian, I think, and it was hard to explain to him why he had to stand in the same place on the second take or do the same things twice. I think in the end we had to box him in with sandbags.' [3]

In an interview with pop magazine *Smash Hits* at the group's Spanish hotel, it was evident that Shane was enjoying the experience, but wasn't taking it very seriously. 'Naaah, it's just a laugh, innit? Sssssss!' he replied when it was suggested that The Pogues couldn't act. The band members were speaking in their own voices and were really playing themselves, he said. When it came to describing the story, he was characteristically childlike in his excitement. 'The Pogues and a few other people play this local family who don't like strangers – they hate them – and all these other people come into the town and everybody starts blowing everybody away, sssssss! Anything that moves, sssssss! It's all gunfights – oh, and there are hangings and drownings as well.' [4]

Asked why there were so many musicians in the movie, Shane said: 'I think that Alex just likes having people that he knows in his films – he knew us from the "Haunted" video. I don't know why he makes films with pop music people in them... maybe for this one he thought we'd like playing around with guns and all that. Sssssss! I dunno, maybe we're mad... I get killed, you know! I'm not allowed to tell you too much but nearly everyone gets killed, sssssss!'

Shane found himself cast with another unlikely collection of musicians in *Eat the Rich*, which was also released in 1987. Paul McCartney, Bill Wyman, Lemmy, Hugh Cornwell and Jools Holland all made appearances in the black comedy directed by Peter Richardson that featured the cast of The Comic Strip Presents... Terry Woods and Frank Murray also appeared. Critics were no more impressed with this than with *Straight to Hell*.

'I did another film for The Comic Strip and that was a load of crap,' says Shane. 'It was fun making it. There was a scene where I was punched, and this huge guy was a stunt man and I had to have faith that he wouldn't batter my face in. I knew he could control it. He was a proper thug and he does a lot of tough guy roles. It was a funny film in bits. But they had me, Terry and Frank cast as Arab terrorists, tsscchh, and I had to say a speech from the balcony of the collapsing town hall. I was held on by a chain with a stunt man holding it for safety or we'd have both gone for a burton. I had to read this awful fucking revolutionary speech, which wasn't even funny, and I was thinking about the balcony giving way beneath me. But I was congratulated on my performance, actually.'

Triumphant tours of America, hit records and movie roles had made 1986 a landmark year in Shane's professional life and, before the year was out, a new chapter had been marked in his personal one. Unlike his previous relationships, this would prove a lasting one. Victoria Mary Clarke had moved to London four years earlier from an Irish speaking village in West Cork, where she had been raised by hippie parents. Then 16, she moved in with her friend Jo Heckett, an heiress who was already living in London, and on nights drinking at their local pub they had got to know Spider Stacy. One evening they had walked in to find Spider with Shane, and Victoria had her first encounter with the man she would go on to marry.

Although they had never met, Shane told Victoria they had spent all their money and demanded that she buy Spider a drink. Unimpressed, she told him to 'fuck off'. Victoria recalls the events of that fateful evening at the end of 1982: 'Shane reckons he thought, Well, we'll get off with this one because she's really rich, but it was actually the other one who was rich, not me. Spider said, "Do you want to go to our gig?" and I didn't know he was in a band, but I was like, "Why not? Might as well go to this gig." So, I went with him and we sat at a table. I think it might have been The Wag Club, but I can't remember. It was Steve Strange's thing anyway.

'Spider was very tired, and Shane came over and said, "Look, you're going to have to wake him up because he's got to get on stage."

'I was like, "I just came along, I didn't sign up for this." But we got him on stage, and I was just amazed at their audacity really. That was the thing that got me, the audacity of it. I was brought up in the Gaeltacht, speaking Irish and listening to real Seán Ó Sé, Peadar Ó Riada, Seán Ó Riada, all the Irish musicians. So, I had never seen it done with that lack of reverence, but also by anyone who wasn't actually fully Irish. I just thought, These guys have got nerve, but I was also really impressed because they were so good.'

Victoria ran into Shane from time to time and went to other Pogues gigs around London. Both of them were in relationships and she didn't feel anything for Shane until she stood watching him on stage in 1985, just as the band was taking off. In that moment, she was smitten. 'I went to see him in the Hammersmith Palais on St Patrick's Day with my boyfriend at the time,' she said. 'He was standing on stage with his hands in his pockets and his eyes closed singing "Dirty Old Town". I was totally mesmerised. I knew Shane but I'd never really noticed him in that way before. The Pogues' gigs were very raucous and wild with a lot of fighting, but this was a more seated, sedate gig and I could really see him. I hadn't thought about him sexually before but felt the need to be around him. I was attracted to his spirit and his energy more than anything. If I fancy someone it wears off after a period of time, but this was unusual; it never wore off.' [5]

On 11 January 1986, the night of her 20th birthday, someone told Shane to give Victoria a kiss. He obliged and, later, in the back of a taxi, they kissed again after having a blazing row about which of them knew more about Irish music. Shane was then in a relationship with Julie Walsh, who had also become part of his close circle of friends, and Victoria was living with Rob McKahey, the drummer from Irish band Stump.

'He had a girlfriend and then I also had a boyfriend, so I had to get rid of the girlfriend and he had to get rid of the boyfriend,' said Victoria when she and Shane were interviewed on RTE Radio 1's *Ray D'Arcy Show* in January 2018. 'The girlfriend actually poured a pint over my head and pushed me down the stairs, didn't she?' she said to Shane.

'Which one?' asked Shane.

'Julie,' replied Victoria, before turning to the camera and waving tauntingly, 'Hi Julie.' The studio audience burst into applause and cheered at this, prompting Victoria to reveal more about the public spat. 'She said to me, "Are you wearing the curtains?" That was her line and then she poured a pint over my head!'

Shane hadn't apparently wanted to upset Rob McKahey. But Victoria had her sights set on Shane and, after a gig at the Mean Fiddler, Harlesden, in January 1986, she seized her chance: 'I shamelessly threw myself at Shane and we collapsed on the floor together in the dressing room and rolled around, amorously, until the club was deserted.'

For their first date, they went to the 100 Club. The bouncers wouldn't let Shane in and, when they also refused his offer of a fight, the couple went back to Shane's bombsite of a flat, where they drank retsina, listened to Van Morrison's *Astral Weeks* and talked about Irish poets of the seventeenth century – a typical night's end at Cromer Street. Victoria was disgusted when she saw the squalid conditions he was living in. The mattress on the floor was hidden beneath dirty washing and Wendy's burger wrappers, and overflowing ashtrays and empty wine bottles covered the floor.

Despite the chaos, Victoria was entranced. 'When I woke up the following afternoon, I didn't want to leave, but I had to go home to my boyfriend,' she said. 'When I got there, somebody had already tipped him off and that was the end of him, but I didn't care, I was in love and I was happy. I went out with Shane again that night and the night after that and eventually we moved in together and that was that.' [6]

Mary Buxton had continued to carry a torch for Shane after they had split up. However, when she saw Victoria with him, long before they got together, she instinctively knew they would never get back together. 'I remember seeing Victoria in a pub in Kentish Town and thinking, It's all over, stop trying!' remembers Mary. 'I realised I was out of the game. Luckily, I had little Mo [O'Hagan] then. Not that I was with Mo, but I had him as my partner in crime, so I could still hang out there and be all right. Something went on and I just knew. Some of that is her character because she's got a strong character. I think she is quite honest in that she came to get him, and I could see that. I have got quite a good antenna, especially when it comes to being done down. I can see it coming a mile off!'

Victoria was nine years younger than Shane and stunning. An added attraction for Shane was that she was Irish and had been raised in a remote community untouched by time, the Ireland he viewed through such rose-tinted glasses. But she had hated growing up in West Cork and while Shane saw life in rural Tipperary as a nirvana, Victoria had glamorised the London she had heard from all her father's East End relatives. When she emigrated, she fell in love with city life and was mystified by Shane's preoccupation with rural Ireland.

'I couldn't really see what he was on about when he talked about how romantic it was to be in Ireland,' says Victoria. 'I thought he was crazy. He romanticises everyone he meets. He makes them into a character, or they become something in his mind, and with some of them it's a positive thing and some it's a very negative thing, for them. They are always bigger than life, so they are always characters in his mind. I think Ireland for him was the Ireland of Yeats or somebody who romanticised it like that.'

In the early days of their relationship, Shane talked often about his childhood visits to The Commons and of his love of Irish literature and history. He was fascinated by Victoria's upbringing in the Gaeltacht, an area where Irish is primarily spoken, and impressed when he found out she had been taught by the son of Seán Ó Riada, one of Shane's greatest musical influences.

Victoria recalls: 'He only talked about it in a romantic way because the fact that I was from Ireland meant I was automatically on a pedestal. So, he would talk to me about Ireland and Irish poetry, Irish music, Irish language. He was really impressed that I spoke Irish – all those things that I didn't really think were in any way cool, he thought were very cool.'

In turn, when she discovered he was the Shane O'Hooligan she had read about as a young punk in the pages of *Melody Maker* and *Hot Press* she was in thrall to him. 'I liked the Sex Pistols and all that kind of music,' says Victoria. 'So, it was fortuitous then that I did meet Shane because he was a link to all the things that I already liked. It does feel like fate.'

As one woman entered Shane's life, another to whom he had once been close left. Cait O'Riordan had been wrestling for some time with her long-term commitment to the band and when Elvis was on tour with The Attractions, she wanted to be with him. So, when she called Frank Murray from Los Angeles in October to announce she was quitting, no one was surprised. Darryl came to the rescue again on bass, but this time it would be permanent.

Jem recalls: 'My memory is phoning her up to see if she was coming to a rehearsal because she hadn't been the day before and her saying, "I'm not coming to rehearsal and I'm not ever coming to any other rehearsal. I'm never coming to anything, so fuck off!" Those weren't her exact words, but it wasn't like, "Look, I'm really sorry I can't carry on." I don't know what had got her goat, but her goat had been got. That was around the time of "The Irish Rover" because then Darryl stepped in and then he kept stepping in. I think he had stepped in before, once or twice. It made it a much better band because he is a much better bass player and he and Andrew became a great rhythm section. So, it really transformed the band.

'I don't think anyone thought it was his [Elvis Costello's] fault. She had obviously made a choice and maybe she had seen a life that she thought was preferable to her life in The Pogues. Cait was a complex person. She could be difficult and she could be very charming, and there was something great about having a woman in the band.'

Darryl might have been the obvious choice, but there had been some agonising about how to fill the vacancy. A list of names was drawn up. Auditions were even discussed. Shane was angling for his former lover Shanne Bradley to join the group, supporting Frank Murray's belief that he 'carried a torch for her for a long time' [7]. She had recently left The Men They Couldn't Hang and Shane saw an opportunity to reunite. Ron Kavana, an Irish singer, songwriter and band leader, was also in the frame.

But Darryl came with certain advantages: 'I had already done it, I knew the set, and they obviously liked what I did, which was a compliment, and Shane seemed to be happy with it,' he says. 'There was a thought that he was really thinking about Shanne a long time before Cait was in the group because they were old lovers. I don't think any particular pressure was on anybody. Ron Kavana was a friend of Terry's and they might have thought he'd do. But Paul Scully said to them, "What's your problem? You've got someone doing it." So, that's how it came about really.' Of Cait's departure, he comments: 'Something obviously wasn't right. She didn't go off with Elvis Costello just because of that. She was obviously unhappy. I can remember her once saying to me, "This band's got one album in it." The other thing she used to say to me was, "Shane's changed a lot, hasn't he?"'

Shane said: 'I always got on well with her. She was a great bass player and we were great friends. You know, I really liked her. Cait was the first one to freak out and it was a freak out. It was an unreal life.' [8]

Her exit marked the end of an era for the group and a perceptible shift in its musical emphasis. Tom Waits' *Rain Dogs*, which had been played to death on the tour bus, had heavily influenced their sound. So too had the addition of Terry Woods' mandola and Shane's bouzouki, which he had really taken to playing. Live shows, which had been dominated by songs from *Rum Sodomy & The Lash*, began to feature new material, such as 'Turkish Song Of The Damned', 'Lullaby Of London', and 'The Broad Majestic Shannon', the last composed by Shane for the popular duo Tommy Makem and Liam Clancy.

'We had always been open to different styles of music and *Rain Dogs* was something we listened to a lot,' says Jem. 'That was quite influential in the way it used all these different styles but was completely cohesive. We were listening to jazz and so much stuff and we were better at playing. And if you listen to something and it really excites you, somehow it starts coming out in the writing. So, it was a natural progression to become more expansive and I think it worked pretty well on "If I Should Fall From Grace With God", and it got a bit out of hand on "Peace And Love".'

The musical standing of The Pogues and respect for Shane's songwriting had never been higher. Christy Moore had taken to playing "A Pair Of Brown Eyes" in his live shows and told audiences the song was written by his 'new hero'. An equally welcome compliment was paid to them by the group that had inspired them more than any other. The Dubliners were recording an album to celebrate their twenty-fifth anniversary and invited The Pogues to perform with them on a couple of tracks, 'The Irish Rover' and 'The Rare Ould Mountain Dew'.

The Pogues had first met their musical forefathers at the Vienna Folk Festival and had instantly hit it off. Each band had a deep admiration for the other and there was a great camaraderie at Elephant, the studio where The Pogues had recorded their debut album. 'It was brilliant,' said Shane. 'It was a big thrill. Us and The Dubliners – great. I mean, we can all arrange ourselves. It's simple, it's minimalistic. That's what it's meant to be all about.' [9]

Jem retains fond memories of the occasion: 'It was fabulous because they're real and they're great characters and brilliant musicians. It just worked and was a really good combination. There was the more direct, rough-and-ready, self-taught approach we had, and then their real virtuoso playing, the way the songs are meant to be played. But they were playing it more from the tradition with their own, hard-edge applied. It was really great, and they were just totally respectful and warm about the whole process. Obviously the five-stringed banjo and the four-stringed banjo are different kettles of fish, but it wasn't a case of, "We only need his banjo." It was the combination of the two totally different styles... They thought what we did and were doing was a really great thing, great music; but also great for Irish music in general, giving it a kick up the arse like they always had. So, it was a perfect combination, really.'

A couple of weeks later, they got the chance to perform the songs together on stage when they found themselves playing at a TV studio near Munich, Germany. The Dubliners played their show and then stayed to see their new friends The Pogues perform. Dubliners guitarist Seán Cannon was watching from the balcony when he realised they were being invited to join The Pogues on stage. 'I clamoured over all the people on the staircase and ran up on the stage and, because I'd had a few too many, I tripped backwards into the drum kit,' remembers Seán. 'I was looking up and the drummer was beating the drums either side of me and I thought, A person of my age shouldn't be doing things like that. They were great times and to be only in your 60s was great!'

The collaboration had mutual benefits. It opened up The Dubliners to a new generation of music fans who knew little or nothing about them and it kept The Pogues in the public eye, particularly in Ireland. Shane and Dubliners' singer Ronnie Drew appeared together on the front cover of *Hot Press* that Christmas and, soon after, The Pogues were back in Ireland for the last leg of their Back To Hell tour.

Sell-out audiences at the Olympic Ballroom and SFX were delirious at the band's return to Dublin and there were more unforgettable scenes at Blooms Hotel in Temple Bar, where the band were staying. The drinks were flowing and Shane was sinking Finnish Rovers – his own Guinness and vodka cocktail. A guitar was produced by Eamonn Campbell from The Dubliners, unleashing a joyous session involving a large group of musicians. Shane made Eamonn's night with a heartfelt rendition of 'Dirty Old Town' that summoned the spirit of former Dubliners' vocalist, the late Luke Kelly. It was daylight when the session finally came to a close. The atmosphere had been convivial, and it had been a night to savour, but somehow Shane had ended up in a violent incident, sustaining a serious gash on his nose. There was talk of an altercation with a basketball player and a dustbin, although precisely what had happened outside Blooms wasn't clear.

Back in London, anti-Irish sentiment was cited as the reason for the beatings meted out to him and on occasion his republican views. This time, he was in Dublin and there were no witnesses to what had happened to him. Shane simply appeared with a bloodied face on a night of bonhomie.

In conversations with me, Shane was keen to portray himself as a man of violence, just as he had in Victoria's book *A Drink with Shane MacGowan*, in which he bragged about beatings he had inflicted. 'I've been forced to fucking fight... y'know, to become a good fighter,' he said. 'There's nothing wrong with that, I'm glad I've become a vicious, savage, fucking aggressive fighter that would beat the shit out of anybody who fucking looked twice at me, because of my childhood experiences... I completely lose it, and I don't care if I kill three or four of them, y'know what I mean? I used to leave them lying in pools of blood. Like, I only usually had to beat up one, then the other three would fuck off.' [10]

In interviews for this book, I asked those who have been closest to him whether they considered him to be violent. They insist this is simply fantasy.

Maurice MacGowan says: 'Shane is not violent at all. He has had absolutely no violent tendencies either in his childhood or, as far as I know, adult life.'

Terry Woods is also equally adamant on the subject. 'He's not violent,' he says. 'I remember in a hotel Shane was making noise and a guy knocked on his door and hit him with an ashtray – split his nose. We were down in the bar and he came down. Murray and myself said to him, "What's wrong with you? What happened?" "Oh, a guy hit me."

Whatever had provoked the attack at Blooms, Shane went on stage battered and bruised the following night at The Top Hat, an old dancehall in Dún Laoghaire, south of Dublin. The lights were kept low to conceal his wounds. A few weeks later The Pogues were back in Dublin to perform 'The Irish Rover' with The Dubliners on the RTE show *Megamix*, with Eamon Carr of Horslips on drums. The show was recorded in January 1987 in front of a live audience at the Cathedral Club in Christchurch Cathedral. Shane's injuries had healed but he was drunk,

(Left) Shane lying in a coffin during a *Sounds* end-of-year party at the Dominion Theatre, London, November 1980 (Justin Thomas).

(Below) The Pogues supported U2 at Wembley Stadium in June 1987. Shane is pictured on stage with friend Tom (Kathy MacMillan).

(Far left) Shane in a kaftan and bamboo hat, recording the video for 'Yeah, Yeah, Yeah, Yeah, Yeah', 1988 (Kathy MacMillan).

(Left) Kirsty MacColl with Shane in December 1987 promoting 'Fairytale Of New York' (Mirrorpix).

(Left) 'Look 'em straight in the eye and say Pogue Mahone.' Shane in a Pogues T-shirt, July 1988 (Mirrorpix).

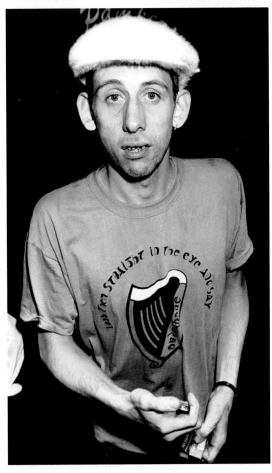

(Right) 'And the bells were ringing out for Christmas Day.' Kirsty MacColl joins Shane on stage at Brixton Academy, London, to perform 'Fairytale Of New York', 19 December 1988 (Justin Thomas).

(Left) The epitome of cool behind his trademark shades (Justin Thomas).

(Below) The Pogues at Brixton Academy, where they played so many legendary shows. L–R: Terry Woods, Philip Chevron, Shane, James Fearnley, Andrew Ranken, Spider Stacy (Justin Thomas).

(Above top) Shane and The Popes decamped to The Commons to rehearse for their first major public performance, at the Fleadh Mor festival, Tramore racecourse, Co Waterford, July 1993. L–R: Shane (in doorway), Rick Trevan (friend), Danny Heatley, Bernie France, Kieran 'Mo' O'Hagan, Leeson O'Keeffe (Bernie France).

(Above) Shane's long-time friend Johnny Depp played guitar on The Popes' debut album, *The Snake*. Pictured together in September 1994 around the time of its release (Mirrorpix).

(Right) Nick Cave and Shane released a cover of Louis Armstrong's 'What A Wonderful World' in November 1992 (Ian Dickson/Shutterstock).

JOE STRUMMER | SHANE McGOWAN | PHILLY RYAN

(Above left) Shane reaches out to the crowd during a Popes gig at The Forum in Kentish Town, December 1993 (Ian Dickinson/Redferns).

(Left) Joe Strummer, Shane and Philly Ryan at Philly's pub, Nenagh (Philly Ryan).

(Below) Therese gets Shane's birthday celebrations underway at Eamonn Doran's in Dublin, after a show at the Olympia Theatre, December 1999 (Josie Montserrat).

(Below) Pouring pints at Rosie's pub in London,
after performing at the annual Fleadh, July 1999
(Josie Montserrat).

(Above) On stage at the Electric Factory,
Philadelphia, May 2004
(Josie Montserrat).

and interviewer Kevin Sharkey elicited no more than a few slurred words from him.

The Pogues' participation in a special *Late Show*, to celebrate twenty-five years of The Dubliners, spoke volumes about the esteem in which Ireland held them. Three years earlier they had been outsiders, castigated for dragging the name of traditional music through the mud. Now they found themselves lined up alongside Irish musical royalty – U2, Christy Moore, The Fureys and other exalted acts. Even Taoiseach Charles Haughey took part in the tribute to the legendary ballad group, which was broadcast in March. The Pogues joined them to play 'The Irish Rover' and re-emerged at the end of the show to join everyone in a rendition of Brendan Behan's 'The Auld Triangle'.

Darryl Hunt says a lot of Irish people who were previously unsure of The Pogues finally 'got' them at that moment. 'They changed their minds a bit when we did that with The Dubliners because they knew them and where they were coming from,' he comments. 'I always thought of The Dubliners as a folk-punk band, because of their attitude. At school, my maths teacher played us Dubliners songs to get us going – this thumping music. When we did that show, Gay Byrne and all these people saw it and finally made the connection. But they couldn't make the connection without Ronnie Drew singing a couple of verses in one of our songs – the penny couldn't drop.'

Soon the two groups were performing in a TV studio on the other side of the Irish Sea. Stiff Records had released 'The Irish Rover', coupled with 'The Rare Ould Mountain Dew', and the single shot into the Top 40. Performances on *Top of the Pops* did the record no harm at all and it climbed to number eight. But as welcome as a Top 10 hit was to those at Stiff's headquarters in Chiswick, it was too little too late for the ailing label.

Stiff was haemorrhaging money, and although The Pogues had represented Dave Robinson's best chance of turning things round, time had been called on the label. Its mounting debts had been an open secret for a while. An unshaven and tired-looking Robinson had unexpectedly turned up during a rehearsal for their Christmas tour of 1985. Slumped on a flight case, he had come clean with the band and begged them not to leave. They stayed, and the *Poguetry In Motion* EP had provided one of Stiff's only two Top 40 singles of 1986.

Publicly, Robinson had been putting a brave face on things and the label's accountants had written to creditors, reassuring them of a rosy future. A creditors' meeting in August 1986 gave the lie to that, revealing that its parent company had debts of £3.5 million. Almost three hundred people were owed money and US magazine *Billboard* reported that this included a debt to Island Records of $1.1 million. The following month, Stiff was sold for £305,000 to Jill Sinclair, the managing director of ZTT Records and the wife of fellow ZTT founder and producer Trevor Horn, allowing it to continue with its existing roster.

Frank Murray was nervous. He knew The Pogues' next album was going to be critical if the group was going to move to the next level and Stiff clearly didn't have the financial clout to support it. Rehearsals had already got underway at Abbey Road Studios and Murray had told the band that, if anyone asked, they were playing on a solo record by Terry Woods, the only member of the group not signed to Stiff.

For the production of the album that Murray knew could send The Pogues' profile into the stratosphere, he brought in Steve Lillywhite. The renowned producer had met Murray when Lillywhite was remixing tracks from U2's *Joshua Tree* album at Windmill Lane Studios, and he had expressed an interest in producing the record. In signing him up, Murray had pulled off a massive coup. Lillywhite had produced U2's first three albums and applied the Midas touch to Big Country's iconic debut *The Crossing* and Simple Minds' *Sparkle In The Rain*. Murray knew that while Stan Brennan and Elvis Costello had captured the band's essence in a small studio, a top-class producer and studio were needed if they were to fulfil their potential.

The question was, could Lillywhite get the best from Shane? The singer had now been drinking heavily for years and his consumption levels had followed the same trajectory as the group's career. He could knock back whiskey and other spirits like water and often drained a full bottle on stage. Meanwhile, class A drugs were also now having a profound effect on his behaviour and noticeably his state of mind. 'I was always taking different drugs to Shane,' says Steve Lillywhite. 'The mid-eighties were the cocaine years, for me, anyway, although Shane wasn't really into coke in those days. I don't know what he eventually got into, but for him it was more speed… Everyone said he was an alcoholic, but I already knew that the alcohol wasn't as important. He was a junkie.'

The Pogues partied hard and their producer, who had recently worked with The Rolling Stones, joined in. From his perspective behind the mixing desk, the ingredients were all there: a unique songwriter, a group collectively on fire, and a sound that had been enriched by the arrival of Terry Woods. His role was to bring his experience to bear in the areas which needed attention and with Shane, striking while the iron was hot.

'He was actually in great shape on that album,' says Steve. 'I got the band when they were at their best. I'm not sure if they were the best songs. I absolutely loved "A Rainy Night In Soho" and some songs from before my era, but what I managed to get was a band who were firing on all cylinders. I had Shane where he was maybe just past his peak, but you needed to get him early, I mean *his* "early", when he wasn't too loaded...

'"Thousands Are Sailing" was a great song, although Shane stopped singing it and Philip ended up singing it all the time. But I remember I got Shane to sing "Thousands Are Sailing". I said, "Look, you're the lead singer of this band, you ought to sing it."'

A marked change on The Pogues' third album, *If I Should Fall From Grace With God*, was the way in which the songwriting was shared. The previous two albums had consisted mainly of compositions by Shane and rearrangements of traditional songs. This one saw Shane and Jem collaborating more than ever before and producing some of its finest moments – 'Turkish Song Of The Damned', 'Bottle Of Smoke', 'Fairytale Of New York' and 'Fiesta'. For the first time, other band members also got in on the royalties, Philip Chevron delivering 'Thousands Are Sailing' and Terry Woods contributing 'Streets Of Sorrow'.

'There was a long, protracted hiatus before the third album because of contractual problems,' says Jem. 'Basically, it was a stand-off between Dave Robinson and Frank Murray. That's really when we started writing songs much more closely together and I suppose that was because I had become better at writing. So, for example, "Fiesta" was a song that I came along with. It was called "Fiesta" and it had the instrumental tunes and verse, but no words... That was quite a simple one to write. For "Turkish Song Of The Damned", I wrote the instrumental bit. The title came from a mishearing of "The Turkey Song" by The Damned. A German said, "Have you no 'Turkish Song Of The Damned'?" and Shane picked up on that and thought, That's a great title. I wrote this tune and said, "I think this is part of 'Turkish Song Of The Damned'." So, that's the way it worked. We bounced ideas around and sometimes it was almost a template like "Fiesta" and other times it was just parts which fitted in with other things and suddenly made them a whole.'

Relations between Dave Robinson and Frank Murray had turned ugly. Robinson had discovered The Pogues were recording their third album behind Stiff's back at RAK Studios in north London, and he initiated court proceedings to get hold of the tapes. At the same time, word began reaching other labels that the group might soon be free of their obligations to Stiff. Chris Blackwell of Island Records was among those circling the band, although his demands to control their publishing brought those negotiations to a swift close. An alternative solution was found when Robinson parted company with ZTT and his replacement, Chris O'Donnell, succeeded in forging a healthy working relationship with Frank Murray. It was agreed The Pogues would set up their own label, Pogue Mahone, as part of ZTT.

As well as exploring new ground musically and creatively, *If I Should Fall From Grace With God* also marked another departure for the group. Although they had been playing Irish rebel songs since Pogue Mahone's embryonic rehearsals and Shane's republican sympathies were well known, they had never been overtly political. They were a good-time band to which people liked to have a drink and wheel joyously around. So, when Shane launched a broadside at the British justice system in a song about the men jailed for the Birmingham pub bombings, it attracted attention.

The IRA attacks in November 1974 killed twenty-one people, but the six men convicted for the atrocity always denied involvement and insisted their confessions were beaten out of them. Five people had died when bombs detonated in two pubs in Guildford, Surrey, just weeks earlier, and the three men and one woman arrested and found guilty had similarly protested their innocence.

Calls to have their convictions quashed had grown louder and more persistent by 1987, and The Pogues had been invited to perform at benefit gigs for the Birmingham Six and Guildford Four. Frank Murray, however, felt the band could lend more weight to the campaign if Shane could write a song about it. He did just that.

Paddy Hill, one of the Birmingham Six, said: 'I thought it was a joke at first, when I heard that MacGowan was going to do a song and the attitude I had was, "I'll believe it when I know it's out,"' he said. 'And eventually when it did, I was absolutely… I couldn't thank him enough'. [11]

Shane's biting lyrics also referenced the Loughgall ambush in County Armagh, Northern Ireland, in which eight members of an IRA unit were shot dead. They had planned to drive a stolen digger carrying a massive Semtex bomb into the RUC barracks in the village on 8 May 1987. The gang would then open fire on the building with automatic rifles. British intelligence forces got wind of the operation, however, and the SAS were waiting for them, launching a deadly attack. As well as the IRA members, a civilian who unwittingly drove into the area on his way home from work with another man were shot. It was the IRA's single biggest loss of life in any incident and the last verse of Shane's song made direct reference to it.

On 15 April 1988, The Pogues were scheduled to perform on *Friday Night Live*, a Thames Television show presented by comedian and writer Ben Elton. They told the producers they would be playing 'Fiesta' and 'Streets Of Sorrow Birmingham Six' *and* ran through their controversial number in the rehearsals that afternoon. Viewers later saw them career riotously through their song of Spanish revelry, covered in party string and against a bizarre backdrop of giant, fibreglass hands. However, as 'Streets Of Sorrow' was about to segue into 'Birmingham Six', the producers cut to a commercial break. The group were livid at being censored and complained bitterly, accusing Thames of suppression.

Friends of the band were also furious at the incident and spoke out in defence of Shane's song. Kathy MacMillan says: '*Points of View* on BBC had a little video cabin and you could go in. I went in and said, "I don't know what the fuss is about. The words are on the album, everybody's heard it, what's going on?" They showed it and Phil [Gaston] and Dee [O'Mahony] wrote a letter. I think I was living with them at the time. So, we did this little campaign, and we did get a good slot on *Points of View* where Ben Elton was called out. He was a bloody hypocrite because they were pretending their show was the coolest thing in town and anti-censorship, and it was just a bloody lie. He was good, I liked him, but I was so disappointed with this episode… The band did get on the show and they let them do the "Streets

Of Sorrow" bit and then up came "End of part one" or whatever it was. So, they censored them.'

Paddy Hill commented: 'This was going to become a big political issue and the last thing that they wanted was people like MacGowan educating the public about the Birmingham Six... The fact that it wasn't heard was a great shame, not just for us but also for MacGowan, for the band itself, because the lyrics were so true to the day.' [12]

The Pogues became the first band to fall casualty to the British government's 'broadcast ban'. Introduced in October 1988 by the home secretary, Douglas Hurd, it prohibited the broadcast of direct statements by representatives or supporters of eleven specific Irish political and paramilitary organisations. The purpose was to prevent Sinn Féin, the IRA's political wing, from using the media to further its cause. The song was banned by the Independent Broadcasting Authority, preventing it from being played by radio stations or performed on TV.

A Pogues statement was issued, via Frank Murray, describing the ban as 'hilarious'. 'Irish people are disadvantaged in British courts of law,' it said. 'The Pogues will continue to write about what they want, and we hope every other artist will do the same.'

On 14 March 1991, the Birmingham Six had their convictions quashed and they walked free after having spent sixteen years in prison. The sight of them standing outside the Old Bailey in London with their hands held aloft was a shameful and damning one for the British justice system. Shortly afterwards, the ban on Shane's song was discreetly lifted.

After their release, the men personally thanked Shane for his part in their hard-fought campaign. 'They all came around one by one to say, "Hello" and to say, "Thanks for giving us a hand to get out,"' said Shane [13].

Paddy Hill recalled: 'I remember when I came in, he got up off the settee and he just threw his arms round me. And he just picked me up and he whirled me around the floor, and he said, "I'm so happy to see you out." I said, "So am I – so happy to be out."'

Some of the greatest songs ever written have undergone unexpected journeys. 'Fairytale Of New York' certainly took a circuitous route – from spurned album track to one of the most cherished Christmas songs in pop history. Had it come out a year or so earlier, it might have saved Stiff from folding. But it was the dusting-down of the song during recording sessions at RAK and the involvement of Steve Lillywhite that led to Shane and Jem's masterpiece being released.

There are different accounts of how The Pogues came to contribute to pop's festive songbook. Shane has said that, when Elvis Costello was producing their second album, he bet them they couldn't write a festive track without it being 'jingly-jangly, "Happy Christmas"' [14]. However, Jem's recollection is that the idea originally came from Frank Murray. 'There was a suggestion made to me by Frank Murray that it might be a good idea to do a Christmas song and he suggested a song by The Band ["Christmas Must Be Tonight"],' says Jem. 'I can remember saying it would be better if we wrote our own one.'

Jem wrote a Christmas duet about a sailor, but when he played it to his wife Marcia, she wasn't convinced. She suggested he go back to the drawing board and write about a couple having a row after the guy gambles away their money. Jem tried again and then showed the results to Shane. He suggested they set the story in New York and together they decided to write about two Irish immigrants who were down on their luck and reflecting on their unfulfilled dreams.

Shane and Spider's long-running obsession with *Once Upon a Time in America* also played a part in the song's development. The first notes of 'Deborah's Theme' from Ennio Morricone's stirring soundtrack were borrowed for the opening music of the first verse ('It was Christmas Eve, babe').

On the original demo, recorded during the sessions for *Rum Sodomy & The Lash*, Shane had duetted with Cait. There was then a discussion in the studio about what it should be called. Shane recalled: 'Costello said, "What are you going to call it? 'Christmas Eve in the Drunk Tank?' Amazing imagination that guy! No, that's not pretentious enough. Yes, "Fairytale Of New York"! I was looking at the book cover, *A Fairy Tale of New York*, y'know?' [15] Shane arranged to meet Irish American author J. P. Donleavy in Dublin and told him his dad Maurice was a great admirer of his work. He asked if he could use the title for the song in recognition of that.

In the event, the song didn't make it on to the album and wasn't released as a Christmas single. 'I don't know why Elvis Costello decided not to put it out as a single, but as a producer that was his shout,' said Shane. 'Cait did a great version of it.' [16] However, Shane was determined to complete it and he did this while suffering from a bout of pneumonia in the Swedish city of Malmö. 'You get the delirium and stuff and so I got quite a few really good images out of that,' he said [17].

The song finally complete, there was now the conundrum of who would sing the female parts. Cait was now living an entirely separate life away from the band, as Mrs Costello, and there was no obvious candidate. Until, that is, they got into the studio with Steve Lillywhite, who was married to singer-songwriter Kirsty MacColl.

Steve says: 'I took the tape home for Kirsty to do the vocal. Not for the record necessarily, but just as a trial, because I think the band had slightly loftier pretensions. It was like, "Well, we want Chrissie Hynde", or "We want so-and-so". But maybe because I was producing the album and Frank had managed Kirsty before, it was a case of, "Oh, let me take it home. I've got a studio at my house, I'll get Kirsty to do a vocal and then we can see what you think."

'Basically, Shane did a lead vocal singing all the parts and then he literally took the lyric sheet and ripped out the lines that he sung. He couldn't have ripped out Kirsty's lines because then she wouldn't have known what to sing. So, he ripped out his lines and handed me the piece of paper and said, "This is what she has to sing." So, we did that, and I spent a whole day on Kirsty's vocals and we really made sure every single note, every little nuance was in there, because it's a very difficult song to sing. Other people who have done covers of that song have certainly not done Kirsty's melody justice – her melody is very intricate, so we spent a long time working on it. I'm very proud of what I came up with for Kirsty. When we took it back to the studio, Shane listened to it and said, "I have to sing the part again," so he had pride. He thought he had done it before, but when he heard how good Kirsty was, he thought, Oh, I've got to up my game.'

Although large amounts of drink and drugs accompanied the recording sessions at RAK, The Pogues were deadly serious about the music they made. As well as being an unforgettable and timeless song, 'Fairytale Of New York' was testament to their dedication to getting things right. When it came to recording Shane, the producer drew on his experiences with other artists to draw out his best performance. 'Sometimes he was a little bit overwhelmed and couldn't really get a vocal and he couldn't sing a song he didn't really feel – like all singers, to be honest,' says Steve. 'I'd learned this trick very early on and it's part of my personality that I'm very empathetic to that sort of thing. I worked with Johnny Thunders on his first solo album and I absolutely had to get him at the right time. Even though at that time Shane wasn't anything like Johnny Thunders, you just have a sense of the right time, and I'm a good captain of the ship. That's what I am, and I think because I'm very confident in the studio, they would do what I asked them to do because the results showed for themselves.'

Ann Scanlon got to witness Shane redoing his vocals against the parts Kirsty had recorded at home, after being summoned to RAK Studios by Frank Murray.

'Steve Lillywhite said, "Ann, come and sit in the control booth with me," and we both listened to Shane and Kirsty's vocals. I said, "This is going to be the greatest Christmas record since "Lonely This Christmas", and it was a bit better than that one... She was such a musical genius herself, with her melodies. That song could not have been done with anyone but Kirsty.'

Another of the first people outside the band who got to hear the iconic record as the finishing touches were being added was veteran publisher and impresario Liam Teeling. He got a phone call one night and was told to get himself down to RAK Studios as soon as he could. What he saw and heard when he arrived has stayed with him: 'I arrived there and went in and Shane was lying in a pool of vomit on the floor. Terry Woods and Steve were standing at the desk and Steve moved this big chair away and sat me down. He pressed the button and I heard, "It was Christmas Eve, babe, in the drunk tank." It was incredible. The only other person who heard it was Chris O'Donnell and the two of us got together and it was mayhem because we both knew it was a stone-dead hit. I was almost in tears because being a publisher, it's not about how you play, it's about – what are you saying? Why do you make records? Why should anyone listen to you? That song goes straight into people's hearts and minds.'

'Fairytale' is a masterclass in storytelling. It is also the most incongruous of Christmas songs. Shane's characters aren't sitting by the fireside and sharing peace and goodwill on Christmas Eve. They are slumped in the drunk tank, musing bitterly on false promises ('You promised me Broadway was waiting for me') and unfulfilled lives ('I could have been someone'). The lyrics are classic Shane: the coarse language; the references to old Irish songs and literature; the focus on the human condition. In presenting New York through the eyes of two Irish immigrants, it doffed its cap to those who, for 250 years had been arriving at the gates of Ellis Island, carrying with them their hopes and dreams of a new and more prosperous life. Shane had not added another gaudy bauble to pop's Christmas tree, but a song of real substance.

'The world of "Galway Bay", the world of John Ford's *Quiet Man*, the world of an imagined Ireland is very much a diasporic world,' observed Martin Burke from City University of New York. 'And that's one that's heavily nostalgic and heavily sentimental and, bang – we're being hit up against this in the very song, where sentiment meets sadness.' [18]

Linda Dowling Almeida, from New York University, added: 'I think it's the timing of it: 1987 was really the peak period of new immigration out of Ireland to the United States. So that young generation of people who would be listening to Shane MacGowan and The Pogues and being in the bars, they relate to it on a very serious level.' [19]

If 'Fairytale Of New York' was to become the commercial success it deserved, however, timing was critical and Stiff ended up hastily putting it out in November 1987. Liam Teeling describes the events surrounding the record's release: 'We did a deal with Warner Bros. and we put it out on Pogue Mahone Records. But the original record came out on Stiff because we rushed it all through. We had the record and we raised a few quid to send the band to New York. Simon Ryan did all the artwork for Stiff and we put it out in a gatefold. I've got number 001. It was a great cover, with the bridge in New York and Spider. It was originally a photograph of Sammy Davis Jr., and Simon Ryan took Sammy Davies Jr.'s face off and put Spider's face on it...

'Later, I was at ZTT and I got a phone call out of the blue from Rob Dickens at Warner. He said to me, "What clearances did you get on that fucking photograph?"

'Pretending, I went, "Which photograph?"

*

'He said, "We're about to be sued by Getty Images," and it cost them a huge amount of money. Somebody came across that picture and the sleeve was put together with a scalpel.'

The record soared up the UK singles chart. All eyes were on it to see if it could emulate festive classics such as Slade's 'Merry Xmas Everybody' by claiming the coveted number one spot. It appeared at number forty on 5 December and was at number eight the week before Christmas. People from the band's circle started laying bets on it, including Frank Murray. 'Before it came out, I went to a bookies in Camden Town and I asked them what they were giving on the Christmas number one single,' he said. 'They said, "Who do you want to bet on?" and I said, "The Pogues." They said, "Who are they?" and I said, "Just put down The Pogues." So, they rang headquarters, and they gave me 50–1. And then one day I went in and it was 20–1, and I'd get braver every day and say, "I'll have a little bit more on that." [20]

'Fairytale' topped the Irish chart at Christmas, where it stayed for five weeks, and Shane was with his family in Tipperary for Radio 1's countdown to the UK number one. Siobhan MacGowan recalls: 'Shane came down here that year on Christmas Eve and we had a "Happy 'Fairytale'" cake for his birthday because it was number one in Ireland. We had a radio with a coat-hanger in it because it wouldn't work. So, we were listening to the English countdown to see if it was going to get to number one. Shane was sitting there, and we were all sitting around staring at the radio as if it would make it work. Then we heard "Fairytale of New York" was number two and the Pet Shop Boys' "Always On My Mind" was number one. "Always On My Mind" is one of the most beautiful songs ever written, but not by the Pet Shop Boys, who did a terrible job on it and robbed it of everything that's beautiful about it. Yet they got to number one. How the hell did that happen?'

Liam Teeling says 'Fairytale' was pressed and distributed by EMI, the label to which the Pet Shops Boys were signed, a scenario that played against them. 'We were vying for number one with the Pet Shop Boys and our distribution deal was with EMI Records,' he says. 'We couldn't print enough records and I got Monty Presky, the old Jewish boy who used to press all the old jazz records, to make some vinyl for us. We ordered some from Germany because EMI were pumping the shit out of the Pet Shop

Boys because they had them. We only had a pressing and distribution deal. So, did we get fucked? In my opinion, absolutely, without a doubt. EMI decided "Always On My Mind" was going to be number one.'

Being number one in his beloved Ireland, however, meant the world to Shane, says Terry O'Neill, The Pogues' publicist in Ireland. 'At the time this was really important to Shane,' says Terry. 'When he thanked me, he said, "Number one in Ireland. That's all that matters to me," and he really meant it.'

More than thirty years on and the popularity of 'Fairytale Of New York' has endured. It has become part of Christmas, played on radio stations and piped around shops, restaurants and bars the world over. It returned to the UK Top 40 in 1991 and has re-entered the Top 20 every December since 2005. In December 2012 it sold its millionth copy, making it the 126th million-selling single in the history of the British charts. A framed disc marking this achievement hangs proudly on the wall in Shane and Victoria's home in Dublin.

Artists who have covered the song include Ronan Keating and Moya Brennan, KT Tunstall and Ed Harcourt, Ed Sheeran and Anne-Marie, Jon Bon Jovi, and Christy Moore, who sang it solo. Although it has never topped the UK chart, it has been named as the best Christmas song of all time in numerous polls and each year people hearing it for the first time fall in love with it.

Shane's first cousin once removed, Lauren Mulvihill, who is now at university, attests to its lasting appeal. 'He's still popular among people of my age and at Christmas, when "Fairytale Of New York" comes on, it's crazy,' she says. 'It was Christmas time in fifth year and my music teacher started talking about "Fairytale Of New York" and I was like, "Oh sure, I'm cousins with Shane," and he's loved me ever since. He was so shocked.'

Shot in a real New York police station, the video was directed by Peter Dougherty during the week of Thanksgiving. Shane had a margarita confiscated when he tried to smuggle it in under his coat. Down in the cells, a real drunk tank developed as the band and their entourage got heavily boozed up as they waited to be called to perform. 'We nearly all got arrested as well because we did the jail scenes in the real nick and we were all getting really pissed,' said Shane [21]. The NYPD were livid at the scenes taking place in their own station and only the presence of a sober

Matt Dillon (who played a police officer) helped keep the peace. And even if the band had behaved, the New York Police Department's Pipes & Drums of the Emerald Society had loaded up their bus with beer and were reputedly already well-oiled by the time they arrived for the filming.

At one point in the video, Matt Dillon had to manhandle an inebriated Shane out of a bar and throw him in a cell. Cautious about how rough he should be with his friend, Shane just told him, 'Just fucking beat the shit out of me, push me through the fucking door and the thing's done, man. You're an actor, tsscchh. In the end he did it properly. It was great, tsscchh.' [22]

'Fairytale Of New York' didn't only do wonders for The Pogues but helped build the fragile confidence of Kirsty MacColl. She was crippled by stage fright, a situation not helped by Frank Murray having previously insisted she do a tour of Irish ballrooms to boost her solo career. She and Shane had recorded their vocals separately, but she got to know The Pogues during filming and promotion, and they managed to persuade her to perform it live with them.

Steve Lillywhite says: 'When it came to the tour, I remember Kirsty said to me, "Steve, they want me to come to Berlin to do one show with them." I said, "Great, that'll be good." Kirsty was very nervous on stage, but to not be the star and to come on to a song that everyone knew was a win-win whatever happened. So, she got really excited after the show. I remember her calling me up at home and saying, "Steve, do you mind if I stay for the rest of the tour?"

'Obviously, Kirsty had kids and could not be quite as bohemian, but she did have a little element of that. She was certainly a free spirit. I'm not at all – I'm just horribly middle-class. She got on great with Shane. I mean, Shane was always trying to shag her, and she said that. But it was always like, "Shane, don't be so stupid. I'm a married woman with two kids." But Shane felt he had to!'

Ann Scanlon says, 'She was part of the gang and when she came out everyone loved her. With that bit, "I could have been someone. Well, so could anyone," the audience were always on Kirsty's side. It was like, "How could you do that to our Kirsty?"'

'Fairytale Of New York' capped off an amazing year for the band and their popularity would never be greater. During the summer they had been

151

invited to support U2 on some of the dates of their *Joshua Tree* tour. As well as performing in front of seventy thousand people at Wembley Stadium, The Pogues performed to huge crowds at Croke Park in Dublin and in the USA: Sullivan Stadium, near Boston, and Madison Square Garden, New York. The love-in between The Pogues and America had reached new heights.

Fortuitously, Ann Scanlon was able to join up with Shane and the rest of the band when they supported U2 in New York. She had received a dream last-minute writing assignment – an interview with Tom Waits in Los Angeles – and before she left, she recalls, 'I went to The Devonshire because I was so excited, and Philip Chevron was at the bar. I said, "What are you up to?" and he said, "We're off to America tomorrow, we're supporting U2 at Madison Square Garden. What are you up to?" I told him and he said, "I want to be you!"

'Anyway, we got to LAX, and I looked at my plane ticket and realised I could change it. I said to the photographer Peter, "The Pogues are supporting U2 on Monday," and he said, "Just do it." I said, "Tony, my editor, will kill me," but he went, "Ann, just do it." I should have been at the printers, but I changed my ticket. I rang Tony up and I don't think he was pleased, but he forgave me a long time ago.

'Tom Waits' PR said I was going to meet him at this Mexican restaurant downtown. She said, "What are you doing? You can stay in the hotel another night."

'I said, "Well, actually, I'm going to go and see The Pogues."

'You know the way Tom Waits would put on personas? But I knew he wouldn't do that with me and that he'd be himself, which he was. He was really quite shy, and he said, "I hear you're off to see The Pogues. Will you take these presents?"

'He wrote Shane a note and gave him some dice that Peter Anderson took pictures of him with and then, for the rest of the band, he handed over a tape of Mexican music. So, of course, I arrive and I'm the most popular person there. "I've got a present from Tom Waits for you all..."'

Shane spent Christmas in Tipperary and reflected on an extraordinary year. The Pogues had made an album that was rich in sound and diverse in its influences and in 'Fairytale Of New York', Shane and Jem had written a stone-cold classic. The stadium shows they had performed had meanwhile underlined the scale and speed of their achievement: The Pindar of Wakefield to Madison Square Garden in less than four years.

But it had come at a cost. The almost non-stop touring was making Shane miserable and he was increasingly using drugs, especially speed, to keep going. Over the dark months ahead, people around him would notice an ominous change in his behaviour. For Siobhan, the brother she had always known and loved was about to disappear.

CHAPTER 7

St John Of Gods

'See the man
The crushed up man
With the crushed up Carrolls packet in his hand
Doesn't seem to see or care
Or even understand'

'St John Of Gods', **Shane MacGowan & The Popes**

The Samurai sword incident raised the bar of Shane's increasingly alarming behaviour. His friend and landlady Kathy MacMillan knew he had been taking huge amounts of LSD in his room. But it was this frightening episode that pushed her over the limit.

'One time I came up to his room and he had a Samurai sword,' says Kathy. 'I mean, when I look back now, I think I was a fool to let him have that, but you can't go to a grown adult and say, "You can't have that." Anyway, when I went in, he had slashed this chair. It was a really comfortable, nice, old-fashioned, Parker Knoll-type chair, and he had slashed it to ribbons. And that totally alarmed me because I thought, He could harm himself; he could harm somebody else; he could set the building on fire.

'He was not in a good state, he was falling apart, and I didn't want the responsibility. It wasn't what I signed up for at all. I didn't sign up to be the nanny, but I ended up doing that a lot. But when he was so far gone, I just didn't want to know, because I couldn't help him. I couldn't do anything.'

Normally she could get through to Shane but terrified about what he might do to himself or her, she picked up the phone and called Paul Ronan. He arrived and managed to calm Shane down. But the massive amounts of speed he was taking to deal with the pressures he was under meant he was becoming impossible to reach.

Victoria had also become troubled by his behaviour: 'He just freaked out on acid for a while – maybe twenty tabs a day. He was always tripping, all the time. It was very scary. It was hell on Earth.' [1]

Shane had needed somewhere to hide from the world and had asked Kathy if he could use her place as a bolthole. She agreed and he turned up on her doorstep sometime later with some carrier bags. That night he went out and returned with a group of friends – instantly making his new-found lodgings the worst kept secret in town. At one point, he lived in a spacious room at the top of the building, the entire floor invisible beneath a sea of bottles, glasses, ashtrays, cigarette packets and other detritus. If Kathy tried to clean it up, Shane would become irritated and start shouting, 'Leave it!'. And when his girlfriend Julie Walsh occasionally called to the Cromer Street flat he was still renting to clean up the devastation, she was met with an equally furious response.

The relentless demands of touring were taking their toll, physically and mentally, and tensions between Shane and Frank Murray had reached breaking point. Shane wanted out of the group. But he would cut off a leg rather than confront a situation, and his solution was to hole himself up at Kathy's and use speed, acid and whatever else to expunge his problems.

'This battle between him and Frank had been going on for a long time and Shane's way of dealing with it was to fight with Frank and take more drugs and booze,' says Kathy.

One night after being out all night, Shane went back to his room at Kathy's. He put on *Madam Butterfly* and started dropping acid tabs, precipitating a trip during which he started eating a Beach Boys' *Greatest Hits* record. Shane recalled: 'Kathy knocked on my door and my mouth was covered in blood and she said that Frank Murray was on the phone and I had to be somewhere, and I said, "Go away, can't you see I'm involved in the future of the world here?" She knew I'd flipped my lid when I threw my green guitar, my favourite guitar, down the stairs after her.' [2]

Kathy comments: 'It wasn't a healthy situation because I could normally communicate with Shane, but sometimes he was so out of it on acid that he would frighten me. He had this green guitar and how much respect he had for his guitar was my benchmark. At one point, I don't know if he threw it down the stairs or if it fell, but he treated the guitar disrespectfully. When he was that bad, I used to have to phone Paul Ronan because I couldn't deal with it. Jimi Hendrix used to live in the mews behind the house. So, Shane would be up in his ivory tower and he would be taking acid all night, and Hendrix would be there with him and he would talk to Hendrix.'

Kathy phoned Victoria this time, in the middle of the night, and asked her to come over. She arrived to find blood pouring from Shane's mouth and him holding the record he had literally bitten chunks from. Victoria recalled: 'He told me that he had taken fifteen or twenty tabs of acid earlier in the evening and had become convinced that the third world war was taking place and that he, as the leader of the Irish Republic, was holding a summit meeting in his kitchen between the heads of state of the world superpowers: Russia, China, America and Ireland. In order to demonstrate the cultural inferiority of the United States, he was eating a Beach Boys album.' [3]

If there were signs that Shane's mental health was failing, the sight that greeted Frank Murray when Shane opened the door to his hotel room in New Zealand left him in no doubt that he needed professional help. The group had embarked on a month-long tour of Australia and New Zealand in January 1988 and it was amid the Antipodean heat that alarm bells about his sanity rang louder than ever.

Shane's erratic behaviour was hardly a news story. But it was getting worse. Other band members had been patient down the years, but they were being sorely tested, especially when it affected the group's performance. Audience members might not have minded what state Shane was in. In fact, some seemed to turn up wanting to see him wasted. But it was a problem some of the band could no longer overlook and after a show in New Zealand he was met with a volley of criticism in the dressing room. Sound engineer Paul Scully rarely lost his cool, but even he was at the end of his tether and increasingly concerned for Shane.

Philip Chevron said: 'Paul Scully came backstage shouting, "Is this how it's going to be? You're just going to watch the guy die in front of your eyes?" It was the tensest it's ever been. That's how it was increasingly coming across, as being that on the edge... Paul went into a corner and wept and then he started talking to Shane. Everybody was taking off in a different direction to cry on each other's shoulders and at 4 a.m. have that conversation in the hotel room yet again – "What's the matter with this band?" We were in ever-decreasing circles of hell.' [4]

Back in his own hotel room in Christchurch, Shane was otherwise occupied. He had taken to bringing pots of paint around with him on tour and during the early hours of the morning, driven by copious amounts of speed, he went into a creative frenzy.

Joey Cashman recalls: 'I went to art school and he does drawing. So, we were on the floor and we had all those pens with indelible ink and these huge pads. I said, "I'm going to have to get some kip, at least a couple of hours," and I fucked off. I came round in the morning and Shane had painted himself with the indelible ink. He'd painted himself blue and the whole room, even the mirror – everything was blue.

'Frank said, "Where's Shane, what's keeping him?" and I said, "Maybe you should have a look yourself." He went ballistic! When I see Shane painting himself and the room blue, I go, "This is quite cool" because I'm ex-art school and I can see a sort of abstract attraction to the décor, whereas Frank didn't know art from a hole in the ground and didn't really appreciate the finer points. That's probably the same attitude the owner would have, although that owner probably called it the Shane MacGowan Room and charges more for people to stay there now!'

Why had Shane done it? He explained: 'This particular night I started getting a very strong, totally real feeling that the Maoris were talking to me. You see, you talk to yourself in your head when you're speeding and you get turned into two people, who talk to each other in your head.' [5]

Siobhan MacGowan was close to the band at this time and was also worried about her brother's worsening state of mind. She was working for The Pogues from Frank's office near Camden tube station, writing and editing the fanzine, *The Ordnahone Missal*, doing admin and going to gigs. A few years later she worked as personal assistant for Van Morrison, travelling with him around Europe and the United States.

Shane's mum Therese absolutely doted on him, and Siobhan tried as much as possible to shield her and Maurice from what was going on. Unlike Shane, Siobhan didn't shy away from situations and, as reports reached her of his deteriorating mental health, she was deeply concerned. By the time he returned from a world tour in the summer of 1988, she knew he was utterly lost and in need of urgent help.

'I was living in Dublin and Shane came over,' says Siobhan. 'We went to a Hothouse Flowers gig and he was there, painted all black-and-white and talking rubbish. He tried to get me to drink a huge concoction of shit. I thought, "He's gone," because he would never do that to me. Then, when we were going back in the car, he threw all his money out the window and he said, "Look, look, money, money." Later, he was on the floor and I called Dr [Niall] Joyce, Shane's doctor, and he said, "If your brother goes on like this, he will have six months to live." I was about 24 and at that age I took it very literally. I said, "Oh Christ."'

With his family, friends and bandmates all at the end of their tether, things came to a head when the group attended sound engineer Dave Jordan's wedding in Youghal, County Cork. During the reception, Frank Murray tried to introduce Shane to Liam Clancy, a hero of Shane's from the world of Irish music. But Shane simply offered a limp handshake and barely acknowledged him, leaving Liam feeling awkward and embarrassed.

Later, after Shane and others had travelled up to Dublin, Frank heard he had painted his face again and he was causing trouble at a nightclub. He had also been seen swallowing a handful of ecstasy tablets. What Frank didn't know yet was that Shane had tried to jump out of a moving car as he was being driven to the apartment Siobhan and their cousin Carmel were sharing in Donnybrook, Dublin. When Shane got there, he had locked himself in a room and refused to come out. Frank rushed to Dublin and was shaken by Shane's appearance when he got there. He took him outside and started remonstrating with him in the street. He then spoke to Terry O'Neill and the two of them decided enough was enough. A doctor was called.

Siobhan describes the upsetting events that followed: 'We called the doctors and talked about committing him. Frank Murray came around and said, "Don't do it, Siobhan, don't do it. I'll get him into a hospital in London."

'I said, "What are you going to do? Are you going to get him on a plane like this and get him into a hospital in London? Are you really going to do it, Frank?" He admitted he wouldn't. It was just dreadful. I committed him, and we went in the ambulance together. They strapped him in, and I really wished they hadn't done that. We were in the ambulance and Shane looked at me and said, "I knew you were stupid, but I didn't know you were this stupid."

'I said, "Look, Shane, I'm doing what Phil Lynott's sister wishes she had done." He didn't answer that. We went to the hospital and they kept

159

saying, "Is he psychotic?" I said, "I don't know. I think he is, but it's drug induced. He's not mad." The emotional strain was absolutely brutal. I had a breakdown after that incident. The irony is he's got a massive sense of self-preservation, so the last person he would want to hurt is himself.'

The parallels with Thin Lizzy's charismatic singer and bassist were particularly painful for Frank Murray, who had been Lynott's manager and friend. The charismatic musician and frontman had become a hopeless drug addict. After a massive drink and drug binge at his home in Surrey on Christmas Day 1985 he collapsed and was taken to hospital with serious kidney and liver failure. He died from heart failure and pneumonia on 4 January 1986, aged 36.

Frank went to see Shane after he was committed to St John Of God, a large psychiatric hospital in Stillorgan, County Dublin. Shane was livid at being sectioned and was demanding that he sign himself out. Not long after, his family received a call saying he had tried to jump out of a window. But after a few days he calmed down and decided that a charm offensive might get him out sooner.

The drama had placed an unbearable strain on his relationship with Siobhan. But for all the anger directed towards her, he wanted her to visit him. 'Shane's a funny one, because he's blaming you in one way and forgiving you in the same breath,' she remarks. 'I thought he wouldn't want to see me in hospital. But I got a call from him the next day and he said, "Are you coming up?" I said, "Well, you know I've just put you in hospital," and he said, "It doesn't mean you can't come and see me." So, I went up and saw him. When I got there, he was craving sugar, and he was really angry with me. He said, "Right, I want you to get me some stuff." I said, "Yeah, right." And he said, "I want ten Kit-Kats," and I just laughed because I thought he was going to ask me to get him drugs, but he wanted ten Kit-Kats, and he said it really angrily.

'That's where our relationship went pretty wrong, actually. I didn't even understand what had happened there myself. He probably didn't quite understand what had happened or where I was coming from. I got a lot of blame from the music business, although Mum and Dad backed me up... Shane said to Mum years later, "I do understand what Siobhan did." But he was angry because on his next album he wrote "Cotton Fields": "They're gonna crucify you," and that was all about that. Shane didn't see it as it really was. I don't think he saw it as a complete act of love. Maybe he did, but he didn't want to see it as that. He was acting out so much, he was almost crying out for it. I think there were a lot of conflicting things going on there. It was a very difficult time and I think it took him a long time to forgive me.'

In an interview the following summer, Shane said of 'Cotton Fields': 'It's a private joke between me and an Irish hospital… Nah, actually I wrote it for Bruce Springsteen thinking he could do a good Elvis job on it. 'Cos it's meant to be about a guy who's washed up; he might have done quite a lot, but he's fucked now. Goes home to commune with his roots and they fucking crucify him!' [6]

His inner hurt at his family's decision to have him locked up was underlined almost ten years later in a song on The Popes' album *The Crock Of Gold*. 'St John Of Gods' began: 'See the man / The crushed up man / With the crushed up Carrolls packet in his hand / Doesn't seem to see or care / Or even understand'. In case there would be any doubt as to who he was writing about, the inner sleeve featured a photo of Maurice in the middle of the lyrics.

Jem Finer comments: 'If someone signs you into an institution, it's not necessarily what you think is best, it's what someone else thinks is best for you. I guess Shane has always had a strong feeling of conflict between what he thinks is best for himself and what other people think is best for him.'

When Shane was eventually discharged, it was agreed his cousin Carmel would accompany him back to London. But they never got out of Dublin Airport. Shane started necking Long Island iced teas after their flight was delayed. Then he launched an unprovoked attack on a man and barged into a woman. She was not prepared to let the matter drop and told the airport police she wanted to press charges. Shane was given a stark choice: he could either go to Mountjoy prison or St John Of God. Back in hospital, he found the doctors' attitudes had hardened and only by agreeing to take part in Narcotics Anonymous therapy sessions did he stand any chance of being discharged again.

Getting Shane out of Ireland and back to the UK would prove no easier second time around, as his exasperated father would discover. His drunken antics first time around had attracted the attention of the Gardaí and, although the complainant withdrew the charges, they were now taking a keen interest in St John Of God's celebrated patient.

'I had a fucking job getting him out of John Of Gods,' admits Maurice. 'I was living in England then. My brother Billy rang me and said, "You'd better come over here and get that son of yours out." I had to talk to the head man there because they weren't too keen to let him go. They had the law on their backs. Billy had a word with the top people and then I saw the head man and he said, "You have to get him out of here and don't let him come back for a while and don't go on an ordinary plane. You'll have to organise something else." So, I had to get a private plane. I organised a taxi and we all got into it. There was Dr Niall Joyce, myself and Shane. We had a private plane booked at Baldonnel airport to get him back. But we ran into a traffic jam in the town and Shane jumped out of the car and went in some place and got an ice cream!'

They did in the end manage to complete the trip and get on the plane. When they landed in London, where Shane's friend Charlie MacLennan was waiting for them, Shane was booked into a private centre near the King's Road. But he kept signing himself out and people were bringing him drugs. So it was decided to move him to The Priory, the rehab centre in south-west London renowned for treating celebrities.

Victoria had missed all the drama. She had stormed back to London after finding Shane in bed, virtually comatose, with a female fan. The Pogues had performed at the RDS in Dublin the night before and afterwards she had gone to stay with her sister. 'In the morning I got the chambermaid to open the door back at Blooms Hotel and I found him in bed with a girl,' she said. 'I went mental. I left him but after a while, back in London I got a call to say he'd been admitted to St John Of Gods. He did a lot of grovelling.' [7] It wasn't the only time she had caught Shane with a groupie. 'I did catch him with other women,' she confessed. 'The first time I behaved with great dignity, I think. It was on the tour bus in France. I found Shane sitting with this girl and, um, they proceeded to get off with one another that night in front of me. They went back to the hotel and slept together right next to my room.' [8]

After Shane came out of rehab in the autumn of 1988, Victoria gave him an ultimatum. If he couldn't be monogamous, it was over. Chastened, he agreed and asked her to go on the road with him. 'I used to go off on tour and leave her behind for ages,' he said. 'That was horrible. I missed her. In the end I started fucking paying for her to come on tour with me, 'cos I couldn't handle the separations any more… I hated it for the last four years, but she helped me… I had to go into hospital several times, but she comes to see me. She doesn't leave me there to rot.' [9]

The Pogues' fourth album, *Peace And Love*, had a deliberately ironic title. There was precious little of either around during the recording and the camp was now riven with dissent. What had started as a band of brothers had degenerated into a severely dysfunctional family. Much of the discontent arose from the disproportionate amount of attention Shane was receiving compared with the rest of the group and how much democracy there was when it came to decision-making. Shane was also becoming more unpredictable, forgetting lyrics on stage or even singing a completely different song from the band, and seemed to be in a parallel universe of drugs and acid house music. At the same time, other band members were wrestling with their own addictions and inner demons.

The real elephant in the room was that Shane wanted out. When he returned from the *If I Should Fall From Grace With God* world tour, midway through 1988, Siobhan had asked him what was wrong. His response was unequivocal: 'I want to leave. I can't handle it.'

'Well, leave,' she implored.

'I can't,' he replied. 'I can't let them down.'

His desire to quit had come as a surprise to her. The Pogues had enjoyed their biggest hit with 'Fairytale Of New York' and were playing to large audiences around the world. The third album had been hailed a triumph and the group had developed and honed an exciting new sound. Siobhan was still working for the band at the time and, believing she might help the situation, she decided to tell Frank Murray. It was to prove a mistake.

Siobhan says: 'Frank just attacked me. He was taking a lot of coke at the time. He said, "You're a fucking lunatic, your brother's a fucking lunatic…"

'Frank was terrified of losing him. I mean they had just made it huge and Shane wanted to leave. Now, I think if Shane had left then of his own accord, you'd see a very different Shane today. I think what happened was he went on with that treadmill and he never came back from there. He changed. He took more and more drugs, more and more drink, and became more and more aggressive and unreachable – basically trying to throw himself out of the band, which is what they did eventually. So, it took him three years to get out of it.

'That's what Shane does. If Shane wants to get out of a situation, he doesn't take the bull by the horns. I think, instead of dealing with a difficult situation, he'll create a scenario that will bring about what he needs or wants, i.e. getting out of the band. He felt very responsible for them, of course he did. He knew that they were counting on him and he didn't want to let them down. But then he made it impossible for them to carry on with him.'

Darryl Hunt corroborates this view: 'He wanted to leave the group for a long time and he'd often get into a state where he tried to express it through his behaviour, just getting completely out of it and making it unworkable. But he didn't want to stand up and say, "I'm leaving because I don't need this anymore," because he thought that would let everybody down. So, he was trapped between two stools, and he ended up being like a caged animal, not knowing which way to turn. "I'm not happy. I don't want to let everybody down. I'm just going to scream instead and see if anybody notices."'

A thick layer of cocaine coated *Peace And Love* and this was cited as one of the reasons for the hotchpotch of ideas and songs being thrown into the mix at RAK Studios. Shane, though, wasn't using coke. He was taking acid and ecstasy and wanted to make an acid-house record. At one point, he tried to record a twenty-minute drum-machine track over which he continually shouted, 'You've got to contact yourself'.

'It was very evident that Shane was going completely in the wrong direction, taking way too many drugs and drinking too much,' commented Philip. 'It was a way of coping with things. He was a shy man who never wanted to find himself in the position he was in. It took him many, many years to be comfortable with being "that Shane MacGowan".' [10]

Recalling the first day of recording, James Fearnley said: 'Shane arrived at the studio, took one step into that control room from the corridor and released the contents of his stomach into a wastepaper bin. He sat on the side of the room struggling to take us all in, a meek expression on his face.' [11]

Victoria vividly remembers Shane's acid phase. She says he became completely immersed in it and was writing new material for the record while tripping, something other members of The Pogues found difficult. 'He was listening to a lot of acid-house music and he was going to acid-house clubs all the time and taking acid all the time,' she says. 'So, he started writing things that were very far out. Even "Summer In Siam", when he first did it, everybody thought, What the fuck is this pile of crap? because he was doing it on a little Casio thing, and he was off his face. He wrote the entire album completely off his face, but none of them were doing acid.

'So, I think they thought it was quite scary and weird and not The Pogues. They thought he was completely insane, which probably he technically was. He was wearing T-shirts that were all multi-coloured and his hair was grown, and he was just mental. He latched on to that because it was like, "Wow, this is really trippy." But they couldn't really handle it because they gave a shit. How did the performance come across? Was it good, did the audience like it? But he never gave a shit. It was like, "No, we're just doing this. We're channelling, man..."

'That's why with some of the songs he wrote, they were like, "Go and do that yourself." They hated "Yeah, Yeah, Yeah, Yeah, Yeah", which is a brilliant song. They thought it was too simple and maybe because it was very different to the previous stuff. So, it was like The Beatles in their *Sgt. Pepper* phase.'

Shane was withdrawing from songwriting and was no longer collaborating as well with Jem as he had done on *If I Should Fall From Grace With God*. Just six of Shane's compositions made it into the final fourteen tracks: 'White City', 'Cotton Fields', 'Down All The Days', 'USA', 'Boat Train' and 'London You're A Lady'. Jem wrote three of the tracks on his own – 'Misty Morning, Albert Bridge', 'Tombstone' and 'Night Train To Lorca' – and collaborated with Andrew on the opening instrumental 'Gridlock'. Terry Woods contributed 'Gartloney Rats' and combined with Ron Kavana on 'Young Ned Of The Hill'. 'Lorelei' fell from the pen of Philip, who also collaborated with Darryl on 'Blue Heaven'.

Shane's voice was noticeably more fragile this time around, which meant his vocals had to be supplemented by others. Terry and Philip provided lead vocals on the tracks they had written. Steve Lillywhite admits: 'Shane's voice was weak, and I always say that my big mistake on *Peace And Love* was hearing Shane's voice being weak and therefore making it very quiet in the mix. And, actually, I find that by mixing something that's not very good down a bit, you actually make it sound worse than it really is. His singing wasn't great and then, of course, there were songs that should never have been on there... It wasn't as strong. All the things that landed butter-side up on *Fall From Grace* ended up butter-side down on *Peace And Love*.'

Jem comments: 'Shane has always had the propensity to hang out with certain people who weren't great for him and, actually, for a while in the band there was a culture encouraged and facilitated for making a lot of substances readily available, which was very damaging not only to Shane, but to other people and to the music as well. *Peace And Love* is a consequence of far too much cocaine if you ask me, and a lot of people starting to think they were better and things were easier than they were.'

Like the curate's egg, the album was good in parts. 'White City' was an excellent addition to Shane's London songbook, a paean to the famous greyhound stadium which was demolished in 1985 and developed by the BBC, before itself leaving the site in the mid-2010s. '"White City" is so brilliantly written,' says Darryl, 'and I was just playing root notes in the studio. Shane says, "Why don't you play in between them?" and he hummed it to me, so he had a bit of Brian Wilson about him as well.' Shane had written it after trudging past the derelict site in the rain on his way to do *Top of the Pops*. 'I was sitting there at the BBC bar getting pissed and it came out,' he said [12].

'Misty Morning, Albert Bridge' didn't do it for Steve Lillywhite, who saw it as '"Fairytale" by numbers'. Musically, though, it was one of the most memorable songs and it got the nod for the first single, with 'White City' following it out of the traps. Shane was full of praise for it. 'It's such a brilliant, beautiful ballad,' he said. 'I couldn't have written that.' [13] 'Down All The Days', which featured Kathy MacMillan's typewriter, was a tribute to disabled Dublin writer and painter Christy Brown and was used on the soundtrack of the biopic *My Left Foot*.

'Lorelei' was a stirring ballad about the siren of Germanic legend whose singing was said to lure boatmen on the River Rhine to their deaths on the rocks. Kirsty MacColl harmonised with Philip Chevron to mesmerising effect, ensuring the track lingered in the memory long after it had faded out.

Many of the songs careered along with a boundless energy that belied the fatigue within the group and there were positive notices in the press, *Q* magazine awarding it four stars. 'If MacGowan's ability to see clearly during times of profound intoxication remains The Pogues' strongest suit, their increasingly textured arrangements suggest a band that still delights in its craft,' said the review.

Sounds writer Keith Cameron, however, said the album was a 'definite letdown compared to the towering brilliance of last year's *If I Should Fall From Grace With God*', and he heard 'the sound of a band hanging on in there, punch-drunk and on the ropes, with only the occasional uppercut recalling their recent golden days'.

A party to toast the album's release was held in the backroom of The Boston Arms in Tufnell Park, north London, the scene of their first rehearsal with Terry. Plenty of well-known faces turned up: Bob Geldof, Joe Strummer and Paul Simonon from The Clash, and former Thin Lizzy guitarist Brian Robertson among them. Shane was on terrific form, wheeling erratically around the bar and revelling in the throbbing acid-house music he had insisted on.

The previous evening, the band had been interviewed by *Q*'s Adrian Deevoy [14] in a pub in south London. They were playing pool and killing time before recording a live performance for the short-lived Channel 4 youth show *Club X*. The Pogues had long become weary of the media's obsession with their drinking and its hackneyed representation of the band in general. Some of the exchanges during the interview suggested their tolerance of journalists was wearing dangerously thin. Spider railed against people who still saw The Pogues as 'a drunken novelty act even now, after four albums and seven years and Christ knows how many successful tours'. Shane vented his spleen at the press for depicting them as cartoon drunks. 'Most papers are a waste of time,' he ranted. 'A waste of trees. Futile. I'd rather read a tree. You even get bowel cancer if you use those papers as toilet roll.'

By way of riposte, Adrian Deevoy said the band were remarkably naive when it came to their public image. Shane would drink heavily during interviews and then complain bitterly when this was reported. Glasses were cleared from tables ahead of the photo session for his article, but as soon as the cameras were put down it was 'doubles all round'. He recounted an interview Shane had recently agreed to do with the *Sunday Times* during which he was accompanied by three friends he had met in the street. 'After ruining what slim chance there was for an interview and running up a £52 drinks bill, one of these friends – a knicker salesman by trade – rounded on the journalist, telling him he "knew fuck-all about rock'n'roll" and should therefore "fuck off".'

The day after the launch at the Boston Arms, they were bound for the west coast of America to support rock royalty. Bob Dylan had asked them to perform on six dates of his Never-Ending Tour, starting in Berkeley and winding up in Los Angeles. After that, The Pogues had a headline tour of their own that would take them across the US.

Bob Dylan was said to be an admirer of The Pogues, having been introduced to them by his son Jesse. Shane seemed interested in the prospect of meeting the legendary songwriter, admitting that he would love The Pogues to play 'Love Minus Zero/No Limit' with him. 'Never Mind Dylan and The Dead,' he said. 'Dylan and The Pogues. Dylan and The Nearly Dead!' But he was also dismissive of Dylan's more recent work. 'You can't really hear the lyrics anymore,' he moaned. 'He was really good on lyrics. But he's hard to keep track of. One week he's into God, the next week it's something else. Listen, I don't blame the guy for maturing and turning his back on everything. He's entitled to do that. But with his early stuff people were really listening to it.' [15]

The night Shane was due to fly to California, his family were over in London. He spent the evening at a hotel near Heathrow Airport with, among others, his dad Maurice and Charlie MacLennan, and the old Irish spirit poitín was said to have been consumed. There are several versions of what happened next, but what is not in dispute is that the following morning, Shane was still out of his mind with drink and banned from boarding the flight. 'I saw Shane being dragged into the airport by two people and I just went, "There's no way he's getting on the fucking plane,"' recalls Joey Cashman.

Frank Murray was rightly incensed, as were the rest of the group, who faced being left to support one of the most revered names in music without their own singer. But it was still early in the morning in the UK and Frank found out there was another flight at six o'clock that evening. He told Charlie MacLennan to get Shane into a hotel room and back to the airport well in time.

Shane never made the flight or indeed the next. Charlie's story was that Shane went to the toilet and vanished, before later going back to the airport. Shane claimed he and Charlie had tried to get on a plane for three days in a row. But in fact, he had taken himself back to Kathy MacMillan's and holed himself up there until the Dylan gigs were over.

Kathy describes what happened: 'It was the middle of the afternoon and my doorbell rang. I went to open the door and Shane literally fell in – he just collapsed in front of me. He was such a mess. I've seen him look really bad, but never as bad as he looked that day. I really was concerned for him. I helped him up and said, "What are you doing here? You're supposed to be in America, what's going on?" But I couldn't get any sense out of him and that was the beginning of a very hellish period, the only really bad period I had with him to be honest.

'Frank was already in America and his wife Ferga started phoning up the flat looking for Shane. But Shane was saying, "I'm not talking to anybody. If anybody asks, I'm not here." So, suddenly I'm stuck between them. I'd known Ferga for a very long time and I felt terrible. He was letting everybody down, but he didn't really have that much of a choice because if he had gone to America, he'd have fucked up anyway.'

On the other side of the Atlantic, Frank believed Shane had deliberately acted up in front of Kathy, professing to be too tired and ill to travel. This line was something to which women were particularly susceptible, he said. While Kathy accepts Shane didn't want to do the shows with Bob Dylan, she also says Frank worked the band 'into the ground'. Shane didn't really want out of the band completely, she says, but needed 'the nature of the band to slow down'. The Dylan debacle was the final showdown in Shane and Frank's marathon battle of wills.

'Shane one hundred per cent didn't want to go – he made that really clear,' says Kathy. 'It was a build-up. Frank and Shane were going up against each other, it was the alpha male struggle and both of them were used to getting their own way; two charismatic guys. I think Frank thought Shane would want to support Bob Dylan because it was such an honour to be asked. But Shane called his bluff. He made sure he was so drunk they wouldn't let him on the plane. Then he was escorted off and Maurice was there. Maurice said, "That's my son. I'll look after him."

'Maurice and Therese had been coming to London quite a lot around then to try and help Shane or make things better. But Shane didn't want the help, sadly. They used to come and ring the bell and he would say, "Don't open the door, don't answer the phone." There had to be a secret code when people phoned or rang the bell. He wouldn't let Maurice in, and he would just be ringing all these different combinations. Awful, isn't it?'

To make matters worse for The Pogues, they couldn't access their instruments when they arrived in California. 'Charlie MacLennan needed to sign for our equipment at an airport, so we had no equipment to play with,' says James. They had landed on Labor Day, a public holiday, and had to scamper around for replacements in the hours before the opening show. 'Friends of Terry Woods went out into Marin County looking for accordions and banjos and stuff like that and then these things would arrive while we were actually playing the opening set at Berkeley University. Charlie obviously went away again, but I can't remember when he came to join us on the tour, and we got all our gear. I rather think that Charlie must have got the next flight out or got one the next day, so there was no excuse for Shane not to have come.'

Jem comments: 'It was a real shame really. It would have been nice to do proper Pogues gigs with Shane singing. But we just had to do Pogues gigs with Spider singing. It wasn't unprecedented that Shane would not turn up or would walk off the stage, so we were used to coping with that. But that was not the way it was meant to be. It was always stressful actually and a bit depressing. It was unfathomable. You would think Shane would have wanted to perform on the same bill as Bob Dylan, from the point of view that most people would like to do that. But really, I have given up trying to second-guess his reasons for doing or not doing things. He seems to be singularly prone to just doing exactly what he feels with often little regard to the consequences or his responsibilities towards other people. With hindsight, one had to accept that you were never going to turn him into a model citizen, and he was the singer of the band and without him it wasn't the same. So, you either had to put up with all that nonsense or not.'

Bob Dylan saw so little of The Pogues over the six shows that he probably wasn't even aware that Shane didn't turn up, laughs Joey. 'Nobody told Dylan – he thinks Shane toured with him!', he says. 'We all looked the same in those days. We all dressed the same, looked the same, haircuts and age and everything, and there's fucking eight in the band. When Dylan comes off stage, he shakes my hand and says, "Great show," and I'm going, "Thanks!"'

Shane flew to America several days later, to join the headline tour, but it wasn't without a fight. 'When he finally got on a plane it took four people to escort him and he screamed all the way to Dallas,' said Victoria [16]. Shane's alibi was that various airlines had frustrated his repeated attempts to get to the US on the grounds he was drunk. Some in the band were more accepting of this explanation than others. Yet no one had a go at him. James Fearnley says: 'It was like, "Well, it's too late to say anything about that. Let's carry on with the fucking tour..." But interesting that somebody like Bob Dylan should seek a band like ours out to give us a leg of his tour and MacGowan would not show up for it. There's got to be something playing there.'

Only hours after arriving, Shane caused another drama. A cigarette was apparently dropped in his hotel room, setting off the fire alarm, and guests were hastily led out of the building and had to wait in the car park. On route to the University of Michigan, the band stopped at a bar in Ann Arbor where Shane got wasted on Long Island iced teas and called the barman a 'dago cunt' when he couldn't understand what he was ordering. He was so out of it after the gig that he had to be carried from the dressing room by his bandmates and dumped on a sofa at the back of the tour bus. What might have once been indulged was becoming maddening.

Shane and Joey had become close, partying hard together, and the no-nonsense Dubliner was often relied on to dig Shane out of his flat or hotel room and on to the tour bus. Kicking the door with his Dr. Marten boots proved the most effective way of rousing Shane from his slumber and when Shane tested his patience beyond what he could stand, Joey pulled no punches.

Joey recounts one such episode: 'We were in Germany and had to make it to an airport. Shane was awake when I went down to the lobby and had probably been up all night. He said, "I'd like to get something to eat," and I said I'd sort it out. There was a really plush restaurant across the road, and I knew they probably wouldn't let him in [on his own]. So, I went with him and got a table and the menu, and everything sorted out. He said, "Thanks, thanks. Get me some wine and some this-and-that,' and I did that. Then I went off to get the other wankers onto this mad bus and when I came back, I said, "Right, we're all ready. We want to go now."

'In the meantime, Shane had got really drunk, and it's usually in the early stages of being drunk when he's a real cunt. After that, he becomes cool again. So, he's sitting back and hitting the plate with his cutlery and saying, "I don't give a fuck."

'And I said, "Oh, you don't give a fuck, do you not?"

'And you know like when you're a kid and you pull another kid's coat over them and they can't do anything? So, I grabbed his clothes, pulled them over his head, kicked the table aside and pulled him right through the restaurant. Tables, chairs, glasses, meals are going flying, the chefs are coming out from the back. The Germans are all upper-class, and saying, "Oh my God, what is this?"

'Meanwhile, I'm punching him, kicking him and going, "You ignorant, fucking cunt, you ungrateful wanker." Then I got him up against the bus and I'm really good at kung-fu and I kicked him. I made sure I stopped just at his chin and I would have loved to have continued with that kick. He was taller than me at that time, believe it or not. He was scared shitless, and then I grabbed him and threw him towards the doors, "Get the fuck in there, you wanker."

'Fifteen minutes later, he came back and said, "I'm really sorry, Joey" and I said, "Oh, who gives a fuck? Let's have a drink!"'

Airports were a minefield with Shane. Other band and crew members braced themselves before passing through departure lounges, passport controls and the boarding gates. Terry Woods knew better than to sit near Shane, especially on a long-haul flight, and would try to find somewhere a safe distance away.

He recalls an episode which happened as The Pogues flew to Scandinavia: 'There were two seats in a row and Shane was on the outside and a little old lady in a blue suit and with a little blue handbag was by the window. The hostess came around and he ordered a bottle of wine, a glass of milk, a cup of coffee – so there was a selection of stuff on his little tray. I know the way he is, and I can tell you he falls asleep after it takes off. But when he wakes up, he always wakes up really suddenly. So, I was sitting there, and I was trying to attract the roadie's attention to come down and clear his tray before he woke up. I failed. He woke up with a start and the red wine and the milk went all over the woman – she was destroyed by the time she got off the plane. I mean it's funny, but it wasn't funny for her.'

Maybe Shane should have left The Pogues after the recording of *Peace And Love*. Years later, he would say he 'didn't think there was a way out' [17] and, despite the rapidly deteriorating situation, no one offered him one. Instead, with gritted teeth, they ploughed on and did everything they knew to keep Shane on board. The other band members had people back home who were dependent on them and, frustrations aside, it was a job they largely enjoyed. The Pogues had spent seven years building up a huge fanbase. From France and Germany to Japan and Australia, they were greeted as returning heroes, and to throw that all away after investing so much was unthinkable. To kick Shane out would have been to risk sabotaging everything they had worked for.

Shane wasn't the only cause of the building resentment. Frank Murray had been responsible for the merciless tour schedule that had brought them to their knees with exhaustion. His failure to give the band any respite from the blur of airports, buses, hotels and venues is blamed by many people in and around the group as the reason for its demise. This situation was especially difficult for Terry Woods. He and Frank had known each other for many years, and it was Frank who had brought him into The Pogues. But Frank's obdurate refusal to give the band a break was threatening to destroy it and testing his relationship with his old friend. So too was Frank's own escalating cocaine addiction.

Terry says: 'We were all chaotic then. There was an awful lot of drink and substances going around. At that point, we were touring a great deal when we didn't have to, and we didn't know that. We didn't know we were earning the money we were earning because we weren't getting it. So, we had the impression that we had to keep working and, unfortunately, Frank was my friend. Frank and I had been friends and working together one way or the other since I was in Sweeney's Men. I had known him for years and it upset me, and I used to have rows with him. I mean, the two of us wrecked a hotel room in Tokyo. Rather than punching each other, we were wrecking the hotel while I was having rows with him over the way he was treating the band and saying he needed to cop on. He didn't cop on and then eventually the shit hit the fan, he got really annoyed with me and we fell out over it for a couple of years. Then we made up because there had been too much water under the bridge for us to carry it on.'

By 1989 nothing had changed. Shane was still in the group that he wanted to leave, and the touring juggernaut rolled interminably on. Shane's way of coping was to blot it out with enormous amounts of drugs and drink, and to spend time in Thailand. In his excellent memoir, James Fearnley recalled how Shane had returned from a trip to the country with Victoria extolling the virtues of his newly discovered Shangri-La. This period of stasis, however, didn't last: 'A glaze of mysticism twinkled in his eyes for a week or two, to be clouded once more by sullenness and resentment,' said James. [18] At a photoshoot on the banks of the Douro River in Portugal, Shane had turned up with an eyepatch he had taken to wearing and appeared to James to be in 'a dark and precarious state'. 'When it came to taking the photograph, he was intractable. He clambered up on board the skiff and screamed at the photographer and screamed at us. We waited, ransom to his dementia.' [19]

Others in the band had their own addictions. Spider and Philip were both trying to overcome alcohol addiction and, back in London, Philip's boyfriend Achim had contracted HIV through his heroin use. Drink and drugs were rife in and around the band as people sought sanctuary from the problems that were fast enveloping it.

Shane has been shy his entire life, but he has always been a social animal. He enjoys company, often not conversing much himself, but content to listen to others and joining in when he wants. By 1989, he had withdrawn into himself, spending more time in his hotel room and removed from those around him. On stage, he would stare out into the crowd, lost in his own world. Lyrics would be forgotten, or he would sing entirely the wrong song. If he was in contact with himself, as per the advice of his interminable acid-house track, then few others were. A pall hung over him. He was more solitary, testy and lower in his mood, especially when the spiritual highs of Thailand had worn off. Ominously, he was also now using heroin. 'There was a lot of coke going on and he was mixing it with all sorts of other things,' says Siobhan. 'Then, of course, the heroin came in and then you're just at nothing. I was still trying to communicate with him as he was. It completely messed up my mind because I was trying to talk to him and not realising that I was trying to fight through a chemical barrage – that he just wasn't there.'

As the 1980s drew to a close, things had reached an all-time low. On a tour of German sports halls and ice-hockey stadiums, Shane was so wrecked some nights that the band left him face-down on the dressing room floor and walked on stage without him. The Christmas tour, a long-held Pogues tradition, was cancelled to give them time to make some demos ahead of recording the next record. They then flew to Australia for a tour that was a disaster. Shane couldn't get through the opening show in Perth. He staggered off to the side of the stage and Spider had to take over. Frank flew at Shane afterwards, threatening to get him barred from his beloved Thailand.

In Wellington, New Zealand, Shane collapsed on stage and then hauled himself up, smashing the microphone stand against the floor. Back in the dressing room, he sat slurring, apparently asking for a cigarette. Andrew's anger got the better of him and he knocked him off the bench he was slumped on and caused him to hit his mouth as he fell. A scuffle broke out. Things were unravelling.

Shane's isolation from the rest of the band had never been so pronounced and his deepening heroin addiction meant things would only deteriorate further. Not until he and Charlie MacLennan had disappeared for a fix could he stagger – or be dragged – onto the stage. 'Charlie would take him into a room and put whatever up his nose that was deemed to be necessary to get him through a couple of hours on stage,' says James. 'I'm not saying that was a regular thing, but I'm not saying it wasn't either. But it was a routine they had that enabled Shane to get onstage and it involved locking themselves in a room.'

It could not go on like this. The end was now in sight.

CHAPTER 8

Sayonara

'OK, it's time for sayonara
So long, Yankee, break my heart
Now there's nothing left but sorrow
Even the best friends they must part'

'Sayonara', **The Pogues**

If any doubts remained about how Shane felt about the band, they were brutally expunged by the lyrics he had been working on.

'Now there's nothing left but sorrow/Even the best friends they must part,' he wrote in 'Sayonara'. 'Finally found a place they could never reach/Sipping Singha beer on Pattaya beach', 'House Of The Gods' began, pointedly. In '5 Green Queens And Jean' he reflected wistfully on a time 'when five green queens on a black binbag meant all the world to me'.

Shane's sojourns to Thailand weren't just about finding inner peace away from life on the road. They chimed – as did his new songs – with his desire to have and feel nothing. 'I think Thailand had made great incursions into his stance toward the world and us,' says James Fearnley. 'It's mindlessness – to give up, to have nothing.'

Material possessions had never mattered a jot to Shane and, although the band were enjoying mainstream success, he was still living between his rented room at Cromer Street and Kathy Macmillan's. He liked having money to spend on drink, Greek food and night out at acid-house clubs. But he didn't pursue wealth for its own sake and was more likely to avoid other famous people rather than gravitate towards them.

Shane and Victoria live in fashionable Dublin 4, but the ground-floor apartment they rent is a modest, two-bed affair. There are a couple of shelves in the sitting room with books and a few records, and a pile of DVDs beside the armchair from which he constantly watches television. I found other records from his collection lying damaged and strewn over the floor in the dilapidated attic at The Commons, along with an acoustic guitar. To Shane, things have always been something to use and enjoy, rather than look after.

Remove the wine, e-cigarettes and other accessories laid out on his little white table, and he will panic. There, on that small plastic surface, is everything he materially wants from life and its continual replenishment gives him peace of mind. Sleep comes when it takes him; food is a low priority. For Shane, it is a good film or the company of friends from which he derives the most pleasure in life. When Paul Ronan, Joey Cashman or other old friends call around, his face lights up.

Steve Lillywhite observes: 'He's certainly one of a kind. In my whole career – and I've been producing for a long time now – I've only ever really met two absolute bohemians. What I mean by bohemian is that if they wake up at seven in the morning, it's purely coincidence. Those two people are Shane MacGowan and Keith Richards. Especially Shane. He has absolutely no need for any order in his life. Most of the rest of us need to have something to hold on to. But he doesn't even have a brand of cigarettes that he likes. We all know he's an alcoholic, but he doesn't have a specific drink that he has to have. A lot of alcoholics will stick to one drink. He'll wake up at midnight; he'll wake up at any time. He doesn't need to hold on to any form of what we sort of look at as reality. I don't know why that is. Keith Richards had a similar sort of thing about him. I remember him [Shane] going on tour and most people take a bag. He got on the tour bus with nothing. It was like, "Well, what are you going to wear, Shane?" "Oh, I'll just get swag…" He never cared about his quality of life. It was never about making money.'

Joey laughs when he recalls the times when Shane did take belongings on tour: 'Shane's luggage used to be a black rubbish bag and you'd look inside it if you had the nerve. He wouldn't even tie a knot in it. There would be CDs, half-drunk bottles of wine, bits of Greek food, broken CD players; anything that he picked up and threw into the bag. I used to tie a knot in it and put it in the overhead locker. One of the cabin crew would say, "What's that?" I'd say, "It's one of my friend's luggage." They'd just go, "Wow!", and I wouldn't point at Shane, I'd point at the best-dressed person, so they'd look eccentric!'

While the simple, disordered lifestyle has never really changed, the Shane MacGowan who stumbled blearily from the 1980s into the next decade did. Siobhan says that up to that point her brother was still recognisable to her. From then on, he 'careered out of control'. Attempts by Siobhan, girlfriends and others to get Shane to curb his drinking and use of hard drugs had been heavily resisted, just as he had always hated journalists asking about his boozing. 'It's nobody's business what I drink,' he said testily in an interview with *Q*. 'It's nobody's business what anybody drinks. It's nobody's business how long they stay up, where they go when they stay up, what they do when they stay up, right? Once that gets stripped away, the last vestige of human dignity is gone, right?' [1]

Steve Lillywhite had turned down an invitation to produce the next Pogues album and at the eleventh hour the band's long-time friend Joe Strummer offered to do it. RAK Studios was meanwhile spurned in favour of Rockfield Studios in Monmouth, Wales, where 'Bohemian Rhapsody' was recorded. It was an idyllic setting and, as the Italia '90 World Cup got underway, the UK was enjoying a warm summer. Most of the band took advantage of the location, rambling through the countryside and along the river into the town, dropping in on local fetes. Charlie MacLennan had set up a south-facing room for Shane, with a view of the hayfields. But after just two weeks Shane returned to London. The others carried on, infuriated and relieved in equal measure.

The scheduling of the tracks on the appositely named *Hell's Ditch* led to a bitter wrangle between some of The Pogues and Joe Strummer, and there were lengthy late-night calls before it was resolved. Shane was left stewing over what he saw as his diminishing influence over the records they were making. He was particularly peeved at the omission of some his songs like 'Aisling' at the expense of 'mediocre tripe' [2]. James Fearnley remembers it as 'a miserable experience'.

A major British tour then followed. At Brixton Academy, Shane was in bad shape and Spider had to take over halfway through. But that didn't stop a 16-year-old Dermot O'Leary being blown away by the occasion. 'It's like walking into a North Sea of people when you go and see a Pogues gig,' says the TV and radio presenter. 'It's like you're two hundred miles off Peterhead. Immediately, I lost all my friends, and I was being tossed around. I'm 16 and I'm in a world of big, beery giants with beards and leather jackets and bald heads and being tossed around to "Streams Of Whiskey" and "Boys From The County Hell". Then suddenly they play "Summer In Siam" and it stops. I looked up and there were these two drunk guys, old rummies with their arms around each other, bawling. I was like, "Who is this guy? How can he do this to this many people? This is magic."'

Shane, however, was increasingly unhappy with the attention he was receiving from press and audiences alike. He had never craved the limelight, even in the nascent days of the group, and rumours of his imminent departure from the band had only intensified the focus on him. Success had brought with it huge expectations and other pressures and so grave was Shane's health at this point that a doctor gave him three weeks to live.

'In the early days of the group when Cait was playing bass, and for the first two years I was playing bass, we really felt we were being appreciated as a team,' says Darryl. 'We still get that in America a lot, but then it started to get more and more about Shane, and I think that freaked him out... There became more attention on him, which on one level he probably felt quite chuffed about, but on another level, it was more pressure. He always wanted to spread the load sideways to the rest of the musicians; not out of any selfishness but just everybody has to share the load a bit. I just remember standing next to Jem looking out at the crowd in America somewhere and nobody was looking at anybody else but Shane, and it was strange for us as well.'

Victoria says performing is 'not his thing' and that Shane always encouraged Spider and Cait to be really noticed, so the attention was not all on him. 'He wanted to be the frontman because he likes being the frontman, but he didn't want it to be about him,' she explains. 'He would probably have liked to have been in something like The Band where, of course, there are brilliant people in it like Robbie Robertson, but it's still The Band. It's not like Van The Man who has his backing band who are in their place and being told, "Stay in the back." U2 are different because they are quite democratic, but it's quite obvious that Bono is the frontman, which isn't Shane's thing at all.'

Some believed Shane remained in The Pogues because he felt a sense of responsibility towards his fellow band members. However, Shane refutes this. 'No. I felt responsible to the audience… It's the fans you play for, not the rest of the band. Certainly not for Frank Murray. I think he tried to talk the band out of sacking me and then he came to me and he said, "Why don't you go and talk to them?" I said, "I don't want to be in this fucking band anymore. I've been trying to get out of it for the past couple of years, at least."'

Despite Shane's behaviour, it was The Pogues' long-term manager who was axed as soon as *Hell's Ditch* was completed and the group's obligations to Warner were fulfilled.

A shrewd manager and a force of nature, Frank had been fundamental in the group's journey from rebellious outsider mob to household name and no one was denying the impact he had made. However, his failure to see their utter exhaustion and allow them to recuperate was short-sighted and the mood in the group had reached rock bottom. Terry Woods says: 'Given the way Frank was pushing the band, there was always a brick wall around the corner. I think one year we did over two hundred gigs. I don't know how my wife put up with me. My marriage was hanging by a thread for a long time, simply because I wasn't there, and when I was there, I was so fucked-up. Luckily enough, I copped on. It was a hiding to nothing.'

A clause in The Pogues' contract with Frank allowed them to cut their ties with his business, Hill 16, if they were without a record deal for a specified period, and that contract was about to expire. A meeting was called at Frank's offices on Kentish Town Road, Camden. Most of the band turned up and Frank assumed they wanted an update about what he had booked over the coming months. He didn't see it coming. When Jem told him they were going on without him, he cried and asked each of them if they agreed. As painful as it was, they all said, 'Yes.' Their relationship with him had soured and the taste left in Frank's mouth became nastier still when he didn't get a mention on *The Best Of The Pogues*, released in the autumn of 1990.

Frank didn't know it, but his replacement was already waiting next door. 'When they fired Frank, they asked me to manage,' says Joey. 'We had worked together as partners and Frank came into the room and told me they had fired him. And the first thing he said to me – and I thought it was very magnanimous, really – was, "Whatever you do, you don't give up your job with them." Instead of trying to encourage me to go, "Fuck you," he encouraged me to stay and keep the job. I did, and we still worked with other bands as well and I never took any percentages from managing The Pogues or Shane ever.'

Shane felt guilty about Frank although, as usual, he had not been the one to confront the situation. But he 'thought everything would be all right if we could get rid of Frank' [3]. Such reasoning was delusional, especially when he was doing everything humanly possible to get himself chucked out of the band.

Shane was now ravaged by drugs and it was rendering him unable to perform. Where other band members had once been able to paper over his shortcomings on stage by jumping in and singing the correct words, a set at the annual Fleadh Festival in Finsbury Park in June 1991 was so shambolic, *Melody Maker*'s reviewer was left with 'a sense of genuine, heartfelt disgust'. James Fearnley recalls: 'We had done a music festival in Harlow and the festivals before that. We didn't know if Shane had had a stroke of some kind because his hand was quivering and palsied, and he couldn't hold onto the microphone very well.'

On 4 August, Shane returned to Tipperary when The Pogues performed at the Féile – festival – in Semple stadium, Thurles, less than an hour from his beloved homestead. Soon they would be flying off to Japan and, incredibly, it would be seventeen years before they would play in Ireland again.

The Japanese had a love affair with The Pogues and two weeks of dates had been lined up, including an appearance at WOMAD in Yokohama on 30 August. But the lead-up to the show had been tumultuous and, unbeknown to the audience, they were witnessing a group in its last throes. The band had arrived at the Pan Pacific hotel, on the city's photogenic seafront, from Tokyo the previous day. Glorious sunshine greeted them, but the connection between Shane and the rest of the band was now completely broken. He lurked in his darkened room, in a self-imposed solitary confinement, adrift from reality, unreachable. On stage he had become a liability, lurching and wheeling about and tarnishing their reputation as one of the world's most exciting live acts with every slurred line and missed cue. It had to end.

Phone calls were made, and the band – minus Shane – gathered in Jem's room. They talked reluctantly, but honestly, about the situation; their personal unhappiness at where things were and the sorry state of Shane. Eventually, Jem asked them what they wanted to do. Andrew wasted no time. 'Let him go,' he said. The others agreed it was time. But who would tell him? Both Spider and Jem, who had known him the longest, said they couldn't do it. Darryl nobly offered to take on the solemn task.

Shane was summoned and Jem let him in. His hair and clothes were filthy, and his skin had a deathly pallor. He sat and listened quietly as Darryl told him of their decision. They had all dreaded how he would react to what they had imagined would be a body blow. But they needn't have worried. Shane simply waited until Darryl had finished and nodded resignedly. 'You've all been very patient with me, tsscchh…. What took you so long?'

Speaking about the painful occasion almost thirty years later, Jem says: 'I think it just got to a point where no one could handle it anymore and I think there was concern that he could actually end up killing himself. So, we came to the conclusion that we couldn't carry on. But the trouble was that we had to carry on because, contractually, we had tours we had to do, and we had just got a new record deal. Whether or not we could ever make a record was another matter, but basically there were lots of complications and, if we had just split up, we would have been financially fucked. So, there was a not-very-pleasant situation where we couldn't really carry on the way we were with Shane, and we couldn't really stop because no one could afford to stop and take the consequences. So, we came to the conclusion that we had to talk to Shane and say, "We can't carry on." It was absolutely horrible. It would have been much better just to say, "Let's just stop the band." He said something like, "You've been very patient." He wasn't going mad and breaking things and insulting people. I would imagine for him it was quite a relief, in some sense, and maybe it was what he had been trying to make happen for a long time.'

Terry Woods found the experience extremely distressing, especially as it could have been avoided: 'The touring fucked Shane up. He was bad enough anyway, but that drove him over the edge. I was in the room in Yokohama and I was actually in tears. It takes a lot to make me cry, but it was sad because I could see the wrecking of something that was so good for everybody. I don't mean just money. I mean the satisfaction, musically, of having an impact like that. We should have gone off the road. The money was there, the record company would have said, "There you go, we'll keep you alive for a year. Take time out." We didn't know that then, so Shane had to leave. With him, it was like going around with a cardboard cut-out. In fact, you'd have had more life out of a cardboard cut-out.'

James Fearnley adds: 'That was the pinnacle of horror for all of us because Shane was totally powerless at that point and we all hated him. We're all in this room and he had no other fucking place to go, and he was totally desperate... I think he was hurt and so totally alone.'

Whatever was going through his mind, Shane did take to the stage with them that night and got through the show. However, he missed the following shows in Osaka and Ngoya and there was still time for one act of self-destruction before they flew home – one that remains etched forever in the memories of those who saw it.

Terry Woods describes the drama: 'We were on the bullet train and Shane discovered that you could get sake. You got a can of sake with a little sword which punched the bottom and whatever gasses were in the bottom they heated up the sake, which is the way you're supposed to take it. When we got to Osaka there were two or three people-carriers waiting. We looked round and Shane was fucking bananas. We had a big gig that night, so the rest of the band went on ahead. The Japanese are so polite. They had the little white doilies on the seats, the drivers had white gloves and everybody's nodding and it's all very nice.

'Anyway, we got to this big, glass-fronted hotel and we were standing at the desk, checking in. MacGowan had had to be carried from the train and put in the back of a people-carrier. When it pulled up outside the hotel, we looked to see what was going on and, before the Japanese man could get around to open the door, it opened, and this fucking figure fell out. He fell with his top lip on the pavement, while his chin was in the gutter. So, whatever was left of the teeth came out and there was blood everywhere. He was then carried into the hotel and, luckily enough, the hotel thought it was an accident. Well, it was an accident, but not the kind they thought. They were very helpful, and he was taken to his room and doctors were called and all the rest of it. The end result was he couldn't do the gig that night, so we had to make it up between us.

'This had been going on and had been getting worse and worse. He obviously didn't want to be there. He had been pushing the boat in his own way and I don't blame him. He just wasn't able to do it. He wanted it to stop and he needed to stop. He didn't necessarily want the band to stop, but he needed some form of rehabilitation.'

Shane injuring himself or having to miss shows was nothing out of the ordinary. He had been sent flying through the air by taxis and even hurled himself out of a moving car, only to be patched up and sent on his way. Hotel receptionists, airline staff and chauffeurs had seen him being carried along like a ragdoll, paralytic with drink. Tales of his wild adventures were ten a penny. But the sight of him crashing face down on the ground was shocking, especially with everyone still reeling from his sacking in Yokohama.

The final two shows in Japan were completed without Shane before everyone returned to the UK. There, they were left to ponder who would front the group on the forthcoming tour of the US and Canada, and for subsequent dates in Europe and Australia. Taking over from any front-person is a tall order. But Shane's bond with the audience was a special one and, when the band walked out onstage, it was his inimitable silhouette, drink in hand, they craned their necks to see. For most fans, if not all, Shane MacGowan was The Pogues.

A solution came in the form of an old friend: Joe Strummer. The Pogues felt unburdened at no longer having to drag Shane around, a question mark hovering over each show. They got on well with Joe and his history with The Clash added a different dimension. While some songs like 'Fairytale Of New York' and 'A Rainy Night In Soho' were too closely associated with Shane to be performed without him, Clash favourites 'London Calling', 'Complete Control' and 'I Fought The Law' were introduced to their live sets. The new line-up and repertoire proved a hit with crowds and so exuberant were the scenes during their two-night stint at the Wilton Theater in Los Angeles that The Pogues were banned from ever returning.

There was no animosity on either side following Shane's sacking. He spoke to Jem and Spider on the phone and asked how things were going. Shane had even lobbied for Spider to be his replacement. 'I thought it would have been a great idea for Spider to take over from me, but the band wouldn't go for it,' says Shane. 'Strummer wasn't that charismatic, but it's just the way things turned out. Spider was really popular with the fans. We were a double-act and that really pissed off the other members of the band. Strummer couldn't do the real Pogues that I did. He didn't have a feel for Irish music. I tried to get it for Spider. I said, "I'm fucking off and you should let Spider take it over. He knows all the songs; the crowd love him."'

In reality, Spider wasn't in a fit state to take it on. 'Generally, I was too messed up at that time,' he admitted. 'Everything was kind of like slipping through my fingers. The times I wasn't drinking too much, I was fine, but you really can't be drinking like that and singing at the same time. It was difficult to maintain focus.' [4]

As for Shane, his health was more precarious than ever. He was using heroin and other class A drugs, including cocaine and speedballs, a cocktail of heroin and amphetamines, in parallel with drinking spirits by the pint. He continued to have problems with his gut – with which he effectively went to war every day – and he ate sporadically.

In the months following his dismissal, Shane and Victoria relocated to Ireland, initially living in a converted Martello tower fort owned by Bono, in the seaside town of Bray, County Wicklow. The U2 singer, who lived in nearby Killiney, generously covered all their bills during their stay. He also spent a long night in a local pub with the couple, sinking pints of Guinness and discussing religion.

There was no shortage of excitement at the nineteenth-century property during their stay. One night, Shane went to hit someone, and they ducked. His hand smashed into the thick wall, causing his arm to be in plaster for three months. He was also caught standing by one of its long glass walls and flashing at another singer who was a near neighbour. 'I would say good morning to Mary Coughlan by waving my donger at her,' he laughed. 'I was spotted by somebody passing on the train, flashing at her, and it was in the papers the next day, but the temptation to do it was unbearable.' [5]

A flat in a Georgian house in Mountjoy Square, on the north side of Dublin, provided their next temporary home. Shane made the most of the free time he had so craved during his touring years, travelling down to Tipperary to catch up with family and friends. The rest of the time he rambled around Dublin's pubs and clubs, adding his face to the gallery of celebrities who could be spotted out and about. Ireland's generous tax laws for artists made it a popular place to live in the 1990s, with Joe Elliott from Def Leppard, Rolling Stones guitarist Ronnie Wood and Elvis Costello among those who had headed to its shores. Soul singer Lisa Stansfield had acquired a stunning period house in Dalkey, and she famously ended up giving Shane a bloody nose after an argument at Lillie's Bordello nightclub on Grafton Street in 1994. Shane said afterwards that she had approached him, and he had asked her to wait a moment as he was in a conversation. According to him, she had got annoyed and punched him very hard in the face, breaking his nose.

Lisa recalled: 'What happened was that he wanted me to read some poetry out of a book and I said, "No, I don't want to." And I started laughing. Then he said, "You silly cow," and pushed me! And I thought, I'm not having any of this,' so I slapped him. I've never punched anyone, but a slap was enough to give him a nosebleed. Yet we made up afterwards. We were all just having a laugh!' [6] Lillie's was clearly a dangerous place for Shane. He had also ended up in a fight there with Oscar winner Neil Jordan, who had directed the video for 'Miss Otis Regrets/Just One Of Those Things', and Terry Neill was called on to break it up.

Back in London, one of those who could be found hanging out with Shane was Nick Cave. They had first met in 1988 for an *NME* front cover shot and interview with Mark E. Smith from The Fall and, not long after Shane's departure from The Pogues, he called Nick and suggested they record a few slow songs together.

The outcome was a cover of Louis Armstrong's 'What A Wonderful World', which they performed on BBC Two's *Later...With Jools Holland* on its release as a single in November 1992. In the official video, Shane sat enveloped in darkness as Nick Cave sang the first verse. When the spotlight was turned on him, he looked like a punch-drunk fighter. Deathly pale, he sat swaying drunkenly and the absence of his trademark black shades exposed eyes which looked like they hadn't been shut for days. Whatever world he was inhabiting, it was far from wonderful.

In a joint interview with *NME* to coincide with the release of the single, Shane spoke of his commonality with Nick Cave, an artist perennially drawn towards the dark side of the street. 'We're both a bit schizoid, you see,' he said. 'He can be a bit of an animal sometimes. And then he'll do something, sing something really tender. I'm like that. I can be tender. But there's a lot of psychotic hatred coming out of me as well. Know what I mean?'

Asked whether listeners might think two such 'poets of the gutter' were being 'ironic' in reprising 'What A Wonderful World', Shane was furious. He launched into a tirade about the cover version that had denied 'Fairytale Of New York' the Christmas number one slot. The 'fucking Pet Shop Boys', he fumed. 'They slaughtered "Always On My Mind". That's a great Willie Nelson song [written by Wayne Carson, Johnny Christopher and Mark James], a classic version by Elvis Presley, and they took the piss. Out of the song, out of the writers, out of the people who bought it. The only people they didn't take the piss out of was themselves. The worst cover version ever. "Wonderful World" is nothing like that.'

Despite his declining health, artistically Shane was continuing to look forward. He had reconnected with his old college mate and bassist Bernie France and guitarist Mo O'Hagan, and he was writing. Bernie remembers: 'Shane was sitting there with lyrics all over the floor and he had written all over the walls and done drawings… there was stuff all over the place. So, we began to rehearse at the flat with Mo. It was just acoustic guitars, and I had a bass and a tiny little amp. I'd go around there and stamp my foot and Shane likes it that way. He always said The Pogues started to go wrong when they got a full drum kit.'

Shane wanted to go back to basics and, by the end of 1993, he had gathered around him the musicians who would help him achieve that. They were guitarist Paul 'Mad Dog' McGuinness, banjo player Tommy McManamon, drummer Danny Heatley (previously of The Boothill Foot-Tappers and punk band The Exploited) and whistle player Colm Ó Maonlai (brother of Hothouse Flowers singer Liam and later an actor). They christened themselves Shane MacGowan & The Popes, signalling that this time there would be no room for democracy.

Some of the songs they rehearsed had been written by Shane and recorded as demos by The Pogues before being discarded. That would not happen again. The Popes were Shane's band, and he would call the shots. 'He just wanted to do it his way,' explains Bernie. 'He said, "Now, there is no democracy – it's a dictatorship," and we were happy with that. He was the songwriter.'

Paul McGuinness confirms that Shane was in charge: 'He used to do all the songwriting. We'd try to put in our contributions, and we'd play. Shane would let us play the way we wanted it and the band would loosely do some of the arrangements, but Shane would do most of the songwriting. I thought, I want to try and get in there, but Shane was adamant – it was his songs.'

'Mad Dog' hailed from Dublin and went back years with some of those in Shane's circle. He had been in the new romantic/soul boy band Tokyo Olympics with Joey Cashman, and it was his former schoolmate Philip Chevron who had taken him to see Pogue Mahone at The Pindar. Later, he had found himself working as a roadie for The Pogues and, when Philip fell ill while they were in Switzerland, he deputised for him on guitar for a couple of shows.

'My first impression of Shane was that I had seen him before from the picture in the *NME* when his ear bled,' he says. 'I remembered him from that and when I saw him, I thought, Oh, that's Shane. When I started talking to him, I couldn't believe how nice he was and that astounded me. I was expecting something different, somebody telling me to go fuck myself, but he just made me feel very comfortable. People don't know that, but he's really intelligent and a very nice person.'

On Valentine's Day 1994, Shane made a rare television appearance. Van Morrison was performing at the Brit Awards at Alexandra Palace, London, and had asked if he would duet with him on 'Gloria'. Shane was a long-time admirer of Van's, especially of early albums like *Astral Weeks* and *Veedon Fleece*, and he was surprised at the invitation. 'I don't know why he asked me,' he remarked modestly, 'Perhaps he likes me.' [7]

He made the comment to the Friends of Shane MacGowan newsletter, started by long-time fan Ingrid Knetsch. Frank Murray had heard of her German fan club and, when he met her at a gig in London, he asked if she would make it international. She agreed and he sent her a large sack of unopened fan mail to sort through. When The Pogues played in Germany, he then organised backstage passes so Ingrid and the friend she ran the fan club with could meet the group. Ingrid admits she was nervous of meeting Shane and felt there was 'something unapproachable about him'. However, she needed photographs of the band for the next fanzine and plucked up the courage to speak to him. She found him 'very friendly and polite' and they would go on to become friends. Sometime after he left The Pogues, Shane asked Ingrid to set up his own fan club and it was her decision to create the website shanemacgowan.com.

'Since I've been taking care of his fans, and that's twenty-eight years now, I've found they have incredible love for him,' says Ingrid. 'Generally, people seem to hate or love Shane. There's nothing in between. But this love is so wonderful it's hard for me to describe it. Shane is their hero in the darkness; his voice comforts them in hard times and helps them celebrate good times. For example, I received a letter from a Croatian soldier during the Croatian–Serbian war. In this letter, he wrote: "When I'm in the trenches and I hear Shane's voice, I'm not afraid of the Serbian bombs anymore." I had tears in my eyes, as Shane did, when he read it.'

Spirituality had always been important to Shane and it hung heavy in the air when rehearsals began that month. Catholic icons and artefacts were scattered around the studio at John Henry's, near Pentonville prison. A picture of a nun with the caption 'Sister Margaret leads a life of chastity, poverty and obedience' was attached to an amplifier, next to a photograph of Phil Lynott. There were crucifixes: one on top of a speaker, another dangling from Shane's microphone stand, and the one he always wore around his neck. On a wall was a voodoo doll. Some of the original compositions that had emerged from the scraps of paper that covered almost every surface of Shane's flat also dealt with matters of faith – 'Old Time Religion' and 'The Church Of The Holy Spook'. Shane explained: 'The mandala of Christ, the crucifix, is a strong protective thing and guide. I feel a lot better with a Gaelic cross around my neck.' [8]

The Friends of Shane MacGowan newsletter reported that he was fit, sober and lucid, and was practising 'moderation in all things'. 'I know that I'm going to live to be 88, at least, and I'm still going to feel cheated... but you can't argue with death,' he said. The dynamic in The Popes was also making him happier. 'I'm doing what I want, and I've got a great band that plays what I ask them to play... And I'm doing what I want, within the confines of this shitty, stinking music business.' [9]

Musically, The Popes were just what Shane needed after the frustrations he had gone through in the latter years of The Pogues, according to

Paul Ronan: 'When Shane wanted to form a new band, he wanted to go back to the beginning, something a lot more earthy and punky, with more feeling in it. The Popes was the name agreed, so we went with that. When I was listening to the demo tracks, it didn't have the sophistication of The Pogues, but it really had the fever that The Nipple Erectors and the early Pogue Mahone were about. Shane was happier at that time because he was revisiting something that he felt he had lost before leaving The Pogues.'

Paul McGuinness confirms Shane's desire to get back to playing the kind of songs The Pogues had been less inclined to play. 'When Shane started The Popes, one of the things that he wanted to do was try lots of the songs he'd written back in the day,' he says. 'That's what we started doing and we started rehearsing at John Henry's. So, we were doing that for a couple of months before we started playing again and doing any gigs at all. I remember that lots of people in the early days used to come along and they were expecting a total Pogues tribute and I think Shane was trying to be more Creedence Clearwater, very basic rock'n'roll with an Irish influence. We started playing lots of songs that The Pogues had refused to do, like "Aisling". I think they were trying to get away from the Irish thing.'

Not only did Shane have a clear vision about the style of music he wanted the band to play, he also had an innate feel for how best other musicians would fit into the group. 'I'd be astounded by Shane,' says Paul McGuinness. 'He used to come along and just say to people, "You're going to change. You're going to play accordion." And he would just change everybody. He knew what to do and what would suit people and it always worked out.'

The embryonic Popes made their live debut at a benefit for the charity Cradle at Cork city hall on 1 December 1993, with Nick Cave making a guest appearance. A few other warm-up gigs in Ireland followed, and another in London at The Mean Fiddler in Harlesden, before they appeared at The Grand, Clapham, on St Patrick's night. Whatever reservations anyone might have had about Shane's new venture, both audience and critics were blown away.

NME's Gavin Martin hailed 'the triumphant return of one of the great talents sired by punk' and was full of praise for his new band. 'More pared, more primal than The Pogues, The Popes are that rebel punk folkabilly thing at full throttle, the missing link between Shane's juvenile punk past with The Nips and his still-wired, unhinged vision of the present,' he wrote. 'Perhaps during years of Poguemocracy Shane lost his grip on the musical steering wheel, but there's little doubt this new band sees the world the way he does.' [10]

The setlist was full of surprises and spanned the breadth of the Shane MacGowan songbook: from The Nips' 'King Of The Bop' and Pogues' favourites 'Streams Of Whiskey' and 'Sally MacLennane' to new compositions like 'Church Of The Holy Spook' and 'That Woman's Got Me Drinking'. Nick Cave joined in late on and he and Shane brought the house down, duetting on Frank Sinatra's 'Love's Been Good To Me', 'The Irish Rover' and 'Fairytale Of New York'.

Another of the songs they played that night had arisen from a bet Shane had made with Ann Scanlon. She remembers: 'One night we were in a place on Pratt Street and Shane said, "I can write a song about anything. All I need is a title."

'So, I said, "Right, I bet you ten pounds you can't," and he said, "Go on, then."

'I went, "'I'll Be Your Handbag'," and he said, "Honestly, Ann, I thought you could have come up with something a lot better than that." He wrote the lyrics on a napkin within a few minutes and another time I saw him he had a different set of lyrics.

'I forgot about it and I probably didn't see him that much towards the end of The Pogues, only occasionally. Then, when The Popes played Clapham Grand, Shane suddenly said, "This is 'I'll Be Your Handbag'. The only bit that had survived was, "You blow my mind away".

'Later he said, "You still owe me for the bet," and I said, "You might owe me some royalties!"'

In glorious sunshine and with an armoury of new songs, Shane and his new entourage decamped to Ireland, practising at The Commons. They crammed into the tiny cottage with the equipment they had brought from London and thrashed out the songs that would make up their first record and live set. Joining them for these sessions was guitarist Leeson O'Keeffe, who would be part of the touring band. For a month, the stone walls of the Lynch family home resounded to the thunderous sound of a band that owed more to The Nips than The Pogues. But their rustic Tipperary retreat had too many distractions. 'It was too bloody chaotic,' says Paul Ronan. 'They wouldn't rehearse unless Shane was there, and Shane would be late.'

By this time, Paul was Shane's new manager. 'Shane was adamant he didn't want a manager and we had an agreement that we would never work together, so as not to interfere with our friendship,' says Paul. 'We were discussing this in his flat on the Blackstock Road. Nick Cave was there and suggested that as Shane trusted me, maybe I could sort out a new deal for him.'

There were plenty of people looking to get a slice of Shane's song rights after he left The Pogues. Among them was Creation Records boss Alan McGee, whose acts included Primal Scream and The Jesus and Mary Chain, both favourites of Shane. However, standing in the way of McGee and other interested parties was Shane's existing publisher, Liam Teeling, to whom 'Fairytale Of New York' had been very kind. Shane is a canny operator and, although he is not greedy, he makes sure he gets what he is due. He also prefers to work with those he likes and trusts.

'Alan McGee was in for the deal and Paul and Shane came to my offices to tell me that the deal with me was off,' says Liam, who was then at ZTT. 'So, we went to this pub in the Portobello Road and we started to talk about all the old times we'd had together and how great it was. At this time, I had the publishing, so I said, "I'll work with Alan and do whatever," and we drank and drank.

'The next thing is somebody comes up and says, "There's a phone call for you," so I went to the bar and it was John Kennedy [Shane's lawyer] on the phone. I said, "Oh, hello, John."

'He said, "What have you done to my artist?"

'I said, "What do you mean?"

'He said, "I've just had him on the phone saying he's going to sign with you and not Creation."'

Liam adds: 'I re-signed Shane about four or five times. Every publisher in town wanted to sign him and I always said to Shane, "You work out what other people are going to give you and I'll give you the same amount of money, so at least it's the devil you know." He always stuck with the devil he knew. He is a very loyal person.'

The Popes had been booked to perform on Sunday 4 July 1994 at the Fleadh Mor, a new two-day festival organised by the Mean Fiddler's

Vince Power at Tramore racecourse, County Waterford. Bob Dylan, who Shane had stood up five years earlier, was topping the bill on the second night. Van Morrison, Joan Baez and Jerry Lee Lewis were also in the all-star line-up. Maybe there were too many big names with big fees because Vince Power suffered major losses as a result, but the high-profile event provided the perfect springboard for Shane's new band.

Emerging to a large crowd, they reprised Pogues favourites like 'Sally MacLennane', covers of well-known Irish songs and three songs that would appear on The Popes' debut album: 'The Snake With Eyes Of Garnet', 'Her Father Didn't Like Me Anyway' and 'That Woman's Got Me Drinking'.

'From where I was on stage it sounded pretty rough,' says Bernie. 'Music on stage always sounds rough anyway, but I was thinking, This is really bitty and messy. But Shane didn't care; it was what he wanted to play.'

Shane is more honest still: 'It was a godawful noise, but it was fun.'

Messier still was the state of the van owned by Phil Gaston and Deirdre O'Mahony that Phil had foolishly allowed Shane to drive around a nearby field later that night. 'We had just moved to Ireland and Shane crashed our van,' says Deirdre. 'Phil let him drive it – can you imagine? At 4 a.m. somewhere on the racecourse, Shane crashed the van!'

Shane says: 'Dee got it off her father's company, who were big book dealers in Limerick. I just wanted to do some driving and we were parked in a field. I'd already had lots of disasters and I always crashed. This time I was really doing well. Phil was guiding me, but I got over-confident and put my foot down on the pedal. I had loads of room, it was a huge field with only one corner of it with parked vehicles. Phil said, "We'll go around this field." I went round a few times and got really confident taking a corner, which meant I ended up in the ditch going really fast and crashed into a tree that was in the ditch – an oak!'

It was the climax to what had already been a highly eventful day. Victoria had become enraged after discovering that Shane had again been unfaithful. An almighty row had broken out between the couple and was played out in front of the festival's headline act. 'Shane and I had a huge fight in his dressing room, in front of Bob Dylan and his roadies,' said Victoria. 'I was bashing Shane around the head with my handbag and Bob was laughing his head off. Then I got very drunk and we broke up – unofficially – for a few months. We ended up back in London and lived together for a while, but I had another nervous breakdown and had to move out. I couldn't function and live with him.' [11]

The wheels had come off in their relationship and those paying attention in the crowd that day witnessed its derailment. As Bob Dylan beckoned to the back of the stage for Van Morrison to sing with him, Van could be seen in a passionate clinch with a dark-haired woman. It was Victoria.

Record companies might have salivated at the thought of acquiring Shane's back catalogue and publishing rights, but there was little interest in his first album away from The Pogues. Warner Bros. had passed on it, as had other labels who had heard about the state Shane was in. Liam Teeling says: 'Word had come to them that everything was fucked up and he was not going to sell any more records, and that's all they care about.'

Shane's addiction to heroin and the company he kept was now of grave concern to those who continued to have his best interests at heart. Liam was among them, but he remained convinced that a great record could still emerge from the darkness engulfing Shane and the band. It was with his money that a studio was booked and the recording sessions for what would become *The Snake* got underway.

The sessions were shambolic. Shane had insisted on using Morgan Studios, Willesden, because it had a bar. But even then, he couldn't be relied on to turn up when the other band members were there. Drugs were a constant presence and hung over the group like a veil. Liam's style was hands-off, knowing all too well there was no point giving Shane orders. But one night, his patience snapped. A row had started about the making of the record during a meal in a restaurant and Liam grabbed Shane by the neck, pinning him to the wall. Tensions were running high.

Shane had asked former Pogues engineer Dave Jordan to produce it and he was struggling to cope. Liam agreed to get him some help, but this had to be kept from Shane, who was adamant his old friend was up to the job. 'Shane was just going, "He's fucking doing it," little thinking that the guy did not have the ability to do so,' says Liam. 'So, I said to Dave, "Here's what we'll do. You do everything and at the end of the night, you leave the tapes and I'll have them collected."

'One of my friends is Steve Brown, who produced that great Cult record "She Sells Sanctuary". He was a big fan of Shane's and I said to him, "I'm going to get the tapes collected and delivered to you. You clean up the tapes and do everything you need to do, then you deliver them back to Morgan Studios in the morning."

'That's what happened, and people went in there and they thought, This is sounding really good. Every day, as regular as clockwork, the guys would go in, they would work, the tapes were taken in a cab straight down to Wandsworth and delivered back, so when people turned up the following day everything was clean. They were so fucking out of it nobody even noticed. Shane was jacking up and drinking. They were a great live band, but a recording band – forget it.'

The Snake was released on ZTT Records in October 1994 and spent one week at number thirty-seven in the UK chart. Reviews were largely positive and the consensus seemed to be that Shane was back to his old self. 'It's one of the records I'm most proud of,' says Liam. 'I had done a record with Seal just before that, which was number one in America, and had a number one single. But this was much closer to my heart.'

The esteem in which Shane continued to be held by other musicians was underlined by the list of guest performers. Barney McKenna from The Dubliners played tenor banjo while bandmate John Sheahan contributed fiddle and whistles and his daughter Siobhan played Irish harp. Jem and Spider found time away from The Pogues to lend their services, along with Rick Trevan, Shane's old friend from King's Cross, who played tenor sax. Brian Robertson also guested on the record, but it was another guitarist whose arrival at the studio caused the biggest stir.

Hollywood actor Johnny Depp was in awe of Shane and they had hit it off after meeting in London after an inauspicious start. 'Shane was in a studio in Camden and Johnny said he wanted to meet Shane,' recalls Joey. 'I said, "He's not in great nick at the moment," and Johnny said, "No, I want to meet him." So, we went down to the studio at Chalk Farm and we walked in and Shane was sitting on a pool table, with a pool cue in one hand and a bottle of something in the other.

'He was standing there, swaying backwards and forwards, and I kept thinking he would fall, but he didn't. I said, "Oh, Shane, there's someone here who would like to say 'Hello' to you."

'Shane goes, "Well, say 'Hello.'"

'I said, "It's Johnny Depp, he wants to meet you," and he said, "So what?"

'I said, "So, Shane this is Johnny, Johnny this is Shane," and he goes, "Yeah, yeah. So fucking what?"

'So, we leave and I'm thinking, Oh bollocks, and I said, "I'm really sorry about that Johnny. He's going through some hard times," and Johnny says, "That was fucking magic, Cashman. Thank you so much," and I go, "Yeah, I suppose it was quite good!"'

Johnny was invited to play guitar on 'That Woman's Got Me Drinking', which was released as a single, and he performed with The Popes when they appeared on *Top of the Pops*. 'I remember he [Johnny] came along to play guitar and at some stage he knocked a bottle of wine over the mixing desk,' recalls Paul McGuinness. 'I think if anybody else had knocked it over they would have made them pay, but with Johnny Depp they said, "No problem, Johnny." He wasn't the best guitarist I've ever seen, and I don't think we recorded an awful lot of him, but he was there.'

Depp also offered to direct and star in the accompanying video, filmed in Los Angeles, in return for Shane performing at the opening of his Hollywood venue The Viper Room. In the clip, Depp staggers into a bar and is served copious amounts of alcohol by Shane, who is a study of cool, with slicked-back hair, sideburns and a cigarette casually hanging from his mouth. Victoria plays the woman who has driven him to drink, kicking and punching him and laying into him with her handbag. When Joey Cashman comes to take over from Shane behind the counter, Shane wanders outside and shares a kiss with Victoria.

'Johnny Depp did a wicked video of that, although the record company fucked it up because there was no band in it,' says Joey. 'They chopped it. Johnny paid for first-class flights for Vicky, Shane and me. He got the location, all the crew, then he acted in it and then he goes, "Cashman, you're in the next scene." Shane leaves the bar, I take over, and I'm talking to Johnny. Then it goes outside to Shane and Vicky. We didn't get permits, so they walk across real traffic and she's swinging her handbag at him and he's going, "Fuck you," and the cars are beeping their horns. Then he [Johnny] goes off into an edit suite, edits it and hands us the finished product that night. He did the whole fucking thing in one day. Johnny's a genius. I love Johnny.'

Irish fans were given a special treat when Shane was among the musicians to contribute to a *Late Show* tribute to Christy Moore, broadcast in October 1994. He joined Christy on the moving ballad 'Spancil Hill' which, like 'Fairytale Of New York', laments the broken dreams of those who left Ireland for America. Written by Michael Considine, it holds a revered place in the Irish songbook. 'Myself and Shane are going to have a go at a song here from a long time ago,' Christy told the studio audience. 'I'm going to sing his version and he's going to sing my version.'

Side by side, they looked an incongruous duo. Shane was dressed in a black suit over a white vest top, with a chain around his neck and his trademark shades. If he seemed a bit unsteady on his feet, his presence in the RTE studio proved a powerful one, physically and vocally, and he and Christy complemented one another perfectly. Shane, of course, knew a great deal about the song and had been clear with Christy as to how he thought they should perform it.

'It was not a case of him wanting me to sing it in a particular way,' recalls Christy. 'He was merely pointing out that I had changed the lyrics from the version he had learned from my earlier recording. I first heard "Spancil Hill" back in 1964 and I recorded it in 1972. When I came to sing it with him, he pointed out that I had changed the lyrics... I had done so unconsciously. It impressed me that he should notice and point it out to me – both seriously and humorously. I recognised that I was dealing with a wordsmith, someone for whom the lyrics were all-important. Lyrics evolve over the years, sometimes without my noticing, I constantly go with the flow and let words change, including some of his!'

Christy has covered 'A Pair Of Brown Eyes', 'Fairytale Of New York' and 'Aisling' and admits to being a little envious of Shane's songwriting. In particular, he is struck by the naked honesty of Shane's writing: 'Shane wears it on his sleeve, shares joy and heartbreak, highs and lows, reveals honesty in his lyrics, violence towards himself in his brutal lifestyle,' he says.

Professionally at least, 1994 had ended on a high note. Shane's first recorded work since leaving The Pogues had been warmly received by the critics and in The Popes, he had a band over which he had full control. But for him personally, and for some of those around him, it was a dark time, marred by addiction and tragedy. *The Snake* had been dedicated to the memory of loved ones who had passed away. They included Shane's uncle Sean Cahill, The Pogues' former lighting man Paul Verner and Paul Ronan's partner Hancey Lynch.

'Shane was there as soon as I called him with a bottle of brandy and was a great support in the aftermath,' says Paul. 'It was due to me finding it difficult to cope that Shane and myself parted ways. I went off to sort my life out.'

With storm clouds circling, Shane was now left to weather them without the reassuring presence of one of the few people he could trust.

CHAPTER 9

Lonesome Highway

'Only you see that I am lazy
Don't care about fame
Nor money like a child
And I'm just like a child
Who's forgotten how to smile'

'Victoria', **Shane MacGowan & The Popes**

Whatever physical or mental harm he had inflicted on himself, the Shane MacGowan his fans loved was back. Rumours about his impending demise had proved unfounded, he was energised by his new band, and *The Snake* had shown he could still write songs that sounded like they had been around for a hundred years. Shane appeared to be in a better place.

Except he wasn't. He was hitting the drink as hard as ever and, when it came to hard drugs, The Popes made The Pogues look like a Sunday school outing. By now, Shane had lost contact with many of his old friends and, when he wasn't touring, he could reliably be found propping up the bar at his new second home: Filthy MacNasty's Whiskey Cafe. The street-corner pub in Islington was opened by Gerry O'Boyle in 1993 and hosted cool literary events. Word quickly spread about the quality of its Guinness, its two dozen whiskeys and the celebrities like Kate Moss and Pete Doherty who could be found at its Vox'n'Roll nights, where writers read from their books and chose their favourite records.

For years, Shane had been famed for his boozing. He was the Brendan Behan of rock, writing about drink and necking it on stage. Stories of his alcoholic antics were legion and tabloid hacks and music journalists were often more interested in what was in his glass than on his records. But what most fans didn't know was that Shane was a hopeless junkie.

In common with so many addicts, Shane would take whatever he could get: heroin, coke, speed, amphetamines, speedballs. He would sit zombie-like in his flat snorting one fat line after another, watching films in a trance, drifting in and out of sleep. The desperate efforts of Siobhan and his parents to get him into rehabilitation and clean of drugs had come to nothing. The Shane they knew and loved hadn't so much faded as completely disappeared from view.

Sinéad O'Connor was among those who saw first-hand the effects of his heroin addiction. She had duetted with him on the song 'Haunted', which had originally been sung by Cait O'Riordan and appeared in Alex Cox's biopic *Sid & Nancy*. When Shane and Sinéad's version was released in April 1995, the single entered the UK Top 40 and during the recording of *Top of the Pops*, a drug-addled Shane could barely stay awake.

'The producers were freaking out because Shane was nodding out on smack in between the verses,' remembers Sinéad. 'I was singing my verse and they didn't believe he was going to wake up and neither did I. But every time he did wake up and sing his verse and the next thing, he'd nod out again and everybody would be terrified all through my next verse. But he always managed to snap out of it just on time, and just when you think he is going to blow it.'

Although his iron constitution meant he would somehow survive the vast amounts of drugs he was consuming, others would not be so fortunate. The Popes had performed a show at the Élysée Montmartre in Paris on 6 March 1995 and afterwards the band and some of the crew returned to the nearby Hôtel Regyn's. In the middle of the night, French promoter Alain Lahana received a call from a member of staff. Someone had been found dead in one of the bedrooms. He rushed to the hotel where he was shown to the room. It was producer Dave Jordan. He had died of a heroin overdose. Lahana called the police and after examining the scene one officer said he believed the body had been moved. Although there is no suggestion the group was in any way to blame for his death, none of the band or crew was around to explain this or to provide any information about their friend's last hours, as they had already packed up and left.

Dave Jordan was an experienced and respected producer who had worked with The Rolling Stones, The Specials and Fun Boy Three before becoming part of The Pogues' set-up. He had also been a heroin user but had been through rehab and got clean. Sometime after Shane formed The Popes, Dave was invited to produce their first album, and Terry Woods tried desperately to talk him out of it. 'I remember Dave Jordan and his wife coming up to visit my wife and myself in Cavan,' recalls Terry. 'He was saying, "Shane has offered me a gig again with The Popes." Now, at this point, Dave Jordan had got himself clean and the two of them were very happy and it was going well.

'I said to him, "Dave, do you really need this?"

'He said, "Well, it's money I could do with," and I said, "Yeah, but you know where this is going to go. Do you really want to go there?"

'He said, "It will be fine." I then met them maybe a year later and Dave Jordan couldn't look me in the eye. The next I heard he was dead.

'I met Alain Lahana, the man who ran that tour, when we did a gig at The Olympia in Dublin. I said, "It's great to see you. MacGowan is in the back, do you want to go in?" And he said, "I don't want to talk to that man. He left me with so much trouble."

'I said, "With Dave Jordan?"

'And he said, "Yes."'

Dave's wife Elizabeth Moynihan, an actress and playwright, had also been uneasy about him returning to Shane's employ and she confided her fears to James Fearnley. 'I want to think that we [The Pogues] saved DJ because we took him back into employment from his rehab from smack in Whitehaven," he says. "Whether it's the truth or not, I don't know. But that's always the way I looked at it. To see the pride DJ had about his life and his own body... he was somebody to look up to. I spoke to his wife on the phone before his death and she said to me, "I'm worried about DJ going off to work with Shane again and getting into that circle and that he's not going to come back to me," and right enough he didn't.'

The time Dave spent touring with the group and working on *The Snake* had soon started to take its toll on their relationship and Elizabeth had begged him to go to London and sort himself out. On the night he collapsed and died of a heart attack, she had woken up in the early hours, sensing something dreadful had happened. His death at the age of 40 left her wracked with remorse.

'When someone you love dies, somehow you can feel responsible and find yourself thinking: If only I'd been there, if only…,' said Elizabeth. 'That feeling hung over me for a long time, even if it had no basis in reality. I still feel that if I hadn't pushed David to produce that album and spend all that time away from me, that he might still be alive.' [1]

Casting his mind back to the tragedy, Shane says: 'Dave was an expert junkie. He could tighten up the muscle in his neck and just jab it in. It was a butch, macho sort of Dave Jordan thing to do, and I think that's how he died that night. We had some white [heroin] from Amsterdam and we'd been doing it, and we were meant to be going up to Charlie's for a party. I said, "I'm going up now," but I knew I'd had enough, yeah? I knew I was going to be drinking and taking speed and smoking dope and having a laugh. I knew I wouldn't need it for a while, but I'd have to have it.'

Just four months later, another friend of Shane's collapsed and died. This time the emergency services were called not to a hotel room, but Shane's own flat. The ambulance crew arrived to find two men clearly under the influence of alcohol and drugs, or both [2]. They pointed them to the body of a young man lying against a chest of drawers. There was no sign of life and a subsequent inquest would find he died of acute alcohol poisoning and morphine overdose. It took over four days to formally identify Bryan Ging, a young man from County Dublin.

Quite what emotional impact this episode had on Shane is impossible to know. When tragedy comes calling, he tends to pull down the shutters and leave others to do the things which may be painful or distressing. He is shy and sensitive, but he's also an addict, and sadness and guilt seem to be blotted out by the very substances that have claimed the lives of so many of those he has known. And then there is the ever-present television, which continually blares out during his fragmented waking hours, forbidding any contemplation. Even as a child, his instinctive response to the passing of relatives in Tipperary was to face the wall and not speak, pointing to a lifelong inability to face up to reality.

Terry Woods observes: 'There has been so much meandering around that his sense of self is lost. But I don't think he likes himself and that's why he watches so many movies because he will do anything rather than sit with himself. You have to learn to sit with yourself and be yourself, in the moment. It's all to take him away from himself.'

Sinéad O'Connor adds: 'The drugs are how he's blotting it all out and TV is what heroin addicts do. If you've ever spent time with heroin addicts, they burn out their cigarettes, they piss on the sofa, they burn your sofa by mistake, and they blare the TV. The drugs make him not have to think or give a shit or a care... Addicts feel nothing. They have no empathy, they don't feel anything, they don't think. They don't feel stuff like you or I do. The TV doesn't stop him feeling anything or thinking, it's the drug. But the drug makes you want to turn the TV up.'

By the time of Dave Jordan's tragic overdose, addiction had claimed the life of another of Shane's friends, Pogues' lighting engineer Paul Verner. He died from alcoholism in October 1991, inspiring the line 'you wouldn't expect that anyone would go and fucking die' in the James Fearnley song 'Drunken Boat' from The Pogues album *Waiting For Herb*. Then, in 1996, Charlie MacLennan passed away in his sleep from a heart attack. He had been up all night celebrating his birthday and traces of alcohol, heroin, cocaine and cannabis were found in his bloodstream. He was 44.

'It was recklessness to the point of suicide,' said Joey Cashman. 'Charlie got a huge amount of heroin and cocaine and he put out these massive lines and that's really what killed him. Now if you'd gone up to him and said, "Charlie, that is ridiculous," he'd just turn around and say, "Why don't you mind your own fucking business? I know what I'm fucking doing, and I don't give a fuck if I die anyway." He'd been taking drugs all his life. He knew his limits. He didn't do it to die, but it's a form of suicide.' [3]

Charlie's death must have left a massive hole in Shane's life. They had been inseparable after he had left The Pogues, living under the same roof and taking drugs together. He had carried Shane's cumbersome frame onto planes when he was comatose, and when Shane needed a hit on stage, he would wander trance-like into the wings where Big Charlie was on hand with his supplies.

Actor Tomi May saw the two of them when he was boarding a plane for Prague at Heathrow Airport in June 1996. He looked on in amazement as Charlie and another man carried Shane on board and slung him into a nearby aisle seat. Shane was slumped forward, dribbling, when the plane took off and three miniature vodkas were set out on the tray in front of him.

When he woke up, he and Charlie began mumbling to each other in 'their own pissed-up dialect'. By the time they arrived in Prague, where Tomi and his friend Jay Chappell were DJing, they had been offered backstage passes to the festival where The Popes were on the same bill as Iggy Pop. Watching the show at Koupaliště Džbán, they saw the Shane and Charlie double-act in action again.

'Shane starts singing and there are two microphones at stage front – one for Shane at mouth height and another at about waist height,' says Tomi. 'They do some songs then there's a song with a massive instrumental. So, Shane stumbles to the back of the stage, Charlie takes him behind a curtain for a minute or two and then he comes bouncing back out, like he's just had a fat line. He goes to the front of the stage and starts singing, but nothing. He puts his hand up to grab the mic and it's not there. Then he realises he's at the wrong mic, looks around, and the crowd are pissing themselves laughing – thousands of them! It was a surreal experience to have witnessed and remains a treasured memory.'

By the time The Popes came to record their second album, *The Crock Of Gold*, Shane had slipped further than ever from the reach of his family and others who cared about him. He had also lost something he had always prized – people around him he could trust. 'There were some strange people around and he didn't always realise who his real friends were,' remarks Bob 'Lucky' Dowling, who replaced Bernie France on bass. 'He is one of those people you'd sit at the bar with and he'd drink with some people all night and others he'd tell to piss off in a second. They wouldn't be real friends, but the people he had around him business-wise and stuff… I don't know if he likes the darkness of certain people around him. I think he'd been hurt early on and it is very hard to come back from stuff like that and trust people.'

Something else had also happened which had rocked Shane's world to its core. Ten years after they first got together, he and Victoria had separated. Without her, he was bereft. So much so that he uncharacteristically talked about the anguish he was going through. 'At the same time that I split up with my missus, Shane and Victoria split up,' says Bob. 'She [Victoria] was with some young guy, so me and Shane were sort of on each other's shoulders for a couple of months. He said to me, "I know what she's about, but I don't give a shit. I just want her back. She can have whatever she wants.""

For two people who seem so different, it might seem miraculous that Shane and Victoria's relationship has survived. Shane cares not one jot about fame, while she openly admits to pursuing it. He drinks through the day and barely eats. Victoria practises yoga and goes to the gym. But they are bound together by a profound mutual need.

If the grief in Shane's eyes was being masked by the dark shades he wore, it was laid bare in his writing. In 'Victoria', he wore his heart on his sleeve and made a barely veiled, but caustic reference to her liaison with Van Morrison. 'Victoria, left me in opium euphoria / With a fat monk singing Gloria'.

Their relationship had foundered and it would do so again. But whenever they separated, Shane longed to get her back. He simply couldn't cope without her and, despite the hurt inflicted by his infidelities, she couldn't give him up. 'If you feel that close, you get angry, but it doesn't separate you,' she said. 'It's just the way of the lifestyle with all the opportunities and being on the road. I'm a very jealous person, but we always came back together.' [4]

One of the reasons for Victoria's attraction to Shane was divulged in a deeply personal piece for the *Guardian*'s family section in January 2009. Entitled 'Looking for a Father Figure', it revealed her unhappy and confusing upbringing in a remote part of Ireland, and her search for the biological father she had never met. Victoria was just 1 when her mother Orla – pregnant with her sister Vanessa – married Dardis Clarke. Her mother later told them both that he was their father. But when Victoria was about 7, her mother left him and into the role of father stepped a man called Dave, with whom her mother was having a baby. Victoria admitted she made his life 'as unpleasant as possible and it was only after I left home that we warmed to one another' [5].

Years later Vanessa needed a copy of her birth certificate and she found herself staring at the words 'Father unknown'. Her mother came clean. They had different fathers and neither of them was Dardis Clarke. Even more of a shock for Victoria was that she had almost been put up for adoption. Her mother, like so many young women who became pregnant outside marriage in 1960s Ireland, had been sent to a home for wayward girls. These homes were the Catholic Church's way of hiding the 'shame' of a fallen woman. Babies born in the homes were put up for adoption and this would have been Victoria's fate had her grandfather not taken her in as a baby while her mother completed her education. When her grandfather died years later, Victoria embarked on a search for her real father.

As it turned out, he would find her first. Victoria revealed in an Irish magazine feature that she was looking for her father when he telephoned their local pub and ended up speaking with Shane. Victoria went on to meet him at a club in Mayfair and, on several occasions after that, in Claridge's.

In the unflinchingly honest piece, Victoria admitted her troubled childhood and sense of desertion had drawn her to men 'who seemed to need me, who clung to me as I clung to them'. And she pointed with laser-like precision to the appeal of her relationship with Shane. 'Once we were together, I felt my own life becoming subsumed by his,' she wrote. 'This was a welcome feeling for me, as I preferred to live someone else's life. I took immediate responsibility for his moods and problems and devoted myself to solving them and to being his personal assistant, as well as his lover. I worshipped him in every possible way.

'In return, I felt that he gave me a sense of purpose, as well as a sense of being wanted. I belonged to him in a way that I had never really belonged to my family. I found my place in the world for the first time. And before long, Shane took over the financial responsibility for both of us, which made me feel supported.'

Without Victoria, Shane felt lost and it caused him to reflect on his lifestyle and his behaviour towards her. Some say his continual abuse of drugs and alcohol suppressed thoughts of guilt and sadness and helped him to avoid confronting the consequences of his actions. But with her out of his life, he couldn't drown out his feelings of self-loathing. 'It seems that I am different / Seems that I am strange / I'm a bumpkin / I'm a lout,' he wrote in 'Victoria'.

Whatever was happening in Shane's life, he never lost his yearning for The Commons and since establishing The Popes he was seen regularly in the bars around Nenagh. Pubs line the long street which runs through the small Tipperary town: The Hibernian, Lily's, The Half Barrel. Shane knew them all, although most often he would be found at the counter of Philly

Ryan's with brothers Noel and Scruffy Kenny and other locals who had become close friends. He was the toast of the town and in 'B&I Ferry' he raised a glass to it, namechecking Noel Kenny, Scruffy, Mick, Jimmy and Brick of 'north-west Tipp'.

Noel Kenny had been a teenager working in one of the local pubs when he first met Shane in the early 1980s. He knew Shane was in a band in England, but it was only when he moved there and saw The Pogues on *Top of the Pops* that he recognised him. He went to see them perform a few times, but didn't get to know Shane until he moved back to Nenagh in the early 1990s and began working in Joe Corcoran's pub, now The Kiwi Bar.

Word would spread like wildfire when Shane was due in town and his friends would gear themselves up for marathon sessions. Sometimes Joey would call Noel from Shannon Airport to let him know the band was on its way to Nenagh. Other times, Maurice would call Philly's and the news would be passed that way. Either way, he knew there would be no sleep until Shane had gone again.

Noel says: 'I'd just book time off work and it would be like, "I'm not coming home!" He'd sleep in our house for a few nights in a row and then he might just go home and say "Goodbye" to the parents and go back to London. He'd often call me before he called his mum and dad. Generally, he'd stay up all night and then go to sleep around eight or nine o'clock in the morning, when everybody else was getting up again. Often, I'd ring his dad or mum and say, "Shane told me to ring you at lunchtime." They'd say, "Oh, he's just gone to bed. You'll have to wait until seven o'clock this evening." He always did it the opposite way – he was a real vampire. He'd be up all night and asleep all day, except when he'd be travelling. Generally, by three or four o'clock in the morning, I would have had enough myself and just go. But he'd keep going! I've often joined him, and I'd be stone-cold sober and by the end of the night I'd be fucked, and he'd still be going. His stamina is unreal. But having said that, he wouldn't be throwing drinks into him. He would just be sipping.'

Shane might have drunk slowly as his mates guzzled their pints, but he made up for it with his extensive orders, filling up an entire table with his own drinks. Noel recalls: 'One night myself, Scruffy and Shane were in Tom's Tavern in Borrisokane, which is down near Carney Commons. Shane went to the counter and said, "A pint of Guinness, a large bottle of cider, a glass of white wine, a cup of coffee, and whatever the lads are having!" But those four drinks were still there two hours later, while we were drinking more and more pints. He'd take a couple of mouthfuls out of the Guinness, then he might have some wine, then he'd have a drop of cider, then he'd drink some coffee. He was always mixing and matching, and you'd never know what he was going to have next: it could be a gin and tonic, it could be a Martini.

'I wouldn't say I would be in a heap or anything, but I'd just know when I'd had enough and go home. But he would sit there 'til dawn, no problem whatsoever, and his brain is always working one hundred per cent. You might just mention something and the next thing he'll rattle off stuff like an encyclopaedia. It could be about a football match twenty years ago or it could be some war that happened two hundred years ago... It's like a photographic memory.'

If they weren't drinking the local pubs dry, Shane and his friends would decamp to The Commons, frequently consuming poitín. Paul Ronan remembers on such occasion: 'We were all sitting around with a bottle of poitín and Noel had just bought a brand-new pair of jeans and he was looking the bee's knees. Anyway, he decided he was a bit cold, so we had the fire going and he lay down in front of it, and he set fire to a leg of the jeans and we had to cut it off! He had to come back into town with all these black patches and one leg missing!'

The cottage sat empty when Shane wasn't around. When he arrived after a prolonged absence, it would take the neighbours by surprise. Noel says: 'We were playing LPs and drinking away and the next thing, this woman barged in the door and says, "What are you doing in here?" and Shane says, "I live here. This is my fucking house." She was a next-door neighbour and she had seen my car outside and thought it was somebody breaking in or something. It could have been twelve months since he was last there.'

Maurice and Therese had returned to Tipperary in 1988 after living in England for more than thirty years. Siobhan and her mum had taken charge of the house-hunting and had instantly fallen in love with a large detached house on an acre of land in the townland of Garryard East, Silvermines, a few miles south of Nenagh. They presented it to Maurice as a done deal and he agreed that they would buy it.

For Shane it was an escape from the distractions of London, and it was in his bedroom there that he had begun writing songs for *The Crock Of Gold*. He felt more at home in Nenagh and its surrounds than anywhere else, and that affinity bled through in the lyrics. In 'Back In The County Hell', he wrote: 'When I've done my patriotic chore / And burnt London to the ground / I'll get back home to Nenagh / And get pissed every night in town.' 'Mother Mo Chroi' found him reflecting on the wrench felt by those of his parents' generation who had to leave their homeland to find work, and his own 'furious devotion' to Ireland.

Maurice had his own pub, 'Mac's Bar', in a downstairs room, known as The Den. The family joked that after smoking was banned in pubs in 2007, it was the only smoking bar left in Ireland. Siobhan also spent a lot of time there as she had already moved back to Dublin before her parents left England. She still has happy memories of parties and sessions at the property. Wherever Shane himself was in the world and whatever was happening in his life, he would always be at the house for Christmas. Drink would flow and music was played until the early hours. There was no roast turkey on the menu, though. Maurice was a vegetarian (he is now vegan) and Shane was close to being one, so Siobhan would cook a vegetarian moussaka for their Christmas Day meal.

Scruffy Kenny says: 'He'd ring every Christmas for years to say he was coming at eight or nine o'clock, but he'd never come until twelve or one o'clock. He'd always come down on Christmas Eve so he could spend time with his mother on Christmas Day. He'd come and sit in our house until two or three o'clock and Siobhan would be ringing for him, wondering where he was and saying his dinner was ready. We'd have to take him down to Siobhan's house or up to Silvermines… He treated Christmas as just another day, apart from he'd always have to go to see his mother. That was his most important thing ever.'

One Christmas morning, the Nenagh gang returned to Scruffy's house, having been boozing all night. They arrived with a bottle of brandy and a bottle of Baileys. But the Baileys got knocked over and spilled all over the coffee table. Scruffy recalls: 'My wife came in with a J-cloth to wipe it and up and he [Shane] took the J-cloth off her, squeezed it back into a glass and drank it! That's his attitude. He'd never see anything go to waste.'

Shane's friends made the most of every minute when he was in town. Sessions at Philly's would go on through the small hours and one morning, a cleaner arrived to find Shane asleep across a seat. She told him it was time to wake up and asked if he would like a drink. 'A triple gin,' came his groggy reply.

Tom Kenneally, who manages Philly's, remembers putting some music on one night while he counted the takings in the main bar. Shane and one of his pals had fallen asleep in the lounge and when Tom put on a recording of the late Liam Clancy performing 'The Broad Majestic Shannon', Shane emerged in a state of confusion.

'The one I put on was a live version of him singing it in New York and instead of Liam Clancy singing, "Take my hand, dry your tears, babe," he sings, "Dry your tears, Shane",' says Tom. 'MacGowan wakes up and he hears Liam Clancy singing, "Dry your tears, Shane", and he comes out into the bar holding his head and says, "Jesus, what's going on?" because he could hear Liam Clancy calling him.

'I said, "It's OK, it's only on YouTube!" So, for the next two hours, he didn't have a beer, he just smoked a couple of fags and we were just standing at the computer picking out songs. It was like a jukebox of his life and we were talking about Paul Weller and the Gallaghers. When you have a love of music and you listen to him like that, completely coherent, you realise, "This man's a fucking genius."'

Philly also runs a funeral business that stands opposite the pub and one night he thrilled Shane by asking him to help prepare a grave. So, in the middle of the night, the songwriter so fascinated with death found himself unexpectedly occupied in a cemetery. 'I had a funeral in Terryglass which wouldn't be far from Carney and is right on the lake,' recalls Philly. 'One thing I don't do too easily is get up in the morning, so I had Shane here in the pub and at two in the morning I said, "Shane, will you give me a hand?"

'He says, "What will we do?"

'"A bit of undertaking," I says.

'"Oh Jesus, no bother," he says.

'So down to Terryglass we went, in the middle of the night. We had all these rolls of carpet and we dressed the grave together! Well, he fucking loved that. Shane would love to think he was in anything bar the music trade.'

Bar staff also had to get used to a different routine when Shane was in town. 'Shane would order drink all day and there would be no money passing hands,' explains Philly. 'There would be different girls and new people serving. I have it rented now and the place changed hands, and you're trying to explain to them, "Just relax, don't worry about Shane MacGowan. He's going to honour everything and give you double."

'I said to Shane. "That's €180 for your drinks, by the way," and he said, "There you go, and there's fifty for yourself." That's the way it works.'

Shane is renowned for his generosity. If he needs driving somewhere, he makes sure anyone who helps him out is handsomely rewarded. He has been known to give £100 to someone begging in the street and he has a compassion for people facing hard times. Noel Kenny says: 'There was a traditional music festival on in Nenagh and Shane happened to arrive in the thick of it. We were walking around town and there was a blind fella busking with an accordion on the side of the street, so Shane pulled out twenty quid and stuck it in the jar. Later that night we were up in Philly's and it turned out Philly had seen this guy playing down the street and he said, "Oh Jesus, come up and play in the pub tonight." So, he played all night and Shane got up and sang "Dirty Old Town" and "The Irish Rover" and a few songs with him, and the blind guy was delighted. He was a Pogues fan and never in his wildest dreams did he believe Shane would come up and sing on stage with him.

'Later on, a woman went around with a pint glass collecting for the guy, and everybody threw a couple of quid in. Shane pulled out this wad of sterling and counted out two hundred and stuck it into the jar. The next thing, Shane disappeared. Five minutes later he came back again behind her and she walked up to the guy and gave him the pint glass and counted all the money out for him. I said, "Where did you go?" and he said, "I just followed her around to make sure nobody took the fucking money out of the glass."'

Bankcards are an alien concept to Shane and his approach to money harks back to the old days in rural Ireland. Once, Noel accompanied him to a bank in Nenagh to withdraw some money. Shane mumbled to the cashier that he wanted to withdraw some money and she said he needed to contact his bank in London to verify his identity. What happened next was classic Shane.

'He had most of the digits [of his account number], but he couldn't remember the last two,' recounts Noel. 'The next thing is he starts pulling things out of his pockets and putting them up on the counter. He pulls out this bag of cocaine and left it there, then a lump of hash and left that there. Next, he found this piece of paper with the phone number and a name, and he gave it to the girl behind the counter. Five minutes later, she said, "No problem Mr MacGowan," and she started counting out fifties. He said, "No, no, I want it in used twenties," so she did all that. Then he put everything back in the pocket and of course the coke and the hash were the last two things!'

Next stop was a shop where Shane bought a holdall and armed with that he disappeared into a second-hand bookshop. Up and down the rows he went, indiscriminately picking up books from the shelves, and filling up his bag. Having paid, he called Philly at the pub and ordered drinks to be delivered to The Commons. Shane then spent three weeks solid voraciously reading through his pile of books.

Noel says: 'There is a pub about two miles from there, John Ryan's, and we'd go up there and have two or three drinks. Then he'd say, "I have to go home, I want to finish reading..." whatever book it was. He'd have four books on the go at the same time – he was on a mission to read them. He'd sit there drinking whiskey or whatever and say, "You watch television, I'm reading this."'

However intoxicated he was, he drank in the words on the page just as heavily. Facts and figures would be filed away and pulled out randomly in conversations years later. At the same time, Shane was observing the colourful characters from the town and the stories he heard them tell. Just as his childhood visits to The Commons had informed his school essays and some of The Pogues' songs, so the people he got to know when he returned in later life inspired lyrics found on *The Crock Of Gold*.

Three years had passed since *The Snake* and by the time The Popes came to record its follow-up, Paul McGuinness and Tom McManamon were the only survivors from the original line-up. John 'The Riddler' Myers had come in on fiddle, whistle and guitar, and Kieran Kiely was supplying accordions, whistles and backing vocals. Bob Dowling meanwhile had replaced outgoing bassist Bernie France.

Bob had been in and out of various bands and had worked on the sound desk at The Sir George Robey in Finsbury Park and The Lady Owen Arms in Clerkenwell, where he got to know Paul Ronan. He still vividly remembers the first time he clapped eyes on Shane at The Sir George Robey, then a staple on the live music scene in London.

Says Bob: 'One night it was empty, none of the bands turned up and MacGowan walks in and there were just three of us sitting at the bar. He was as mad as a march hare, but like a beacon. Not because he was Shane MacGowan, but because of his character. He used the pub as his local and I was there five nights a week, so we became friendly. I remember walking in one weekend when I wasn't working, and he had a broadsheet – I think it was *The Sporting Life* – and he was just tearing chunks off it and eating it. I thought, What's going on here?'

Bob's invitation to join The Popes didn't come from Shane, however, but Danny Heatley, who he knew from a previous band. There was an American tour coming up in November 1995 but as there was no time to rehearse, Bob was simply sent a live tape from which he had to learn the songs.

The recording of *The Crock Of Gold* at Wessex Studios in London was beset with problems. Brian Robertson produced the original sessions, only to be replaced by Adrian Sherwood and engineer Alan Branch. Shortly after they took over, Shane fell off a barstool at Filthy's during one of the literary events and broke his hip. Richard Thomas, Shane's old friend from King's Cross, says: 'Publishers had a lot of money in those days and they had put five hundred quid behind the bar. If it was another author from a different publisher, then they'd say, "Well, we'll find five hundred quid as well." It went really daft at times. One evening there was about two grand behind the bar and Shane took advantage. When he broke his hip, I remember the hospital saying, "He's got the hips of a very old man."'

Bob says, 'Tommy and Paul used to go down there every day for a couple of hours and come back to Wessex Studios. How it was ever done is amazing. We did the backing tracks ourselves and Shane healed up a bit and came in and put in some great vocal performances, even though he was just out of hospital. At the time it was fun. I wouldn't like to be doing it now at 50, but in my mid-twenties it was like, "Yeah, this is fucking rock'n'roll."'

Perhaps unsurprisingly, the record wasn't received as positively as its predecessor and didn't perform as well commercially. Released in November 1997, *The Crock Of Gold* reached number fifty-nine in the UK chart and promptly sank like a stone. 'Justly praised by the likes of Christy Moore on a recent BBC documentary for the originality of his writing with The Pogues, MacGowan these days is principally a master of cliché,' wrote Neil Spencer in *Mojo*. 'While it helps that he coined at least some of the clichés – the tales of demented ceilidhs and ne'r-do-wells on drinking binges that his audience expects – his celebration of modern Celtic mythology on, say "Paddy Rolling Stone", is never enough to deliver *The Crock Of Gold* from predictability.'

ZTT put out 'Lonesome Highway' as a single, but it didn't bother the Top 75 and 'Rock'n'roll Paddy' similarly flopped. Then again, by the late 1990s, CD singles were an irrelevance for groups like The Popes, having nothing like the impact of their vinyl predecessors. The previous year The Popes had released the *Christmas Party EP* which featured 'Christmas Lullaby', 'Paddy Rolling Stone', 'Hippy Hippy Shake' and 'Danny Boy'. However, its highest chart placing was eighty-six, proving that even a Christmas release by Shane could be a festive turkey.

He did, however, feature on a number one record for the first and only time in his career before the year was out. Lou Reed's 'Perfect Day' was recorded to raise money for BBC Children in Need. Shane joined Bono, David Bowie, Elton John, Emmylou Harris and Tammy Wynette, among others to contribute to the charity record. It entered the chart at number one and spent thirteen weeks in the Top 40.

The Popes' popularity was driven not so much by record sales as by their live performances and the fans' love of Shane. Despite the fact that The Pogues' unremitting tours had taken a huge toll on Shane, The Popes travelled extensively and would do so with him until 2005. They proved a big draw at events all over the world, from the Montreux Jazz Festival in Switzerland and Pinkpop in the Netherlands to the Byron Bay Bluesfest in Australia. They never commanded the top billing enjoyed by The Pogues, except when they headlined the 1997 Fleadh in Finsbury Park, replacing an unwell Bob Dylan. Van Morrison was also on the bill and it was the first time he and Shane had crossed paths since his dalliance with Victoria three years earlier.

Bob Dowling says: 'Bob Dylan took ill and no one knew who was going to headline. Van was on before us and you could tell Van wasn't happy that MacGowan was going to be closing the show. He was in the next portacabin and he was shouting at the sax player for playing some bum notes. I've never heard Van Morrison argue for that long before. Of course, there was the personal thing between him and Shane, and I bet Shane got a kick out of that. Also, there was the irony of what happened with The Pogues and Bob Dylan. It was like, "Ha, I'm standing in for Dylan now!"'

Offstage, Shane was beginning to reflect on the impact his lifestyle was having on his physical health. Despite the damage he had inflicted on his body over the years, he has a fear of dying. He is insistent that he wants to live and treasures the time he spends with his friends. When faced with the prospect of leaving them behind, he becomes emotional, holding their hands for ages and looking at them tearfully.

Noel Kenny remembers one such moment: 'Shane had done the Olympia Theatre with The Popes and he came down home the following day and stayed around for Christmas. Shane said, "Noel, this is the last Christmas we're ever going to meet," and we both burst into tears. He was bad on the drugs at the time and you could see he had one eye looking one way and one in the other direction. I thought, Jesus, he's fucked.'

An article in *Hot Press* in December 1996 sounded a more positive note, with some of The Popes describing the period since Charlie MacLennan's passing as 'a fresh start for Shane' [6]. But their optimism proved misplaced and Shane sank deeper still into addiction. Inside his rented flat in Gospel Oak, near Hampstead Heath, he sat snorting thick lines of heroin and coke, numbing whatever feelings he was experiencing. And before the decade was out, another harrowing event would cast a spotlight on Shane's wretched world.

CHAPTER 10

Back In The County Hell

'We watched our friends grow up together
And we saw them as they fell
Some of them fell into heaven
Some of them fell into hell'

'A Rainy Night In Soho', **The Pogues**

Shane's notoriety and ready access to hard drugs made him a magnet for other users. Add to that his almost inhuman constitution and their temptation to keep pace with him, and there was a high risk that history would repeat itself. On 17 May 1999, it did.

An emergency call was made and an ambulance sent to 82 Savernake Road in Hampstead. Inside, a young man lay dead. He was Robbie O'Neill, the son of The Pogues' former publicist Terry O'Neill. He was 25 and, like Bryan Ging, he had overdosed in Shane's flat.

Shane and Robbie had socialised back in Dublin, going to parties together. He had seen first-hand Shane's capacity for hard drugs and Shane's recollection of one such occasion suggests he was keen to impress his young friend.

'He [Robbie] would take me to a party where there were lots of young idiots and there would be a big idiot who was "the man". I passed out for a while at this party and it was the one where he shaved my eyebrows while I was asleep. I woke up and I didn't mention it. Then this crowd came around with this big guy, who was as tall as me and built like a bricklayer. That's because he doesn't do hard drugs and he was into making money out of it.

'So, I did a great one on him because I was sure he'd fucking suggested cutting my eyebrows. He was saying, "Do you want to buy any speed?" because everybody knew I was a speed freak.

'I said, "Yeah, sure, but I've got to try it first, yeah?" He gave me a gram of speed to try and I scarfed it, tsscchh, and it was a great blast. I managed to conceal it, but I was buzzing! I was trying hard not to piss myself laughing.

'He said, "How's that? Give me the money."

'I said, 'It hasn't done anything, mate. You'll have to give me another one to try." And he did it – and then he gave me another one. Three grams of speed and it was quite good speed for a change. I was just pretending I wasn't feeling it and I had to try and avoid grinning.

'I just sat there and said, "This is not really doing anything. Where did you get that stuff?" That was the best speed I'd had for ages in Dublin because it's not that good usually. So, he actually gave me a fourth one, right? I said, "I'm sure it will take in a minute and I also want to get some smack." He wanted to say he'd sold me as much speed and smack as possible. Eventually he left in a huff because he was a big guy, but he was a sissy and I'd finished his speed. All the kids were looking at us and they were really learning something, and Robbie was pissing himself.'

Bob Dowling says that, while Shane may seem nonplussed about such tragic events, Robbie's death hit him badly. 'All I know is Robbie had nowhere to stay and Shane was the one who let him have somewhere to stay... I think that really affected him. He will come across as, "Yeah, that's life," but you know there's that bit of humanity that's in him and he probably feels more than most people would. But he has a mechanism.'

The details that emerged at the inquest into Robbie's death were achingly sad [1]. He had tried to make his way in the music world and had worked as a sound engineer at The Mean Fiddler and other venues owned by Irish impresario Vince Power. But in pursuit of something more exciting, he had given this up and started to drift. Living with his dad had led to rows and after moving out, he had ended up being taken in by Shane and Victoria.

Despite a post-mortem finding that Robbie had taken four times the fatal dose of heroin, the absence of heroin in his urine proved he was not a regular user. Whatever he thought he was taking, and however much he thought he could safely use, he had probably died within half an hour of taking it.

News of yet another fatality in Shane's flat soon reached the press and the fact that Robbie was the son of one of his long-time friends only added to the public interest. SHANE'S TRAGEDY read the headline in the Irish tabloid *The Star*, which quoted Paul McGuinness from The Popes saying Shane had been left in 'deep shock'. 'He is devastated by what has happened and is very distressed by Robbie's death,' he said. 'Shane and Terry are great friends – they have been for a long time. I spoke to Terry myself yesterday, but he was too upset to talk to me about Robbie.' Shane's failure to attend the inquest, and the lack of respect he showed Terry and his family at the memorial service, created a deep rift between them. Some years would pass before Shane and Terry spoke again.

A Scotland Yard spokesman said the 'householder and people who were there at the time of the death' had been interviewed. No arrests had been made, however, and it was not being treated as suspicious. At that stage, formal identification had still not taken place and the post-mortem had proved inconclusive. However, if there seemed to be no legal consequences for Shane from this second fatal overdose at his home, further than another stinging admonishment from a coroner, that was about to change.

Sinéad O'Connor had been disgusted by Shane's no-show at Robbie's inquest and was distraught that another young man had overdosed at his home. So, in November 1999, when she called to see him and found him taking heroin, she took drastic action. She reported him to Kentish Town police station and had Shane arrested.

Shane railed against Sinéad when the story hit the papers, accusing her of seeking publicity for herself, and when the police followed up her allegation he called his former girlfriend Mary Buxton, then a practising solicitor. Not for the first time, she came to his aid. Mary says: 'He was quite lucky because I was working in London then anyway, so I knew a lot of the prosecutors, some of them were quite fond of The Pogues and I'd see them at gigs. He needed to just get a caution for entry to America, so that he didn't have a recent drug conviction. Sinéad thought she was being kind – but what an idiot. I mean, sort out your own addictions and leave other people alone. The police did charge him, but I went along and said, "He'll go into rehab," and they eventually agreed. He went to The Priory for twenty-eight days to get his caution. I don't know how much good it did him. I heard a lot of drink was being smuggled in.'

Sinéad had known Shane for about thirteen years and regarded him as a close friend. Speaking about her motives for reporting Shane to the police, she is characteristically candid: 'That was a desire not so much to help the addict but to stop him dying. It was also to stop Victoria from starting because she was beginning to consider taking the drug so she could be on his level. So, that wasn't necessarily trying to take care of him or take care of the addict. It was to create a situation where I knew he would only be cautioned. But then if he got caught again, he would get locked up. I also did it because he wouldn't go to the inquest into Robbie O'Neill's death and that was very disrespectful because Robbie died, like several people around Shane, from sniffing heroin when, so it was said, he thought that it was cocaine...

'Reporting him for possession of heroin meant he got cautioned, and if then he got caught again with heroin on him, he was fucked. He would have gone to jail. It was a slow path to put him on, but it put him on a path which he then had no choice but to follow.'

Shane would later concede that Sinéad's unwanted intervention did have the desired effect. Asked if the episode had ended his relationship with Sinéad, he replied: 'No, but it ended my relationship with heroin'. In an interview in 2003, Shane insisted he was totally clean from the drug. 'I'm not recommending to people that they should rat their friends out to the police, you know what I mean? At the time I was furious, obviously, but I'm actually very grateful to her now.' [2]

Sinéad's bid to get Shane to change his lifestyle resonated with Siobhan, who had intervened on numerous occasions to try to help her brother. 'I did a lot of things like that,' comments Siobhan. 'I just kept on and on. With all that drug stuff, Vicky used to ring me and say, "Come over here," and I used to fight and fight with him. I spent a lot of my twenties trying to get him off and trying to change him, until I realised I can't. So, his addiction had a really bad effect on our relationship and that's the same as any addict in any family. It's just how it is, and I understand that now.'

Victoria also entered the clinic at the same time. By now, she and Shane each had been battling their own demons for years: Shane his rapacious heroin addiction and Victoria the depression she put down to her failure to become a success in her own right. She wrote about her experiences in a 'Priory Diary' for the *Evening Standard*.

'Shane's having dinner with me in the restaurant,' she wrote. 'I'm highly anxious, because I think everyone's staring at us. I have a phobia about being embarrassed in public. Shane always gets stared at, but he doesn't give a shit. He's got no shoes on and his suit is covered in filth and cigarette ash and he's reading to me, out loud, from a book of Irish history. I hate this, because I secretly have a desperate craving for fame and success, which I can't do anything about, because of my fear of embarrassment. I want to watch telly now.' [3]

Victoria admitted she had checked into the private clinic after becoming 'suicidally depressed' because she 'wasn't famous or important' [4]. A novel about her spiritual journey, an accompanying screenplay and a pitch to Channel 4 to turn it into a TV show had all been rejected, dealing a devastating blow to her confidence and lifelong ambition to be recognised.

Speaking about it almost twenty years later, Victoria says: 'The Priory was never something [Shane] took seriously. He only went there because people made him go there. I wanted to go there myself, but Sinéad O'Connor got him busted and they said, "You can either go to The Priory or go to prison, which do you want?" So, he went to The Priory, although he considered prison because I think he thought, Oh no, it's group therapy!

'It was very weird being in there together. We didn't have the same therapy groups or anything because I was being treated for depression and he was being treated for drugs, so it was different. I wrote about that very facetiously because I found that for me, being funny about it... would take the power out of it. But actually I wanted to die. I was suicidal. I had been seeing a counsellor every day and it hadn't helped and I still wanted to die. So, I thought, Well I don't really want to have to kill myself. I'd rather try being institutionalised and see if that worked. But I did write a funny piece for the *Evening Standard* which they [The Priory] were very angry about because they said I was trivialising it and being facetious and frivolous.

'I was trying to explain to them that my way of coping was to make a joke of it. I didn't really want to address the serious side of it, so I addressed the funny side. I found The Priory very useful because I actually wanted to be there. Shane didn't think there was anything wrong with him, but I knew there was something wrong with me.'

Not long after her treatment there, she left Shane and moved into a cramped bedsit in Dublin where she continued to feel 'hopelessly depressed'.

Shane meanwhile was as miserable without her as she was without him. Looking back on her decision to leave him, Victoria comments: 'I felt like I did have to try and stand on my own two feet and I suppose I did have to try to face my own demons. It's quite easy when you're with someone else who seems to have more demons than you do, to just face their demons. That distracts you from your own until it drives you crazy. I think I was just driven crazy enough to need to go to hospital and then when I got out of there I was like, "I can go back to bullying Shane to stop taking heroin or I can try and fix myself." And so, I decided to try and fix myself and that took quite a long time.'

Victoria had also been upset by Sinéad's decision to have Shane arrested. But later she came to appreciate her actions had been born out of love for them both. Victoria said, 'I did believe she did do it because she genuinely felt that our relationship was worth saving and she saw that I love Shane and that Shane loves me, and she could see that very clearly. Even though l couldn't really at that point see it and I was ready to give up. I thought, Right, I'll cut my losses and see if I can find some more satisfactory relationship. It may well have helped because I think it did force Shane to think – even if he didn't want to think – about what was going on and what I was unhappy about and what he was doing and stuff.' [5]

An ominous glimpse into Shane's declining mental state came in February 2000 when he appeared on RTE's *The Pat Kenny Show*. The presenter hinted at the direction the discussion was going to take in his introduction when he said Shane had been 'in the news for all the wrong reasons'. Before he began an interview that was painful to watch, Shane performed Hank Williams' last ever song, 'The Angel Of Death', accompanied only by Tom McManamon on banjo and Bob Dowling on bass. 'Can you truthfully say with your dying breath / That you're ready to meet the Angel Of Death?' he slurred. Some of those in the studio audience, which included Maurice and Therese, must have wondered if Shane would soon be having to answer that very question himself.

Shane had the gait of a man considerably older than his forty-two years as he shuffled slowly from the stage to the waiting chair. But as he sat himself down, glass in hand, and gazed out blearily at the audience, he looked in that moment like a lost child. His defences were down, and his host sensed an opportunity for some tough questions. 'What kind of shape are you in these days?' Pat asked bluntly.

'Um... about the same shape as you really, tsscchh', Shane slurred through gravestone teeth.

Pat laughed, but Shane and everyone there knew what was coming next. He said he had been reading about Shane's falling out with Sinéad O'Connor, remarking that they were pretty good friends. 'No – I didn't like her anyway', Shane replied disdainfully, prompting laughter from the audience. But he had no such glib response when he was asked point-blank what had happened when Sinéad had called to his flat. He sat speechless and nervously cleared his throat, his eyes flicking around the audience as if looking for the answer. After a prolonged silence, he replied: 'Well, she told me she was a priest and if I didn't do what she said, me being a Catholic...'

When Pat said Sinéad had 'shopped' him to the police for having heroin, Shane was quick to point out he had not been convicted of anything, and anyway the case was sub judice, meaning he could not legally discuss it. However, the presenter was not letting the matter rest. He pressed Shane on how he had felt about the police going to see him because of someone he had known for a long time. Shane stroked his scruffy beard and another agonising silence ensued. A man who had come to rely heavily on other people to do his bidding and solve his problems was suddenly exposed and alone.

'Well actually I'd like to say something more important than any of this rubbish', he said, before hesitating again. 'It's a very dangerous drug, heroin, and you should think very carefully before you take it, yeah? But the same goes for alcohol or nicotine. But I'm not... I'm not a regular heroin user, yeah? OK?'

Shane conceded he had used the drug occasionally in his own home and the police were aware of that. Trying to shift the focus away from himself, he pointed out that schoolchildren in Ireland were taking heroin. When Pat Kenny questioned the kind of role model he presented to them, Shane blamed Sinéad for publicising it. He cut a pathetic figure throughout, incoherent in his answers. Here was an erudite man, renowned for his sharp-wittedness, and reduced by his addictions to a rambling mess.

Yet there was sympathy from the audience and when he said Sinéad would do 'anything for publicity', it drew a round of applause. From his parents, who also contributed to the show, there was unswerving loyalty and love. Asked what she thought of what was happening to Shane and what had been in the papers, Therese was clear and firm in her reply: 'As far as I'm concerned, Shane is a son who is very, very talented, loved very much by us, extremely trustworthy, and of whom, of course, we're very proud. As regards your question about the papers, I do not think that in going to the police to report Shane, Sinéad O'Connor did the right thing. And may I make a point? If Sinéad did it as a friend, as she claims, why all the publicity? That's not the action of a friend. She should not have spoken to the papers.'

Maurice's loyalty towards his errant son was equally unerring: 'I never comment on Shane's private life. There is so much more to comment upon. His magnificent genius that I've had the privilege to have custody over during the formative years.' When Pat Kenny asked whether they worried about him all the time, his father simply observed: 'What parent doesn't worry about their children? You're a parent, you must know.'

Shane said his boozing would be regarded as 'sissy-drinking in Ireland' and Maurice also sought to give his son's behaviour a wider context.

'The whole bloody country drinks, you know?' remarked Maurice. 'Alcohol is the most dangerous drug in the world – everybody knows that. It creates all the violence, most of the violence. You know, heroin is sissy stuff – to use Shane's expression – as regards violence. The only reason heroin is a problem is because people can't get it at a reasonable price.'

Sinéad O'Connor was watching the show and was deeply hurt at the criticism levelled at her by Shane. Her riposte was the song 'Big Bunch Of Junkie Lies', which would appear on her 2003 album, *She Who Dwells In The Secret Place Of The Most High Shall Abide Under The Shadow Of The Almighty*.

Sinéad remarks: 'He was going around on telly saying I was ordering him around, and maybe he said I did it for publicity, which is horseshit because why would I want bad publicity? And anyway, I didn't need the publicity. If I want publicity, I get my tits out! Then what happened was, quite sweetly and quite dutifully after a few years, he began to understand when he came off heroin... because it did get him off heroin, ultimately.

I don't know if he ever went back on it, but it certainly got him off because he got a fright and they got him on methadone. And as he began to come off it, he changed his heart about why I had done it. He began to realise that I had done it to save his life and then I believe he began to go around saying that, in fact, I had saved his life.

'A therapist once told me a husband should be very unflattered if his wife is not throwing plates, and that's the way I felt about Shane. Not like a wife, but like a sister. I was throwing plates because I just wasn't having my brother go down like that, I wasn't having him act like that, I wasn't having him treat other human beings like that, and I was not having Victoria start taking smack...

'I would go round to the apartment and it was covered in black mould, you know the way it is with smackheads. A woman can't live like that. So, it was also out of love for her that I did it. The unrequited love I have for her.'

If Shane had been shaken by the tragic events that had happened in his flat, he hid it well. Any direct questions on the subject were casually shrugged off. When asked in a 2003 interview about the number of friends he had lost to drink and drugs, he replied, 'Who hasn't?' He also pointed out that drugs had played no part in the untimely deaths of Joe Strummer and Kirsty MacColl. 'So, I've lost a lot of people to other things as well,' he said. 'People die, you know? It's a fact of life, tsscchh.' [6]

A small crack in his apparent insouciance was glimpsed briefly when he was interviewed about his painting of leprechauns sitting around a fire, used on the cover for *The Crock Of Gold*. Shane admitted: 'I've been through a lot, yeah, right, a lot of people have died over the last few years and I suppose after that *Crock Of Gold* album is when it started happening, you know? And I've been pretty down in a lot of ways.'

Amid the blackness enveloping Shane, filmmaker Sarah Share embarked on a documentary about his life for Irish production company TG4. This time Shane was filmed in London – not in The Commons as he had been for the BBC documentary three years earlier. However, the focus was firmly on the cottage and the time he had spent with his mother's family. As he had always done once he had taken on his ultra-Irish identity, he painted Tipperary as a heavenly playground. England, the country in which he had been born and raised, was cited as the cause of his ruin. Looking unkempt and sounding incoherent, he said: 'I started off as a healthy fucking Tipperary farm boy, you know what I mean? I came over here and degenerated into a... into a... into a school truant... um... drunkard and drug user and thief.'

Living in London had not only warped his character, but soured his relationship with his dad, he said. 'We got on until I got kicked out of school because I was such an obnoxious little turd in England and I was obviously turning into a complete scumbag, you know what I mean? The more time I spent in England, you know what I mean? From being a decent person and he'd noticed it.'

By all accounts, the documentary-maker was plagued by the frustrations faced by anyone seeking to get Shane to open up. 'On many occasions we sat outside his flat waiting for hours for him to answer the phone or the door,' she said in an interview to promote the film. 'I'd arrive at twelve noon and finally get him out to do something at twelve at night,' she said. 'Plus, he was frequently incoherent. I have hours and hours of incoherent footage. In the end it was best to just follow him around waiting to get a little nugget of something. My cameraman described it as being like wildlife photography.' [7]

If I Should Fall from Grace with God: The Shane MacGowan Story was an 'unflinching' look at Shane, according to the promotional blurb. The ninety-minute film certainly didn't sugar-coat the pill, scrutinising his addiction to drugs and drink, as well as his extraordinary prowess as a songwriter. Maurice spoke candidly about his son's drug-taking as a youngster and his expulsion from Westminster. He was on the verge of tears when he alluded to the damage wrought on his mind by so many years of abuse. 'He had a brilliant brain... still has, about a billion cells later,' he said [8], his voice laden with regret.

Shane came across as troubled. Chatting with friends outside a bistro in fashionable Primrose Hill, he claimed he had been declared clinically insane in about seven different countries and spoke about the psychiatric treatment he had received after Therese had suffered her mental breakdown.

As was so often the case, Shane's recollections fused fact and fantasy. Describing gleefully the meeting at Westminster where he had been expelled, he said Maurice got the headmaster 'by the fucking throat against the wall' and afterwards that the head had 'exiled himself to somewhere pretty far away'. There had, of course, been no such violence and John Rae had remained in his role at Westminster until 1986. Siobhan MacGowan comments: 'He will take a real story and embellish it, start rewriting it in his mind. The whole family are good at making up stories, but Shane's creative process keeps going, into the sphere of real life!'

Professionally, Shane was busy when the documentary was broadcast in Ireland in 2001. In an interview with *Rolling Stone*, Shane had confirmed The Popes were working on a double album. Before that, there would be a live LP taken from both the St Patrick's Day show at the Webster Hall in New York City and one at the same venue two days later. *Across The Broad Atlantic* was released the following year on Eagle Records with twenty tracks recorded not only in New York but at the Olympia Theatre in Dublin. ZTT separately released a Popes' compilation entitled *The Rare Ould Stuff*.

However, the double album didn't materialise. In fact, Shane MacGowan & The Popes continued to drift, and while his reputation as one of the most gifted songwriters of his generation was assured, the imagination that had produced 'A Pair Of Brown Eyes', 'Fairytale Of New York' and 'Rainy Night In Soho' seemed to be in retreat as the new millennium dawned.

The 'fresh start' for which *Rolling Stone* said he was hoping had never come, and the legacy of his sordid lifestyle was now inescapable. Sinéad O'Connor's intervention may well have contributed to him kicking his heroin habit over the next few years. However, its effect was far from immediate, as exposed by the ravaged state in which the documentary had captured him.

Jem Finer hammered on the old wooden door of The Commons, trying to make himself heard above the din coming from inside. He had just driven from the airport, negotiating the narrow lanes leading to the remote cottage. It was autumn 2001 and he was on an important mission: to ask Shane about rejoining the band that had sacked him ten years before.

'Jem took it upon himself to be the one to go over and find out from Shane if he was interested in doing some pre-Christmas shows,' says James

Fearnley. 'So, he flew over to Ireland and must have rented a car to go down to this fucking cottage. He could hear Cashman and MacGowan inside and he's banging on the door and there is all this noise and shouting. He ended up ringing the cell phone with them on the inside saying, "Can you come to the fucking door?"'

Regrouping for a one-off series of Christmas shows had been the idea of the band's accountant Anthony Addis and initially Jem hadn't been keen. Reunions had been mooted before and never come to anything, and for Jem to contemplate taking part, Shane would have to be involved. He said: 'I thought, I don't want to do it if Shane doesn't want to or if he's going to be completely crap and horrible to work with. I didn't want to go back to what we had before.' [9] Jem put the proposal to Shane over the phone and he had said he would be interested, in theory. Heartened that his old friend was at least open to the idea, he suggested he visit him in Ireland so they could discuss it further. 'I went over, I think in September that year, and visited him and we talked about it,' he recalled. 'I just thought it was worth a try. I thought maybe something could be healed. It seemed very sad the way everything had ended up.'

Spider was up for it, although he was amazed to discover that both Jem and Shane were too, especially after some of the things Shane had been quoted as saying about his former bandmates. 'I thought he'd put himself beyond the pale a bit with Victoria's book,' he said [10].

The Pogues had continued to make albums after Shane's departure, releasing *Waiting For Herb* in 1993 and *Pogue Mahone* in 1995. However, they were dropped by Warner the following year, a blow from which they didn't recover. They performed in the UK and all over Europe until the summer of 1996, when they ended with a show at the Boston Arms pub in Tufnell Park.

Anthony Addis and his son Mark had formed Brontone Management that year when they began managing Muse and The Pogues. Initially, there had been little appetite within the group to perform together again. And although Jem's role as emissary had succeeded in getting Shane to a meeting in London to explore the idea, he exhibited no interest once he was there.

'I think everyone was sat there and they were going through the details of it all and Shane was pretty much asleep in the back on the couch,' says

Mark. 'He didn't really take part in much of the meeting. The whole summary of it was that everyone was talking about what this tour would consist of and invariably how much money they would get... Shane was there in person but nothing else.'

Anthony's pitch to the band was that they would do a handful of pre-Christmas shows and see how it went. If it was an experience they enjoyed, then they could take it from there. If not, then everyone could go back to whatever they were doing. Eventually, it was agreed they would give it a go and Anthony's friend and leading promoter Simon Moran booked eight shows.

'For one week only,' read the trade press advert, which confirmed that the same line-up from which Shane had been summarily dismissed in 1991 was finally back together. Such was the demand for the opening show at Manchester Apollo on 16 December that another date was added at Manchester Academy the day before. Tickets were like gold dust for the other shows in Glasgow, Birmingham and Dublin and three nights at the Brixton Academy in London, a venue synonymous with the band's heyday. The gigs were a roaring success and the following summer the group reconvened at the Fleadh in Finsbury Park and the RDS in Dublin. However, for the time being that was it, with Shane and The Popes continuing to perform regularly abroad, despite not having released any new material since *The Crock Of Gold*.

Shane was content to go out on the road, so long as he didn't have to endure the unremitting tour schedules Frank Murray had once inflicted on The Pogues. Occasionally, he would appear on TV chat shows or do press interviews. But for the most part he was hunkered down at The Commons, his new base, where his days were taken up endlessly watching films, drinking and taking drugs. Creatively, Shane was spent.

He had lost so many of those close to him in tragic circumstances and he was no longer in contact with Paul Ronan, who had left his old lifestyle behind and was now working full-time in England. So, Shane sought refuge in the one place where he felt at peace, and with someone who had remained a constant in his life.

Joey Cashman loomed larger than anyone in Shane's life after his permanent move back to Ireland. The pair were inseparable and before they settled into The Commons, they lived with Shane's parents. Therese would wait on them hand and foot while they sat around, never offering to help. Joey says their disrespectful behaviour at the house angered Maurice and rightly so. 'Before we moved into the cottage, we'd spend fairly long periods of time in the house, maybe a month or two,' he says. 'I had my own room and if I got a bit pissed off with any rowing or anything, I'd go up to the room, take out the heroin and lie on my bed. I had my own DVD player and everything set up there. They'd be going, "Why is he up there all the time?"'

Joey and Shane spent some two years in The Commons, drinking and arguing and feeding their heroin habits. Anyone passing the cottage would have been forgiven for wondering what was going on, as raised voices competed with thunderous music. One day blurred into the next, their rapacious consumption interrupted only by sleep or trips to the pub.

Joey describes a typical night from this time: 'I used to drive a big Merc that Therese gave us. It was in my name because Shane can't drive. I can't sit and look at the optics in a bar all night, but he can. So, I started off bearing with him for a while, then I said, "Look, I'm going out to the car. I don't give a fuck what time you leave. You can stay until fucking nine tomorrow morning. Just knock on the door when you're ready and we'll go home."

'But he thought it was my way of protesting and he said, "No, stay here."

'I said, "I don't want to stay here." I'm not complaining – I like the car. So, I put the seat back, I put on the radio. I get out the tin foil and I whack in the heroin and I fall asleep in the seat. So, then he would knock on the door at four or five in the morning and I'd drive him home or to some other mad place. I drive extremely fast and one time we were going along the main road out to his place and the ditches were more like banks. We were driving along, and I felt him digging me in the side. I said, "What, what?" And he said, "I don't think we're on the road."

'I look up and I can see a signpost for Dublin and somewhere else coming at us at about a hundred miles an hour and we are on the grass bumping along. I just swerved and carried on, back on to the fucking road. I'm pretending to be calm, but inside I'm like, "Jaysus Christ."

'Then, a couple of minutes later, Shane says, "Do you know what, Joey? You're a fucking amazing driver!" I just went, "Ah, thanks Shane."'

Joey and Shane's friendship went back a long way and, despite often tumultuous times, they had an intense loyalty towards each other. Joey was still responsible for managing The Popes, a role he had assumed following the death of Charlie MacLennan. Shane was also on his own again and he had come to rely on Joey, who had been by his side during a previous split from Victoria. During that earlier period, the two friends had lived together in Howth, on the north Dublin coast. Joey says: 'We shared one room for two years. We just watched films and argued over the remote. I used to say, "What time is it, Shane?" and he'd say, "I don't fucking know. It's... ten."

'And I'd say, "Is that the morning or the night?"

'"The morning."

'"Oh, right, OK. That's brilliant. I'm going to go swimming tonight."

'There was a swimming pool, sauna and everything below us, and in the two years we were there, I never made it for a swim. By the time the evening would come along, I'd say, "What time is it Shane?" and he'd say, "I don't fucking know. It's twelve o'clock" and I'd look at the window to see if it was dark and I'd go, "Is that the eyening?"

'"Yeah, I think so."

'"Fucking hell, I'm going tomorrow."'

Joey's influence on Shane and his running of the band proved divisive. Some believed Shane would never kick his drug habit while he was hanging out with Joey and that his career was going nowhere. Concern for his health and frustration at his professional inactivity was growing and in spring 2004, things came to a head in a very public way.

A petition was posted on the Friends of Shane MacGowan International Fan Club website calling for the removal of Joey as his manager: 'We have noticed that your career has taken a serious turn for the worse in the last few years. We have had to suffer shows being cancelled. We have had to wait, on occasions for two hours or more, at venues when you were due on stage. There are times when we have felt ripped off. Yet, we have continued to support you. We now feel that things have gone too far.'

When Maurice MacGowan lent his support to the campaign, a bitter public row followed. 'Shane is now at best a middle-ranking artist – and declining all the time – when he should be up there with the majors,' said Maurice. 'He still has the huge talent that brought him fame. It just needs to be unlocked and a fresh start with a new set-up might be the key. I hope that Shane will bring in an expert, or team of experts, to look at and eliminate very serious weaknesses in the current set-up such as financial control, gig management, tour management, administration and PR and publicity.' [11]

Shane had been scheduled to perform shows with Terry Woods and former Dubliners Ronnie Drew and Eamonn Campbell as The Hellfire Club, and they had appeared on Eamon Dunphy's RTE show the previous year, performing 'The Irish Rover'. After jamming together at Dobbins restaurant in Dublin in January 2004, an enthused Shane welcomed the idea of playing some shows. Jim McKee, booking agent, told *Hot Press* he had called Shane in Glasgow and received confirmation that he would take part in four shows he had lined up. Several weeks later Joey phoned and told him Shane had done no such thing, and he could not do them as he had a gig to play at that time in Poland.

Maurice was furious: 'The disastrous decision to cancel the dates approximately two weeks after confirmation by Shane personally, and when tickets had been on sale for some time, is symptomatic of some of the weaknesses I've referred to. It exhibits a breathtaking contempt for the fans and is bound to limit gig opportunities. It also puts paid to a venture which would probably have led to new material, and certainly new versions of old material, being put out. I'm delighted that fans are showing their teeth, and long may they continue to do so.' [12]

A spokesperson for the website said the absence of any 'proactive management' had made it difficult for fans to find out about forthcoming live shows and TV appearances. This had led to the website, which was run voluntarily on Shane's behalf, being flooded with complaints when gigs were cancelled or rearranged.

Almost seven years had passed since the release of *The Crock Of Gold*. The Popes continued to perform, but shows consisted of old songs, Pogues favourites and random cover versions. Whoever was at fault, there was no avoiding the fact that Shane's writing had dried up and his public profile was diminishing. So, how did he react to the calls from his own father for Joey to be replaced? For someone whose default position was to shun confrontation, his response was unequivocal. Joey had his full backing.

'No business matters relating to Shane MacGowan should be conducted or discussed with Mr Maurice MacGowan or any other person claiming to represent him,' read his statement. 'All issues should be directed through Mr Shane MacGowan in person, or via his representative and long-term manager, Mr Joey Cashman. This can be either direct or through the administration office. Any issues, agreements or arrangements not made as directed can be deemed to be unreliable and unconfirmed, and Shane MacGowan and his management take no responsibility for any situation arising as a result.'

It wasn't all about cancelled gigs or Shane being late on stage. He had spent years being late for soundchecks, gigs, interviews and other appointments. There was genuine concern that the amount of drugs he was now taking would kill him.

Former Popes drummer Danny Heatley was among those who backed Maurice. He cited the names of those who had died during his time in the group and expressed his fear about the damage Shane was continuing to do to himself. 'People have been saying he's got six months to live for the past twenty-five years, you know?' he said. 'He's always had the constitution of an ox – but how strong an ox he is these days I couldn't tell you. It'd be a hugely sad thing if the world lost somebody like Shane MacGowan through drink and whatever else he gets up to these days.' [13]

Commenting on the controversy fourteen years later, Joey accepts responsibility for the rift between him and Maurice, which he says stemmed from an incident backstage one night. It is not known what Maurice said, but Joey admits his overreaction, along with his behaviour at Maurice's house, led to the public row that followed.

Joey explains: 'I love Maurice and the reason we fell out was more my fault than Maurice's. I overreacted to something he did, and he wasn't really to know because he doesn't live on the road with bands and he didn't understand it... I disgraced him in public and he couldn't handle it and he just went off the rails. I don't hold anything against him for doing it at all. As far as I'm concerned, I overreacted. I was the cunt. I could have gone down to him, been really calm and sorted it out, as I should have done as the fucking tour manager because he is part of the family, and there wouldn't have been anything else.'

In the run-up to Christmas 2004, Shane re-joined The Pogues for a few gigs, including the by-now obligatory three nights at Brixton Academy, the band's second home. The shows sold out, but Shane's visible deterioration drew comment from some reviewers. As he duetted with Cait O'Riordan on 'I'm A Man You Don't Meet Every Day', he cut a 'slightly sad figure, tired and old and deflated', remarked one [14]. Another write-up of Brixton said, 'The state of his mouth now renders few of his eloquent, if inelegant, lyrics intelligible' [15]. One critic, however, sounded a positive note. 'Even by Shane MacGowan's standards, it's not been an easy few years for him – what with broken limbs, infamously poor performances and relationship bust-ups. He needs a break of a positive nature. This Pogues reunion tour appears to be it.' [16].

A rare insight into Shane's state of mind at this time came when he appeared as a guest on *The Frank Skinner Show* in November 2004. Dapper in a white jacket and a black shirt with a flame design, he seemed incoherent and, in his response to one line of questioning, lonely.

Frank: 'Have you got any ambitions left, Shane?'

Shane: 'I had a twenty-year relationship with a young lady, you know, and I'd like to patch it up.'

Frank: 'This is Victoria you went out with for ages?'

Shane: 'Yeah, yeah.'

Frank: 'And is there any chance of you sorting it out?'

Shane: 'I dunno.'

Frank: 'Well, maybe she's watching and it's good to know you still love her.'

Shane: 'She knows that.'

Victoria was going through detox on a health farm when the interview went out. She later watched a recording of it and found it 'deeply moving'. But Shane's anguished plea did not have its desired effect. I'LL NEVER GET BACK WITH MY SOULMATE SHANE read the headline on a brutally honest piece by Victoria for the *Sunday Independent*.

'Shane is very dear to me and I don't know if I will ever again meet a man that I feel so connected to,' she said. 'I don't know what would have happened if he had chosen to change his lifestyle, too. Possibly we would be together now. There is no doubt in my mind that abusing alcohol and drugs destroys even the closest of connections. But whatever might have been, I know that I made the right decision and I'm sticking to it. Sometimes the price of staying together is too high to pay.' [17]

In the article, published three years after *A Drink with Shane MacGowan*, she reflected ruefully on the squalid life they had come to lead. The consequences of their chosen lifestyle had become 'more than obvious', with Victoria drinking heavily with him and taking whatever she was offered. A documentary had shown them sitting at home in a sea of empty bottles, overflowing ashtrays and the tell-tale remains of lines of coke. At the time they had thought it was funny, 'kind of like the Osbournes on a much lower budget'.

'The only problem was, it wasn't really funny, anymore,' she confessed. 'Shane had been in intensive care and had been very sick; I was seeing a counsellor because I no longer saw the point in living, and I was begging to be locked up. Nature was taking its inevitable revenge and our life together was unravelling into a very, very sticky mess indeed. With bailiffs hammering on the door and dead friends on the living-room floor.' [18] It was a harrowing appraisal of the life they had shared and the private hell into which it had descended.

As broken as his heart was without Victoria in his life, the dark, brooding clouds that had appeared to envelop Shane in the preceding years did begin to recede, giving his family and close circle of friends cause for optimism. The new millennium had seen him reconvene with The Pogues for the first time in a decade and he had moved into Gerry O'Boyle's spare room at The Boogaloo, the pub in Highgate, north London, which he had opened at the end of 2002. Surrounded by friends who offered support and looked out for him, he lapped up the live music sessions in the pub and went out to The Groucho and other social hangouts in London. Naturally, the television in the room was rarely off and he binged on films for hours on end. Martin Scorsese's 2006 movie *The Departed* was a favourite, while a long-time obsession was *The Wind That Shakes The Barley*, Ken Loach's film set during the Irish War of Independence, starring Cillian Murphy and Pádraic Delaney.

'When Shane and Victoria split up, Shane spent a lot of time at The Boogaloo,' says Ann Scanlon. 'The Pogues were a family, and so was The Boogaloo. So, Shane always had people around him and Shane is a man of faith, so I think in his heart he always had faith that he and Victoria would get back together.

'In those years at The Boogaloo, I do believe he was very happy. There were great nights; Bap Kennedy played on Sunday nights with his band and Shane would regularly get up and do "Cupid" and other songs like that. Gradually Victoria would come over and spend more time in London and The Pogues were back together at that time.'

Gerry O'Boyle says of his friend: 'He was then, and still is, the most interesting and best company you will ever meet. I must add that I don't drink myself, so my threshold for drink can be low, but good company always wins, and he has that in abundance.' He adds: 'Shane is a very loyal person and has been a good friend to me. I know he is inherently a good soul that sometimes went astray, but I wouldn't fault him for that.'

Significantly, before moving into The Boogaloo, Shane had been through a spiritual experience and one that had led him to finally kicking his heroin habit. If Sinéad O'Connor's controversial reporting of him to the police had been the catalyst for him getting clean, he believed his cure came on a visit to a visionary in the west of Ireland. The House of Prayer is a Catholic retreat situated on Achill Sound on the windswept coast of Mayo and word had reached Shane of the healing powers of its founder, Christina Gallagher. In June 2002, he and his mum Therese and Gerry travelled to Mayo to meet the self-proclaimed visionary. Christina Gallagher is not without her sceptics, the Catholic Church included, but Shane was set on meeting her and he spoke and prayed with her.

On 28 September, Shane returned to see Christina, this time in the company of Gerry and Ann. She remembers the trip well. 'Gerry was back from Filthy's and living in Sligo and picked me up at Knock Airport. A driver delivered Ireland's National Treasure to Sean Walsh's and you know what Ireland is like and with mobile phones, within seconds the whole of Charlestown was in the pub. It was like "Quick, we'd better get to the House of Prayer, it closes at five." So off we go, and Shane is on crutches. He goes, "Will you hold my drink in the back?" It was a white Russian and we're on country roads and I'm wearing black – not a good look. Anyway, we pull in with the open-top Saab with Gerry driving, Ireland's National Treasure in the front and me in the back. This older couple came over and she just peered in and said, "Shane, it is really you? We heard about you being here and we're praying for you every day."

'After Shane saw Christina, he said that he felt like she just looked into his eyes and down into his soul and sucked all the badness out. In a way, that was part of his Damascene moment. You can't forget about Sinéad [O'Connor] and that turned out to be a blessing, but this was a physical, spiritual thing.' Gerry O'Boyle lived with Shane for several years and remembers this as a time of contentment for Shane. He also testifies to him staying heroin-free after the trips he had accompanied him on to the House of Prayer. 'He wasn't doing smack when he lived with me and hasn't since 2002 or thereabouts, and he has had a golden period of being content in himself since. Shane lives in his head most of the time, he communes with the spirits of those who have gone on ahead on a daily basis, and he sees souls not bodies in people. This is why he has survived so well with falls and all kinds of scrapes over the years. He is a hybrid, spiritual being.'

By the end of 2006, with The Pogues' reunion by now a permanent one, Shane called time on his involvement with The Popes. It was eight years since they had released a studio album, Tommy McManamon was gravely ill, and Shane's focus had clearly shifted back to The Pogues. The Popes were on the road and heading for a gig when they got the news that Shane wouldn't be joining them. Bob Dowling says: 'We were on our way up to Manchester to do a benefit gig and we stopped at some services. Joey rang up and said, "Shane's not turning up. No more gigs; that's it until further notice." I knew that was it, because there were Pogues gigs going while we were still doing Popes gigs; obviously, there was a lot of money involved. So, we headed back to London.'

Ruminating on Shane's relationship with the group he fronted for more than a decade, Bob says: 'The Popes was more of a gang like he wanted The Pogues to be and maybe it had been in the beginning. There was a lot of drink in The Pogues, but The Popes would have blown The Pogues out of the water when it came to naughtiness... and Shane kind of liked that. For some reason he felt comfortable in it. He had great players. He always said that pound-for-pound The Popes were far better players. Unfortunately, I don't think Shane had the songs by then.'

At Brontone it was decided that Mark would take over responsibility for the group, while his father concentrated on Muse, whose third album, *Absolution*, had topped the UK chart. Mark had been around bands since a young age and, despite the group's reputation he wasn't daunted by the prospect of touring with them. 'To be honest with you, it needed someone with a lot of patience and who had a lot of energy and, me being younger, I fitted the bill,' he says. 'The rest of the guys were sensible, and they knew what they were doing and how the business worked. But Shane is more cocooned in his own world which works differently from everybody else's, so it needed someone to work in both worlds really.'

In March 2006, The Pogues returned to the US with Shane for the first time in about fifteen years. They played six dates on their favoured east coast, culminating in three nights at the Nokia Theatre in New York. Before the year was out, they flew out to the west coast and to Japan. Their first shows in New York with Shane after such a long absence brought out the rich and famous, Kate Moss among them.

Over the years, The Pogues had all had issues to deal with. Philip and Terry had developed serious alcohol problems and gone through treatment for their addictions. Terry had become teetotal and Spider had also sought professional help for his drink and drug addictions and succeeded in getting clean. The Pogues' story was ultimately one of survival.

'It's really great to look around at them,' commented James Fearnley of their reunion. 'Spider and Philip could easily be dead now from alcoholism. They were handing themselves the black spot, so to speak. Terry was having a hard time too, but I don't think I feared for his life as much as I did for Spider and Philip.' [19]

Philip Chevron said they were all still alive and their lives had 'changed for the better in many ways'. 'We've learnt over the years that we're all indispensable, that the only way it really works is when the eight of us are together.' [20] There was one even more important caveat, however, as former Stiff Records boss Dave Robinson pointed out. 'If Shane can get it together, and when he has a little respect for the music he's performed, it's got to work better.'

The Pogues' reunion seemed a positive development for everyone. The band were better with Shane and he was better with them. There were no new songs in the set, no label pressures for a new record, and the band and fans alike were content with a trawl through the old favourites. While Shane and Jem could rely on the handsome royalties from 'Fairytale Of New York' to ensure their financial security, playing live at decent-sized venues represented a welcome payday for the others. They were also able to do tours on their own terms and they were happier in each other's company.

'One of the conditions was that we weren't going to do it 24/7 for months and months,' explains Mark Addis. 'The whole premise was three weeks at a time: then everyone goes home, we clear our heads and then we go again several months later. And it kind of worked. Whatever everyone was stewing on in those three weeks, it just dissipated.'

Jem found the reforming of the group 'a wonderfully cathartic and healing experience. It was wonderful because most of the problems that had existed kind of sorted themselves out. Other people in the band who had problems with addiction and stuff had confronted them and come through them. It was actually a real pleasure to all hang out together, which it hadn't been for many years.'

Being around Shane still required boundless patience. His unreliability and pure obduracy maddened his fellow band members, and their solution was to follow the path of least resistance. Shane wasn't given sight of setlists to avoid him insisting on last-minute changes to the running order. Rehearsals and soundchecks were done without him. The pre-show routine was simply easier if he wasn't around and they all hoped he wouldn't turn up early and join in. All they asked of their wayward singer was that he deliver the goods on stage.

Terry Woods says that in the thirteen years of The Pogues' reunion, they never missed a show because of Shane. Getting him through each show, however, required a team effort. 'I like soundchecking, it's part of the whole thing, but we gave up with Shane,' he says. 'So, we developed a way of soundchecking without him, which was grand. Then we had to find a way of getting him from the hotel on time, so there was a selection of people who knew how to do that. Some of the other band members weren't involved and didn't want to know and that's fair enough.

But there were little quirks that had to go on. He was known as "The Sheik". So, it was, "Is The Sheik in the tent yet? Does he have his camels?" and all this.

'Ross Duncan was one of our tour managers and without him I don't know how much work we would have done. He went above and beyond to make sure it worked. The rest of the humans would be there and doing their thing. But the odd man out was Shane and you had to dance through hoops to get him to the stage. When he got up on stage, he was fine. It used to drive me nuts. When I say he was fine, he used to deliver. It would come from somewhere. Now there were a few occasions when he would be singing one song and we would be playing another and I'd have to go over to him and say, "That's the wrong song. You need to be singing this," and we'd get by that.'

Negotiating Shane through airports was no less stressful than it had ever been. On one occasion, Terry and Mark Addis were on an escalator in Dublin Airport behind Shane, who was carrying a bag, with Joey Cashman having gone on ahead of him. Terry says: 'We were on the other escalator talking and suddenly we noticed Shane had fallen backwards. I said, "Ah, fuck, Shane's after falling." He was on his back and his arms and legs were flailing about – he was like a beetle going down the escalator.

'Mark said, "I'm going to jump and go and help him." But Shane hit the bottom and he just went straight up with the bag behind him and walked off as if nothing happened. The two of us were dying laughing!'

At other times, Terry found Shane's behaviour intolerable. When the band played the Wolf Trap, an ornate open-air amphitheatre in Virginia made from wood, they were asked not to smoke on stage. Shane flagrantly ignored this request, causing Terry to reflect on the reasons for his recalcitrance. 'That is when it dawned on me, he does not understand the word "No",' he says.

Terry has known Shane for more than thirty years and admits he still doesn't know 'what makes him tick'. However, he believes his legendary lack of co-operation and insistence on doing whatever he likes goes back to the problems he had in adolescence.

'I know he had a breakdown when he was a young lad and I doubt, and I know this from experience, if it was ever treated,' remarks Terry. 'One of the problems with mental illness is it is always diagnosed by psychiatrists, but psychiatry isn't empirical. There is no science behind it as there is with other illnesses. It's only recently they are beginning to cop the effects of labelling people and treating them with tablets without ever getting to the root of what the problem really was or is. I don't think Shane ever got properly treated and I think it has stayed with him all his life. I think his mother was very good to him in the best possible way, but the wrong way. She indulged him and he doesn't understand the word "No". If you say, "You can't do that," he'll just do it anyway... When I met him first, I saw a very tall guy who had this talent but was very shy and he got over his shyness with alcohol. I remember that because that was something I did myself when I was young to a degree. But Shane did it to a huge extent, to his detriment, and I think it was to block stuff out.'

A year later, Victoria stretched out her hand so the camera could pick up the large stone on her ring finger. 'We got that from Liz Taylor', she joked as she and Shane made an appearance on *The Pat Kenny Show* on RTE. Not only were they reunited but engaged. Of course, the ring hadn't come from Elizabeth Taylor: Victoria's dad Tom had helped her pick it out in Dublin. But a wedding was now in the offing.

Asked what had taken him so long, Shane replied: 'I've been popping the question for quite a while and so has she, but never at the same time.' Victoria confessed she had been the first to ask. She had gone down on one knee and presented him with a ring, only for Shane to throw it back at her. On this occasion, neither had really asked the other. Bemused, the chat show host enquired how it had happened. 'Telepathic, tssscchh,' sniggered Shane.

To say their relationship had been turbulent would have been an understatement. They had separated on numerous occasions since becoming a couple twenty-one years earlier and had been living apart not long before their engagement became public in March 2007. They had even had a row and broken up after Shane had made his proposal – at Christmas, following shows with The Pogues. Victoria had caught him smoking in the kitchen of their home on the South Circular Road in Dublin, despite a ban she had imposed after she accidentally started a fire two weeks earlier. But by the time they returned from a holiday in Tangier in the new year, they had told their respective parents they would be getting married that September.

'It was at Spider Stacy's wedding to Louise in Las Vegas last summer that I realised how much I wanted to marry Shane,' said Victoria. 'Shane sang Elvis songs that night. At our wedding, he will have the night off. I'm hoping Nick Cave will write and perform a special song for the occasion. It's going to be heaven.' [21]

A wedding venue had yet to be chosen, but it would be in either England or Ireland in 'a muddy field like Glastonbury with people queueing up for beer and champagne', Victoria said. An engagement party was held at The Boogaloo, but as for the wedding, that would not take place for eleven years.

So, why had Victoria got back with Shane after ruling out a reunion two years earlier? She explains: 'As I got better myself, I realised that I'd missed what we had, which was really quite special. It's important to find out who you are on your own if you've been with the same person your whole life. It wasn't fun and it wasn't easy, but I was able to do stuff that was mine. So, the work I did had nothing to do with him, like writing for the *Sunday Independent*. I wrote the health page for two years, interviewing sick people all the time. So, I learned a bit more about life from people who were dying or incapacitated, so I was like, "Maybe my life's not so bad and I'm good at this."'

Victoria and Shane were back at The Boogaloo on 9 December 2007 to mark his 50th birthday. Despite Shane's total lack of interest in celebrity culture, there were plenty of famous musicians there to help him demolish his cake. Dexys' frontman Kevin Rowland, three of the Arctic Monkeys, The View, The Horrors and members of Madness were among the guests. Kate Moss had been lined up to sing 'Happy Birthday' to him, although the model ended up singing it down the phone after missing her flight. The partying continued into the wee hours with a short set from Shane, in which he included a cover of Van Morrison's 'Gloria'. 'We danced all night, and laughed a lot, and most importantly, even though he hates birthdays, Shane really enjoyed himself,' wrote Victoria afterwards. 'Even leaving aside his legendary alcohol and drug consumption, he had been run over several times, been attacked and kicked in the head countless times, he had overdosed, been in intensive care, been in loony bins, jumped out of moving cars, pretty much any way a person could endanger their own life he had tried.

'And, although I never did think he was suicidal, most of the time I was terrified that I would wake up one morning and find myself going to his funeral. I had pictured it many times, but never been able to imagine the horror of it actually happening. And here we were, more than twenty years later, and he had reached 50. Was, in fact, middle-aged.' [22]

CHAPTER 11

Wandrin' Star

'Rock and roll you crucified me
Left me all alone
I never should have turned my back on
The old folks back at home'

'The Church Of The Holy Spook', **Shane MacGowan & The Popes**

Shane had gone missing. He was due to perform with Sharon Shannon's Big Band for the first time, but there was no sign of him in the run-up to the show on 27 December 2007.

Only when one of Sharon's group went out looking for him was he eventually found, and fears that he wouldn't show up banished.

'We had booked a full-day rehearsal with Shane the day before the first gig,' says Sharon. 'None of us had ever really worked with Shane before, so we hadn't anticipated that he was going to be about five hours late for the rehearsal. By the time Shane arrived, most of the band had already left. We were faced with the nerve-wracking prospect of a huge gig to do with little or no rehearsal.'

Shane's inaugural performance with Sharon's popular live band was at the TF Royal Theatre in Castlebar, County Mayo, and it was to be a memorable one for a variety of reasons. The legendary Irish showband singer Joe Dolan had passed away the day before, aged 68, after being ill for some time. Shane was a huge admirer and when he heard the news, he decided to sing one of Dolan's songs as a tribute.

Sharon remembers: 'We were all very sad to hear the news as we were all fans, including Shane, and he suggested that we do a brilliant Joe Dolan song called "You're Such A Good Looking Woman". The only problem was that he didn't actually know the song, but he was adamant that he wanted to do it. We had singer Joyce Redmond also guesting with us and I reckon that Shane just assumed Joyce would be able to carry the song and he'd just sing along. But Joyce didn't know the song either so, as you can imagine, it didn't work out too well on stage. Apart from that mini disaster and a few other small teething problems with the way we as a band accompanied Shane, the show went very well overall.

'We learned a few valuable lessons that night as regards playing with Shane... mainly that if the band played our parts identical to the recorded versions with The Pogues and The Popes, there would be zero problems with Shane musically. He knew that stuff upside down, inside out. He could do it in his sleep. So, from then on it just got better and better and everyone was very happy, including Shane.'

In her twenties, Sharon had shared a house with other musicians, one of whom was a Pogues fanatic, and she had become familiar with his songs, learning the music inside-out. So, she had been 'thrilled and honoured' to find out years later that he was going to do some guest spots with her. Her manager John Dunford had previously worked with Joey Cashman and The Pogues, something that had done no harm when it came to convincing Shane to perform with the band. 'Sharon and I were honoured to have Shane join Sharon's Big Band as a guest vocalist,' comments John. 'And as I knew Joey well, he and Sharon got to know and have great respect for each other, and Joey joined the band on stage playing whistle and beating a tray off his head!'

Adding Shane's name to the bill naturally created an additional buzz around the shows. Audiences also had the opportunity to see other well-known acts from the Irish music scene: Damien Dempsey, Mundy, Tanya McCole, Wallis Bird, Imelda May, Camille O'Sullivan, Joyce Redmond, Eleanor Shanley and Dessie O'Halloran. Shane had been looking to perform with other artists and, following his not-to-be-forgotten debut in Castlebar, he became a regular feature on the tour, performing five or six songs a night, such as 'A Rainy Night In Soho', 'The Irish Rover', 'Fiesta', 'Sally MacLennane', 'Fairytale Of New

York', and joining Mundy and Dessie O'Halloran for 'Galway Girl', and 'Courtin' In The Kitchen'.

The band played gigs at Vicar Street in Dublin, Leisureland in Galway, and other large venues around Ireland. Collaborating with such accomplished musicians and singers and engaging fans, some of whom had never seen him before, reinvigorated Shane. The opportunity to play and socialise with a fresh group of musicians lifted him professionally and personally. Coming on stage towards the end of a show was also less demanding and gave him more time to sit backstage drinking.

Mundy observes: 'It was great because Shane was at a little bit of a loose end career-wise. The Pogues had maybe done one or two tours and I think they'd fallen out again. So, this was a new gang for him, and he seemed to be really refreshed by it. It seemed like it turned him on and he was in great shape back then. More than anything else he was really enthusiastic. He didn't have to be there soundchecking all day. He did his five or six songs, and we would have probably all sang "Galway Girl" together at the end. But he wasn't obliged to hold it all up on his own. There were new friendships there for him as well and there was no bad blood. He did his songs and went off stage and we'd all have a good drink and a chat. He would be able to function the next day without having to do a whole gig and a soundcheck and travel.'

Shane was driven to and from the gigs by Brendan Fitzpatrick in his red van and he sat behind the driver's seat with his own drinks table and fridge. Joey was continuing to manage Shane and they remained an incorrigible double-act, engaging in furious debates and on occasion coming to blows. Sharon Shannon's producer John Dunford recalls their dramatic arrival at The Rose of Tralee festival: 'We were doing a show with Shane and Mundy as part of the entertainment for TV and Shane and Joey were having a huge row in the van. We were all down at the venue when they arrived outside the hotel where all the Roses were doing their PR. Next thing the door opens, and Joey and Shane roll out on the ground and Joey's belting him with a cup, and then he breaks the cup, and he says, "Now you've broken my favourite fucking cup!"

'Shane is a gentleman and I really like him as a person. Incredibly informed on history and music, he rivals the likes of Burroughs, Kesey, Donleavy, Behan and Hunter S. Thompson, not only in intellect and talent but also in their reputations for causing mayhem and chaos, and enjoying a sherry or two, and really not being concerned with perceived genteel manners of polite society or what anyone thinks of them. Say what you will, but I see great honesty in that approach, and it typifies the true artist.'

John relays another vintage Shane moment: 'At an open-air gig with Sharon at Dungarvan Racecourse, Brendan's van pulled up and Shane climbed out, and staggered on to the stage wearing a plastic bag over his head. The musicians assumed it was part of his act, until they heard him complain to Joey that he couldn't see. During the first song, Shane ·fell backwards on stage, like a tree being felled, his head narrowly missing the keyboard behind him. He carried on singing, while lying flat on his back with the microphone stand on top of him, as if nothing had happened. When he got up at the end of the song and saw Sharon beside him, he said, "Oh... Sharon." I don't think he realised until there and then that he was actually on stage in front of an audience!'

When the Christmas shows arrived, Shane would arrive spick and span, in beautiful tailored suits with his hair freshly shampooed. He would get to know and remember the names of everyone who was on the road and buy them all drinks at the bar. 'Seven days later he would still be in the same clothes as the first day, with cider and beer and spirits spilled all over them, having barely seen a bed the whole time!' recalls John with a laugh.

Those in and around the band were also exposed to another endearing side of Shane's character: his respect for the older generation and the ways of old Ireland. John says: 'One of the defining moments for me was one of the Christmas shows in Ennis when Sharon's mother and Shane's mother were in the dressing room. There was a fucking massive music and drinking session going on, but Shane and Sharon and the two mammies were there, drinking tea and eating sandwiches at two o'clock in the morning.'

Shane's personal warmth and lack of ego made a deep impression on Mundy, who had seen Shane in The Pogues when he was 14 – his first live gig. They developed a close friendship as the shows went on and, to his surprise, Shane agreed to sing on his song 'Love Is A Casino'. They recorded it one evening in a Dublin studio, Shane working ever more quickly as Mundy announced that last orders beckoned. Mundy also saw the depth of Shane's kindness when Sharon's long-term partner Leo Healy died suddenly from a heart attack in May 2008, aged 46. Sharon was on tour at the time and was left devastated.

'Shane visited Sharon in Galway two months later and brought all sorts of trinkets and stuff for her,' says Mundy. 'He gave her this charm necklace with a crystal on it, and he was really supportive.' Sharon and other traditional musicians played Leo's favourite songs at his funeral and later they went into a studio to record them for a private commemorative CD for family and close friends. Shane was sent a copy and loved it, playing it constantly in the van. He also sang at a memorial concert for Leo a few months later at the Róisín Dubh, Galway, where the same songs were performed. He stayed over at Sharon's house for a week or two and was at the centre of the music sessions and drinking that went on into the night.

Sharon says: 'When there are live music sessions going on, Shane is always very happy, and everyone in Galway was really excited to have Shane around. People were calling the whole time and it was like a big, long music festival because everyone knew he was there.

There was no sign of Shane going back to Dublin and I was concerned that Victoria might be worried about him. I called her to let her know that I was heading away to do some gigs in Spain and I could organise for one of my friends to bring him back to Dublin. I think she might have assumed that I was trying to get rid of him out of the house, which wasn't the case at all. She told me that it was probably going to be difficult to persuade him to leave Galway, but if I really wanted him gone that I could try a bit of crying. Ha ha! Anyway, she seemed easy-going about it and I didn't mind having Shane staying while I was away.

'There were a few friends around looking after him and bringing him out for dinners and making sure he was okay and happy. When I got back a week later, he was still there. Even though I had made up a fresh bed for him upstairs, he didn't go to bed at all the whole time. I think he was beginning to have problems with his feet at that stage, so the stairs were too much of a challenge for him. He preferred to sleep on the couch, and when he woke up in the morning, one of my dogs was there, cuddled up with him. She was a stray that I had taken in and she really took to Shane. Dogs are great judges of character.'

In common with most people who get to know Shane, Sharon found him kind and sensitive and generous. She also detected an inner torment.

'Often, when he sang "A Rainy Night In Soho", he would point at me for the "Some of them fell into heaven", lyrics and then he'd point at himself for the "Some of them fell into hell" lyrics. That made me sad for him.'

Backstage, there was consternation. Shane had vanished the night before and extensive searches of New Orleans and calls to police stations and hospitals had failed to locate him. The Pogues' daytime slot at Voodoo Fest had now arrived and they had no option but to walk out on stage without him. They greeted the crowd at City Park and Spider took centre stage, as he had done on so many other occasions. It was 1 November 2009 and Shane was missing in action.

The previous day, he had hooked up with an acquaintance from Canada and gone drinking. Normally, this would have given the band and crew no cause for concern as Shane regularly left hotels and went off boozing in the company of people from outside their touring party. He didn't need to be at soundchecks or meet other pre-gig requirements, but he did need to be delivered to venues in time for the shows.

As the night wore on, there was no sign of them, and Shane's friend wasn't answering his phone. When he was finally found, the news wasn't good. He was back at his hotel, having been on a heavy drinking session, and he had left Shane in the bar.

Mark Addis describes the bizarre events that unfolded in New Orleans: 'We sent out a search party. We got the coach driver who knew the area very well, and the tour manager was calling police stations and hospitals. I was searching for hours and a couple of the band members were walking the streets until the very early hours. Obviously, you are always thinking the worst because Shane doesn't know where he is going, and people can take advantage. He is a bit naive to the world around him and you never know. Anyway, we went to the gig and Spider had to take the lead. We all went on stage and we're telling the promoters, "This is what it is. He should turn up, but we're not a hundred per cent sure at this stage because we've not seen him."

'Then lo and behold, three songs in, we heard a noise and Shane turned up on stage. It transpired he had managed to get himself to a hotel lobby, thinking it was the hotel he was staying at, but it wasn't. It was literally two minutes' walk away from it. He stayed in the hotel lobby and the next morning a fan came down and saw him and said, "Aren't you supposed to be on stage?"

'Shane said, "Yeah, yeah." So, he said, "Right, I'll take you there."

'So, he got him in a taxi and took him there and they went through the gates as normal punters. He said, "Look, this guy is supposed to be on stage," and eventually Shane got to the stage. We got through the gig – although we didn't really get through it, because he wasn't there, he was like a puppet. He was there, but he wasn't making any noise.

'That was it, and we got back in the bus and away we went. It was our worst gig because it was the only time we had lost him in any country, and we'd been to a fair few. But again, that comes down to the people around him. Afterwards, the others were saying, "I've had enough – this is it." They were massively pissed off. But it's the same scenario you always have. Shane is a law unto himself, he's in a different world. He does care about people and he does care about letting them down, but at times it doesn't even enter his head.'

Nick Skouras, a session guitarist, says the fan who saved the day was his nephew and godson Spiro. Nick had taken him to see The Pogues in Seattle and had planned to go with him to New Orleans, but he had to pull out at the last minute. So, Spiro had flown off on his own, along with the clothes Nick had packed for himself and in the lobby of his hotel he discovered Shane lying on the floor, passed out. Not knowing what to do, he pulled out his phone and called his uncle.

Nick recalls, 'I told Spiro, "OK, I'm gonna walk you through this. Get him up, get him to your room, throw him in the shower and get my fresh clothes on him," which he did. I told him to call the concierge downstairs and explain that Shane MacGowan of The Pogues was headlining the festival imminently and to organise a car or taxi to get them both to the venue immediately. Which they did. I was on the phone with the both of them throughout the entire ordeal.'

Shane has been helped and even carried on stage in some wild states of intoxication down the years. Musicians and crew members who have worked with him throughout his career have been astounded at his ability to get through a gig after marathon drink and drug binges. However, the shambolic affair that played out at Voodoo Fest was the exception, not the rule, during the reunion days.

Mark Addis accompanied The Pogues on some two hundred shows, but only remembers three or so that were a write-off. Whatever state Shane was in, sometimes with only hours to go, he managed to get on stage and see the show through. Keeping Shane's hangers-on out of backstage areas, his hotel room or anywhere else he could be found before a show posed one of the biggest challenges, especially when he performed in Ireland. These hangers-on had less interest in Shane fulfilling his tour obligations and more in having some entertaining stories to dine out on, says Mark.

Shane's natural inclination to go with the flow and to avoid confrontation at all costs made the task of keeping them at bay even harder. During UK or Irish tours, one of his most notorious hangers-on would stay in his room every night, getting everything paid for, says Mark. 'He is literally a leech and he always has been. But the thing about Shane is that he never likes to say "No" to anybody... Over the years, there have been plans to get them away from the hotel, but invariably they will find a way in. It's literally a case of how they can help themselves and Shane can be naive. For an incredibly clever, educated guy, he would always fall for that because he just likes company. He never likes to sit alone. Even if he's having a conversation with you and he's fallen asleep for half an hour, someone being there is comfortable. You know, he's a lonely guy.'

Victoria admits Shane's unswerving loyalty and forgiveness allows people to take advantage of him. 'He's loyal to a fault, so he'll be loyal in a way that hurts him – many times,' she says. 'Someone can hurt him, and he wouldn't ever stop them. He always sees it and names it in his mind. He doesn't name it to them, but he'll think, I know he's ripping me off, or I know he's doing that. It doesn't matter to him; he forgives that stuff. He forgives basically anything. He's very accepting.

'He might have a friend who is annoying him, and he might tell them to fuck off or shut up. But it doesn't mean he's not going to give them money or sort them out in whatever way they need sorting out. It just means he doesn't want them to annoy him.'

One fan who had shown enormous kindness and loyalty to Shane after they became friends was Dave Lally. Like Shane, he had grown up in an Irish family in London and was deeply proud of his heritage. Quietly spoken and shy, he had got to know Shane at gigs over the years and had earned his trust and respect. Later, after Shane's accident rendered him immobile, he travelled to Ireland to care for him when Victoria was away. He was great company on my visits to Dublin and we became firm friends. We regularly spoke on the phone and he was very supportive of this book, putting me in touch with people to interview and acting as a sounding board. Tragically, he passed away at his home in north London on 15 March 2020, less than two weeks before his 34th birthday.

Dave had seen first-hand people using Shane for their own ends and believed Shane's tolerance of it was due to feelings he had about some of his own past behaviour. 'He knows who is bad and when they're up to something in one way or another, whether it's taking a bit of money or using him for drugs or fame. He also knows people like me, Paul and Scruffy, who he totally loves, are all out for him. He is very loyal. He always had bad people around him, long before my time. Junkies, users, whatever. Shane has always called himself a scumbag and he fucks up. He's a junkie, he's cheated, he's beaten people up. He's done loads of shit. I think the reason why he has a lot of bad people around is because he'll look at them and think, Well I'm a scumbag, but at least I'm not like that. If he's around good people all the time, he is the bad egg and it will make him feel worse. Shane's like that and he does take things to heart. He's a little boy behind it all, whatever rock'n'roll image he might have.'

Shane isn't comfortable in his own company and is reassured by the presence of others, according to Mark Addis. He has no wish for their approbation or respect. It is the simple presence of someone else in which he finds comfort. During a Pogues reunion tour, a cleaner arrived at his hotel room. Shane apologised to her for the state of the room, which was as dishevelled as he was, and instead asked her to sit and chat.

'He wouldn't let her clean the room because he was embarrassed,' comments Mark. 'But he was happy to have a conversation with her and give her a tip – a really good tip, as he always does. He can chat about anything and you could see her smiling, happy to have a five-minute chat, although she probably didn't want to because she would have been on a schedule. That's the side of Shane that no one else sees. He's a kind-hearted person.'

If Shane was writing any new material, there was still no sign of him recording it. When he wasn't performing his old songs with The Pogues or Sharon Shannon's Big Band, he would sporadically get together with other musicians. But it was never a serious endeavour. For a songwriter and artist of international repute whose admirers read like a *Who's Who* of rock'n'roll, Shane seemed content to drift, recording old covers with local musicians. When he was jettisoned from The Pogues, he had a clear vision of what he wanted to do next and had collaborated with other iconic artists: Nick Cave, Van Morrison, Christy Moore. Now, he seemed to be looking, misty-eyed, into his musical past.

Fans of The Nipple Erectors were given an unexpected treat when the band reformed for a secret gig at the 100 Club in London on 6 May 2008. Shane O'Hooligan was back, hollering down the microphone and exuding punk swagger alongside his old flame Shanne Bradley, guitarist Gavin 'Fritz' Douglas, and drummer Eric 'Le Baton' Baconstrip. Shanne's 15-year-old daughter Eucalypta was in the audience and she got up on stage at the end to sing 'Gabrielle' with Shane. At Shane's suggestion, the band reconvened at Philly Ryan's in Nenagh the following year. Shane appeared on the tiny stage wearing a trilby and an eye patch, and footage of the chaotic affair shows him completely rat-arsed. At one point, he stumbles off the stage and has to be helped back on his feet.

Behind the drum kit was Shane and Victoria's friend Michael Cronin who, with his brother Johnny, had tasted success in Ireland with their band The Aftermath. Recalling a memorably drunken day, Johnny says: 'We went out to The Commons and Shane was watching Daniel O'Donnell on RTE and drinking poitín. We carried on drinking and went into Philly Ryan's and watched a hurling match. We had great craic that day because a lot of Shane's record collection was there. He was playing "Love" by John Lennon on seven-inch and "Some Of Your Lovin'" by Dusty Springfield. We listened to that four or five times. "The Year Of The French" by The Chieftains was a big influence on him and I remember he was playing that. So we did this gig and Shane was pretty drunk from the jam-jar.'

Of The Nips' first ever performance in the Irish Republic – 32 years after they formed – Shanne says: "It was just a rehearsal to try out this drummer, but Philly Ryan got a film crew in and all of a sudden it was all over social media and Shane was holed up in the cottage... It was just a happening – you have to look at it like that. It was a dreadful gig, terrible.'

About a week after the surprise gig in Tipperary, the group did something even more unexpected. They assembled at the Cronins' studio in Drumlish, County Longford, to re-record some of their original songs. 'The band were down for about two days waiting for him and I was thinking, This isn't going to happen,' says Michael. But on the third day, Shane finally arrived.

Johnny says: 'He turned up with Paul McCartney's 'Russian Album', a Tipperary hurling stick, [Eamon] de Valera's biography and a bodhrán with 1798 on it [the year of the Battle of Ballinamuck, in which a Franco-Irish force was defeated by the British]. We're down the road from Ballinamuck, so "The Year Of The French" by The Chieftains and the TV series is always in his head. We recorded "Gabrielle", "Happy Song" and "All The Time In The World", but they've never been released.'

One studio session that Shane took part in, and which did see the light of day, was a cover of Screamin' Jay Hawkins' 'I Put A Spell On You'. Proceeds from the single by Shane MacGowan & Friends went to the Dublin-based charity Concern Worldwide after the earthquake that ravaged Haiti on 12 January 2010. Shane was accompanied by Victoria as he arrived at the London studio to join a line-up which included Chrissie Hynde, Johnny Depp, Paloma Faith and former Sex Pistols bassist Glen Matlock.

Glen says: 'I got down there and there was Bobby Gillespie, Nick Cave and Shane, and some other people started turning up. Mick Jones came down later on and played the fire extinguisher. They'd already recorded the music, so they had a go at singing, which I did, and Mick Jones took over the production a little bit. Shane was asleep on the sofa and as soon as the film crew appeared to do the video, he miraculously came to life and said something cool.

'What was funny was Chrissie Hynde came in and we were doing "I Put A Spell On You", which everybody kind of thinks they know a bit, and Chrissie was singing it totally wrong. Not out of tune, but there was a bit where the verse comes in and she was singing it in time but double the speed. I looked at Nick Cave and Nick Cave looked at me and Shane, and we drew straws as to who was going to tell her. Nick lost and he had to go out and we were watching through the glass. It was funny.'

The record didn't chart, overshadowed by two other songs released for the Haitian appeal. However, *Channel 4 News* was invited to the recording session and interviewed both Shane and Victoria. 'It just popped into my head as a great alternative to what Simon Cowell's doing, as an alternative for Haiti,' she explained. 'I thought it sounded like it was a cool idea and I thought he [Shane] would be brilliant doing it, and I thought Nick would be brilliant doing it.'

Asked if the song was an appropriate choice given its voodoo connections, Shane said: 'Casting a spell on you doesn't mean a bad spell, it's casting a spell on you because I love you,' he replied.

The recording session was a rare one for Shane. While artists like Van Morrison and Elvis Costello had remained prolific, continuing to write and release new material, Shane had produced nothing for thirteen years. But, by the end of 2010, there were signs that his songwriting hiatus might be over.

Dublin was experiencing the coldest December since records began when Shane headed to the warmth of Lanzarote to record with a new band. Some bungalows had been rented out and they planned to spend four weeks on the island writing and recording an album. The Shane Gang was comprised of drummer Paul Byrne, from Celtic rock band In Tua Nua, bassist Jack Dublin, and Shane's old pal Joey Cashman on whistle. They had done a few impromptu gigs in Ireland, starting at The Summit Inn in Howth, and Shane was buoyant when talking about the new line-up.

'It's a long, long time since I've got such a positive vibe from a band like I get from this one and I can't wait to get into the studio with them,' Shane told the *Irish Daily Star*. 'I know there's a brilliant album just lurking there, ready to be recorded.' Joey was also upbeat about the project: 'I really believe we're going to see the "a new old Shane", if you like, with this band, and if the few small gigs we've done so far are any indication, there's a special album on the way.' [1]

In the event, no recording took place at all. Shane and a few mates, including Paul Ronan, flew out to the Canaries for what was basically a holiday. The Shane Gang did appear on the bill for Vince Power's London Feis Festival at Finsbury Park the following summer, but video footage of their set shows them playing Pogues tracks 'Sayonara' and 'London Girl' rather than new material. Shane saw out the rest of 2011 performing with The Pogues and as a tour guest for Jools Holland. The Shane Gang was quickly forgotten.

(Above) Chilling on holiday in Ibiza (Paul Ronan).

(Below) Shane and Victoria after returning from a holiday in Malta, June 2004 (Tony Gavin).

(Below) Sharon Shannon was 'thrilled and honoured' when Shane joined her Big Band as a guest vocalist in 2007 (Sharon Shannon).

(Above) Shane with the unusual piece of art he offered to the ISPCC (Irish Society for the Prevention of Cruelty to Children) in September 2010 (Tony Gavin).

(Below) Chatting with his late friend Dave Lally.

(Below right) '...this was a new gang for him, and he seemed to be really refreshed by it.' Shane and Mundy backstage after performing with Sharon Shannon's Big Band (Dave Lally).

(Above) The Pogues performing one of their thirtieth anniversary shows at The Olympia, Paris, September 2012. L–R: Terry Woods, James Fearnley, Philip Chevron, Andrew Ranken, Shane, Darryl Hunt, Spider Stacy, Jem Finer (Paul Ronan).

(Right) Pete Doherty and Shane became friends at Filthy McNasty's pub in the early 1990s and they appeared on the same bill when The Pogues and The Libertines performed at London's Hyde Park, 5 July 2014. Pictured backstage L–R: Michael Cronin, Shane, Victoria Clarke, Pete Doherty, and Johnny Cronin (Johnny Cronin).

(Left) A bedroom at The Commons with a home-made banner celebrating Shane's fiftieth birthday (Richard Balls).

(Below) Members of Shane's family with the author at The Commons. James Mulvihill, Vincent Mulvihill, Lauren Mulvihill, Mary Taylor (née Lynch), Richard Balls, Anthony Hayes, Tom Donnelly, Debra Donnelly, Vicky Cahill, Siobhan and Lisa Mulvihill (Paul Ronan).

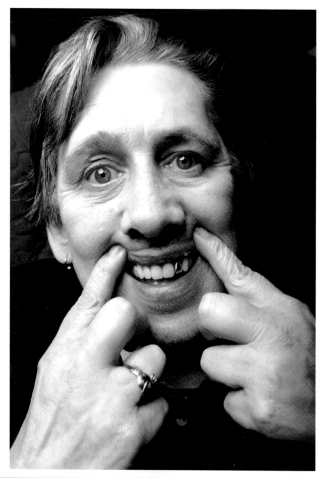

(Above) So notorious were Shane's rotten teeth that Sky Arts made an hour-long documentary about the making and fitting of a set of implants, complete with a gold tooth (Mark Large/ANL/Shutterstock).

(Left) 'He always stuck with the devil he knew. He is a very loyal person.' Publisher Liam Teeling (left) has worked with Shane for years, re-signing him several times (Liam Teeling).

(Above top left) All smiles as Shane and Therese pose backstage after a Sharon Shannon's Big Band show (Dave Lally).

(Above top right) Reunited – Shanne Bradley and Shane (Dave Lally).

(Left) Shane joined Chrissie Hynde to duet with her on 'I've Got You Babe' at the RDS in Dublin, June 2019. Chrissie and Pretenders guitarist James Walbourne also spent time with him at his home (Dave Lally).

(Above) Maurice MacGowan pictured on his 90th birthday.

(Above) Shane receiving a National Concert Hall Lifetime Achievement Award from the President of Ireland, Michael D. Higgins. L–R: Carl Barat, Glen Matlock, Nick Cave, Bobby Gillespie, Jesse Malin, Johnny Depp, Bono, Glen Hansard (Johnny Cronin).

(Below) Shane with his old friend Paul Ronan at the Grosvenor Park Hotel, June 2018 (Paul Ronan).

(Above) Eleven years after getting engaged, Shane and Victoria got married at Copenhagen Town Hall on 26 November 2018. Johnny Depp delighted the couple by joining the small group of family members and friends for the low-key ceremony.

(Below) A fan touches the glass carriage carrying Shane's remains through the streets of Dublin ahead of his funeral service in County Tipperary on 8 December 2023 (Charles McQuillan/Stringer/Getty)

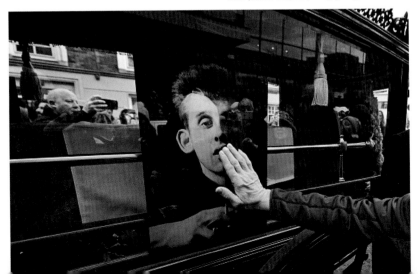

In 2012 Shane returned to Drumlish to record a remake of The Dubliners' song 'The Rocky Road To Dublin' with The Aftermath and others. 'The Rockier Road To Poland' was released to celebrate Ireland's qualification for Euro 2012 in Poland and Ukraine, the first time the country had qualified in twenty-four years. All profits went to the homeless charity, Simon Communities of Ireland. It had been the Cronins' idea to do a fun reworking of the song and they had wanted Shane to be involved. After an initial recording, they brought in others to finish the track, including comic actor Joe Rooney from *Father Ted*, and a video was filmed at the National Wax Museum in Dublin. What they didn't know was that The Dubliners were recording the official anthem, 'The Rocky Road To Poland', with members of the Irish team.

On 8 October 2013, there was some sombre news. Philip Chevron had died six years after being diagnosed with oesophageal cancer. He was just 56. His passing was mourned not only by his former bandmates from The Radiators From Space and The Pogues, but across the Irish music community. His last public performance had come at a testimonial concert at the Olympia Theatre in Dublin that summer. Shane and other members of the band took part in the show, as did other Irish musicians, including Paul Brady, Mary Coughlan, Hothouse Flowers, Camille O'Sullivan, and writers Patrick McCabe and Joseph O'Connor. The Pogues gave a poignant performance of Philip's song 'Thousands Are Sailing'.

Philip had curated the evening and invited *Game of Thrones* and *Peaky Blinders* actor Aidan Gillen to compere it. 'We had some mutual acquaintances, and he knew I was a Radiators fan,' explains Aidan. 'I'd never MC'd a night like that and I was nervous, as I think anyone would be, but I got through. I don't know how emotional Shane was. I think on nights like that, or any night, singing the song is what you do.'

Shane confirmed The Pogues were no longer active less than a year later. As had been the case in 1991, they had grown tired of each other all over again and Shane had had enough. They played their final show at the Festival Fête du Bruit in Landerneau, France, on 10 August 2014. 'I just meant to do one gig, to get out of a bind,' Shane told *Uncut*. 'I didn't intend it to go on this long. No, this is it. This is the last year.' [2]

Back in Ireland, Shane was making a new record with Johnny and Michael Cronin, at their suggestion. Better still, he had picked up his pen again. 'I've written a few songs, yeah,' he confirmed. 'But I've been going through a mental block.' [3] The interviewer asked if Shane faced the same challenge as Jerry Dammers from The Specials, who had said that it was hard to top 'Ghost Town' when he was asked why he hadn't released a new song in thirty years. Shane replied: 'What, he thinks it's hard to top "Ghost Town"? I have to top fucking "Fairytale Of New York". It doesn't scare me! I'm already writing new stuff. When it's ready you'll be informed.'

The Cronins corroborated the return of Shane's writing muse and said there were fifteen songs ready for an album which were 'classic MacGowan'. Covers were also being worked on during the sessions in Dublin, including 'Come Out, Ye Black And Tans', the Irish rebel song by Dominic Behan, and old traditionals 'Wild Mountain Thyme' and 'Raggle Taggle Gypsy'. Shane enjoyed the experience, but it was another false dawn, and it was followed by an event that would cause more than his creativity to stall. Shane has been in and out of hospital like a 'yo-yo' over the years, breaking arms, legs, his pelvis and hips. He had always recovered but when he fell over in Dublin during the summer of 2015, the injuries he sustained would have a lasting impact on his quality of life. He was still on crutches when he attended a charity busking event in the city on Christmas Eve, supported on either side by Victoria and her nephew Olan. Eventually, he would need the use of a wheelchair to get around and now, six years later, he is still unable to walk.

Media reports said the fall had happened outside the studio where they were recording. In fact, it took place as the Cronins dropped him off at the house he and Victoria were then renting in Sandymount. Michael explains: 'He had got out of the van and he sent me around for his bottle, and he just fell over on the pavement. That's what happened.'

When Ireland again qualified for the UEFA European Championships in 2016, Shane and the Cronins did get to record the official song. 'Je t'aime Irelande' fused 'Endless Art' by Irish band A House with Jane Birkin and Serge Gainsbourg's risqué duet, listing legendary Irish players and other national icons.

A glittering charity event that year saw Shane perform 'Streams Of Whiskey' with Johnny and Michael at Ronnie Scott's in Soho. The fundraiser marked the tenth anniversary of the Hoping Foundation, in aid of Palestinian refugee children. Van Morrison, Chrissie Hynde, Kate Moss, Noel Gallagher, Jools Holland and Rob Brydon also graced the bill at the legendary jazz club, with Naomi Campbell, Bill Nighy and Monica Lewinski among the celebrities in attendance. Shane stood with the aid of a stick and looked to be in some discomfort.

Songwriting has always been a spontaneous process for Shane. In the early days of The Pogues, he would suddenly leave Victoria and his friends in the pub and go home to write when an idea came to him. Now the well from which some of pop's finest storytelling had been drawn had dried up, something Shane found 'very frustrating', says Victoria. 'I've talked to Nick Cave about it and he says that he sits down at his desk promptly every day and he works and works. He'll write what he considers to be rubbish and throw it all out until he finds some things that seem to work. But Shane's never done that. He just gets it all, it comes through, he's hearing the tune, the words are coming. Sometimes it seems to him that they're coming from a dead person or another being. So, for him to have that sense that it wasn't coming through meant he was cut off from his channel.'

Shane's inability to get out and about has also removed him from the situations from which he took his inspiration, says Victoria: 'A lot of the material came from socialising, so he would be sitting there, and he would be listening to you, but not really in the way you might think. He might be listening for an idea or get a couple of words or get something that might end up in a song. A lot of that happened all the time, so socialising was part of the research.

'I don't think the block is a bad thing. I think he sees it as a bad thing, but I think it's probably not. I think it's more about him questioning who he is without that, without being the performer. "If I'm just me, who's that?", instead of, "Who am I as Shane MacGowan?"'

Dave Lally observed: 'People always talk about him being pissed, but Shane was hard-working. 'He would go home and put on the TV or the radio. He would have somebody in the room talking and he'd have a few books he would be going through. He would be doing all this at the same time as writing a song. He was still working. Drink and drugs come into it and the more famous you get, that will come in. You need that. People think he kind of blagged it, but Shane worked his bollocks off and he doesn't have that anymore. He doesn't have anything to inspire him at all.'

Musing on the self-destructive lifestyle chosen by Shane and the physical state he now finds himself in, Julien Temple remarks: 'Obviously what he has done has taken its toll. It's the reason he fell over. It's a lifestyle that is going to have consequences and it's a cautionary tale on one level. To create something as strong as his body of work, do you have to go that dark and deep into losing yourself or not? That's a big question that he throws up. Did he need to be that on the edge and that fucked up a lot of the time? He proudly says he writes better when he's fucked up, which may be the case.'

Over the years, Shane's fans could have been forgiven for believing that he had long since become past caring about his appearance. His clothes were dishevelled and stained with food and drink, the skin around his eyes grey from lack of sleep, and his face unshaven. And then there were his teeth or, more famously, the lack of them. Shane was a dentist's worst nightmare, large gaping holes separating crooked tombstones. They rotted before his fans' very eyes, his two remaining stumps giving up the ghost in 2008, leaving him with the gummy look of a man twice his age. The decaying state of his mouth had made his the most talked about gob in rock'n'roll. 'Is he the guy with the teeth?' people often say when his name crops up. His gruesome gnashers had come to define him.

In fact, Shane is quite vain. In his younger days he was acutely aware of fashion, paying particular attention to the clothes which accompanied punk, northern soul, mod and other musical styles. He appreciates well-made suits and has a keen eye for a jacket or shirt or a cool pair of shoes. But even Victoria was surprised to discover that after neglecting his teeth and living without them for so long, he announced he wanted a new set.

Shane had apparently had some dentures made in 2009, but he hated them and described them as a 'botch job'. When Victoria had some work done on her teeth by dental surgeon Darragh Mulrooney, Shane asked for his own appointment at the practice in Mullingar, County Westmeath. Dr Mulrooney commented: 'It was the stuff of legends told amongst dentists that, when he had teeth early in his career, he went to get crowns done in some surgery in London and had never gone back to get them fitted, and the teeth just continued to deteriorate.' [4]

This unexpected move by Shane set in train a lengthy and complex process. Dr Mulrooney and his team worked with him for six months, gradually rebuilding the foundations of his mouth. Technicians were flown in from Portugal and they used old photographs, videos and other material to help replace the teeth that had rotted away so publicly. Shane had also made clear he wanted to retain some of the character of his old ones, with the inclusion of a gold tooth.

'I went to the Greek islands years ago on holiday and I was really impressed with the Greek fishermen,' he remarked. 'I drank a lot with them. They had really rotten teeth, but they all had one gold tooth – that was their bank account. If they were ever stuck for money, they had gold in their mouth.' [5]

No fewer than twenty-eight implants were installed into a titanium frame which was then fitted in a nine-hour operation. So monumental was this feat of dentistry and so notorious the patient that Sky Arts made an entire documentary about it entitled *Shane MacGowan: A Wreck Reborn*. His old friend Johnny Depp was among those interviewed for the hour-long programme, which aired on 20 December 2015.

Therese was also interviewed, in the kitchen at The Commons, before he underwent his surgery, and she spoke of her great pride in him for going through with it. She said: 'I admire him for having the courage to do everything he had to do to get to this stage because it's been a long haul and his dentist is marvellous. He loves his dentist.' [6]

After the gruelling operation was completed, the team gathered around their celebrated patient and clapped. They gave him another round of applause when he bit into an apple to put his new teeth to the test. He seemed pleased when he admired them in the mirror for the first time. But despite his initial protestations that he didn't want a gleaming Hollywood smile, he subsequently had them replaced with a whiter set.

Aesthetic considerations aside, there was one thing that neither he nor his dentist could influence – how he would sound. 'Shane recorded most of his great works when he had some teeth to work with,' said Dr Mulrooney. 'The question on everyone's lips is how it will affect his voice. The tongue is a finely attuned muscle, and it makes precise movements. We've effectively retuned his instrument and that will be an ongoing process.' [7]

For all the predictions of his own demise, Shane has motored on, outliving so many of those close to him. Dave Jordan, Charlie MacLennan, Tommy McManamon, Joe Strummer, Kirsty MacColl, Philip Chevron – all taken too young. Shortly before Christmas in 2016, Frank Murray joined that list after suffering a suspected heart attack at the age of 66. But it was as the new year dawned that Shane was to receive the most shattering news of all.

Therese had been to Mass in Nenagh, as she did every Sunday, and was driving home when her car left the road and smashed into a wall. No other vehicles had been involved and it was thought she may have gone into cardiac arrest at the wheel. It was three o'clock in the afternoon on New Year's Day and Shane's mother had become the first person in 2017 to die on Ireland's roads.

As the local undertaker, Philly Ryan had got the sombre call from the gardaí. He drove to the scene on the Silvermines Road and began making the arrangements. Through his friendship with Shane he had become close to the family and was fond of Therese. He also knew better than most the devastating impact her passing would have on them all.

Victoria was told the news before Shane and didn't know how she could break it to him. 'I was very, very, very shocked,' she said. 'I bawled my eyes out thinking, How am I going to say it to him? I couldn't figure out what to say to him. It took me at least an hour to say it. At first, he didn't believe it. He said, "No, couldn't have happened. Not possible." Then he began thinking.' [8]

Therese was 87. She had not been ill, and her death was a huge shock in the close-knit community where she was well-known and liked. The previous August, she and Maurice had celebrated their sixtieth wedding anniversary with a reception at the Abbey Court hotel in Nenagh. Now, just months later, her family and friends were back there for her wake.

Shane cut a frail figure as he arrived in a wheelchair for the funeral service, held exactly a week after the accident, at Our Lady of Lourdes church in Silvermines. Sorrow was etched on his face, his pallor magnified by his dark shades. Photographs online and in the following day's papers captured him stricken with grief.

Siobhan and her husband Anthony led the pallbearers as the coffin was carried into the church that was packed with mourners. Like Shane, Siobhan was exceptionally close to her mother and her passing had come as a terrible shock. In her eulogy, she spoke of Therese's upbringing in Carney Commons, a tiny hamlet that produced 'big characters'. The Lynches' home was renowned in the area for 'its open door, its hospitality and generosity of spirit'. There would be 'sparks flying off the floor' of the cottage with all the music and dancing, but it was also a 'very holy place', filled with kindness, and where tears flowed easily.

Therese had been 'strikingly beautiful and gregarious' when she and Maurice had met in Dublin, said Siobhan. When she decided that Maurice wasn't paying her enough attention, 'she set out to dazzle him – and dazzle him she did'.

'Our mother and father were the best parents in the world,' said Siobhan. 'They encouraged in us a fierce sense of individuality, to question, and to think for ourselves. My mother nurtured and supplied us with an abundance of love to the day she died. All who knew her talked of her grace. It was not just grace of movement or manner but true grace – a grace of the spirit. An open heart, a great compassion and wisdom, which she shared with all who passed her way. Many who have written to us have talked of this dignity, this grace, but also of her great sense of humour and fun. She had a childlike joy and a sage mind. She gave counsel, spread joy, and impacted many lives with her magical spirit. People felt richer for having known her. The mark of a life well-lived.'

The parish priest, Father Brendan Maloney, told the mourners that the day Therese died had been a 'New Year's Day of sadness', but that was eased by 'the joy of having Therese in your lives for so many years'. He paid tribute to her talent for singing, which she inherited from her family, and recalled how she had won awards in her younger days. 'So many people said she could have made a professional career, her singing was so good. She passed that international stardom to Shane and, of course, Siobhan you acquired the literary skills of writing.' [9]

Mundy was among those to pay their respects. He had seen her with Shane and been struck by the strong bond they had. 'I think Shane was just turned upside down,' says the musician and singer. 'He looked really sad and like he hadn't slept for a long time. His mother used to come to the

Sharon Shannon gigs. If we were playing in County Clare, which is not far from Tipperary, she would come over with Siobhan. They'd sit there with their stash of drinks and cigarettes to share. They wouldn't be drinking all of it, but it was just like, "What's the point going up and down to the bar all evening when we're going to be here?" It was like sitting in an old Irish kitchen. They would talk, and she used to speak about him when he was a little boy. He used to be very well-behaved around her. It was kind of cute to see it and not many people would get to see that.

"I would say his mother [dying] broke his heart in a big way. I met her one time down in Terryglass in Tipperary with his sister. I think he [Shane] might have had some physio or been in a clinic trying to get better from his fall and he hadn't drunk in a while. She said, "If you meet him, don't encourage him. He's doing very well." That was not long before she died.'

Dublin's National Concert Hall was packed to celebrate Shane's 60th birthday and his contribution to Irish music. A stellar line-up of artists had been brought together to pay tribute, but now it was Shane's turn. Through a sea of mobile phones and raised hands, Shane came into view, pushed in his wheelchair by Victoria. Nick Cave welcomed him to the stage and took a seat beside him to duet with him on 'Summer In Siam'. A hush descended as Shane sang the opening lines and those fortunate enough to get hold of tickets for this special night at the National Concert Hall in Dublin strained to hear his unmistakable voice. The presence of former Pogues Jem, Spider, Terry and Cait in the band assembled for the occasion only added to its poignancy.

Shane sang beautifully and, as the high-water mark of the group's final record with him came to an end, Nick wished him a happy birthday and lent over to embrace his long-time friend. He took his bow and left Shane to perform, the audience bursting into an impromptu rendition of 'Happy Birthday'. They then joined him in singing the chorus of the traditional folk song 'Wild Mountain Thyme'. 'Will you go, lassie, go, and we'll all go together to pluck wild mountain thyme, all around the blooming heather...' There wasn't a dry eye in the house.

'I just wanted to perform a song with Shane,' says Nick. 'We had recorded "Wonderful World" together years ago, so it just felt right to sing again with my old friend. I have never, in all my years of performing, felt such a palpable sense of euphoria emanate from an audience as when lovely Victoria escorted Shane on to stage. Shane raised his glass to the crowd and began his verse of "Summer In Siam" – that exquisite ballad of spiritual acceptance and love – and the crowd simply melted. The love from the audience and from his fellow performers was overwhelming. It was a very emotional moment for us all, and one I will never forget.'

Admiration for Shane, as both writer and performer, runs as deep as the River Shannon, and the roll-call of artists who filed out on stage for the evening's grand finale served as testimony to the breadth of his appeal: Bono, Johnny Depp, Sinéad O'Connor, Bobby Gillespie of Primal Scream, Clem Burke from Blondie, Catatonia singer and radio presenter Cerys Matthews, Libertines co-frontman Carl Barat, Finbar Furey. There were lots of familiar faces in the audience too: film director Neil Jordan, actors Stephen Rae and Cillian Murphy, and Sinn Féin president Gerry Adams. They had travelled from near and far to mark Shane's 60th birthday and also to see a huge honour bestowed on him.

Compere John Kelly, the writer and broadcaster, told the audience: 'Ladies and gentlemen, this has been a quite remarkable evening, a celebration of one of our greatest writers. And, as you know, we could have filled this hall ten times over, such is the regard in which we all hold Shane MacGowan. But there is one more tribute tonight. The National Concert Hall is at the very heart of music in this country, a place where music in all its forms is celebrated and performed, whatever its genre. And the highest accolade that this institution can bestow is its lifetime achievement award. So, I'm delighted to announce that the National Concert Hall is tonight making a special lifetime achievement award to Shane MacGowan in recognition of Shane's unique contribution to the art of songwriting.'

The venue erupted with roars of approval as Ireland's president and National Concert Hall patron, Michael D. Higgins, presented Shane with his award, a sculpture in the shape of a harp. The outsider whose lyrics and music had once been seen as heresy by some in Ireland was being lauded as one of its most celebrated sons. By any standards, Shane's journey has been a remarkable one.

Says Sinéad O'Connor: 'He got very weepy when he got his award, so me and Victoria were hugging him. He was very moved by the whole thing. He is very republican, so it would have meant a lot to him to get that award. Ireland means a lot to him and he is very much a Sinn Féiner. Politically, it would mean a lot to him to be honoured by the Irish state.'

The decision to hold an evening in Shane's honour had been the brainchild of Gerry O'Boyle in the wake of Therese's death, and months of preparations went into the event held on 15 January 2018. 'Gerry has been such a good friend to Shane,' says Ann Scanlon. 'He really looks out for him and it was Gerry who made his birthday concert happen. You don't think you're going to say when you get a bit older, "The greatest night of my life", but honestly and truly, there was never more love in a room. It was such a beautiful, brilliant night, and Gerry came up with that. He said, "We should do something to cheer Shane up," because it was after his mum died.'

Few songwriters whose style is so rooted in the Irish tradition have spoken to such a diverse constituency. Shane's admirers are drawn from punk, heavy rock, folk, pop and every musical staging post between. Nick Cave, Paul Weller, Bono, Tom Waits, Van Morrison, Christy Moore, Chrissie Hynde... The list goes on. The high esteem in which he is held underlines how powerfully his timeless and poetic songs resonate with people. Like Shane himself, they are real.

'There is a universality about Shane's writing, an understanding of the commonality of things that is unparalleled among his generation of writers,' says Nick Cave. 'It feels as if he is writing the story of our own lives. Within that great love he has for humanity itself, his words have extraordinary poetic power – not only for the marginalised and the dispossessed and the beaten down – but for all people. There is never any pretention in Shane's words; they are deeply authentic, as is the music that accompanies them and the unique way he delivers them. He writes straight from the heart, but with real craft and skill and in doing so touches all people. He is the great songwriter of our generation.'

Bruce Springsteen, too, is in awe of Shane's gift for words and the abiding quality of his songs. Speaking on *The Late Late Show* in October 2020, he said: "He's the man, you know. As I said on my radio show, I truly believe that a hundred years from now most of us will be forgotten, but I do believe that Shane's music is going to be remembered and sung. It's just deep in the nature of it. So, he's the master for me and I have a deep appreciation of his work and the work he did with The Pogues."

Christy Moore is a long-time admirer and says that Shane ranks alongside some of the greats of songwriting. 'More important than any awards, Shane is loved... sometimes pitied, but always loved. Most people think kindly of him, some are frustrated by him, of how his talents might be perceived to have been squandered. He has connected with the hearts and emotions of many, he is part of our culture, our underbelly, our soul, our crack. I can only speak for myself. I rate him as being up there on my top shelf... Shane, Ewan MacColl, Bob Dylan, John Spillane, Wally Page, Jimmy MacCarthy.'

Gems from Shane's songbook were revisited for his birthday concert. A band that included New York rocker Jesse Malin, former Sex Pistol Glen Matlock and Blondie drummer Clem Burke got the night off to a thunderous start, with songs like 'That Woman's Got Me Drinking' and 'Hot Dogs With Everything'. A 'house band' then backed the array of performers who stepped up to play the numbers Shane had carefully chosen for them.

Bono was joined on guitar by Johnny Depp to perform 'A Rainy Night In Soho' and Bobby Gillespie gave 'A Pair Of Brown Eyes' the Primal Scream treatment. It fell to Glen Hansard and Lisa O'Neill to duet on 'Fairytale Of New York', while former Libertine Carl Barat got people out of their seats with 'If I Should Fall From Grace With God'. Damien Dempsey, with whom Shane had so often sung in Sharon Shannon's Big Band, also contributed to the occasion. 'This is for all those people who said Shane wouldn't see 30,' he said, before leading a gallop through 'Bottle Of Smoke'.

Sinéad O'Connor received a rapturous welcome from the audience, and when the whooping finally died down, she delivered a hauntingly beautiful rendition of 'You're The One' (written by Shane and Michael Kamen), accompanied only by piano and flugelhorn. The emotion of the evening had been made rawer still by the sudden death of Dolores O'Riordan earlier the same day. The Cranberries singer had been found dead in her hotel bathroom, aged just 46. A tragic end to a troubled life. Introducing Cerys Matthews to reprise 'The Broad Majestic Shannon', John Kelly dedicated it to Dolores – to the evident shock of some in the audience who had not heard the news.

Songs written by others were also chosen by Shane. Terry Woods performed 'Streets Of Sorrow', which segued as it did on the record into

Shane's 'Birmingham Six'. Imelda May duetted with Finbar Furey on 'When You Were Sweet Sixteen', the evergreen that gave The Fureys and Davey Arthur a surprise UK hit in 1981. Finbar also produced one of the most poignant moments of the night when he sang 'Kitty', a song about a Fenian bidding goodbye to his sweetheart from his prison cell. It resonated strongly with Shane, who had learned it as a boy from his mother. In the BBC's 1997 documentary, *The Great Hunger: The Life and Songs of Shane MacGowan*, Shane was filmed singing it in a bar and Therese sang it for the camera in her interview.

When Shane and Victoria appeared on *The Ray D'Arcy Show* on RTE Radio 1 a few days later, he was asked if he had a favourite performance. Victoria suggested he couldn't have a favourite, but after a moment's thought, Shane replied: 'If I was pushed, I would say Finbar.'

'I think that was very generous of him,' says Finbar. 'It was beautiful, and I thanked him very much. When I got his version of the song, I wanted to do it like he would do it. But I cannot be Shane MacGowan. I'm Finbar Furey and I did it in the way I felt it and he got that, and I think that was lovely. All we had was guitar and a cuatro between us, myself and Peter Eades. It's such a beautiful song and I felt every word of it.' Commenting on the love for Shane that night, Finbar says: 'All it was short of was putting a crown on his head, they love him so much. Even with the heavy, pseudo-traddies, the perfectionists, they'd have to throw the towel in and say, "Yeah, you're right." You cannot deny him, he's just amazing and I'll fight his corner any day of the week.'

Brendan Fitzpatrick, who watched the show with Shane on a monitor backstage, says Finbar's delivery of 'Kitty' hit him hard. 'I remember sitting in the dressing room with Shane, and Finbar Furey was playing "Kitty" and I could see that was a moment when a few tears started coming because Shane was thinking about his mum,' says Brendan. 'It was a very touching moment in the concert for him and he went on to say afterwards it was one of his favourite songs of the night. Even though it was a big celebration night for him, he was thinking of his mother and she wasn't there to see it. She had been there for him throughout his career. I put my arm around him and gave him a hug because I knew exactly where he was.'

The occasion made a lasting impression on fan and actor Cillian Murphy, best known for his portrayal of Tommy Shelby in the BBC drama *Peaky Blinders*. 'I think I would rate that evening as one of the great musical events of my life,' he says. 'There was such electricity in the air that evening. The whole audience were such devoted fans and to have that calibre and range of musicians, from original Pogues like Cait O'Riordan to Sinéad O'Connor to Nick Cave to Bono to Glen Hansard to Glen Matlock to Damien Dempsey to the president of Ireland himself, and a myriad of others, all presided over with such calm and good nature by John Kelly. It was a beautiful evening I'll never forget.'

The celebrations continued afterwards in an upstairs room, with guests taking it in turns to do a song. 'Mundy and Glen both sang and me and Steve Wickham played as well,' says Sharon Shannon. 'At one stage, Glen started calling Bono up and I knew he was down in the very back corner with Johnny Depp and there was no moving him. In the end, the Concert Hall called time and we were all fecked out.'

Just months after being honoured in Ireland, Shane's towering legacy was acknowledged at the music industry's prestigious Ivor Novello Awards in London. The awards have been presented every year since 1956 by the British Academy for Songwriters, Composers and Authors (BASCA) and represent peer recognition for exceptional achievement across classical, jazz, screen composing and songwriting. The citation for Shane's inspiration award said he had not only inspired bands like the Dropkick Murphys and The Libertines, who had followed in The Pogues' riotous wake, but iconic figures such as Joe Strummer and Tom Waits whose careers had preceded his own.

It read: 'Ever since MacGowan emerged from the punk scene (his band The Nipple Erectors were a stalwart support act during punk's first wave), the raw reality of his work has been obvious to anyone who heard it, whether the songs date from his time with The Pogues or his solo career. This, after all, is the man who brought bittersweet authenticity into the cheesy world of the Christmas song, with the most cherished festive single of all time, "Fairytale Of New York". A man who can do wild-eyed party songs ("Fiesta", "Sally MacLennane") or sad-eyed, wistful ballads ("A Rainy Night In Soho", "A Pair Of Brown Eyes") with equal effectiveness. And a man who deserves to be hailed for much more than his well-documented love of a drink.'

Former Stiff boss Dave Robinson was among those at the Grosvenor House hotel to see Shane honoured, thirty-four years after he saw The Pogues at The Pindar of Wakefield and decided to sign them. Gerry O'Boyle and Victoria accompanied Shane on stage for the presentation, which was made by actor Aidan Gillen.

'I was flattered that Shane had asked me to present it and very happy that he was getting proper recognition for his songwriting because a songwriter is what Shane is more than anything,' says Aidan. 'He's a frontman, a singer, but mostly – and this is really apparent now – he's a songwriter, the likes of whom don't come along that often. I had written a few early drafts of what I was going to say on the day, and it seemed like the hardest bit would be cutting out superlatives and references to Nick Cave, Bob Dylan or whoever; the other best songwriters around who've already all amply endorsed Shane.'

Aidan's partner Camille O'Sullivan was also there to see Shane honoured. She has toured with The Pogues and sung the parts in 'Fairytale Of New York' that Kirsty MacColl seared into pop's consciousness. The first time she had been called on to sing the track, she had been given just an hour's notice. Therese MacGowan had been unable to perform with Shane at the Olympia Theatre in Dublin and Victoria called Camille, who was at a friend's house, and made a dash for the theatre.

'I know the song like everybody else, but I realised I didn't know it well enough,' said Camille. 'I got someone to print out the lyrics and I cycled down to Dame Street trying to read it on the way. The first time I met Shane was singing with him onstage. It was terrifying. His mum usually sang it, but she couldn't that night. It was the most mental introduction I've ever had to anybody.' [10]

Aidan has developed a friendship with Shane and Victoria and calls round to their Dublin flat. He's watched westerns and horror films with Shane and shared a few drinks with him, so much so once that he couldn't put his shoes back on when he came to leave. Asked about the man he is still getting to know, Aidan replies: 'There's plenty I don't know about him yet. But if I had to nail down some attributes, I'd say: quick, cool, funny, real and shy.'

The Dublin-born actor is among those to whom Shane's lyrics spoke so directly as an Irish person living in London. Explains Aidan: 'The whole

London Irish culture that The Pogues could only ever have come out of was something I understood well, having moved over there as a teenager and then stayed for twenty years. It seems like it might be a simple enough scene to explain, but it's really not. The thing of being an outsider in both countries, but also getting the best of both worlds and making a lot of noise if you wanted. It's a particular and potent niche to be in… those streets of King's Cross and Camden and Kilburn and Soho that I walked endlessly myself from the late eighties. It was a lonely enough situation a lot of the time. But I wanted to make a career as an actor and those songs often kept me sane.'

Shane's lyrics are visceral and real. Death, violence and guilt loom large, and flawed characters inhabit seedy streets and bars. It's no surprise then that so many actors have been drawn to his music: Johnny Depp, Matt Dillon, Matthew McConaughey, Robert De Niro, Sean Penn. Some were in bands themselves and the music they made was informed by The Pogues.

Actor Cillian Murphy was in a group with his brother Páidi when he was growing up in County Cork. Traditional Irish music was played at home and his parents took him and his siblings to sessions. But it was The Pogues who made Irish music cool.

'The drummer in our band and one of my oldest pals, Bob Jackson, invited me to his gaff after school and turned on *Rum Sodomy & The Lash* really loud in his garage,' remembers Cillian. 'All of a sudden there was this synchronicity between punk and trad exploding in my ears. It was unlike anything I had ever heard before – and it made total sense. All teenagers adore a rebel and Shane's lyrics, the way he sang them, and the wildness of the playing, made him an instant hero.'

For a teenager growing up in rural Ireland, songs about whiskey and Soho's neon-lit streets were 'mythical', conjuring a world that seemed fictional rather than real. 'His songs feel like they have been passed down through the ages,' says Cillian. 'Each one feels like a story. The poetry of the lyrics set against the savagery and abandon of the playing was definitely what did it for me initially. The way the songs were brutal and tender and often in the same song, "A Pair Of Brown Eyes", for example. The way the lyrics reveal themselves with every listen. They are full of all these classical and literary allusions which were way beyond me at the time, probably still are!'

While songs with such eternal resonance have not flowed from Shane's pen for more than two decades, his influence on other songwriters and musicians has never waned. From Boston-based punks the Dropkick Murphys and Irish American outfit Flogging Molly to The Libertines and The Decemberists, the stark realism of Shane's words and the intensity of The Pogues can be heard. Contemporary artists born long after the heady days of *Rum Sodomy & The Lash* and *If I Should Fall From Grace With God* continue to take inspiration from the songs.

Singer Joy Crookes is 23 and grew up in London. Her Bangladeshi mother introduced her to Sufi music and her dad to The Dubliners and The Pogues. He also impressed on her from a young age the importance of her Irish heritage. The emerging artist, nominated for a Brit Award in 2020, explains: 'My dad used to say to me growing up, "I don't care about your English accent, the fact your skin is brown and how you want to dress – you're Irish!" As a child he would make me recite Yeats with him before bed, send me to Irish dancing lessons – in which I achieved Grade D – and play me everything from Sinéad to Van and The Chieftains' take on Paddy Kavanagh's "Raglan Road". He loved The Pogues and that music seeped into my young bones.'

At 15, Joy recorded herself playing guitar and singing 'A Pair Of Brown Eyes' and posted it on YouTube. So, when she began to forge her own writing style, she thought about how and why Shane's songs spoke so strongly to her.

'I learnt a lot about Ireland and Irish ways of communication from Shane,' says Joy. 'His voice and lyrics would always make me immediately set a scene in my head – be it "Summer In Siam" or "A Pair Of Brown Eyes". As I got older, the lyrics meant more to me; I felt as though I could relate and – more importantly – I understood Shane was a storyteller. His vision is both broad and intimate, sometimes like he is talking to us, the children of Irish emigrants.'

Shane's friend Ann Scanlon says he had always believed Irish music to be cool and his mission to see other artists fervidly express their Irishness and tap into the country's poetic soul had been fully accomplished. 'When Shane was living in The Boogaloo, he said to me, "I'm going to set up this thing 'Hip Eire' because we've always been hip,"' says Ann. 'As I understood it, his vision was for all the young bands to pick up the mantle and, in a way, this has happened because we would talk about people doing "Raglan Road" really fast and you've got Lankum, Lisa O'Neill and people like that. For me, the band that I think are really doing it are Fontaines D.C. Grian [Chatten] has got that thing Shane has, that quiet sensitivity, the poet soul. He sings in an Irish accent and he was born in England. I remember he said something like, "It feels nice to wear our Irishness on our sleeve because it's a voice that's been downtrodden", and that's like Shane.'

CHAPTER 12

A Furious Devotion

'There is always one thing
That I'll keep within me
Deep in my heart a furious devotion
The Love of old Ireland
And Mother Mo Chroi'

'Mother Mo Chroi', **Shane MacGowan & The Popes**

That Shane had received such accolades for his poetic and enduring songs shouldn't have caused anyone to knock their Guinness over in surprise. But the news that hit the press in November 2018 really caused jaws to drop. Shane and Victoria were finally getting married.

Rumours swept the internet after Victoria posted a Facebook picture taken through the window of a plane, with the cryptic message: 'Off on a secret mission.' The following day the *Irish Sun* carried an exclusive, confirming the couple were to tie the knot: 'Shane MacGowan will end the longest engagement in rock'n'roll history by finally marrying Victoria Mary Clarke this Monday,' it revealed. The wedding would not be in his beloved Ireland, however, but the Danish capital of Copenhagen. It was to be an 'intimate occasion', an unnamed friend told the paper, with no celebrity friends.

If fans were amazed, some of those close to the couple were equally taken aback. After all, eleven years had passed since Victoria had flashed her engagement ring on *The Pat Kenny Show* and they had separated several times since, with little further talk of any wedding, publicly at least. In the summer of 2016, they had split up again and Shane had taken it badly. Maurice was so worried about him he phoned Paul Ronan and asked him to fly to Ireland to be with Shane. Therese, ever the doting mother, had sat up with her son all night. In the end, just like always, Victoria took him back.

As the wedding approached, Maurice was himself being treated at the Mater Private hospital in Dublin and Siobhan was staying in a hotel so she could see him each day. Her husband Anthony was also travelling up and down from their home in Tipperary to support Siobhan and help keep Maurice's spirits up. Maurice's ongoing treatment meant that neither he nor Siobhan could attend the wedding, but Shane did go to see him and discussed his forthcoming nuptials.

Originally, the plan had been to fly to the Bahamas, where their Hollywood A-list friend Johnny Depp was to perform the ceremony. But with Shane confined to a wheelchair such a lengthy flight was impractical, and it was a long way for Victoria's family to travel. Instead, they decided on a low-key civil ceremony in Copenhagen city hall. There would be no flower girls or page boys or matrons of honour, Victoria explained in her *Sunday Independent* column. They wouldn't even exchange wedding rings.

So why, thirty-two years after they first got together and eleven years after getting engaged, were they finally tying the knot? Victoria explains: 'I proposed to him just after we met because it was a leap year and he said that he didn't want to get married. I don't think I proposed again for a long time, but then he proposed to me after I dumped him. He was like, "No, let's get married," and I'm like, "No, I've broken up with you now and I've found someone else." So, that was obviously why he wanted to get married. So, then, when we got back together, we both decided it was actually a good idea to get married. But once we got engaged, we didn't really feel the need to go through with it because I don't think either of us really wanted the fuss. Neither of us actually enjoys fuss; we like to deflect fuss to someone else. So, the idea of all that fuss and all the questions… Oh, God, too many questions and all these people we don't even know… It was a nightmare, so we couldn't do it.

'The idea of going to Copenhagen was mine because I thought, We do not know anyone in Copenhagen, so we could just go there, and no one would know. I could bring my sister to be the witness, and then if I'm bringing my sister, I'm going to have to have my mum… but also, just people that we feel really comfortable with, so comfortable with that we might as well be at home.'

Shane and Victoria were married on Monday 26 November 2018. Victoria's parents, sister Vanessa and other family members and friends were witnesses. Despite suggestions that their famous acquaintances would not be joining them, Johnny Depp jetted in, ensuring pictures were shared around the world. Victoria wore a beautiful red Bella Freud gown with long-sleeves and a floral headband. Shane was dressed in shirt and tie, a dark overcoat and a black trilby hat.

Johnny and Michael Cronin serenaded the couple and their guests with 'A Rainy Night In Soho' after the couple tied the knot, Johnny Depp joining in. The Cronins had grown close to the couple and were honoured to be invited to perform at the ceremony. Johnny recalls: 'That morning, we were in the car with Shane and we were going on about songs off *Veedon Fleece*'. We started singing "Linden Arden Stole The Highlights" and Shane started telling me who Linden Arden was. Also, The Beatles – on the road to his wedding he was singing "If I Fell", and it was beautiful just how excited he was, going to meet Victoria. It was just a beautiful moment. We went back to the Tivoli Gardens, which is like a winter wonderland, and we had a meal and then we had to do some songs. "Astral Weeks" is one of Shane and Victoria's favourite songs, so we played that with Johnny Depp. Shane didn't want to hear "A Rainy Night In Soho" because he's written so many other amazing songs.'

The next day, Shane and Victoria flew home as Mr and Mrs MacGowan. For Victoria, the picturesque setting in the Danish capital and friends making the trip to celebrate with them had made for a magical occasion. She was also pleasantly surprised at the impact it had had on Shane.

'It was so much better than I imagined possible because it was like magic, every minute,' says Victoria. 'I think it was partly the location because the Tivoli Gardens is like a fairy tale. It is the oldest fairground in the world, but it looks like something out of a movie, a Disney movie. It's like magic with snow and Christmas trees. Then, obviously, having Johnny [Depp] and the Cronins singing, that was so beautiful. It really made it. I think Shane was genuinely moved by it, really moved, and he became different after it. He actually softened and I think he felt more loved because of it.'

Shane looks up and beams. He is sitting in his favoured armchair and he instantly starts nattering. He's in great form and it is the first time I've seen him holding a notebook and scribbling down ideas. Paul Ronan and I have gone straight round to see him after landing in Dublin. It's November 2018 and Shane is clearly delighted to see us. The man I have got to know doesn't care for his own company. Even if there is silence in the room, he likes to know people are there, just as the bottle of white wine in front of him is a reassuring presence. I'm glad we've come.

For most of his life Shane has been surrounded by people. His inherent shyness can still be glimpsed in a crowded room or when he meets people for the first time. He is no extrovert and never dominates situations. He is happiest listening to the voices of others. Jem regularly flies over from London to see him and Joey is still a constant caller. Friends from Nenagh also keep in touch and travel up to Dublin to spend time with him.

Victoria dotes on him and for all they have been through, it is impossible to imagine him without her. Since injuring his hip, he has become increasingly dependent on her and others. His physio Paddy Pio O'Rourke, a fellow Tipperary man, has meanwhile been helping him build up his strength.

In April 2019, the *Irish Sun* ran a picture of them both, Shane standing with the aid of rails, beneath the headline FAIRYTALE OF NEW WALK. Paddy Pio described how he had used music to encourage Shane to do his exercises and reported that he was making great progress. 'Since I started working with Shane, he has been very motivated to get back on his feet and he's doing really well,' he said. 'He's a huge Post Malone fan now! His [Post Malone's] song "Rockstar" came on through my playlist during one of our first sessions and he couldn't stop laughing at some of the lyrics. And now he loves the rest of his music, so we usually throw him on as loud as we can, and Shane does his best work.' Victoria was delighted with the impact Shane's trainer was having. 'I think psychology is a huge part of getting people moving when they have had mobility issues. He's great.' [1]

Public performances have become a rarity in recent years, but Shane got to sing with his old friend Chrissie Hynde in June 2019. The pair duetted on 'I Got You Babe' when The Pretenders supported Fleetwood Mac in a sold-out show at the RDS in Dublin, and Chrissie spent time with him at his nearby home. The previous summer Shane made a brief appearance at the Liverpool Feis, leading the crowd in a singalong of 'Dirty Old Town'.

Having mostly seen Shane since his accident, I often wonder how he copes with the life he is now forced to lead. I have detected a reluctance on his part to leave the flat, perhaps because it is simply too much effort and he is more comfortable at home. As we were talking one night, however, he was vehement in his determination to get an operation and walk again: 'I'm going to force them [doctors] to do it. I'm going to the papers. They won't operate on my hip and I can't walk and it's ruining the rest of my life. I love walking, I loved running, I love kicking the shit out of people and that includes them! It's not that much of a risk and I'd rather take it. I used to break all sorts of things and recover in a week. But this time, because they didn't do anything, nothing changed. Now I don't know what the situation is. I've got an uncle who is 91, who really knows his stuff, and I'm going to go to him and ask him what kind of operation I need. I don't care if it's long and involved, but I don't see why it should be. It's a broken hip – that's nothing – and in this country it's mad because everybody is athletic, does GAA [Gaelic Athletic Association – promoting Gaelic games], and fights a lot, and runs after women, and runs after guys with spades in their hands, tsscchh… I'll have it done in England if I have to. If you're in hospital, who cares?'

After suffering his fall, Shane was treated at two private hospitals in Dublin and his fractured pelvis did heal. Several months later he was sent home, with a view to his hip being operated on when his body was up to it. But it never happened and while friends hate to see him unable to walk, some blame his refusal to prepare himself for surgery.

Terry Woods comments: 'When he was in the Mater Private, Mark [Addis] and I went to visit him. They were detoxing him and it was taking time. They couldn't do it quickly because his body couldn't cope with a quick detox. So, they said, "He should really go home. We'll keep the detox going. He's suffering from malnutrition as well, and his body needs to be physically repaired before we can do an operation. His body wouldn't be able to cope with an anaesthetic."'

Sinéad O'Connor says Shane has been reluctant to undergo surgery on his hip because he won't be able to get his drugs (the illegal kind) in hospital and his continued use of them gives his stated desire to get better a hollow ring. 'He doesn't want to live, or he wouldn't be doing all the drugs,' says Sinéad. 'Nobody doing those things wants to live, whether it's the tramp in the street or the guy in the apartment or whether it's Shane. They want to be undead: not dead or alive. If he wanted to live, he would be doing his physiotherapy to get up and walk. There is no reason for him not to be able to walk right now, except that he gave up… I saw five years ago a man that had given up. His bed is faced towards his television, it looks like a coffin.

On one side he's got his drink, on the other side his drugs. He's got the remote, and he just sits there 24/7...

'The amount of shite he's taking... I'd be in hospital if I took one of those Valium, never mind taking them to get out of bed in the morning and a ton of drink. You can die [from that] and if he's saying he wants to live, he's a liar. He doesn't want to live. Over the years, I've watched a lot of TV shows, particularly in Ireland, where they all feel sorry for him and they all feel like, "Oh, poor Shane. If only he could get his shit together." But this is chocolate and vanilla.

'There are millions of people in the world, different types of people, and he is exactly as he should be. It's not for us to pity him or feel sorry for him and change him or want him to be different. He is 60 years of age and he's chosen to be what he is. So, we have to respect and admire him for it, and for the fact that once he did get the foot up his arse, he took it. In a way, he has been responsible ever since.'

We are discussing his health one evening when out of nowhere Shane changes the subject. This is something he does a lot; sometimes as an avoidance tactic and sometimes as a way of switching the conversation on to one of his favourite subjects. On this occasion, the topic is one which has preoccupied his mind since childhood. The Troubles.

'I don't want to die just yet. I don't want to die at all. But the idea that other people wasted so much of their lives blowing up other people who wasted their lives and the fact that there's no redress. They've got to give redress to the hundreds of people and their friends and relatives on both sides of the divide, which is a completely fucked up divide.' Sit with Shane for any length of time and the conversation will turn to Northern Ireland. For most of his life he has been both fascinated and pained by its bitter struggles and it is a subject that can trigger the angry outbursts which have become part of his personality. This is safe ground for him. He knows his Irish history inside out and is a staunch republican who counts former Sinn Féin president Gerry Adams as a close friend.

It was on his holidays at The Commons that Shane heard about how his ancestors had fought for 'the cause' and that a whole division of Black and Tans were killed and buried near the cottage. He was given a copy of *My Fight for Irish Freedom* by Dan Breen which was 'very violent and very graphic' [2]. Breen was involved in the ambush and killing of two

RIC policemen, an act regarded to have started the War of Independence, and fought in the third Tipperary Brigade of the IRA. He became the first republican to enter the Free State Parliament and represented Tipperary for more than thirty years.

As Shane got older and his 'furious devotion' to Ireland deepened, it gave him the identity he never had growing up in England. When he found fame with The Pogues, his family's republican credentials came to form a keystone in his backstory.

Although neither The Pogues nor The Popes were overtly political, Shane has made his own contributions to the rebel songbook. In 'Skipping Rhymes' from *The Crock Of Gold*, he sang: 'We put a hood round his head / Then we shot the bastard dead / With a nick-nack, paddy-wack give a dog a bone / Send the stupid bastards home'. The chorus repeated the same line four times: 'The nation's gonna rise again'. 'Paddy Public Enemy No. 1' from the same record was inspired by the story of Dominic 'Mad Dog' McGlinchey, the republican paramilitary. He became chief of staff for the Irish National Liberation Army after being expelled from the IRA and was later shot dead.

The release of that album had come just two months after the start of the peace talks in Northern Ireland that would culminate in the Good Friday Agreement. In interviews to promote it, Shane didn't shy away from expressing his republican views. 'I think it should happen now – the English should get out,' he said. 'We've talked enough, they should let the Irish run their own country. I've always said that the Brits have no right to be there. I believe in a republic, a socialist republic.' [3]

That summer, Shane had met Sinn Féin leader Gerry Adams at the Féile an Phobail, the West Belfast Festival, set up in response to The Troubles and taking place on and around the Falls Road. Talking about the meeting in an interview for the *RTE Guide*, Shane said he thought there had been 'mutual respect' [4] between them. The two have remained friends and Gerry Adams still writes to Shane.

This chance encounter with Adams was still fresh in his mind when Victoria began recording conversations with him for her book *A Drink with Shane MacGowan*. When she asked what being Irish meant to him, his reply was striking. 'The Pogues would never have existed if I wasn't Irish,' he said. 'Ireland means everything to me. I have always felt guilty because I didn't lay down my life for Ireland, I didn't join up. Not that I would have helped the situation, probably. But I felt ashamed that I didn't have the guts to join the IRA. And The Pogues was my way of overcoming that guilt. And looking back on it, I think maybe I made the right choice.' [5]

Quite how the republican movement would have viewed someone who once dressed in a Union Jack shirt in the very streets where they were planting bombs is open to question. Shane's evolution from punk with a London accent to ardent Irish republican is one which has drawn comment over the years. John Lydon remarked in his 1995 memoir: 'Shane MacGowan used to come and see us play all the time. He'd be down in the front totally pissed out of his head in his Union Jack T-shirt. When he joined The Pogues, he traded it in for [an Irish] tricolour.' [6]

Filmmaker Julien Temple, who directed the 2020 documentary *Crock of Gold: A Few Rounds with Shane MacGowan*, was the first ever person to interview him, filming him in the lift of a block of flats in 1976. Back then, he detected nothing of the Irish background which would become pivotal to his identity. "He was like Joe [Strummer]; very thick London street accent, probably forced – the mockney style,' says Julien. 'But you had to be like that to be a punk. It was very much about covering your past and reinventing yourself, which I think suited Shane down to the ground, as it did Joe and many other people... There wasn't a hint of Irishness if you didn't know his name. A lot of Irish people were very London at that time, and you wouldn't have known that he was Irish, and certainly, you would have had no inkling that he would go on to do what he did.'

Siobhan, however, sees no contradiction between his republican sympathies and his punk attire. 'I do think the Union Jacks that were on the ripped punk shirts were a form of mockery and anarchy against the flag," she says. 'I think that's the spirit in which Shane wore it.'

Violence is another prominent theme in the Shane story as he tells it, from his role as 'minister for torture' and his associations with Charlie Kray while at Westminster to people he had left lying in a pool of blood years later. I found him at his most animated when telling these stories. I also couldn't help wondering how many of them were the product of his extremely fertile imagination.

I asked him if he was apprehensive as a teenager at consorting with dangerous underworld figures like Kray. 'Of course fucking not,' he snapped. 'I'm from a criminal race, a criminal family.' I ask him to elaborate. 'The older ones had been in the IRA and the younger ones were still hanging out with the IRA and foot soldiers,' he says.

'The Commons had also been used as a safehouse?' I ask.

'Yes, years before I was born. My great-granddad who went to the house was the head of the local IRB, the Irish Republican Brotherhood – the Fenians, they were called when he started. They became the IRA.'

Terry Woods' family were involved in the 1916 rebellion and, like Shane, he is well-versed on Ireland's turbulent history. So, Shane has always been keen to discuss the subject with him. Says Terry: 'Shane homes in on that. We used to have conversations about it and it got ridiculous. But he does believe an awful lot of this shit... When you consider there is this thread going through his life, all the drink and drugs he's taken from a young age. So, his mind is not clear in any shape, make or form, and it wouldn't surprise me what he'd believe to be the truth about anything.'

For several years now, Shane has existed in a bubble, removed from the outside world. He rarely, if ever, looks at a computer. He does not have email. A mobile phone sits beside him, but he doesn't call people, preferring to watch TV. Any public appearances are arranged and coordinated by Gerry O'Boyle and Victoria, who have played a key role in maintaining his profile since he stopped performing with The Pogues.

Over the past few years Victoria has pursued her ambition of bringing her relationship with Shane to the big screen. She spent two years co-writing a script with her director friend Maeve Murphy, and towards the end of 2019 announced her husband would be played by the award-winning *Dunkirk* actor, Barry Keoghan. Even more exciting for fans, Shane was back in the studio recording the soundtrack.

'Most of those rock biopics are really from the point of view of the rock star, so it's kind of interesting for me to have the opportunity to write about Shane, but from my point of view – and he hasn't seen any of it,' Victoria revealed in a TV interview. 'He just hasn't seen the script. I guess I asked him, "Can you just give me permission to do it without interfering?", because I don't try and write the songs, you know what I mean?' [7]

Asked whether the movie would be a warts-and-all look at their relationship, Victoria replied: 'Absolutely. That's the one thing he did say: "Look, make sure you put in all the violence and all the drugs and all the danger, and all that stuff. Don't make it schmaltzy, don't make it like a Hugh Grant film."

Maeve got to know Shane and Victoria towards the end of the 1980s through Frank Murray. He had supported Trouble And Strife, the theatre company she founded and for which she co-wrote and acted. She says the seeds of the film project were planted when she had a dream about Shane. He was in the same room as the actor who had played a prison officer in her 2001 film *Silent Grace*, and she walked in and felt comfortable. She emailed Victoria the following morning. 'At first, I thought it was going to just be about Shane,' explains Maeve. 'But when I started doing the research and talking with Victoria, I quickly realised their love story was just a great story.'

There is a mystery about Shane and Victoria as a couple that 'fascinates and touches' and makes their story compelling, says Maeve. The volatile nature of their relationship is central to its big-screen appeal and the script chronicles the dark as well as the happy times they have had as a couple. 'It is compelling because it's an edgy love that is cinematically exciting," says Maeve. 'Wild and fun at times, dangerous at times, doomed at times. I love that when it is doomed, we can't see how it can ever work and yet...'

Victoria's love of publicity and pursuit of celebrity has always been at odds with Shane's own total disinterest. He remains intensely private, with a small coterie of friends. Joey Cashman is larger-than-life, the perfect foil for an introverted man who does his storytelling through his songs. If Shane isn't in the mood to talk, Joey is as likely as anyone to draw him out. But most of the time, Shane is happiest watching a gangster film with the reassuring presence of a friend.

Dave Lally observed, 'Shane just wants love and company. I would often bring him a gift over, and he'd get all excited and say, "What, for me?" He'd be in total shock and hide it in case it went missing. Whenever we meet up and we've not seen each other for a while, he always asks after my mother. He hates hearing bad news and will take it to heart if I say she hasn't been well. Shane's very sensitive... I'm quiet anyway and when I'm with him, we'll sit there together watching a movie. In the first hour we might only say a few words. He just wants me there; he wants the company. He'll fall asleep and when he wakes up, he doesn't know where he is, and he'll look around to see who's in the room. He'll see me and he won't say anything and go back to watching the TV. But I'm there.

'He is still living life the same way. Just the TV and a few pounds to get him drink and smokes through the day. That's all Shane wants. He lives a very basic life and I think all he wants is his friends and loved ones around.'

Victoria says Shane has never been able to cope with terrible stories in the news, especially if they involve people suffering in any way. 'I think he does feel connected to people, so if something is happening to somebody that's bad, he feels it,' she says. 'Not just people he knows, but the First World War, the Second World War, Vietnam – he takes them very seriously. Even though they happened in the past, to him they're very real and those people are real people suffering, dying, being tortured. To him, it's not like that is something that happened to someone else; it's happened to a person, a human being. He's a humanitarian.'

If there is a violent side to Shane, it is manifested in a temper that can erupt from nowhere, as many of those who have tried to interview him can testify. Victoria says he hates questions and has never been comfortable talking about his music and career. In such situations, he can become aggressive and cutting in his tone. Friends have also ended up on the sharp end of his tongue over the years. But Shane is not unkind and feels terrible when he knows he has offended someone he cares about.

Paul Ronan recalls one such episode: 'I was round at his flat and he upset me. He was being obnoxious, like Shane can be sometimes, and I remember storming out and saying, "You can just go and fuck yourself."

'I just went home and when I got in, the phone was ringing and it was Shane. "Look, Paul, I'm sorry. Can we go down Le Mercury?", which was a French restaurant in Upper Street, Islington. "I'll buy you a meal and we'll have a few drinks and a chat. I'll come round and pick you up by cab."

'I said, "No. I'll come over to you or I'll meet you down there."

'So, he said, "Get yourself a cab, I'll look after it." That shows Shane. He doesn't like upsetting people close to him. He might take the piss, but if he feels he has overstepped the mark or been impolite he becomes very apologetic.'

During a drinking session in Nenagh one night, Shane had begun teasing Dave Lally and calling him a 'West Brit' – an Irish person who is more British in their outlook – even though he himself had been born in the UK. Nothing was said afterwards and Dave had not dwelt on it. Several years later, Shane suddenly brought it up. 'Out of the blue he turned around and said, "I'm sorry about upsetting you that time,"' recalled Dave.

'I said, "What time?"'

'He goes, "When I was taking the piss down in Nenagh and calling you a West Brit. I didn't mean it."'

'I said, "Shane, forget about it. I wouldn't be here if I was angry about it."'

'He said, "Well, I was only joking, I didn't mean it. I'm sorry."'

One day, Paul and I were in a Dublin pub with Shane when a fan joined us at the table and asked me who I was. I told him I was a friend of Shane's.

'You're not a friend of mine,' said Shane, looking at me.

'Okay, you're right. I'm not a friend of yours,' I said.

A few seconds passed before Shane said, 'Actually, you are a friend of mine.'

A bottle of white wine and a glass sit in front of Shane all day. He will sometimes fill his glass to the brim and it will sit there for half an hour or longer without him having a drop. As each bottle is emptied, another is opened and even when he goes to bed it is within his reach.

Alcohol has been his constant companion for more than forty years. His flat at Cromer Street was a sea of empties long before he was downing bottles of whiskey on stage with The Pogues or pints of gin or martini in the Popes years. When he performed with Sharon Shannon's band, his wine was often set up on a small table beside his microphone stand, never beyond his reach. Even as he received his prestigious awards in 2018, he had a glass in his hand.

But Shane has given up drink and once stayed on the wagon for six months. That dry spell began in the middle of 2016 when he was readmitted to hospital with excruciating pain in his hip and contracted pneumonia. His doctors ordered a total detox and Shane spent several months in his private room without touching a drop. Even when he got home, he remained teetotal. Victoria was amazed: 'This is the longest that Shane has been sober since we met, and we are getting on very well. I would not have dreamed that it was possible for Shane to be happy and sober.' [8]

Shane has always staunchly defended his right to drink, telling journalists that it was no one else's business what he did. Siobhan, Victoria and others have begged him to stop over the years. However, they have come to accept that when it comes to his lifestyle there is only one voice to which he will ever listen. His own. Siobhan says: 'I have tried over the years to give him wake-up calls, but you might wake him up for five minutes. It doesn't last.'

The mere fact he is still alive after decades of self-abuse seems to have imbued him with the belief that, whatever dependencies he may have, he is not entirely in their grip. His limits may dwarf those of most people, but he has always known to stay within them. 'When I say you've had enough, you've had enough,' he witheringly told an inebriated woman who attached herself to his party in a London hotel.

'One drink will set you up and you could be an alcoholic,' says Shane. 'You have one in the morning and one in the afternoon and try and get it down. That's the only way to get off the booze for any time at all. You can't sleep if you are withdrawing and alcohol is a powerful drug. It is the worst of the lot. It makes you ill if you haven't got it, and you don't enjoy it after you've had more than a couple of glasses. Nobody drinks for the taste. I drink for the fucking hit. I drink slow and I don't like to hit it that much anymore. I need it, but I'm not an alcoholic.'

Asked if she thinks Shane is an alcoholic, Victoria says: 'He probably isn't. I think if they gave him a different drug and said, "This drug is going to actually do the same thing," he would probably take that. It's whatever drug is going to make him feel normal. I think he also romanticises drinking in that sense of hard men drink and Irish men drink, and if you can't drink there's something wrong with you.'

Victoria has seen peaks and troughs in his drinking over the years. She says his alcohol intake went off the scale when The Pogues began to taste success and the pressure on them to tour increased. She says: 'He used to get very stressed on tour and that's when he used to drink a lot. He really found it difficult. I remember one day we were driving around Dublin in my car and I noticed that he didn't have a drink. I thought, 'That's very odd, he normally has a drink'. I said it to him, and he said, "Yeah, but I've got nothing to worry about." He wasn't stressed, we weren't on tour, he didn't have to be anywhere or do anything. So, I think he feels pressure very strongly, even if it's pressure just to go anywhere really.

'He drinks to medicate. I used to drink a lot more than him when we met, and he was actually quite shocked by it. I didn't drink to medicate. I drank to get wasted and he thought that was a bit much. He'd be like, "Oh, why are you drinking so much?" and he would drink a white wine spritzer and I would drink a double whiskey or a triple whiskey. So, I noticed the difference when The Pogues took off and, when he was under pressure, he totally changed. He became stressed and he couldn't cope with the guilt of not doing the whole thing that they wanted him to do, and the responsibility of all these people whose jobs depended on it. He couldn't just leave. It was really horrible. So, then he began to drink, kind of passive-aggressively, to get at them because his only way to communicate it was to fuck it up. It was like, "OK, I'll show you. You want to see what's going to happen?" He couldn't just knock it on the head. Now he doesn't go crazy. He just keeps topped up.'

Shane's drug use has also diminished since the dark days when addicts were overdosing in his flat. It is also many years since he kicked the heroin addiction which prompted Sinéad O'Connor to go to the police.

Shane says: 'I went on to medicine, the soup, the shit. That's what I went on originally and I managed to talk them into putting me on morphine, which is an active ingredient of heroin. The ones I'm taking at the moment are the same as MST [Methadone Substitution Therapy], they just look different. At one point I was on five grams of heroin, I suppose. I wasn't really counting. At a certain point, you give up playing it safe. If you can get four big lines up you, you might as well take five. I often injected when I got a chance because that's the best rush. I find smoking makes you drowsy. I was always doing speedballs, but if I ran out of heroin, the speed would keep me going for a while. But when the heroin was there, I'd be fucked. You're yearning for it.'

Drink and drugs have robbed the lives of many of his friends while he has survived it all. Quite how he is still alive is one of life's great mysteries. But his consumption levels today bear no comparison to those of the past and given that his father and his uncle Billy are in their nineties, he may have inherited the MacGowan constitution.

Jem Finer remarks: 'I think he has made compromises. It's possible to spend a lot of time with Shane. He might not be everyone's definition of sober, but I would say he is pretty sober most of the time and articulate, sharp and good company... He must have an amazing constitution. I don't know what makes that happen, but I suppose some people are just very strong and they are very adaptable to any kind of diet, like some weird creature living around a volcanic vent – and can extract nutrition from anything!'

Shane listened with deep pride and humility as friends and admirers spoke about his gift for songwriting and why his music spoke so directly to them.

He was back on *The Late Late Show*, for a special tribute filmed in December 2019. RTE had cast the net wide to bring together guests who would not only illustrate the profound respect in which he is held as an artist, but the extraordinary reach of his songs – geographically and culturally.

Singers, actors and others whose paths had crossed his talked with host Ryan Tubridy about their lasting admiration. Shane, dressed in a white shirt and smart navy suit, sat between the presenter and Victoria listening carefully and occasionally interjecting when his own memories challenged theirs. Studio 4 was given a bar-room makeover with guests sitting around tables of drinks, a move heavily criticised by Alcohol Action Ireland. However, the atmosphere during the recording was one of reverence.

Shane's return to *The Late Late Show* as a national hero brought him and the programme full circle. In the same studio thirty-four years earlier, iconic presenter Gay Byrne had charged Shane and The Pogues with giving Irish music a bad name. Shane had been just as bemused at that accusation as he now seemed overwhelmed to be honoured by so many respected performers from Ireland.

Shane MacGowan's place in the history of Irish music has long been secured. His face appears alongside Luke Kelly, Phil Lynott and Sinéad O'Connor on the wall of fame at the Irish Rock'n'roll Museum Experience, in the heart of Dublin's Temple Bar. The role played by The Pogues in expanding the Irish music tradition and introducing generations around the world to it was acknowledged many years before he was honoured with the special lifetime achievement award at the National Concert Hall.

The Late Late's tribute underlined Shane's significance in the story of Irish music and the intrinsic relationship between his songs and those he heard as a child on Raidió Telifís Éireann and Raidió Na Gaeltachta on trips to Tipperary. Legendary storyteller and singer Seán Ó Sé's presence on the show was proof positive that the origins of Shane's poetic songs go to the very marrow of Irish traditional music. Shane was visibly humbled by the presence of the 83-year-old, describing him as a 'huge hero'. Ó Sé's was one of the first Irish voices picked up by his young ears, as well as being the best friend of Seán Ó Riada, one of the biggest influences on Shane's music. Ó Sé said he considered it 'a privilege' to be in Shane's company and he spoke of the part he had played in adding to the Irish tradition.

'When I was very young... in the very early forties, I remember hundreds leaving west Cork to go to get work in England,' he commented. 'Then later on, when I was singing in places like the White Hart in Fulham Broadway, I met those people and they played Irish music, but they had added a dimension. Like the Clare style and Donegal, the Irish in England added their own dimension. For instance, they made the piano accordion respectable, which was kind of taboo until then.

'Shane has been a hero of mine and there is one thing that sets him apart; that if anybody writes a song that would be performed as long as there's Irish people or Americans on this planet, that's a unique achievement, and that's what "Fairytale Of New York" has done.'

Shane listened in awe as Sean sang a section from 'The Body Of An American', accompanied by a group of musicians. Before leading the song – famously featured in the hit US series *The Wire* – Seán said its opening lines stood on their own as 'as a wonderful poem, as a requiem for a paddy'.

In contrast to other appearances on RTE chat shows, Shane was alert and in good humour. He had also been keen to perform and was backed by more than a dozen musicians who included Jem Finer and Terry Woods from The Pogues, Steve Wickham, a renowned fiddle player and relative of Shane, and Fiachna Ó Braonáin, guitarist with Hothouse Flowers. 'White City' and 'Sally MacLennane' were plucked from The Pogues' extensive songbook before seasoned country singer Philomena Begley joined him to sing 'Fairytale Of New York'.

In the fireside-style conversation led by Tubridy, Siobhan recalled their childhood, and Shane spoke, as he had so often, about the influence of his mother's family at the cottage in Tipperary and the music he listened to there. As they did so, a screen displayed black-and-white photographs from those holidays, so loved by Shane.

As well as tracing the origins of Shane's songs, the show also explored why they came to form the connective tissue between Irish people living outside Ireland and their musical and cultural roots. Despite becoming known the world over as an 'Irish band', The Pogues were a London group and none of the original six were born in Ireland. Jem was from Stoke-on-Trent, James from Worsley, Manchester, and Andrew from west London, while Spider hailed from Eastbourne, Sussex. Cait was born in Nigeria to an Irish father and Scottish mother, and Shane was the only band member whose parents were both Irish. Only when Philip Chevron and Terry Woods joined did the group have any Irish-born musicians.

As Seán Ó Sé pointed out, it was The Pogues' emergence from London rather than Ireland that gave them such a furious energy and saw them add an edgier dimension to Irish traditional music. Their treatment of traditional songs like 'The Auld Triangle', 'Waxie's Dargle', 'Poor Paddy' and 'Kitty' provided the London Irish with a gateway to and pride in their cultural heritage.

Songwriter Glen Hansard was born in north Dublin but experienced first-hand what The Pogues meant to the Irish in London. 'What made Shane's music and The Pogues' music different for me was that it was speaking to the broad diaspora – and the word diaspora means the scattered tribe,' he said on the programme. 'I remember seeing The Pogues in London in the late eighties in the Town & Country Club, and there was an energy in the room that was really terrifying. I was actually freaked out because it was mental energy. I have cousins in Birmingham, and they used to sing Irish songs with much more gusto than me or my parents ever sang them. And it had something to do with being away from Ireland and not being quite English and not being quite Irish, and so kind of leaning into the identity. So, when The Pogues came along, there was just this shock of passion and devotion.'

Far from just speaking to the Irish in Britain, The Pogues also gave those with Irish ancestry living in the US a band they could embrace as their own. Martin O'Malley, a former US presidential candidate and governor of Baltimore, met The Pogues when they toured America and his band O'Malley's March supported them. He flew to Ireland to take part in the special tribute show and spoke powerfully about the impact of Shane's lyrics on Irish Americans.

Martin commented: 'I have, for so long, admired this man: his passion, his range. And I'm not talking about the amount of notes he sings, I'm talking about the fact that as an Irish American kid growing up in the seventies and eighties in the United States, our kind of portal to an awareness of things Irish through music was mostly the Clancy Brothers and Tommy Makem. And it was great, but it was always our parents' music. But when this guy came along with the passion and the fierceness, it changed it, and it wasn't just a young guy singing the old songs, you know? It was him making the old songs new again. I had gone out to see him many times at the 9:30 Club and the Guinness Fleadh up in New York. He has just done so much for Irish music and Irish music throughout the whole diaspora.

'I know a lot of the conversation has been about the Irish in the UK, but songs like "The Body Of An American" and other sorts of songs – "Thousands Are Sailing" – I mean, that was a real connection for us. That made this music passionate and it made it ours. I went to the 9:30 Club and I remember walking in there, we were late, and there was this crowd of young Irish American kids all jumping up and down like the waves of the sea to "Roddy McCorley". It was like, "My God, it's all new again," and with that our music took a kind of different direction; we added drums and electric guitar.'

Shane's worldwide fan club has always included well-known actors, and some have become friends. Aidan Gillen and Patrick Bergin both appeared on *The Late Late Show* to acknowledge his influence, while Tom Vaughan-Lawlor and Liam Neeson both recorded video messages. 'You took aspects of Irish culture and Irish music, kicked it up the arse with a great sense of pride and joy and rebelliousness, and sent it out into the world,' said Liam. 'And it was feckin' great and it stopped us all moping into our pints or into our Baileys Irish Cream and we took pride in ourselves.'

Bobby Gillespie also recorded a tribute, as did another celebrity fan whose friendship with Shane is less well known – Paul Simon. 'I'm here to tip the hat to my friend Shane MacGowan, whose voice revealed something deep and beautiful about the Irish soul,' he said.

Victoria told me how Paul formed a bond with Shane after paying him an unexpected visit. 'He was playing in Dublin and he asked the driver if he knew Shane MacGowan, and the driver happened to know us,' she said. 'He said, "Look, I'd love to meet him. Can you help me to meet him?"'

'So, the driver rang me and said, "Look, Paul Simon wants to come round to your house."'

'So, he came round and spent the whole day chatting to Shane and playing music and having a really nice time, and he said it was the best day he'd had in his living memory. He noticed that Shane had a really crappy record player, so he sent him a state-of-the-art one and now every time he's here, he comes and hangs out. He's a really nice guy and he's a songwriter's songwriter, so they can talk forever about music.'

An after-show party at RTE went on until the early hours, with Shane and friends sharing memories and singing songs. Some of his pals from

Nenagh, including Noel and Scruffy Kenny, were also there to raise a glass to him on his special night.

The Late Late Show generated widespread media coverage in Ireland and proved a tonic for Shane. Speaking to me the following day, Victoria said she was delighted he had been so determined to perform: 'I think he will get back on his feet and he will get back out there and he will be playing. 'He was demanding gigs, but he was also demanding that RTE let him sing more songs and give him his own show. He wanted to keep doing it and I was surprised because I thought it would be hard to get him to do even one song. But actually, he wanted to do the whole bloody thing. He didn't want anyone else to have to sing. He was like, "No, I want to do all of it." He was annoyed that other people were singing, he really was. So, I think he's definitely got that back.'

The creative block that stifled his productivity for so long has shown signs of loosening its hold and Victoria is hopeful he will start writing some new songs. 'I think he's only ever been motivated to get moving by being motivated to write and perform,' she says. Commenting on the award he received in 2018, she adds, 'So, now he's kind of got that back. It's only been in the past year, even towards the later part of this year. I think it was partly helped by the Ivor Novello award. I think that motivated him. He would probably deny it, but I think he is motivated by getting that music out there, still.'

This rediscovered desire to record new material was corroborated in March 2020 by media revelations of a comeback solo album. *The Irish Sun* reported that five songs had been recorded by Shane, with the backing of Johnny and Michael Cronin and their fellow band members Fiachra Milner and Brian Murphy. 'Shane is in such fine voice,' said Johnny Cronin [9]. 'He's been blasting his way through vocal takes and amazing everybody with his energy. It's incredibly exciting to be recording with Shane. Not only is he great craic but he has such presence, and so many ideas, they're spilling out of him.'

Restrictions imposed following the outbreak of Covid-19 curtailed these studio sessions and kept Shane confined at home for the rest of 2020, with the exception of an appearance on *The Late Late*'s annual Christmas busk for the Simon Community. He joined John Sheahan, Glen Hansard, Lisa O'Neill and Finbar Furey for a moving rendition of 'Raglan Road', Patrick Kavanagh's poem about the celebrated tree-lined street not a mile from Shane's home in Ballsbridge.

The release of the film *Crock of Gold: A Few Rounds with Shane MacGowan* put him back in the spotlight as the most extraordinary of years came to an eerily quiet close. Produced by Johnny Depp and directed by Julien Temple, it was shown in cinemas, although largely streamed by fans online. It is a visual feast, which knits audio and video footage with stunning animated effects to tell his story and examine what has made him who he is. We enter the film through parting clouds and see a map of Ireland with its ancient legends, before being swooped into the farmhouse where Shane's young imagination was fired. 'God looked down on this little cottage in Ireland, and said, "That little boy there, he's the little boy that I'm gonna use to save Irish music and take it to greater popularity than it's ever had before."' 'Why would God do that?' we hear Victoria ask. 'Cos God is Irish,' comes the reply.

Cobwebbed religious statues, the Sacred Heart of Jesus and footage re-enacting his childhood visits to The Commons are used to powerful effect in the opening scenes, summoning the 'old Ireland' in which his songs are steeped. The combination of these sepia-tinted scenes with animation and old interview footage gives the film an originality and a kaleidoscopic quality, in keeping with the subject's own restless mind.

However, in making the film, the director faced a titanic challenge. Even though it had been Shane's idea and Johnny Depp had to persuade Julien to take on the project, Shane refused to be interviewed. Worse still, he was irascible, argumentative and, on occasions, aggressive towards Julien and the crew. 'The main skill for me was to learn how to try to let the abuse roll off – become a duck, basically,' admits Julien. 'It swings from one extreme to another, in a way, so you have just got to be able to deal with it. My main fear was taking people's money and then not having anything to deliver.'

Numerous attempts were made to capture footage of Shane at his home, without success. Infuriated, the director decided to film people with whom Shane was more comfortable chatting to, in the hope they would draw him out. This also proved a challenge. Says Julien: 'We asked all The Pogues but they didn't want to go near it with a bargepole. So, we ended up getting this strange collection of people that basically Shane was happy to speak to, but also who were happy to speak to Shane, because it was equally difficult to convince people.'

The first time they tried to film Shane and Johnny Depp together, Johnny didn't turn up. The next night, Johnny appeared but there was no Shane.

When they both showed at the third attempt, the eight hours of footage recorded yielded only a few minutes that could be used. Other friends who tried to elicit some usable clips experienced contrasting reactions. A polite enquiry from Bobby Gillespie about when Shane had moved to England hit a raw nerve. He was accused of 'interrogating' him and told to 'get off the subject'. However, when Gerry Adams visited his Dublin flat, Shane was politeness itself. 'You have to write more songs – there's no excuse,' Gerry told him. 'No, I'm doing my best, you know,' Shane replied. 'Are you writing now?' he pressed. 'I've run out of inspiration at the moment,' confessed Shane.

This rare admission of his struggle to write was particularly sad, especially when contrasted with comments from old interviews. 'Songs are just floating around in the air,' he had once remarked. 'That's why we call tunes airs. All we have to do is reach out and grab 'em. That's why I'm always grabbing cos if I don't reach out and grab it myself, it'll go on and get to Paul Simon.'

For all the obstacles that Shane put up during the making of *Crock of Gold*, Julien Temple has no regrets and says the way in which the story ended up being told was ultimately to its benefit. 'I wanted to show these different versions of him, this fractured sense of the contradictions in him. These different characters are at the root of his creative power. I wanted to let people make their own minds up, show these different fragments of him telling the same story in radically different ways: that unreliable narrator thing is a big part of Shane.

'In a way, it doesn't matter if it is objectively true. At times, it's more important that he believes it's true because that allows him to be who he is. If he wasn't allowed to believe things that weren't true, again he wouldn't be Shane MacGowan, and it's wrapped in the mists of Irish mythology and legend and literature. It's all part of an organic sense of who he has created. But I think everyone does that to an extent.'

Crock of Gold also shone a light on something that had occupied Shane's febrile mind since he was a child: death. On visits to The Commons, he slept in his aunty Nora's bed and because of her chain smoking he was 'always terrified she'd die in her sleep'. He had developed a morbid fascination with the slaughtering of the geese and turkeys at the farm and how they looked as they died. When Therese was on heavy drugs to calm her nerves at the Barbican, he would go into her room every morning and 'kick her to see if she was alive'.

His anxiety around loss and death, including almost certainly his own, was presented as one of the reasons behind his strong Irish Catholic faith. 'One day, I'd been reading Marx and Trotsky and I think that's the moment I lost my faith,' he said [10]. 'It just hit me like a thunderbolt. I just thought, Supposing it's a load of crap? And I lapsed. I tried and tried to fucking regain my faith, but you can't. I became an atheist. Frightened the shit out of me. It meant that I'd never meet the wonderful old people again after they'd died, and some of them had already died.'

Ann Scanlon has a strong Irish Catholic faith and knows as well as anyone how important Shane's own devotion is to him. She says: 'Shane would always say, "I pray to Mary and I pray to Jesus, and Saint Martin and Saint Francis, but I also pray to my dead relatives who I regard as saints." That's the same for me. I could only cope with the loss of my mum by knowing that I will see her again one day and my faith has been the greatest gift in my life to me and that's what Shane has as well. At the end of his 60th birthday concert, it was very moving when he just raised his glass and said in Gaelic, "For God and Ireland". I mean, that is Shane: his country and his faith.'

Many have interpreted Shane's hedonistic extremes as evidence of a death-wish. However, Shane refutes this, and while he may look frail for his 63 years, he is still here – the ultimate survivor. 'He says in the film, "If I wanted to die, I'd be dead already," and I don't see him having a death-wish in any shape or form,' says Julien Temple. 'You almost get the idea he is pickled, that he is preserved in some way from the substances, as long as he keeps a kind of balance on it. He's not drinking to get drunk, he's kind of topping up a system that keeps him in a good space.'

It has, of course, come with a heavy price. For almost five years, he has not walked. His days are spent in an armchair, his eyes glued to his beloved television. Carers get him in and out of bed. His physical frailty, laid bare in *Crock of Gold*, saddens some who know him. Ann Scanlon, however, sees beyond his disabilities to the erudite and philosophical man she has always known, and one fortified by his faith.

She remarks: 'He's had lots of scrapes over the years and that's his body, but with Shane, people have always focused on the way he looks, even back in the day. I never see that. Shane's quite a divine being. Gerry [O'Boyle] says he is like a cross between the composer Turlough O'Carolan and Saint Francis, and you might think that's an exaggeration, but I can see it – the

Irish Mozart and Saint Francis dealing with humanity. Shane does have that sense of divinity and his Irish Catholicism is absolutely essential to him; that's his spiritual scaffolding.'

Shane's standing as one of Ireland's most gifted writers and performers is recognised the world over. To fans, he has been an inspirational figure for more than thirty-five years, a legend who made Irish music cool and instilled among the diaspora an even greater pride in their heritage. As some of the groups who found fame alongside The Pogues posed on luxury yachts and embraced the yuppie ethos, Shane presented the flipside of eighties England, with songs that were visceral and violent. The characters who inhabited his songs spewed up in church, lay penniless in doorways or were haunted by war. The writer who drew his inspiration from old Ireland put into song the kinds of stories he'd once written in his schoolbooks. In doing so, he sparked an interest in Irish music that had once seemed impossible but changed how many people perceived Ireland itself. By celebrating the richness of its culture and its violent struggles and fusing it with punk's insurgent spirit, he opened the door to a country many fans had never been to and knew little about.

The prospect of another 'Rainy Night In Soho' or 'Fairytale Of New York' falling from his pen remains a tantalising one, and fans continue to hope his muse can be rediscovered. When Victoria asks him towards the end of *Crock of Gold* whether there is anything he would love to have happen in his life, he replies: 'Yes, I'd like to start prolifically writing songs again.' Following a pause, he adds: 'And I'd like to be able to play pool.'

In Victoria, he has a rock of support. She provides constant encouragement, as do his family and friends. However, they know that any motivation to walk again and write new songs has to come from him and no one else. For his part, he insists he wants the operation that would restore his mobility and independence, and his writing pad is never far away. Shane MacGowan is not done yet. He is, after all, a man of extremes, and his 'furious devotion' for life remains as fervent as his love of a drink.

CHAPTER 13

The Parting Glass

'And all I've done for want of wit
To memory now I can't recall
So fill to me the parting glass
Good night and joy be with you all'

'The Parting Glass', **The Pogues**

Shane's health was failing him. No stranger to hospital wards over the years, his visits were now becoming more frequent and serious. Victoria remained as upbeat as ever, posting regular updates for his fans on social media, celebrating his small improvements and brighter days. However, while his long-held desire to live was as strong as ever, his body was weakening and his ability to bounce back had diminished. The situation was becoming grave.

'Hi fans,' said Shane, from behind a pair of black sunglasses in a video posted on Twitter on 31 December 2022. 'I'm sitting here suffering from encephalitis. The light is killing me, but I wanted to wish you all a Happy New Year and Happy Christmas, and many more of them to all of you, and all the luck in the world and all the love.'

Just a couple of months earlier Shane had celebrated the publication of a book spanning four decades of his art, entitled *The Eternal Buzz and The Crock of Gold*. He sported a smart blue suit, a white, open-necked shirt and sunglasses at a launch party thrown at the Andipa Gallery in London's Kensington, in what was a rare public outing. Kate Moss was amongst his old friends who turned out for the event, where several pieces were on sale for between £5,000 and £32,000.

Shane had scrawled his imaginative creations on scraps of paper, napkins and air sickness bags, often while hallucinating on drugs. Many of these pieces had returned with him from his tours – somehow salvaged from the detritus of his luggage.

'Shane MacGowan's Thai Boxers' featured himself as one of two gloved fighters and dated from one of his many trips to the country where he drank the mind-altering Mekhong whiskey, took on prostitutes at pool and watched boxing bouts. 'Squid Pro Quo Kandinsky' was the outcome of a heavy acid trip in New Zealand and reflected his obsession with squid and octopuses and his admiration for the Russian abstract artist.

Love notes, handwritten instructions as to how The Pogues should behave and Shane's own cocktail recipes were also included in the limited-edition book made available via his official website, and was priced at €1,000. Gerry Adams and actors Patrick Bergin and Peter Coonan were among those to read extracts from the treasure trove at its unveiling in a Dublin restaurant in November. Shane appeared to throw himself into the project, giving several interviews to support its promotion; it had proved a surprising tonic.

'Shane can get away with being unfriendly, but he actually really enjoyed it,' Victoria said of his art exhibition [1]. 'He doesn't normally like to be told he is good at things, but he's beginning to like the idea his art is good.'

However, the high provided by the reaction to his artwork was short-lived. Shane was readmitted to hospital in early December, initially with shingles in his face which spread to his eye and then viral encephalitis, an inflammation of the brain. Victoria urged fans to pray for him and send healing vibes as he faced another serious health battle. Antivirals were administered intravenously and he responded well enough to be allowed home for Christmas, where he watched football. Fans went online to welcome the news and send their good wishes.

In May 2023, one staunch admirer gave Shane a welcome lift – a surprise visit that made headlines. Bruce Springsteen was performing at the nearby RDS in Dublin that month and took the opportunity to call in to see his hero. Victoria took a photograph of the occasion, with Shane gazing up from his armchair at his celebrated guest as Bruce leaned down and put an arm around him. 'He was very ill, but still beautifully present in his heart and spirit,' The Boss was to recall later.

The following month, Shane's health took another nosedive and he was admitted to St Vincent's University Hospital suffering from pneumonia. Initially treated in the intensive care unit, he was then moved to a room of his own, but his progress was slow. Photos shared by Victoria revealed how thin and frail he had become. It was harrowing for all to see.

Siobhan travelled every week from Tipperary to see him. Bandmates Jem Finer, Spider Stacy and Terry Woods, as well as his old friends and celebrated artists, including Bono, Edge, Bobby Gillespie, Moya Brennan and Imelda May, ensured an almost constant flow of visitors. Shane watched television, just as he did at home, and he smiled in the pictures taken by Victoria. Month by month went by with no sign of him being discharged from hospital and, through fear of aspiration, he continued to be fed by tube. Unable to put on weight and build himself back up, he had little, if any, resilience to the infections which kept coming in waves.

Finally, on Thursday 23 November, there was some good news. 'Shane's got out of hospital!' announced a delighted Victoria on X (formerly Twitter), talking of Shane's discharge two days earlier. 'We are deeply and eternally grateful to all of the doctors and nurses and staff at St Vincent's – it's the best.' Shane was pictured smiling in his hospital gown and black bobble hat, with pals Brian Corscadden and Tom Creagh at his bedside, preparing to leave. He spent the following three nights at home and fans were overjoyed he had made it out of hospital in time for Christmas.

But tragedy was to follow. On Friday 24 November he was rushed back into St Vincent's with septic shock resulting from pneumonia. Six days later came the announcement everyone was dreading. 'It is with the deepest sorrow and heaviest of hearts that we announce the passing of our most beautiful, darling and dearly beloved Shane MacGowan,' read a statement from Victoria, Siobhan and Maurice. 'Shane died peacefully at 3.30 a.m. this morning (30 November 2023) with his wife and sister by his side. Prayers and the last rites were read during his passing.'

In life, Shane had loomed so large, and his Herculean stamina had led us to believe that he would somehow outlive us all. Now, at 65, the light that had once burned so fiercely and so bright had finally gone out. He was gone.

Friday 8 December 2023

Nenagh has had a long and proud association with Shane MacGowan. The Tipperary town is just a few miles from The Commons, where he spent some of the happiest days of his childhood. As a man, he drank in its pubs and made lifelong friendships with Noel and Scruffy (Brian) Kenny, Tom Creagh, Philly Ryan, and others. The connection with St Mary of the Rosary Church was more poignant still. Therese had attended Mass there every Sunday, accompanied by Shane when he was home, and she often lit a candle at Our Lady's shrine.

A group of press photographers had lined up, waiting for the funeral cortège and the celebrity faces emerging from cars. People were already crammed into the doorways at the rear of the building a good hour before the service was due to begin, desperate to get a glimpse. At one corner at the front of the church, musicians were busy tuning up and making last-minute technical checks for a service that would be streamed live around the world. Among them were members of The Pogues, Sharon Shannon, John Sheahan of The Dubliners, Finbar Furey, Imelda May and Glen Hansard, the man tasked with choreographing the extensive musical programme. On pews reserved for family and close friends, Andrew Caitlin's black-and-white photo of a young, fresh-faced Shane stared out from the cover of the order of service. It was hard to believe we would never see him again.

It was heartbreaking to see Shane's elderly father Maurice, 94, being helped out of a wheelchair and taking his place in a pew at the front of the church, as we waited for the coffin and the rest of the family to file in. For a few minutes he sat alone, looking straight ahead.

Anticipation mingled with reverence as Shane's wicker coffin adorned with the Irish tricolour was carried down the aisle to the mournful refrain of Peadar Ó Riada's Coolea Choir. It was then covered with white cloth and a wreath of red roses at the altar where another of Caitlin's black-and-white photographs of him in heady days, holding a cigarette and raising a glass, stood tall. The time to pay our respects had now come and the chatter subsided, giving way to a peaceful calm as Father Pat Gilbert uttered his opening words.

'At his baptism, Shane was clothed in a white robe, the outward sign of his Christian dignity. This afternoon, friends of Shane placed a towel on his coffin as an outward sign of our respect for his mortal remains. In life, Shane cherished the gospel of Christ. May Christ now greet him with these words of eternal life: "Come blessed of my Father". In baptism, Shane received the sign of the cross. May he now share in Christ's victory over sin and death.'

The presence of the president of Ireland, Michael D. Higgins, his official entourage and camera crews in position to capture every moment, gave the occasion the look and feel of a state funeral. No other Irish artist had been treated to such a send-off. The scenes that had unfolded just hours earlier, as Shane's coffin was driven through the streets of Dublin before heading to his cherished Tipperary, spoke to the profound way in which he had touched people's lives. The Artane Boys Band in their bright blue-and-red uniform had played his music and marched in front of the glass, horse-drawn carriage as it made its way along a route presaged in the national papers. Thousands of fans had turned out to witness their hero's final journey, thronging the pavements and applauding as the cortège passed. Some had brought guitars and other instruments with them and 'Fairytale Of New York' and 'Dirty Old Town' rang out as Dubliners broke into song.

Shane had always been discomfited by adulation. However, his eyes would surely have welled up at such a public show of respect and outpouring of grief. Ireland was a central part of who Shane was and that connection had been reciprocated. On that cold December day, it felt like Ireland herself was crying. Dubliners bade their final goodbyes at Westland Row, the birthplace of Oscar Wilde. The procession then began its two-hour journey to Nenagh, where more crowds were waiting. These scenes would be shared with the world, underscoring the breadth and depth of Shane's legacy, prompting a rather unusual message from the priest officiating at his funeral Mass.

'I welcome you who are watching on the web, people listening on radio, people watching and listening to the broadcast being streamed today,' said Fr Gilbert. 'We also remember people who cannot be here for one reason or another but are with us in spirit. We welcome the world; we welcome the world of people this great man influenced, encouraged, entertained, and touched. Your presence here is very important and a huge statement of the love and esteem we all had, and have, for this great man.'

First to pay tribute to Shane in the extraordinary service was former Sinn Féin president Gerry Adams, who had regularly written letters to Shane and had visited him in hospital. The seasoned orator did a reading from Song of Songs and then delivered an eloquent and stirring homage. Victoria had asked him to say a few words as it was Shane's wish.

'My words are words of gratitude. Gratitude for Shane's genius, for his songs, for his creativity, for his attitude. Gratitude for his humour and his intelligence and his compassion. Grateful for his vulnerabilities, his knowledge, and his modesty. Gratitude for his celebration of the marginalised, the poor, our exiles and the underdogs. Grateful for The Pogues and for all our music makers, and all our dreamers of dreams, and thankful for Shane's carers.

'Proud of how Shane deepened our sense of Irishness and our humanity. Grateful for his rejection of the revisionism of time-serving fumblers in greasy tills. Glad that he stood by the people of the North in war and in peace, and that he was proud of Tipperary's fight for Irish freedom and for his family's role in this.

'Thankful for his poet's eye for words of love and betrayal, justice and injustice, rejection and redemption. Grateful that Shane lifted us out of ourselves and that he never gave up. Delighted that he empowered us to dance and sing, to make fun and to shout and yell and laugh and cry, and to love and to be free.

'*Ár laoch thú Shane. Ár ghile mear. File, Ceoltóir, fear uasal* [You are our hero, Shane. Our quick wit. Poet, musician, gentleman]. Your music will live forever. You are the measurer of our dreams. *Go raibh maith agat* [Thank you] Shane MacGowan.'

The musical tributes stirred up a mix of emotions; a sadness that Shane would never again sing them and a gratitude for their timeless beauty. Imelda May and Declan O'Rourke summoned tears as they reprised 'You're The One', the song Shane had originally sung with Moya Brennan. Every moment of quiet in the song could be felt as the congregation listened, rapt. Then, when it reached its exquisite finale, applause and whoops of approbation filled the place, setting a celebratory tone that would infuse the occasion.

Camille O'Sullivan and Mundy's 'Haunted' was delivered with intensity, and its performance, on what would have been Sinead O'Connor's birthday, only added to the raw emotion of hearing it at her friend's funeral. Nick Cave was late to arrive, prompting a reshuffle in the order of performances. When he took his seat at the piano and played the opening notes of 'Rainy Night In Soho', it was one of the standout moments of the service.

Cait O'Riordan, accompanied by John Francis Flynn, performed 'I'm A Man You Don't Meet Every Day', the traditional song included on *Rum Sodomy & the Lash*, while James Fearnley, Jem Finer, Spider Stacy and Terry Woods reunited to deliver 'The Parting Glass' as a fitting finale. 'Fairytale Of New York' brought some to their feet and produced perhaps the most memorable moment of the day. Glen Hansard and Lisa O'Neill delivered the lyrics that Shane and Kirsty MacColl had enshrined in our musical consciousness and were joined by The Pogues, John Sheahan from The Dubliners, and the other musicians assembled for the service. Phones were held aloft and the congregation swayed. Maurice looked on with pride, with Shane's aunt Vicky and his cousin Lisa joining him at the front of the church. Camille and Imelda began dancing and gestured to the family to follow suit. Siobhan and Anthony, and Victoria and Liam Ó Maonlaí partnered up and joined in, dancing beside Shane's casket. It was a spontaneous and magical moment.

Symbols from Shane's life were brought forward by family and friends and held up by the priest. The offerings included a Tipperary flag, The Madonna, a bodhrán, a box of tea and a photograph from Shane and Victoria's wedding. Spider presented a tin tray and banged it on his head, as he had once done so energetically on stage during The Pogues' more frenzied numbers.

In a profoundly moving eulogy to her brother, Siobhan spoke of his hopes and dreams and the scale of what he had accomplished through his music. She spoke of how the Lifetime Achievement Award presented by Michael D. Higgins had meant more to him personally than any other and the how the occasion at the National Concert Hall had brought him to tears.

'I remember him as a little boy, a bit gangly in a blue anorak, who whenever we came home to Tipp would rush to retrieve a cap from one of our uncles. Proudly he would twist it on to his head and run out into the fields. At sunset he would sit down by the fire and listen to the songs and old stories. And those long summer days and nights and that love and devotion to Tipperary and Ireland gave birth to a dream. He dreamed of one day being the teller of stories, the singer of the songs. He dreamed of following in the footsteps of those great Irish lyricists and musicians he so admired. He dreamed of continuing this proud tradition. He dreamed that one day he might add his name to those that had gone before him. So, when the president put that award in his hand, he knew he had achieved that dream.'

Turning to face the casket and speaking directly to her brother, Siobhan said: 'So Shane, you did what you dreamed. You did what you said you were going to do in those long-ago days in Tipperary, and you did it with such heart and fire. A fire that is not dimmed by death, for you have lit that fire and it burns now in Ireland and all over the world. And so, Shane, with words from Dad and I, your little sister and your father, we are so proud of you, so very proud of you our darling. And I whisper farewell to you, but only for now in your own words. "And as the sunset came to meet the evening on the hill, I told you I'd always love you. I always did and I always will".'

Shane's widow Victoria spoke candidly of his addictions and his rock'n'roll excess, as well as his deep spirituality and exploration of multiple religions. She also described how he had mellowed in later life and become more tolerant and forgiving of those to whom he would have been hostile in his younger days. 'When I first met him, he was very much a humanitarian and a socialist and he loved people,' she recalled. 'But he didn't necessarily demonstrate that to his friends always. He could be quite cantankerous and rude and sometimes hostile, and I'm sure The Pogues will attest to that. But towards the end he just told everybody how much he loved them. Like nurses in the hospital were almost shocked because he would say, "I love you", and he'd never even met them before.

'One thing that had never wavered was Shane's compassion for his fellow human beings. His own addictions had made him slow to judge others and, in that, he had served a valuable lesson to us all,' said Victoria.

'He could never pass a homeless person without stopping and pulling out a wad of cash and giving them a cigarette or whatever it was that they wanted, and he would never in any way judge them or patronise them. If they wanted a drink, he would give them a drink – he totally respected their choice, their freedom of choice. I think that's a very beautiful thing because we're very quick to judge in our society people who are marginalised and people who live on the street and think, "Oh you know it must be somehow their own fault – that addiction is somehow their own fault."

'So, I think he also did something very powerful for addiction and people with addiction. He demonstrated that it's possible to be a multiple-drug abuser, not just an alcoholic – every kind of drug known to man, there wasn't a single drug he didn't take – and to still be a genius and a beautiful soul and make a massive contribution to the world and be loved. So, next time you see somebody you are thinking, "That guy's just an alcoholic or a drug addict", stop, give thought to it and let yourself just consider giving a bit of compassion and respect to that person. That would be my final message.'

Locals, who had stood outside during the service, poured in as it finished, using their phones to take pictures of the large black-and-white photograph of Shane at the front of the church, wanting to be part of the occasion. Nearby streets thronged with people and the music of The Pogues was piped around the town, cutting through the crisp December air. They watched as the hearse made its solemn journey from the church to the undertakers owned by Shane's friend Philly Ryan. As the coffin was lifted out and carried inside, Shane's songs blasted out from Philly's pub opposite, and his face could be seen on all the screens. The Guinness flowed and the singing and craic would go on into the early hours. Such a packed place, and yet such a void.

Tight security surrounded the private reception held at The Thatched Cottage pub in the village of Ballycommon, where a large amount of money had been put behind the bar. Guest lists were carefully checked as cars arrived from the church and old friends started catching up. The Pogues were gathered around a table, reliving old times. Dave Robinson, Julien Temple and other well-known faces who had played a part in Shane's colourful story had also made the journey to Ireland for his emotional send-off.

The large back room of the pub provided the perfect setting for a night of music performed by those who had so often shared a stage with him. The band Cronin, along with accordionist Andy Nolan, played for several hours, shuffling Shane's own songs with those he loved by others. B. P. Fallon joined them for a euphoric rendering of Van Morrison's 'Gloria'. Shanne Bradley picked up the bass, and her daughter Eucalypta took the mic, for 'Gabrielle' by The Nips. Spider reeled in the years, belting out 'Poor Paddy' – minus the beer tray. Johnny Depp looked on from a table in the corner of the room where he sat with Victoria. Shane would have loved it.

The following day, while family and close friends were attending Shane's cremation in Shannon, County Clare, his music was still being played from every street corner in Nenagh as people were out doing their Saturday shopping. A copy of the *Poguetry In Motion* EP had been placed among the traditional instruments in the window of a music shop, an elaborate cake bearing Shane's face in the window of the bakery, and a massive picture of him adorned a whole shop front to greet anyone travelling into the town from Dublin. 'Farewell To Our Shane', read the front page headline of the *Nenagh Guardian*, with a photo of him taken in the town. Shane had left an indelible mark here and national newspaper front pages, dominated by images from his funeral procession, confirmed his status as a cultural ambassador for the whole of Ireland.

In life, and now in death, Shane brought people together. Part of punk's appeal had been its egalitarianism, and scenes of joyous camaraderie had been the order of the day at Pogues' gigs. Shane had encouraged an atmosphere of inclusivity – whether that was backstage after a show or in the quiet of his sitting room. Everyone was equal in his sight: from the homeless to the celebrated, the marginalised to the privileged. Shane had come to an accommodation with his own shortcomings, and so had accepted them in others.

His republican fervour that had been awakened at The Commons and energised by the bloody events of The Troubles had not faded. However, the years had mellowed him, and his attitude had softened. 'Although in the early days when I first met him, he was a little bit slow to forgive the Brits,' said Victoria in her eulogy, 'he kind of came round to it and he started to really forgive everybody and everything, immediately.'

There was still a tendency to be difficult and irascible, even in his twilight years. However, his piercing blue eyes betrayed the child within; the Shane who grew up straddling the contrasting worlds of middle England and rural Ireland and whose boyhood passion for the motherland never dimmed.

The Shane who struggled to find his place before the Sex Pistols and punk saved him and who was forever drawn to life's underdogs.

He was an idol to fans the world over. But he was also 'one of us', a man whose songs spoke to compassion and empathy. Shane MacGowan's legacy isn't simply the timeless nature of his music, but its enduring message of love.

Shane in their words

'The Shane MacGowan I know is exactly as he appears to be – generous, outrageous, highly intelligent, very funny, spiritual, brutally honest, compassionate, unbelievably politically incorrect, hopelessly sentimental and completely off-his-face, usually all at the same time. We spent a lot of time together back in the day – eating, drinking, partying, talking, fighting, singing and it was the greatest fun, unbelievable chaos and a wonderful blur. These days we sit and watch *Ready Steady Go!* together on the TV and that is beautiful too. Shane is the real deal. There is no one like him. I love him.' – **Nick Cave**

'His music has transcended everything, and people just love him because of the music, they don't see any of the other things. People from all walks of life love him; everyone loves him. It doesn't matter what kind of music you're into, whether you're old or young, gay or straight, boring or interesting, square or round – the songs are why people love him.' – **Sinéad O'Connor**

'Shane weaves his tapestry seamlessly in and out of Tipperary, Soho, Almeria, Siam, New York. For me, he is a storyteller like no other, his songs always fulfilling and a joy to sing.' – **Christy Moore**

'He's certainly one of a kind. In my whole career – and I've been producing for a long time now – I've only ever really met two absolute bohemians. What I mean by bohemian is that if they wake up at seven in the morning, it's purely coincidence; and those two people are Shane MacGowan and Keith Richards. And especially Shane. He has absolutely no need for any order in his life.' – **Steve Lillywhite**

'Shane means more to Irish people than we could have imagined twenty or thirty years ago, and it's not just my generation or the one behind. My aunties or uncles from Sligo or Wexford or wherever would admire the honesty and would put him in the same place now as Brendan Behan or Johnny Cash or more local heroes like Joe Dolan or people like that.' – **Aidan Gillen**

'It had to be good enough. It couldn't just be representative of a second-generation culture and that's where the song craft comes through. The lyrics are just layered and nuanced and raw, and yet subtle. There is this unbelievable tenderness to his songwriting.' – **Dermot O'Leary**

'The lyrics are very brave; they catch you in the throat. There is no one with the Irish background being so brave and honest and straight up. He's the voice of Emigrant Ireland. You've Van Morrison and then there's MacGowan.' – **Mundy**

'He has a gift of putting words together in such a way that people enjoy them, and everybody is happy. When you sing a Shane MacGowan song, it doesn't matter if it's a sad song, people feel good inside.' – **Finbar Furey**

'I don't think he's really changed. He's not someone that has suddenly affected airs and graces or changed his behaviour. Any bad traits were always there and the good ones too. He's always been someone where the boundaries of his normal, walking around life and stage don't really exist. He's not someone who gets into a character: what you see is what you get.' – **Jem Finer**

'I think we all see him as a fiercely important artist; one of our most important artists. A writer in the tradition of Behan, who is one of his heroes, of course. We see him as an iconoclast. A rebel. And I think we worry about him and have spent the last thirty years as a nation worrying about him, but he keeps on proving us wrong!' – **Cillian Murphy**

'Shane's songs have affected the way I write; in both the way he tells stories and raises emotional connections. His words are full of pathos, longing, revelry and lament that moves you deeply. I try hard in my own way to reach out in this way too.' – **Joy Crookes**

'Shane's fascinating, unsettling, seemingly chaotic exterior belies a sensitive, highly tuned, imaginative intellect that fires with a singular sense of history, a poet's vision and a creative impulse that still blows my mind. I've been lucky to share the stage with him a few times, for which I'm forever grateful... he knew exactly what he wanted... always. And he put his smoke out when he came to visit my new-born twins three decades ago! I'll never forget that.' – **Fiachna Ó Braonáin**

Discography

Recordings featuring Shane MacGowan.

7-inch singles, 12-inch singles, EPs and CD singles

The Nipple Erectors

7-inch single
King Of The Bop/Nervous Wreck
Soho SH 1-2 (limited edition single) (1978)

The Nips

7-inch singles
All The Time In The World/Private Eye
Soho SH4 (1979)

Gabrielle/Vengeance
Soho SH9 (1980)

Gabrielle/Vengeance
Chiswick CHIS 119 (reissue, 1980)

Pogue Mahone

7-inch single
Dark Streets Of London/The Band Played Waltzing Matilda
Pogue Mahone Records PM1 (1984)

The Pogues

7-inch singles
Dark Streets Of London/And The Band Played Waltzing Matilda
Pogue Mahone Records PM1 (limited edition single) (1984)
Stiff BUY 207 (1984)

Boys From The County Hell/Repeal Of The Licensing Laws
Stiff BUY 212 (1984)

A Pair Of Brown Eyes/Whiskey You're The Devil
Stiff BUY 220 (1985)

Sally MacLennane/The Wild Rover
Stiff BUY 224 (1985)

Dirty Old Town/A Pistol For Paddy Garcia
Stiff BUY 229 (1985)

Poguetry In Motion EP: London Girl/The Body Of An American/Rainy Night
In Soho/Planxty Noel Hill
Stiff BUY 243 (1986)

Haunted/Junk Theme
MCA 1084 (1986)

(With The Dubliners)
The Irish Rover/The Rare Ould Mountain Dew
Stiff BUY 258 (1987)

(A-side with Kirsty MacColl)
Fairytale Of New York/Battle March Medley
Pogue Mahone NY 7 (1987)

If I Should Fall From Grace With God/Sally MacLennane (live)
Pogue Mahone FG 1 (limited red vinyl release) (1988)

Fiesta/Sketches Of Spain
Pogue Mahone FG 2 (1988)

Yeah Yeah Yeah Yeah Yeah/The Limerick Rake
WEA YZ 355T (1988)

Misty Morning, Albert Bridge/Cotton Fields
WEA YZ 407 (1989)

White City/Everyman Is A King
WEA YZ 409 (1989)

(With The Dubliners)
Jack's Heroes/Whiskey In The Jar
WEA YZ 500 (1990)

Summer In Siam/Bastard Landlord
WEA YZ 519 (1990)

(With Kirsty MacColl)
Miss Otis Regrets / Just One Of Those Things / Do I Love You? (last performed
by Aztec Camera)
Chrysalis CHS 3629 (1990)

Sayonara / Curse Of Love
WEA YZ 458 (1991)

A Rainy Night In Soho / Squid Out Of Water
WEA YZ 603 (1991)

(A-side with Kirsty MacColl)
Fairytale Of New York / Fiesta
WEA YZ 628 (reissue) (1991)

Honky Tonk Women / Curse Of Love
WEA YZ 628 (1992)

12-inch singles
A Pair Of Brown Eyes / Whiskey You're The Devil / Muirshin Durkin
Stiff BUYIT 220 (1985)

Sally MacLennane / The Wild Rover / The Leaving Of Liverpool
Stiff BUYIT 224 (1985)

Dirty Old Town / A Pistol For Paddy Garcia / The Parting Glass
Stiff BUYIT 229 (also picture disc) (1985)

Poguetry In Motion EP: London Girl / A Rainy Night In Soho / The Body Of An
American / Planxty Noel Hill
Stiff BUYIT 243 (1986)

Haunted / Hot Dogs With Everything / Junk Theme
MCAT 1084 (1986)

(With The Dubliners)
The Irish Rover / The Rare Ould Mountain Dew / The Dubliners Fancy (last
without The Pogues)
Stiff BUYIT 258 (1987)

(A-side with Kirsty MacColl)
Fairytale Of New York / Battle March Medley / Shanne Bradley
Pogue Mahone NY 12 (1987)

If I Should Fall From Grace With God (remix) / If I Should Fall From Grace
With God (7-inch remix) / Sally MacLennane (live) / A Pair Of Brown Eyes (live)
Pogue Mahone FG1 12 (limited red vinyl release) (1988)

Fiesta/South Australia/Sketches Of Spain
Pogue Mahone FG2 12 (1988)

Yeah Yeah Yeah Yeah Yeah (long version)/The Limerick Rake/Honky Tonk
Women/Yeah Yeah Yeah Yeah Yeah
WEA YZ 355T (1988)

Misty Morning, Albert Bridge/Cotton Fields/Young Ned Of The Hill
(dub version)
WEA YZ 407 T (1989)

White City/Everyman Is A King/The Star Of The County Down
WEA YZ 409 T (1989)

(With The Dubliners)
Jack's Heroes/Whiskey In The Jar/Whiskey In The Jar (extended version)
WEA YZ 500 T (1990)

Summer In Siam/The Bastard Landlord/Hell's Ditch (instrumental)/
The Irish Rover (7-inch version with The Dubliners)
WEA YZ 519 T (1990)

(With Kirsty MacColl)
Miss Otis Regrets/Just One Of Those Things/Do I Love You? (last performed
by Aztec Camera)
Chrysalis CHS 12 3629 (1990)

Sayonara/Curse Of Love/Infinity
YZ 548T (1991)

A Rainy Night In Soho/Squid Out Of Water/Infinity
WEA YZ 603 T (1991)

(With Kirsty MacColl)
Fairytale Of New York/Fiesta/A Pair Of Brown Eyes (live)/The Sick Bed Of
Cuchulainn (live)/Maggie May (live)
WEA YZ 628 TG (re-issue, limited gatefold sleeve) (1991)

Honky Tonk Women/Curse Of Love/Infinity
WEA YZ 673 T (1992)

CD singles
(A-side with Kirsty MacColl)
Fairytale Of New York/Battle March Medley/Shanne Bradley
Pogue Mahone CD NY 1 (1987)

If I Should Fall From Grace With God (remix)/If I Should Fall From Grace
With God (7-inch remix)/Sally MacLennane (live)/A Pair Of Brown Eyes
(live)
Pogue Mahone CD FG1 (1988)

Fiesta/South Australia/Sketches Of Spain
Pogue Mahone CD FG2 (1988)

Yeah Yeah Yeah Yeah Yeah/The Limerick Rake/Yeah Yeah Yeah Yeah Yeah
(long version)/Honky Tonk Women
WEA YZ 355 CD (1988)

Misty Morning, Albert Bridge/Cotton Fields/Young Ned Of The Hill/
Train Of Love
WEA YZ 407 CD (1989)

White City/Everyman Is A King/Star Of The County Down
WEA YZ 409 CD (1989)

Summer In Siam/The Bastard Landlord/Hell's Ditch (instrumental)/
The Irish Rover (last with The Dubliners)
WEA YZ 548T CD (1990)

(With The Dubliners)
Jack's Heroes/Whiskey In The Jar (extended version)/Whiskey In The Jar
(7-inch version)
WEA YZ 500 CD (1990)

(With Kirsty MacColl)
Miss Otis Regrets/Just One Of Those Things/Do I Love You? (last performed
by Aztec Camera)
Chrysalis CHS CD 3629 (1990)

Poguetry In Motion EP: A Rainy Night In Soho (remix)/London Girl/The Body
Of An American/Planxty Noel Hill
WEA YZ 603 CD (reissue) (1991)

(With Kirsty MacColl)
Fairytale Of New York/Fiesta/A Pair Of Brown Eyes (live)/The Sick Bed Of
Cuchulainn (live)/Maggie May (live)
WEA YZ 628 CD (reissue) (1991)

Honky Tonk Women/Curse Of Love/Infinity/The Parting Glass
WEA YZ 673 CD (1992)

Shane MacGowan & The Popes

7-inch single

Christmas Party EP '96: Christmas Lullaby / Paddy Rolling Stone / Hippy Hippy Shake / Danny Boy
ZTT ZANG 88 (1996)

12-inch singles

That Woman's Got Me Drinking / Roddy McCorley / Her Father Didn't Like Me Anyway / Minstrel Boy
ZTT ZANG CDX (1994)

The Song With No Name / Nancy Whiskey / Cracklin' Rosie
ZTT ZANG 60 T (1994)

CD singles

The Church Of The Holy Spook / Rake At The Gates Of Hell / King Of The Bop / Nancy Whiskey (numbered, limited edition single)
ZTT ZANG 57 CDX (1994)

That Woman's Got Me Drinking / Roddy McCorley / Her Father Didn't Like Me Anyway / Minstrel Boy
ZTT ZANG 56 CDX (1994)

The Song With No Name / Nancy Whiskey / Cracklin' Rosie
ZTT ZANG 60CD (1994)

Christmas Party EP '96: Christmas Lullaby / Paddy Rolling Stone / Hippy Hippy Shake / Danny Boy
ZTT ZANG 88 CD (1996)

Lonesome Highway / A Man Called Horse / Joey's In America
ZTT MACG 001 (1997)

Rock'n'Roll Paddy / She Moves Through The Fair
ZTT MACG 003 CD (1998)

Shane MacGowan

CD single

My Way / Song With No Name* / Aisling* / My Way (Your Way – Away With You) (*Shane MacGowan & The Popes)
ZTT ZANG 79 CD (1996)

Collaborations and contributions

7-inch singles

Nick Cave & Shane MacGowan
What A Wonderful World / A Rainy Night In Soho (sung by Nick Cave) /
Lucy (version #2) (sung by Shane MacGowan)
Mute 151 (1992)

12-inch singles

Nick Cave & Shane MacGowan
What A Wonderful World / A Rainy Night In Soho (sung by Nick Cave) /
Lucy (version #2) (sung by Shane MacGowan)
Mute 151 12 (1992)

CD singles

Nick Cave & Shane MacGowan
What A Wonderful World / A Rainy Night In Soho (sung by Nick Cave) /
Lucy #2 (sung by Shane MacGowan)
Mute 151 CD (1992)

Shane MacGowan and Sinéad O'Connor
Haunted / The Song With No Name* / Bring Down The Lamp* /
Cracklin' Rosie* (*Shane MacGowan & The Popes)
ZTT ZANG65 CD (1995)

Shane MacGowan and Máire Brennan
You're The One / Aisling* / Victoria* (*Shane MacGowan & The Popes)
ZTT ZANG 68 CD (1995)

Various artists
Perfect Day / Perfect Day (Female Version) / Perfect Day (Male Version)
Chrysalis NEED 01 (1997)

Shane MacGowan, The Aftermath & Friends
The Rockier Road To Poland / The Rockier Road To Poland (trad mix)
Live Transmission Records (limited edition) (2012)

Albums

The Nips'N'Nipple Erectors
Bops, Babes, Booze & Bovver
King Of The Bop/Nervous Wreck/So Pissed Off/Stavordale Road, N5/
All The Time In The World/Private Eye/Gabrielle/Vengeance
Big Beat/Soho WIKM 66 (1987)

Bops, Babes, Booze & Bovver
King Of The Bop/Nervous Wreck/So Pissed Off/Stavordale Road, N5/Venus
In Bother Boots/Fuss & Bother/All The Time In The World/Private Eye/
Gabrielle/Vengeance
Big Beat/Soho CDWIKM 66 (2003 reissue)

The Pogues
Red Roses For Me
Transmetropolitan/The Battle Of Brisbane/The Auld Triangle/Waxie's
Dargle/Boys From The County Hell/Sea Shanty/Dark Streets Of London/
Streams Of Whiskey/Poor Paddy/Dingle Regatta/Greenland Whale
Fisheries/Down In The Ground Where The Dead Men Go/Kitty
Stiff SEEZ 55 (1984)

Rum Sodomy & The Lash
The Sick Bed Of Cuchulainn/The Old Main Drag/Wild Cats Of Kilkenny/
I'm A Man You Don't Meet Every Day/A Pair Of Brown Eyes/
Sally McLennane/Dirty Old Town/Jesse James/Navigator/Billy's Bones/
The Gentleman Soldier/The Band Played Waltzing Matilda
Stiff SEEZ 58 (1985)

If I Should Fall From Grace With God
If I Should Fall From Grace With God/Turkish Song Of The Damned/
Bottle Of Smoke/Fairytale Of New York/Metropolis/Thousands Are
Sailing/Fiesta/Medley (The Recruiting Sergeant/The Rocky Road To
Dublin/The Galway Road)/Streets Of Sorrow–Birmingham Six/Lullaby Of
London/Sit Down By The Fire/The Broad Majestic Shannon/Worms
WEA (Pogue Mahone NYR1) (1988)

Peace And Love
Gridlock/White City/Young Ned Of The Hill/Misty Morning, Albert
Bridge/Cotton Fields/Blue Heaven/Down All The Days/USA/Lorelei/

Gartloney Rats/Boat Train/Tombstone/Night Train To Lorca/London
You're A Lady
WEA (Pogue Mahone NYR-2) (1989)

Hell's Ditch
The Sunnyside Of The Street/Sayonara/The Ghost Of A Smile/Hell's
Ditch/Lorca's Novena/Summer In Siam/Rain Street/Rainbow Man/The
Wake Of The Medusa/House Of The Gods/5 Green Queens And Jean/
Maidrín Rua/Six To Go
WEA (Pogue Mahone 9031-72554-2) (1990)

CD reissues

Red Roses For Me
Transmetropolitan/The Battle Of Brisbane/The Auld Triangle/Waxie's
Dargle/Boys From The County Hell/Sea Shanty/Dark Streets Of London/
Streams Of Whiskey/Poor Paddy/Dingle Regatta/Greenland Whale
Fisheries/Down In The Ground Where The Dead Men Go/Kitty
Bonus tracks: The Leaving Of Liverpool/Muirshin Durkin/Repeal Of The
Licensing Laws/The Band Played Waltzing Matilda/Whiskey You're The
Devil/The Wild Rover
WEA 5046759582 (2004)

Rum Sodomy & The Lash
The Sick Bed Of Cuchulainn/The Old Main Drag/Wild Cats Of Kilkenny/
I'm A Man You Don't Meet Every Day/A Pair Of Brown Eyes/Sally
MacLennane/Dirty Old Town/Jesse James/Navigator/Billy's Bones/
The Gentleman Soldier/The Band Played Waltzing Matilda
Bonus tracks: A Pistol For Paddy Garcia/London Girl/A Rainy Night In
Soho/The Body Of An American/Planxty Noel Hill/The Parting Glass
WEA 5046759592 (2004)

If I Should Fall From Grace With God
If I Should Fall From Grace With God/Turkish Song Of The Damned/Bottle
Of Smoke/Fairytale Of New York/Metropolis/Thousands Are Sailing/
Fiesta/Medley: (The Recruiting Sergeant/The Rocky Road To Dublin/
The Galway Races)/Streets Of Sorrow–Birmingham Six/Lullaby Of
London/Sit Down By The Fire/The Broad Majestic Shannon/Worms
Bonus tracks: The Battle March (medley)/The Irish Rover/Mountain Dew/
Shanne Bradley/Sketches Of Spain/South Australia
WEA 5046759602 (2004)

Peace And Love
Gridlock / White City / Young Ned Of The Hill / Misty Morning, Albert
Bridge / Cotton Fields / Blue Heaven / Down All The Days / USA / Lorelei /
Gartloney Rats / Boat Train / Tombstone / Night Train To Lorca / London
You're A Lady
Bonus tracks: Star Of The County Down / The Limerick Rake / Train Of
Love / Everyman Is King / Yeah Yeah Yeah Yeah Yeah / Honky Tonk Women
WEA 5046759612 (2004)

Hell's Ditch
The Sunnyside Of The Street / Sayonara / The Ghost Of A Smile / Hell's
Ditch / Lorca's Novena / Summer In Siam / Rain Street / Rainbow Man / The
Wake Of The Medusa / House Of The Gods / 5 Green Queens And Jean /
Maidrin Rua / Six To Go
Bonus tracks: Whiskey In The Jar / Bastard Landlord / Infinity / Curse Of Love /
Squid Out Of Water / Jack's Heroes / A Rainy Night In Soho
WEA 5046759622 (2004)

Compilations

The Best Of The Pogues
Fairytale Of New York / Sally MacLennane / Dirty Old Town / The Irish
Rover / A Pair Of Brown Eyes / Streams Of Whiskey / A Rainy Night In Soho /
Fiesta / Rain Street / Misty Morning, Albert Bridge / White City / Thousands
Are Sailing / The Broad Majestic Shannon / The Body Of An American
WEA (9031-75405-2) (1991)

The Rest Of The Best
If I Should Fall From Grace With God / The Sick Bed Of Cuchulainn / The
Old Main Drag / Boys From The County Hell / Young Ned Of The Hill / Dark
Streets Of London / The Auld Triangle / Repeal Of The Licensing Laws / Yeah
Yeah Yeah Yeah Yeah / London Girl / Honky Tonk Women / Summer In Siam /
Turkish Song Of The Damned / Lullaby Of London / The Sunnyside Of The
Street / Hell's Ditch
WEA (9031-77341-2) (1992)

The Very Best Of
Dirty Old Town / The Irish Rover / Sally MacLennane / Fiesta / A Pair Of
Brown Eyes / Fairytale Of New York / The Body Of An American / Streams
Of Whiskey / The Sick Bed Of Cuchulainn / If I Should Fall From Grace With

God/Misty Morning, Albert Bridge/Rain Street/White City/A Rainy Night In Soho/London Girl/Boys From The County Hell/The Sunnyside Of The Street/Summer In Siam/Hell's Ditch/The Old Main Drag/The Band Played Waltzing Matilda
WEA (8573-87459-2) (2001)

Dirty Old Town
Streams Of Whiskey/A Pair Of Brown Eyes/Dirty Old Town/Sally MacLennane/Dingle Regatta/Turkish Song Of The Damned/Metropolis/Thousands Are Sailing/A Rainy Night In Soho/Misty Morning, Albert Bridge/I'm A Man You Don't Meet Every Day/Gridlock/Young Ned Of The Hill/Tuesday Morning/Paris St Germaine/Drunken Boat/Love You Till The End
Warner (5101-10404-2) (2005)

The Ultimate Collection
A Rainy Night In Soho/Sally MacLennane/The Irish Rover/Dirty Old Town/Fairytale Of New York/Streams Of Whiskey/If I Should Fall From Grace With God/Fiesta/The Body Of An American/Misty Morning, Albert Bridge/Repeal Of The Licensing Laws/Boys From The County Hell/The Sunnyside Of The Street/A Pair Of Brown Eyes/Summer In Siam/The Sick Bed Of Cuchulainn/London Girl/Tuesday Morning/White City/Hell's Ditch/Young Ned Of The Hill/Thousands Are Sailing
Bonus disc: *Live At The Brixton Academy*
Streams Of Whiskey/If I Should Fall From Grace With God/Boys From The County Hell/The Broad Majestic Shannon/Young Ned Of The Hill/Turkish Song Of The Damned/A Rainy Night In Soho/Tuesday Morning/Rain Street/A Pair Of Brown Eyes/Repeal Of The Licensing Laws/The Old Main Drag/Thousands Are Sailing/The Body Of An American/Sally MacLennane/Lullaby Of London/Dirty Old Town/Bottle Of Smoke/The Sick Bed Of Cuchulainn/Fairytale Of New York/Fiesta/The Irish Rover
Warner (2-56462254-2) (2005)

Just Look Them Straight In The Eye And Say... Poguemahone!! The Pogues Box Set
Disc One
The Kerry Polka/The Rocky Road To Dublin/Boys From The County Hell/NW3/The Donegal Express–The Hen And The Cock Are In Carrickmacross/Do You Believe In Magic?/Hot Asphalt/ Danny Boy (BBC *John Peel Show*)/Haunted/The Travelling People/Eve Of Destruction/My Baby's Gone/North Sea Holes/Garbo (aka In and Out)/The Last Of McGee/Afro Cuban Be-Bop (Joe Strummer and The Astro-Physicians)/Young Ned Of The Hill/

Pinned Down–I'm Alone In The Wilderness/When The Ship Comes In/
Waxie's Dargle
Disc Two
Repeal Of The Licensing Laws/Dark Streets Of London/Greenland Whale
Fisheries/Streams Of Whiskey/The Auld Triangle/Poor Paddy On The
Railway/Sea Shanty/Transmetropolitan/ Kitty/Boys From The County
Hell/Connemara Let's Go! (aka Down In The Ground Where The Dead Men
Go)/Billy's Bones/The Old Main Drag/Sally MacLennane/The Town That
Never Sleeps/Something Wild/Driving Through The City/A Rainy Night In
Soho/Fairytale Of New York [demo extract 1]/Fairytale Of New York [demo
extract 2]/Fairytale Of New York [demo extract 3]/Navigator
Disc Three
The Aria/The Good, The Bad And The Ugly/Haunted/Love Theme From
Sid & Nancy/Junk Theme/Glued Up And Speeding/Paris/A Needle For
Paddy Garcia/JB 57/Bowery Snax–Spiked/Hot Dogs With Everything/
Rince Del Emplacada/The Rake At The Gates Of Hell/Turkish Song Of
The Damned/If I Should Fall From Grace With God/Battle March/Lullaby
Of London/Shanne Bradley/Streets Of Sorrow/Thousands Are Sailing/
The Balinalee/Nicaragua Libre/Japan
Disc Four
Sally MacLennane/A Pair Of Brown Eyes/Kitty/Maggie May/Dirty Old
Town/The Sick Bed Of Cuchulainn/Fiesta/If I Should Fall From Grace With
God/Johnny Come Lately (Steve Earle)/Boat Train/Night Train To Lorca/
The Mistlethrush/Got A Lot Of Lovin' To Do/Victoria/Murder [version 1]/
Lust For Vomit/The Wake Of The Medusa/The Black Dogs Ditch/Aisling/
Murder [version 2]/Yeah Yeah Yeah Yeah Yeah/Maidrín Rua/Johnny Come
Lately
Disc Five
Johnny Was (Sexy Bongo)/Miss Otis Regrets–Just One Of Those Things
(Kirsty MacColl and The Pogues)/All The Tears That I Cried (Kirsty
MacColl)/The One And Only (Kirsty MacColl)/Afro Cuban Be-Bop (Joe
Strummer and The Astro-Physicians)/Turkish Song Of The Damned (The
Pogues featuring Joe Strummer)/London Calling (The Pogues featuring Joe
Strummer)/I Fought The Law (The Pogues featuring Joe Strummer)/The
Girl From The Wadi-Hammamat/Moving To Moldova/Call My Name/The
Sun And The Moon/Living In A World Without Her/Who Said Romance
is Dead?/Sound of the City Night/Four O'clock In The Morning/The Star
Of The County Down/White City/Medley: The Recruiting Sergeant–The
Rocky Road To Dublin–The Galway Races/The Parting Glass–Lord Santry's
Fairest Daughter/Goodnight Irene
Rhino (5144281352) (2008)

30:30 The Ultimate Collection
Sally MacLennane/If I Should Fall From Grace With God/Love You 'Till the
End/Fairytale Of New York/Dirty Old Town/The Irish Rover/The Body Of
An American/A Pair Of Brown Eyes/Streams Of Whiskey/The Sick Bed Of
Cuchulainn/Fiesta/Boys From The County Hell/Kitty/The Sunnyside Of
The Street/Summer In Siam/Whiskey In The Jar/A Rainy Night In Soho/
Misty Morning, Albert Bridge/Rain Street/Tuesday Morning/Greenland
Whale Fisheries/The Old Main Drag/The Parting Glass/Young Ned Of The
Hill/Yeah Yeah Yeah Yeah Yeah/Thousands Are Sailing/Turkish Song Of The
Damned/The Broad Majestic Shannon/Repeal Of The Licensing Laws/The
Limerick Rake
Rhino (5053105660353) (2013)

Shane MacGowan & The Popes

The Snake
The Church Of The Holy Spook/That Woman's Got Me Drinking/The
Song With No Name/Aisling/I'll Be Your Handbag/Her Father Didn't Like
Me Anyway/A Mexican Funeral In Paris/The Snake With Eyes Of Garnet/
Donegal Express/Victoria/The Rising Of The Moon/Bring Down The Lamp
ZTT (4509-98104-2) (1994)

The Crock Of Gold
Paddy Rolling Stone/Rock'n'roll Paddy/Paddy Public Enemy No. 1/Back
In The County Hell/Lonesome Highway/Come To The Bower/Ceilidh
Cowboy/More Pricks Than Kicks/Truck Drivin' Man/Joey's In America/B&I
Ferry/Mother Mo Chroi/Spanish Lady/St John Of Gods/Skipping Rhymes/
MacLennan/Wanderin' Star
ZTT MACG002 (1997)

Across The Broad Atlantic (Live on Paddy's Day – New York, Dublin)
If I Should Fall From Grace With God/Rock'n'roll Paddy/Nancy Whiskey/
A Rainy Night In Soho/Poor Paddy Works On The Railway/The Broad
Majestic Shannon/Popes' Instrumental (My Ballyvourney Love/The Limpin'
General/Bag Of Chips)/Dirty Old Town/Mother Mo Chroi/The Body Of
An American/Granuaille/More Pricks Than Kicks/Aisling/A Pair Of Brown
Eyes/Streams Of Whiskey/Lonesome Highway/Angel Of Death/Sick Bed
Of Cuchulainn/The Irish Rover/Fairytale Of New York
Eagle Records EAGCD192 (2002)

Compilations

The Rare Ould Stuff
You're The One (Shane MacGowan and Máire Brennan)/The Song With
No Name/Nancy Whiskey/Roddy McCorley/Rock'n'roll Paddy/Christmas
Lullaby Edit/Danny Boy/Minstrel Boy/Rake At The Gates Of Hell/Victoria/
Donegal Express/Ceilidh Cowboy/Paddy Rolling Stone/Paddy Public Enemy
No. 1/Back In The County Hell/The Snake With Eyes Of Garnet/Cracklin'
Rosie/Aisling/Spanish Lady/Come To The Bower/St John Of Gods
ZTT ZTT178CD (2001)

End notes

Unless referenced, quotes are taken from original interviews with the author.

Chapter 1 The Little Man
1. *Shane MacGowan: A Wreck Reborn*, Sky Arts, 20 December 2015
2. *If I Should Fall from Grace with God* (dir. Sarah Share), TG4, 2001
3. Ibid.
4. Ibid.
5. The *Guardian*, 20 December 2013
6. *The Great Hunger: The Life and Songs of Shane MacGowan*, BBC, 1997
7. Ibid.
8. Ibid.
9. 'Shane's Tale Earns Prize', *Kent & Sussex Courier*, 19 March 1971

Chapter 2 Shane O'Hooligan
1. *If I Should Fall from Grace with God* (dir. Sarah Share), TG4, 2001
2. *A Drink with Shane MacGowan*, Victoria Mary Clarke & Shane MacGowan, Sidgwick & Jackson, 2001
3. *If I Should Fall from Grace with God*
4. *Q*, February 1993
5. *Independent*, 10 October 2008
6. John Kelly, *Irish Times*, 26 August 2000
7. *The Story of The Jam: About the Young Idea*, Sky Arts, 2015
8. *Daily Star*, 3 July 2014

Chapter 3 King Of The Bop
1. *NME*, 27 October 1979
2. *Kiss My Arse: The Story of the Pogues*, Carol Clerk, Omnibus Press, 2006
3. *If I Should Fall from Grace with God* (dir. Sarah Share), TG4, 2001
4. reverbnation.com
5. Clerk

Chapter 4 Pogue Mahone
1. *Kiss My Arse: The Story of The Pogues*, Carol Clerk, Omnibus Press, 2006
2. Ibid.
3. Ibid.
4. *Be Stiff: The Stiff Records Story*, Richard Balls, Soundcheck Books, 2014
5. Ibid.
6. Clerk
7. *Crock of Gold: A Few Rounds with Shane MacGowan* (dir. Julien Temple), 2020
8. Balls

Chapter 5 Farewell To New York City Boys
1. *Kiss My Arse: The Story of the Pogues*, Carol Clerk, Omnibus Press, 2006
2. Ibid.
3. *Rum Sodomy & The Lash*, The Pogues, liner notes
4. Ibid.
5. *The Pogues: The Lost Decade*, Ann Scanlon, Omnibus Press, 1988
6. Lynn Barber, the *Guardian*, 11 March 2001
7. *Be Stiff: The Stiff Records Story*, Richard Balls, Soundcheck Books, 2014
8. Ibid.
9. Ibid.
10. Ibid.
11. Scanlon
12. Ibid.
13. Balls
14. Clerk
15. *The Quietus*, 26 November 2012
16. Scanlon

Chapter 6 Straight To Hell
1. *The Pogues: The Lost Decade*, Ann Scanlon, Omnibus Press, 1988
2. Ibid.
3. Ann Scanlon, *Mojo*, September 2004
4. Eva Hall, Extra.ie, 23 December 2017
5. Sylvia Patterson, *Smash Hits*, 24 September 1986
6. *A Drink with Shane MacGowan*, Victoria Mary Clarke & Shane MacGowan, Sidgwick & Jackson, 2001
7. *Kiss My Arse: The Story of the Pogues*, Carol Clerk, Omnibus Press, 2006
8. *Be Stiff: The Stiff Records Story*, Richard Balls, Soundcheck Books, 2014
9. Clerk
10. Clarke and MacGowan
11. *Top 10: X-Rated*, Channel 4, 2001

12. Ibid.
13. Ibid.
14. Fiona Ellis, *Irish Sun*, 21 December 2017
15. *The Great Hunger: The Life and Songs of Shane MacGowan*, BBC, 1997
16. Balls
17. *The Great Hunger*
18. *The Story of 'Fairytale of New York'*, BBC Three, 2007
19. Ibid.
20. Ibid.
21. Ibid.
22. Ibid.

Chapter 7 St John Of Gods
1. Miranda Sawyer, *Select*, August 1993
2. *A Drink with Shane MacGowan*, Victoria Mary Clarke & Shane MacGowan, Sidgwick & Jackson, 2001
3. *Rock Wives*, Channel 4, 1996
4. *Kiss My Arse: The Story of the Pogues*, Carol Clerk, Omnibus Press, 2006
5. Clarke and MacGowan
6. Keith Cameron, *Sounds*, 29 July 1989
7. Eva Hall, Extra.ie, 23 December 2017
8. Sawyer
9. Ibid.
10. Clerk
11. *Here Comes Everybody: The Story of The Pogues*, James Fearnley, Faber & Faber, 2012
12. Adrian Deevoy, *Q*, September 1989
13. Adrian Deevoy, *Q*, May 1988
14. Deevoy, 1989
15. Ibid.
16. Clerk
17. Clarke and MacGowan
18. Fearnley
19. Ibid.

Chapter 8 The Parting Glass
1. Adrian Deevoy, *Q*, May 1988
2. *Kiss My Arse: The Story of the Pogues*, Carol Clerk, Omnibus Press, 2006
3. *A Drink with Shane MacGowan*, Victoria Mary Clarke & Shane MacGowan, Sidgwick & Jackson, 2001
4. Clerk

5. Clarke and MacGowan
6. Joe Jackson, *Irish Times*, 18 April 1997
7. Friends of Shane MacGowan newsletter, May 1994
8. Ibid.
9. Ibid.
10. Gavin Martin, *NME*, 26 March 1994
11. Clerk

Chapter 9 Lonesome Highway
1. Joe Jackson, the *Irish Independent*, 8 May 2005
2. Michael Sheridan, the *Irish Independent*, 26 March 2000
3. *Kiss My Arse: The Story of the Pogues*, Carol Clerk, Omnibus Press, 2006
4. Eva Hall, Extra.ie, 23 December 2017
5. Victoria Mary Clarke, the *Guardian*, 17 January 2009
6. Liam Fay, *Hot Press*, January 1997

Chapter 10 Back In The County Hell
1. Michael Sheridan, the *Irish Independent*, 26 March 2000
2. Concertlivewire.com, 4 March 2003
3. Victoria Mary Clarke, *Evening Standard*, 2000
4. Victoria Mary Clarke, *Sunday Independent*, 19 March 2018
5. *If I Should Fall from Grace with God* (dir. Sarah Share), TG4, 2001
6. Concertlivewire.com
7. *Rake at the Gates of Hell: Shane MacGowan in Context*, Robert Mamrak, Pin Oak Bottom Press, 2011
8. *If I Should Fall from Grace with God*
9. *Kiss My Arse: The Story of the Pogues*, Carol Clerk, Omnibus Press, 2006
10. Clerk
11. Hotpress.com, 3 March 2004
12. Hotpress.com, 24 March 2004
13. Ibid.
14. Ciaran Ryan, BBC, 20 December 2004
15. *The Times*, 22 December 2004
16. Danny McElhinney, *Ireland on Sunday*, 19 December 2004
17. Victoria Mary Clarke, *Sunday Independent*, 5 December 2004
18. Ibid.
19. Clerk
20. Ibid.
21. *Irish Independent*, 4 March 2007
22. Victoria Mary Clarke, *Sunday Independent*, 16 December 2007

Chapter 11 Wandrin' Star

1. Keith Falkiner, the *Irish Daily Star*, 21 November 2010
2. Nick Hasted, *Uncut*, August 2014
3. Ibid.
4. *Shane MacGowan: A Wreck Reborn*, Sky Arts, 20 December 2015
5. Leonie Cooper, Vice.com, 24 December 2015
6. *A Wreck Reborn*
7. Richard Jinman, the *Independent*, 19 December 2015
8. Jim Gallagher, *Irish Sun*, 24 January 2017
9. Conor Kane, *Irish Times*, 8 January 2017
10. Eamon Sweeney, *Irish Times*, 13 January 2018

Chapter 12 A Furious Devotion

1. Barry Moran, *Irish Sun*, 19 April 2019
2. *Crock of Gold: A Few Rounds with Shane MacGowan* (dir. Julien Temple), 2020
3. Tonya Henderson, the *Irish World*, 21 November 1997
4. Alan Corr, *RTE Guide*, 19 December 1997
5. *A Drink with Shane MacGowan*, Victoria Mary Clarke & Shane MacGowan, Sidgwick & Jackson, 2001
6. *Rotten: No Irish, No Blacks, No Dogs*, John Lydon, Hodder & Stoughton, 1994
7. *Six O'clock Show*, Virgin Media One, 14 November 2019
8. Victoria Mary Clarke, *Sunday Independent*, 30 October 2016
9. *Irish Sun*, 13 March 2020
10. *Crock of Gold*

Chapter 13 The Parting Glass

1. The *Guardian*, 23 October 2022, Vanessa Thorpe

Permissions

Image Credits

Chapter 1: In school uniform, with Therese. *MacGowan family archive*
Chapter 2: With the prize-winning *Holmewoodian. MacGowan family archive*
Chapter 3: On stage with The Nips. *Justin Thomas*

Chapter 4: Early days of The Pogues. *Ray Vaughan*
Chapter 5: In France. *Frédéric Reglain/Gamma-Rapho/Getty*
Chapter 6: In Barcelona. *Andrew Catlin*
Chapter 7: In shades. *Andrew Catlin*
Chapter 8: With Siobhan, on stage at Fleadh Mor. *Tony Gavin*
Chapter 9: In Montreal. *Josie Montserrat*
Chapter 10: With Sinéad O'Connor. *Des Willie/Redferns*
Chapter 11: With Victoria. *Tony Gavin*
Chapter 12: With Victoria, on their wedding day. *The Mega Agency*
Chapter 13: A photograph of a young Shane holding a cigarette and raising a glass of wine was displayed at his funeral service in Nenagh, County Tipperary. *Richard Balls*

Index

Author Biography

Richard Balls is a die-hard music fan who stumbled upon The Pogues on their first nationwide tour in 1984. An established writer and rock biographer, Richard was a newspaper journalist for twenty years – almost half of which he spent in Ireland. His previous books are *Sex & Drugs & Rock'n'Roll: The Life of Ian Dury* and *Be Stiff: The Stiff Records Story*. He lives in Norwich where he works in communications.